EMERGING HORIZONS IN FINANCE

EMERGING HORIZONS IN FINANCE

Editors

A.K. PURI
KANHAIYA SINGH

FORE School of Management
New Delhi

BLOOMSBURY
NEW DELHI • LONDON • OXFORD • NEW YORK • SYDNEY

First Published, 2015

BLOOMSBURY PUBLISHING INDIA PVT. LTD.
New Delhi London Oxford New York Sydney

ISBN: 978-93-85436-83-3

10 9 8 7 6 5 4 3 2 1

Published by Bloomsbury Publishing India Pvt. Ltd.
DDA Complex LSC, Building No. 4, 2nd Floor
Pocket 6 & 7, Sector – C
Vasant Kunj, New Delhi 110070

Typeset by FORTUNE GRAPHICS, Naraina, New Delhi

Printed at ANVI COMPOSERS, Paschim Vihar, New Delhi

Contents

Foreword

For a quarter of a century, beginning in early 1980s, finance enjoyed its golden age. Thanks to financial globalization, capital spread more widely; financial institutions and markets evolved; raising finances for businesses became easier; and ordinary people had unprecedented access to borrowing. Indeed, modern finance improved countless lives. To a great extent shaping this extraordinary development was the research in the emergent field of financial economics. It will be interesting to revisit the developments in finance as a chronology of research work that provided the conceptual underpinnings for the practice of finance.

Something went wrong in recent times, leading to an unprecedented global financial crisis. This crisis has seriously exposed the limitations of the rational finance that held sway over finance practice and public policy and underscored the need to blend rational finance with behavioural finance. This paradigm shift has the potential of having an important bearing on research, policy making and practice in finance, in the years to come.

In mid-1960s, Eugene Fama introduced the idea of an 'efficient' capital market to the literature of financial economics. Put simply, the idea is that the intense competition in capital market leads to fair pricing of debt and equity securities. This simple idea has had a profound impact in several ways.

1. The evidence on market efficiency helped in establishing a receptive climate for three seminal developments in financial theory:
   (a) Modigliani-Miller theories of corporate financial policy,
   (b) Capital Asset Pricing Model,
   (c) Black-Scholes Option Pricing Model.
   Each of them influenced the practice of finance in significant ways.
2. Important practical developments like indexing, asset securitisation, performance measurement and disclosure of different earnings numbers are based on the notion of well-functioning security markets.
3. Empirical evidence on market efficiency coincided with growing

> respect for free markets that began in the 1970s, initially among economists and then among politicians. As Ray Ball put it: 'Indeed, the market efficiency literature has helped pave the way for what has proved to be a worldwide "liberalisation" of financial and other markets... In a surprisingly short time, academic attitudes toward stock markets had shifted from one extreme to the other, from suspicion to almost reverence.'

Even when the rationalist model was on the ascent in the world of economics and finance, the not-so rational aspects of human nature began to find its ways into economics. Major challenges emanating from behavioural economics were in the form of deviation from rationality, divergence between market prices and fundamental values and pervasiveness of irrational forces.

In 1950s, Herbert Simon, a Nobel laureate in economics, argued that people don't have the brainpower and time to make decisions so they 'satisfice' (a combination of 'satisfy' and 'suffice') rather than 'optimize'. Daniel Kahneman and Amos Tversky, two cognitive psychologists, argued that the expected utility theory, the workhouse of rational finance, was not an accurate description of decision making under risk. They developed an alternative model called prospect theory. It is a purely descriptive model that seeks to document and explain systematic violations of the axioms of rationality in choices between gambles.

An important early challenge to the idea of efficient markets hypothesis came from Robert Shiller's work on stock market. In a paper published in *American Economic Review*, 1981, he developed an innovative inequality relationship to examine volatility and found that stock prices fluctuate far too much relative to fundamental values. To argue that stock prices were right because it was hard to predict them was, according to Shiller, 'one of the most remarkable errors in the history of economic thought. It is remarkable in the immediacy of its logical error and the sweep and implication of its consequences.'

According to Andrei Shleifer and his co-researcher, Robert Vishny, the pervasive force, which causes market prices to deviate from intrinsic values, is the presence of 'noise traders' and the 'limits to arbitrage'.

At a session honoring Irwing Fisher during the 1997 meeting of the American Economic Association, Richard Thaler, a star behavioural economist, described how the writings of Irwing Fisher, the forefather of modern finance, were infused with behavioural reasoning. 'Fisher... helped... introduce mathematics to economics. Young economists are taught modern concepts (equations, diagrams and the like) but rarely go back and read the surrounding text... It is time to stop neglecting the words and time to start updating our equations to include these behavioral factors.'

Many financial economists heeded the advice of Thaler and research that combined rational and behavioural factors blossomed. It gained further fillip with the award of 2002 Nobel Prize in economics to Daniel Kahneman, a cognitive psychologist, who had considerable influence on behavioural economics and the growing reputation of people like Robert Shiller, 2013 Nobel laureate in economics. While behavioural economists found a lot of holes in the edifice of rational markets finance, they didn't abandon that edifice and they continue to use the equilibrium framework imposed on the field by Irving Fisher a century ago. They still trust Merton Miller's 'pervasive forces'. Economists of Austrian tradition and American institutionalists were not comfortable with equilibrium analysis. However, they were marginalised as their approach lacked the precision and clarity of equilibrium economics – the precision that was inspired by 19th century physics.

1980s onwards economists have been taking steps away from relying more or less exclusively on equilibrium. Economists describe the dynamics of growth and change better by abandoning the concept of equilibrium while sticking with mathematics. In the new growth theory the key word is 'endogenous' – something which arises from within. Earlier it was assumed that growth was caused by 'exogenous' factors. Applying the concept of endogenously generated change to explain short term market fluctuations, however, seems to be a more difficult task. In recent years, some researchers have begun to do just that. Their models are typically populated by rational but half informed agents who make mistakes, but learn and adapt. As a result, the market never settles down into a stable equilibrium. Instead, it constantly changes and occasionally goes bonkers. '*Adaptive market hypothesis*', '*adaptive rational equilibrium*', '*efficient learning*', and '*rational belief equilibria*', are a few such market models.

While a lot of interesting and exciting research is happening, particularly in the U.S., to understand the intricacies of financial markets and financial institutions, not much work has been done in the Indian context. Efforts of FORE School of Management, New Delhi, to bring together group of researchers at FORE International Finance Conference 2014, are commendable.

I am happy to learn that the select research papers presented at this conference, on varied themes like Operational Efficiency, Capital Structure, and Risk Management in Banks, International Financial Markets, Corporate Governance Issues and Behavioural Finance, Corporate Finance, and Banking and Finance have been included in this publication, aptly titled *Emerging Horizons in Finance*. It presents a welcome addition to the contemporary literature thereby providing a peep in to the developments in present day finance.

Prof. Prasanna Chandra
Former Professor, IIM Bangalore

Introduction

In the dynamic global world of present times the way business is conceived and conducted has been undergoing dramatic exponential change. Finance has been at the centre of this transformation, thanks to emerging global linkages of investors, financial service providers, financial markets and businesses. As the interactive markets evolve in both developed and emerging regions of the world, finance has assumed centre stage influencing destinies of countries and its population alike. Independence of economies has been replaced with interdependence to the extent that no country seems to stay immune against developments taking place across the world in the hyperactive financial markets. With the changing times and practices there is a constant revision in regulatory and policy aspects which make the underlying philosophies and contexts of business world both exciting and challenging.

In its quest to decode the developments in emerging business world and humbly contribute to creation and dissemination of new knowledge through research, FORE School of Management organizes International Conferences on a chosen field as part of its Foundation Day celebrations. FORE International Finance Conference (FIFC) 2014 was held on 27-28 November 2014 at its campus in New Delhi. The conference aimed to provide a forum to analyze, discuss and debate the underlying logic of events, actions, practices and perspectives in the financial domain through presentation of research papers in finance. The august international gathering of eminent researchers, academicians, practitioners and regulators in the conference had lively presentations and thought provoking discussion over sharing of diverse spectrum of viewpoints. Through collective wisdom of learned speakers and research paper presentations the conference provided an opportunity to learn and develop participants worldview of logic and reason.

Research papers presented at the conference have been selected by subject experts through blind review process and being included in this book *Emerging Horizons in Finance*. The book is a compendium of research papers presenting outcome of research on financial aspects of business, markets, regulations and economy. The research papers have been grouped in to the following broad areas:

1. Operational Efficiency, Capital Structure and Risk Management in Banks
2. International Financial Markets
3. Corporate Governance Issues and Behavioral Finance
4. Corporate Finance
5. Banking & Finance

SECTION I: OPERATIONAL EFFICIENCY, CAPITAL STRUCTURE AND RISK MANAGEMENT IN BANKS

This section contains six papers. The paper titled "Intellectual Capital disclosure trends. Evidence from Indian banking sector" authored and presented by Meena Bhatia and Vandana Mehrotra, focused on intellectual capital and emphasizes on growing importance of Intellectual Capital (IC): a need for reporting and regulatory aspects.

The paper titled "Efficiency Mapping of the Indian Banking System using Data Envelopment Analysis" has been presented by P.K. Gupta and Sandeepa Kaur. This paper traces the trends in development of Indian banking system, focusing on the dynamics of bank efficiency. Enticed by the reform of Indian banking sector in early 1990s and further slowdown in the economy as a result of global financial crisis in late 2000s, the paper analyzes the performance of Indian banks using data envelopment analysis. The performance is measured in terms of technical efficiency, returns-to-scale, and Malmquist Productivity Index for a sample of 33 banks.

The paper titled "Low Risk Anomaly- Evidence from India" by Nehal Joshipura makes an attempt to investigate the presence of low risk anomaly in Indian stock market. It highlights evidences of low risk anomaly in US and other global markets, where portfolio of low volatility stocks deliver superior risk adjusted returns as compared to market index and high volatility stocks portfolio. The study is based on construction of low and high volatility portfolios using volatility of historical monthly returns of stocks and holding portfolios for the next period on iterative basis.

The paper titled "Basel III: Implications for Indian banks" by Siddharth Shukla analyses the guidelines of Basel III. It explains new regulations which make capital requirements stiffer with specific liquidity requirements. The paper examines suitability, compliance and possible impacts of implementation of Basel III regulations among Indian Banks. The issues and challenges faced by Indian banks are dealt with in the paper.

Shalu Mahajan and Madhu Vij in their paper analyze the impact of risk management capabilities on profitability of banks in India in post nationalization era. The paper explains that risk management directly influences the financial performance of the banks. The paper is developed on the basis of quantitative analysis in terms of Return on Assets regressed on risk management capabilities of banks, comprising of interest rate risk management (NETIM), natural hedging (NOTIM), provisions (PROV) and solvency risk management (CAR). The study suggests that risk awareness of banks increased during the sample period.

Neelam Tandon and Deepak Tandon analyze Basel III norms implementation in Indian banking sector. It emphasises that the very objective of Basel III capital requirements is to improve banking sector's ability to absorb shocks. Greater transparency, disclosures and improved governance and risk management are key areas for improvement. According to the study Indian banks have learnt to be robust and resilient through Capital, Leverage, and Liquidity maintenance. Thus they would gear themselves for Basel 3 implementation by 2019. The authors have emphasized the need for regulatory compliances, proactive actions by Indian Banks to assess their business lines, level of risk profiles, economizing Capital and drawing up strategies to raise further capital.

SECTION II: INTERNATIONAL FINANCIAL MARKETS

This section includes four papers. Paper by Freda Swaminatnan titled "To be or not to be- a Financial Perspective to Brand Equity" focuses on Brand Equity that adds intangible value to a brand in the market. According to this study, the brands are recognized as an asset of an organization where the value in some cases has gone up considerably, between 20-25 times. This study looks at annual reports of some brands listed in Inter brand's Top 100 Global brands, and raises the marketing and financial issues of brand equity. The intangible values in the annual report have been analyzed from marketing and finance perspective. The paper recommends that brand equity should be looked at as an integration of marketing and finance orientation of an organization.

Paper titled "Macro-Economic Determinants impacting Exchange Rate in India" presented by Pooja Misra and Tanvi Babbar, explains the role of exchange rate in determining trade levels. According to this study the primary goals of any economy whether developed or developing is to maintain a stable exchange rate. Volatile exchange rates negatively impact international trade and exchange rate risks discourage foreign financial investors from investing into a country. The volatility of the exchange rate of Indian Rupee has been the focus of study. The paper analyzes macroeconomic determinants that impact exchange rate of the country's currency as against dominating currencies in the international market. It also establishes the correlation between strength of the relationship and macroeconomic determinants with specific reference to the exchange rate of the Indian Rupee against US dollars.

"Impact of Global Capital Flows on Indian Real Estate and Stock Markets" has been presented by Taral Pathek. This paper examines impact of foreign capital flows on BSE Index, its volume, return and market capitalization. It also looks into the variations caused in the housing prices (as measured by CPI Index of the housing sector) and bank credit due to Foreign Direct Investment flows. The author has applied Granger-causality approach to investigate the causality between FII flow, FDI flow and other macroeconomic variables like foreign exchange reserves, money supply and foreign exchange rates.

"Stock Price Reactions to Cash Dividend Announcements" has been presented by Pawan Kumar Jha. This paper examines stock price reactions around cash dividend announcements The research paper examines significance of mean abnormal return on and around the announcement date. The results indicate that most of the t-statistics of AARs and CAARs during event window period are not close to zero, which indicates that stock price of sample companies mostly react to cash dividend announcements during the event in window period. In general, the findings strongly support the dividend signaling hypothesis in explaining the stock price reactions to an announcement of cash dividend.

SECTION III: CORPORATE GOVERNANCE ISSUES AND BEHAVIORAL FINANCE

In all, four papers have been included in this section. In the paper by Ambrish Gupta titled, "Corporate Governance- Enacting Financial Discipline and Reporting" the author has made an in-depth review and analysis on the subject considering various issues and policy matters related to corporate governance. The paper traces enactment of The Accounting Industry Reforms Act, 2002, popularly known as Sarbanes-Oxley Act and explain various aspects of it. It analyses corporate governance norms through clause 49 being followed in India. This paper also examines the extent of compliance of these norms by listed companies to ascertain the corporate sector's response towards voluntary compliance.

Paper titled "Inter Linkages of Ownership Structure, Corporate Governance and Firm Performance" is jointly authored by Namita Rajput, Richa Kumar and Bharti. It explains fair principles and high ethical values of the companies that help in reducing costs and benefitting the organizations in a long way. The study concludes that better corporate governance practices can reduce agency costs, help easy access in competitive and global markets, improve their financial performance and thus lead to wealth maximization of the shareholders for listed companies. The paper examines and addresses noticeable gaps relating to corporate governance practices in Indian literature.

Paper titled "An Analytical Study of Behavioural Biases – An Investors' Perspective" has been jointly authored by T V Raman and Neha Agarwal. This paper stipulates that investors are loaded with information to choose an appropriate portfolio. According to this study several unconscious drivers affect the way investors make decisions about money as behavioural biases. Behavioural finance plays a crucial role in determining the behaviour of investors in market place and very often they act irrationally due to influence of psychological factors. The study analyses as to how portfolio choice depends on well- known behavioural phenomena: herding and overconfidence and optimism.

The paper jointly authored by Mukta Mani and Anupam Narula is titled "Financial Exclusion in India – Causes and Remedies". This paper investigates the causes of financial exclusion and suggests solutions for better financial inclusion. The study analyses and investigates large number of factors responsible for the high level of financial exclusion in India inclusive of market factors, societal factors and behavioural factors. The study also suggests certain remedial measures such as appropriate government policies, financial literacy and marketing strategies that can be taken up to deal with the situation.

SECTION IV: CORPORATE FINANCE

Paper authored by Himanshu Joshi is titled, "Correlation Structure, Portfolio Size and Diversification Benefits – Means Variance Optimization vs. Market Model". According to this study portfolio diversification benefit and optimum portfolio size depends upon internal correlation structure of the market as well as its correlation with other economies. The study analyzes correlation for stocks in Indian (Nifty) and US market (Nasdaq) to know the optimal size of portfolios, where results show higher correlations for the Nasdaq 100 in comparison to Nifty 50. According to findings of the analysis, the study concludes that Indian equity market provides better opportunity for international diversification for U.S. investors. The findings are also compared with a single factor market model.

The paper titled "Determinants of Corporate Credit Ratings in India" has been jointly authored by Rachan Sareen and Madhu Vij. According to this study Credit Rating Agencies (CRAs) play a key role in financial markets by helping to reduce the information asymmetry about creditworthiness of companies between investors and issuers. The paper empirically analyzes the relationship of financial characteristics and corporate governance measures with the credit ratings in 218 companies in three industries in manufacturing sectors of India- Textile, Steel and Paper. The paper develops a model that depicts a significant relationship between the credit ratings and the selected variables.

The paper titled "Financial Determinants of Firm's Value-Evidence From Indian Firms" is authored by Pushpendra Singh. This paper investigates empirically the determinants of firm value creation. The study examines various factors such as net sales, profit, fixed assets, dividend pay-out ratio and capital structure as the financial variables affecting firm's value. Appropriate tools have been applied to identify multiple correlations among variables and a test applied to check stationarity of data. Pooled Regression Model (PRM) has been applied to identify the significant factors. Findings of the paper match with the proposition of Modigliani and Miller, i.e. Capital structure doesn't influence value of a firm. The research outcome also suggests that WACC has a significant impact on value of the firm.

SECTION V: BANKING AND FINANCE

This section on Banking and Finance has four papers. The paper titled "Dividend Signaling Effect" is jointly authored by Pervin A. Gandhi and Neha Taneja. The paper investigates the Dividend Signaling effect of selected 20 companies which are part of S&P BSE MID CAP Index and announced considerable dividend for a particular time period. The study concludes high increase in the frequency of Dividend announcements and the amount of Dividend per share (DPS) in two different periods. The study finds significant wealth effects around dividend changes as proposed by the signaling models.

The paper titled "Effect of Merger on Financial Performance in Banking Industry" has been authored by Megha Aggarwal. The author has made an analysis of mergers and acquisitions considering the case of ICICI Bank with an experience of having many mergers in the past. The study analyzes financial performance of ICICI bank in pre and post-merger periods to analyze how significant benefits were achieved by ICICI Bank after the merger. To find out the benefits of merger, the author considered important factors such as Profitability, Liquidity and Leverage to determine the significance differences in financial performance under these components.

The paper authored by Poonam Singh is titled "Imperative Call for Mergers of Public Sector Banks in India". The paper emphasizes that in the changing scenario of banking with pace of globalization and higher degree of competitiveness, consolidation of banks seems to be more imperative not only for better business growth but also to compete globally more successfully. The paper assesses health of public sector banks over a period of time. To analyze various factors and their outcome, discriminate analysis is used in this study to make distinction as regards health of banks to be fragile and distress bank. The author also used Logit model to construct the Altman Z-score for public sector banks to bring more efficiency.

The paper titled "Size Premium or Liquidity in Drag?" has been authored by Ashok Bhardwaj Abbott. The author in this paper has taken an exhaustive view of various research studies undertaken in the past on the subject and analyzed their significance in the present context and raised several issues about their validity. The author made an empirical study to suggest a strong role for liquidity in explaining higher raw and excess returns realized by investors in smaller, less liquid stocks.

We trust and believe that the research work on divergent issues presented by learned experts in finance will provide a useful insight to policy makers, financial and business organizations, institutions, academic bodies and professionals. We are confident that the findings of research papers compiled in this book will contribute its bit of knowledge to the ever emerging complex field of finance.

SECTION I

OPERATIONAL EFFICIENCY, CAPITAL STRUCTURE AND RISK MANAGEMENT IN BANKS

Intellectual Capital Disclosure and Determinants

Evidence from Indian Banking Sector

Meena Bhatia and Vandana Mehrotra[1]

Birla Institute of Management Technology (BIMTECH), Greater Noida, Uttar Pradesh

[1] GD Goenka World Institute, Gurgaon, Haryana

e-mail: meena.bhatia@bimtech.ac.in; vandana.mehrotra@gdgoenka.ac.in

ABSTRACT

The intellectual capital disclosures of banks in India are largely unexplored in spite of significance of the banking sector to the economy. The study attempts to explain the extent of Intellectual Capital Disclosure (ICD) by the Indian banking sector, and to examine the relationship of ICD with nine independent variables. A disclosure index is created to study the extent and the Multiple Regression Model is used to examine the relationship of disclosure index with independent variables, namely Bank size, Bank risks, Efficiency, Bank age, Human capital pressure, Ownership pattern, Leverage level, Structural complexity, and Board composition. The results reveal that there is no clear pattern of ICD in the Indian banking sector. Intellectual Capital Disclosure is influenced by Size, Risk, Human capital and Board composition. The study concludes that banks in India must improve on ICD practices, as these disclosures will reduce information asymmetry between insiders and other stakeholders and make capital markets more efficient.

Keywords: Intellectual Capital Disclosure, Determinants, Content Analysis, Correlation Analysis, Multiple Regression Analysis, Banking, India

INTRODUCTION

In a continuously changing environment; the competitiveness of each firm has become the key to its survival. A firm creates competitive advantage in this knowledge-based world through its employees, customers, processes, infrastructure, information systems, innovativeness, and such other assets called intellectual assets. As a result, the growing research interest in recent years is the area of Intellectual Capital (IC). As observed by Abeysekara (2006), the shift in the focus of management from tangible to intangible capital while considering 'value creation' processes in the firm, has highlighted the importance of IC within the firm. Value creation is the process of transforming or improving corporate routines and practices (Mouritsen et al., 2001; Abeysekara, 2006).

The traditional financial statement model, based on historical pricing, concentrating mainly on the measurement of material measurable values, and the financial effects of executed transactions omit certain key factors for determining the value of an enterprise, such as the significance of intellectual capital, and the capacity for creating future value. The result of this is a gap in the disclosed information between the value of the company estimated by the capital market, and its adequate balance sheet value (Helin, 2001). As claimed by Abeysekera (2008), 'disclosure of IC in annual reports helps to make capital markets more efficient by reducing information asymmetry between "insiders" and investors.' Shareholder value and market value of an organization is enhanced by disclosing IC information in the annual reports to capital markets (Abdolmohammadi, 2005).

Banking industry being truly representative of a knowledge-based industry, where value creation is mainly through intangible assets and resources, has therefore been taken for study. The present paper focuses on the extent of level of Intellectual Capital Disclosure (ICD) and the factors influencing ICD in the Indian banking industry. To the best of our knowledge, this is the first research on intellectual capital disclosures in Indian Banking sector. The objective of this study is summarized below:

1. To examine the extent of IC disclosures in the Indian banking sector.
2. To examine whether there is any relationship between the IC disclosures and Bank size, Bank risks, Efficiency, Bank age, Human capital pressure, Ownership pattern, Leverage level, Structural complexity, and Board composition.

LITERATURE REVIEW

In recent times, research on IC and its disclosure has seen a growth in case of corporate and banks across developed and developing nations. These studies have frequently investigated the status of IC disclosure in a particular country (usually cross-sectional). Examples comprise study by Guthrie and Petty (2000) on Australia, Bontis (2003) on Canada, Abeysekera and Guthrie (2005) on Sri Lanka, Li et al. (2008) on UK, and Yi and Davey (2010) on China. Studies with regard to a specific industrial sector have also been conducted. Such studies include White et al. (2007) on bio-technology firms, Campbell and Rahman (2010) on a single company (Marks & Spencer), and Cohen et al. (2014) on the Small and Medium-sized Enterprise (SME) sector. It was observed by most researchers that the level of disclosure by firms across different countries was low and generally in qualitative form (Goh and Lim, 2004; Guthrie et al., 2006; Whiting and Woodcock, 2011).

Literature also shows that some studies were undertaken to compare ICD practices across different countries. These studies include studies undertaken by Vergauwen and Alem (2005) on France, Netherlands and Germany; Vandemaele et al. (2005) on Sweden, Netherlands and UK; Guthrie et al. (2006) on Australia and Hong Kong; and Abeysekera (2008) on Singapore and Sri Lanka. This type of research resulted in a better understanding of ICD practices in an international context.

Some researchers attempted to study the trend of ICD in a particular country or industry by undertaking a longitudinal research. Such researchers include Williams (2001); Petty and Cuganesan (2005); Brüggen et al. (2009); Abeysekera (2010); and Campbell and Rahman (2010). They analysed the annual report over a period of time and observed that the level of disclosure was on the rise.

There are also a few studies where researchers have made an attempt to examine the factors that determine the level of ICD in a particular country or industry (García-meca et al., 2005; White et al., 2007; Li et al., 2008; Abeysekera, 2010; Whiting and Woodcock, 2011). The most commonly used determinants of ICD included Industry type, Size of company, Listing status, Profitability, Level of leverage, Structure of ownership, Proportion of independent directors, and Type of auditor.

It is observed that most of the earlier research regarding ICD focuses on developed countries and very few on developing countries (Goh and Lim, 2004; Abeysekera and Guthrie, 2005; Kamath, 2008a; Xiao, 2008; Abeysekera, 2010; Yi and Davey, 2010; Singh and Kansal, 2011). Research on IC and its disclosure in the context of India is truly in its nascent stage. Earlier studies have focussed on examining the ICD practices followed in a few specific sectors, as well as across sectors. Examples comprise studies conducted by Ubha and Joshi (2009) on IT companies; Kamath (2008a) on IT, Entertainment, Communication and Knowledge companies; Bhasin (2011) on IT companies; Singh and Kansal (2011) on Pharmaceutical companies; and Sen and Sharma (2013) on Pharmaceutical and Software companies. As observed by most researchers internationally, it was observed in India too that the level of disclosure of IC by Indian firms was low and primarily in narrative or discursive form (Sen and Sharma, 2013).

Very few studies have been conducted in India comparing ICD practices followed by Indian firms with other countries Joshi et al. (2010) identified ICD differences between Indian and Australian firms. They observed that disclosures by Indian companies were more than Australian Software and Technology Sector companies.

As can be observed, research on ICD has been conducted in case of corporates across developed and developing nations. However, very limited literature is available on ICD in the context of banking sector in India. It fills the gap in the literature of ICD since there is no prior study of ICD in the banking sector in India which finds the extent of ICD and relationship between ICD and the various factors.

THE DETERMINANTS OF INTELLECTUAL CAPITAL DISCLOSURE OF INDIAN BANKING INDUSTRY

Bank Size

Brüggen et al. (2009); Kamath (2008b); White et al. (2007); Guthrie et al. (2006); Garcia-Meca et al. (2005); Ousama (2012); and El-Bannany (2013) found that the size of the organization has a positive relationship with the extent of ICD. It has been argued that large companies disclose more information than small companies because of factors including the cost of preparing information for disclosure, better internal management information systems, higher visibility, and exposure to political attacks and pressure to exercise social responsibility (Ousama et al., 2012; Gárcia-Meca et al., 2005).

Based on the above argument, the first hypothesis is:

H1: There is a relationship between Bank size and ICD level.

Bank Risks

Hossain (2008) and Jameel and Weerathunga (2013) have argued that banks with higher risk, that is, higher Non-Performing Assets (NPAs) may be reluctant to disclose more information in their annual reports, especially voluntary disclosure. Non-Performing Assets have a negative effect on the profitability of the financial institutions (Vighneswara, 2013). High level of NPAs disclosed in the financial statements of a bank may lead to a negative perception caused by bank's high risk (Hossain, 2008). It can thus be argued that the level of NPAs of a bank may impact the disclosure of intellectual capital in the annual reports.

Basedon the above argument, the second hypothesis is:

H2: There is a relationship between risk and ICD level.

Efficiency

Business of banks is primarily concerned with expected returns. The profit earning mechanism thus depends *inter alia* on how effectively these banks conduct their lending and borrowing activities (Hossain, 2008). The Net Interest Margin (NIM) is considered to be an important measure of Efficiency of banks (Kunt and Huizinga, 1998). It indicates as to how effectively the banks deploy their funds to generate income from credit and investment operations (Das, 2013). Efficient organizations are keen to disclose more voluntarily.

Based on the above discussion, the third hypothesis is:

H3: There is a relationship between Efficiency and ICD level.

Bank Age

Owusu-Ansah (1998) and Akhtaruddin (2005) suggested that the age of the organization is a potentially important explanatory variable in relation to the extent of disclosure. Based on research conducted by Suchman (1995), it can be argued that old companies as compared to newer ones might disclose more information about intellectual capital in their annual reports in order to retain their image in the society.

Hamid (2004), for Malaysia, found a positive relationship between the level of disclosure and the age of the firm. El-Bannany (2007) and Hossain (2008) found no relationship between the level of disclosure and the age of the firm. It is not possible to reach a conclusion that long-established banks disclose more information than newly-established banks.

This leads to the fourth hypothesis:

H4: There is a relationship between the age of the bank and the ICD level.

Human Capital Pressure

Abeysekera (2008) defines human capital as the combination of factors possessed by individuals and the collective workforce of a firm. Human capital encompasses knowledge, skills and technical ability, personal traits, share information, participate in a team, and focus on the goals of the firm (Bontis and Fitz-enz, 2002). Edvinsson and Sullivan (1996), Graham and Pizzo (1998) and O'Donnell et al. (2006) consider that human capital is important because its extraction creates capital accumulation of firms.

Subbarao and Zeghal (1997) stated that Human resources information disclosed in annual reports is considered an indicator of the importance of human resources to a company.

This suggests the fifth hypothesis of this study:

H5: There is a relationship between the Human capital pressure and the ICD level.

Ownership Pattern

Eng and Mak (2003) and Said et al. (2009) have documented a significant association between government ownership and corporate disclosures. Mohd Ghazali and Weetman (2006) suggested that companies where governmental bodies hold substantial portion of shares may be forced to provide additional information in the annual reports because of their accountability to the public at large.

The following is the hypothesis formulated:

H6: There is a relationship between ownership pattern and ICD level.

Leverage Level

As per White et al. (2010) and Dhaliwal et al. (1982), companies willing to debt-finance, face pressure in the context of global reporting. In order to satisfy the information needs of existing lenders, there is more emphasis on value-added voluntary reporting. This is supported by the managerial stakeholder theory as well. As suggested by Jensen and Meckling (1976), the traditional agency theory, firm managers are predicted to have motivations for particular accounting policy choice and voluntary disclosures because of obligations to lenders in existing debt covenants.

Based on the above discussion, the ninth hypothesis is:

H7: There is a relationship between leverage and ICD level.

Structural Complexity

Hossain (2008), Haniffa and Cooke (2002) and Speigal and Yamori (2004) argued that an important factor that influences the extent of disclosure is the structural complexity of the firm. Such complexity requires a firm to have an effective management information system for monitoring purposes (Ahmed and Courtis, 1999; Cooke, 1989). The availability of such a system helps in cost reduction of information availability, thereby providing the expectation of higher disclosure.

Based on the above discussion, the eighth hypothesis is:

H8: There is a relationship between structural complexity and ICD level.

Board Composition

The board of directors is an important tool to create, develop, leverage, and manage IC of a firm and thus, affect its performance (Abidin et al., 2009; Ho and Williams, 2003). According to Williams (2001), boards of directors can structure relevant strategies and policies on how to obtain and best utilize the required resources underlying IC. The decisions of inside directors or executive directors would focus on policies that 'maintain or improve product quality and innovation through increased research and development spending' (Johnson and Greening, 1999).

A study by (Rashid et al., 2012) concluded that ICD is negatively related to the proportion of independent directors on the board, which is in contrast with the results of (Chen and Jaggi, 2000; Eng and Mak, 2003).

Thus, we hypothesise the following:

H9: There is a relationship between board composition on board and ICD level.

DATA AND METHODS

This section discusses the data collection procedure.

Scope of the Study

The Indian financial system comprises a large number of commercial banks and these are governed by the RBI, the central bank of India. As the study focuses on only the banking companies in India, all the listed banks on stock exchanges have been included. There are 40 banks listed on the Bombay Stock Exchange (BSE) and/or National Stock Exchange (NSE). The study attempted to study the entire population in examining the IC disclosures of banks in India. One foreign bank listed on the Indian stock exchange is excluded from the sample as it is subject to different regulation. Table 1 and Table 2 show the constituents of the study.

Table 1: Constituents of the Study

Sl. No.	*Name of the Bank*	*Type*
1	Allahabad Bank	Public Sector Bank
2	Andhra Bank	Public Sector Bank
3	Axis Bank	Private Sector Bank
4	Bank of India	Public Sector Bank
5	Bank of Maharashtra	Public Sector Bank
6	Bank of Baroda	Public Sector Bank
7	Canara Bank	Public Sector Bank
8	Central Bank	Public Sector Bank
9	City Union Bank	Public Sector Bank
10	Corporation Bank	Public Sector Bank
11	Dena Bank	Public Sector Bank
12	Dev Credit Bank	Private Sector Bank
13	Dhanlakshmi Bank	Private Sector Bank
14	Federal Bank	Private Sector Bank
15	HDFC Bank	Private Sector Bank
16	ICICI Bank	Private Sector Bank
17	IDBI Bank	Public Sector Bank
18	Indian Bank	Public Sector Bank
19	Indusind Bank	Private Sector Bank
20	ING Vysya Bank	Private Sector Bank
21	Indian Overseas Bank	Public Sector Bank
22	Jammu and Kashmir Bank	Private Sector Bank
23	Karnataka Bank	Private Sector Bank
24	Karur Vysya Bank	Private Sector Bank
25	Kotak Mahindra Bank	Private Sector Bank
26	Lakshmi Vilas Bank	Private Sector Bank
27	Oriental Bank	Public Sector Bank
28	Punjab National Bank	Public Sector Bank
29	Punjab and Sind Bank	Public Sector Bank
30	State Bank of India	Public Sector Bank
31	South Indian Bank	Private Sector Bank
32	State Bank Bikaner and Jaipur	Public Sector Bank

Sl. No.	Name of the Bank	Type
33	State Bank Mysore	Public Sector Bank
34	State Bank Travancore	Public Sector Bank
35	Syndicate Bank	Public Sector Bank
36	Uco Bank	Public Sector Bank
37	Union Bank	Public Sector Bank
38	United Bank	Public Sector Bank
39	Vijaya Bank	Public Sector Bank
40	Yes Bank	Private Sector Bank

Table 2: Constituents of the Study

	Type of Banks	Number	Percentage
1	Private Sector Bank	15	37.5
2	Public Sector Bank	25	62.5
	Total	40	

Scoring of the Disclosure Index

Content analysis can be fruitfully employed to examine virtually any type of communication (Abrahamson, 1983). Content analysis is a technique for making inferences by systematically and objectively identifying special characteristics of messages (Holsti, 1968). Many studies around ICD have used content analysis (Bukh et al., 2005; Cordazzo, 2007; Haji and Mubaraq, 2012). The selection of content is done according to consistently applied criteria; this requirement eliminates analysis in which only material supporting investigator's hypothesis are examined (Holsti, 1968). Content analysis is conducted on annual reports of listed banks in India. This study uses a 44-item disclosure index used by Haji and Mubarak (2012) for banking sector. The disclosure list contains three major heads namely:

1. Internal Capital with 10 items;
2. External capital with 16 items; and
3. Human capital with 18 items.

The familiarization exercise begins when researchers read annual reports individually before scoring the disclosure (Haji and Mubarak, 2012). To capture information pertaining with ICD, the following steps were conducted:

1. The annual report of each of the bank was studied in detail individually by both the researchers.

2. The list, as used by Haji and Muabrak (2012) is now used to capture information on 44 intellectual capital items. The IC information is now recorded in the coding list.

For constructing the disclosure index, each bank is given a score of 1 for item disclosed and a score of 0 for items not disclosed. Disclosure index is made by dividing the total number of items disclosed by the denominator of total items measured, that is,44.

$$\text{Disclosure score} = \sum_{i=1}^{n} d$$

where $d = 1$ if the ratio is disclosed and 0 if it is not, n = number of items.

The extent of the ICD index is quantified using the following formula:

$$\text{IC Disclosure Source (ICDS)} = \sum_{i=1}^{m} di / m \qquad ...(1)$$

where di expresses item i when the item's value is 1 with disclosure and 0 when there was no disclosure, and M is 44 (the total number of items being measured).

Regression Model

Multivariate analysis is appropriate when there are two or more independent variables, and the variables are analysed simultancously. This technique is concerned with the simultaneous relationships among two or more independent variables and a dependent variable. In multivariate analysis, all the variables that have interrelationships that preclude the interpretation of the effect of each variate separately are considered random variates (Krishnaswamy et al., 2006).

Keeping in view the objective of the study multiple regression analysis is considered as an appropriate model. It studies the relationship between ICD level and its potential indicators. Following is the model:

$$Y_{ICDS} = \alpha + \beta_1 X_{Size} + \beta_2 X_{Risk} + \beta_3 X_{Eff} + \beta_4 X_{Age} + \beta_5 X_{Hcap} + \beta_6 X_{Opat} + \Sigma\beta_7 X_{Lev} + \beta_8 X_{Scom} + \beta_9 X_{Bcom} + \varepsilon \qquad (2)$$

Table 3 provides a description of dependent and independent variables measured and analysed during the course of this study.

Table 3: Dependent and Independent Variables Measured and Analysed

Title	*Description*
Dependent Variable	
ICDS	Intellectual Capital Disclosure score represented by the ratio of the number of IC items disclosed by the bank to the total number of IC items.

Title	*Description*
Independent Variables	
A	Embodies the influence of such variables as have been excluded from the model but exercise some influence on ICD. It may also be interpreted as the minimum autonomous value of Y, which is not affected by any change in the value of other variables.
Size	Size represented by the market capitalisation of the bank as on 31 March 2013.
Risk	Risk Represented by the percentage of gross NPAs to total advances as on 31 March 2013.
Eff	Efficiency Represented by the Net interest Margin in percentage terms as on 31 March 2013.
Age	Age represented the age of the bank since formulation, as on 31 March 2013.
Hcap	Human Capital pressure represented by number of employees with the bank as on 31 March 2013.
Opat	Ownership pattern represented by dummy variable. Dummy variable equal to one if the bank is private and zero in case it is a public sector bank.
Lev	Leverage Represented by the percentage of debt to total capital as on 31 March 2013.
Scom	Structural Complexity represented by number of subsidiaries of a bank as on 31 March 2013.
Bcom	Board Composition represented by the percentage of executive directors to total directors as on 31 March 2013.

RESULTS AND DISCUSSIONS

This section presents the results of the study. In the first part of the analysis information pertaining with each item on the disclosure index is discussed and analysed. Analysis is also carried out with respect to three categories used for ICD. The second part deals with descriptive analysis, followed by multivariate analysis, wherein results with respect to correlation and regression are presented and discussed.

IC Disclosure Analysis Item-wise and Category-wise

Bank's intellectual capital disclosure item-wise in percentage terms in three major categories is reflected in Table 4. For the category Internal capital, Information Systems (technology) is the highest disclosed item followed by Corporate Philosophy. Within external capital the highest disclosed item is Customer services; this is the highest disclosed item overall. The lowest disclosed item amongst the 16 items of external capital are Business collaboration, Favourable contracts, Brand development, and Customer knowledge with no score. Of human capital the most disclosed is Employee education and training, with Work related knowledge, Geographical distribution, and Entrepreneur spirit being the lowest with no score. This is also supported by Table 5.

Table 4: Intellectual Capital Disclosure Item-wise in Percentage

Sl. No.	*Intellectual Capital Items*	*Percentage of Banks Making Disclosure*
Internal Capital		
1	Patent	0
2	Copyright	0
3	Trademarks	0
4	Corporate Culture	2.50
5	Corporate Philosophy	92.50
6	Leadership	62.50
7	Information Systems (Technology)	95.00
8	Financial Relations	2.50
9	Innovation	55.00
10	Research and Development	7.50
External Capital		
1	Business Collaboration	0
2	Joint Ventures	37.50
3	Favourable Contracts	0
4	Brands	47.50
5	Brands Recognition	5.00
6	Brand Development	0
7	Goodwill	17.50
8	Distribution Channels	7.50
9	Market Share	35.00
10	Information about Customer (Type/Number)	2.50
11	Customer Services	97.50
12	Customer Loyalty	5.00
13	Customer Relation	47.50
14	Customer Satisfaction	55.00
15	Customer Feedback	20.00
16	Customer Knowledge	0
Human Capital		
1	Number of Staff	65.00
2	Employee Education and Training	90.00
3	Employee Know-How	2.50

Sl. No.	*Intellectual Capital Items*	*Percentage of Banks Making Disclosure*
4	Work related Knowledge	0
5	Expertise	57.50
6	Professional Qualification	10.00
7	Academic Qualifications	37.50
8	Age and Gender	17.50
9	Geographical Distribution	0
10	Safety and Health at Work	15.00
11	Employee Succession Path Training	2.50
12	Knowledge Sharing	2.50
13	Employee Retention	15.00
14	Employee Engagement	17.50
15	Motivation	25.00
16	Employee Satisfaction Survey	2.50
17	Employee Communication	2.50
18	Entrepreneur Spirit	0

The average score for each category is reflected in Table 6, which reflects that internal capital disclosure is most preferred with the average score of 31.75 per cent.

Table 5: Disclosure Pattern as Per Items in Intellectual Capital Disclosure Category

Category	*Most Disclosed*	*Second Most Disclosed*	*Least Disclosed*
Internal Capital	Information Systems (technology)	Corporate Philosophy	Patent
			Copyright
			Trademarks
External capital	Customer services	Customer satisfaction	Business collaboration
			Favourable contracts
			Brand development
			Customer knowledge
Human Capital	Employee education and training	Number of staff	Geographical distribution
			Work related knowledge
			Entrepreneur spirit

Table 6: Intellectual Capital Disclosure Per Three Categories

	Major Categories of Disclosure Index	*Average Percentage Score*
1	Internal Capital (10 items)	31.75
2	External Capital (16 items)	23.59
3	Human Capital (18 items)	20.14

Table 7: Frequency of Banks with Intellectual Capital Disclosure

Number of IC Items Disclosed	*Frequency*	*Percentage*
0 to 4	4	10.00
5 to 8	8	20.00
9 to 12	16	40.00
13 to 16	9	22.50
16 to 20	3	7.50
20 to 44	0	0.00
Total	40	100

Table 7 presents information about frequency of intellectual capital disclosure items by 40 banks. The results reveal that of 44 items, 9 to 12 items are being disclosed by 16 banks. None of the banks are disclosing more than 19 items. Only three banks of 40 listed banks are disclosing more than 16 intellectual capital items.

Descriptive Analysis

Descriptive statistics summarises large quantities of data and present it in simple form. The descriptive statistics for the dependent and explanatory variables are presented in Table 8. Out of the total number of items in the intellectual capital disclosure list (44 items), the banks disclose on an average, 0.24 (24 percent), that is approximately 11 items, varying from highest as 43.2 per cent (19 items) and the lowest being 4.5 per cent (2 items) of the proposed voluntary intellectual capital items. The low frequency of ICD suggests that there are certain factors which may restrain banks from disclosing more information on intellectual capital.

The average size of a bank is INR 19,381.826 crore (3,200 million US dollars, 1 US dollar = INR 60). Risk of Indian banks is low, average being 2.9 per cent. Efficiency of the bank is within the range of 2.12 per cent to 4.7 per cent and average is 3 per cent. In India we have a bank which is 148 years old and the youngest listed bank is 5 years old. One of the banks is the largest employers in India with 2,28,296 employees, with the average numbers of employees with listed banks in India being 25,781. The Ownership pattern reflects that 37.5 per cent of the sample is private sector banks. On an average, banks borrow 8.7 per cent of the total capital, and they have close to three subsidiaries; of the total board, an average 22.9 per cent are executive directors.

Table 8: Descriptive Statistics of Dependent and Explanatory Variables

Variables	*Mean*	Σ	σ²	*Kurtosis*	*Skewness*	*Range*	*Minimum*	*Maximum*
ICDS	0.240	0.089	0.008	−0.187	−0.253	0.386	0.045	0.432
Size	19381.826	36305.504	1318089599.221	7.346	2.836	148406.264	389.516	148795.779
Risk	0.029	0.013	0.000	−0.800	0.047	0.054	0.002	0.056
Eff	3.000	0.588	0.346	1.080	0.859	2.580	2.120	4.700
Age	71.850	35.636	1269.926	−0.680	−0.386	143.000	5.000	148.000
Hcap	25781.425	36867.807	1359235169.892	24.137	4.511	226196.000	2100.000	228296.000
Opat	0.375	0.490	0.240	−1.805	0.537	1.000	0.000	1.000
Lev	0.087	0.065	0.004	3.994	1.899	0.297	0.015	0.312
Scom	2.700	4.553	20.728	2.981	1.950	17.000	0.000	17.000
Bcom	0.229	0.081	0.007	−0.234	0.235	0.354	0.091	0.444

Multivariate Analysis

Multivariate analysis is conducted on the data using correlation and multiple regression techniques.

Multi-collinearity

While using the Multiple Regression Model it is essential to test that independent or explanatory variables are not perfectly linearly correlated. To achieve the underlying assumption of the Multiple Regression Analysis, the variables were checked for multi-collinearity in two ways. One is by examining the correlation coefficients between the independent variables. The values of Pearson correlations show the relationships between independent variables, and are a method for diagnosing the multi-collinearity (Allison, 1999). It is shown that the highest correlation coefficient among independent variables is 0.630. A general rule is, if the correlation is between −0.7 and 0.7 there is not a problem using both of the independent variables (Lind et al., 2008). Results, as reflected in Table 8 confirm this. To check further, the Variance Inflation Factor (VIF) test was also conducted. It is generally believed that any VIF exceeding 10 and tolerance value lower than 0.10 indicate a potential problem of multi-collinearity (Hair et al., 2010; Gujarati, 2004). The results, as given in Table 9 show that the coefficients of independent variables and the tolerance value are quite below the rule of thumb. As a result, multi-collinearity was not a serious problem for the regression model.

Correlation Matrix Analysis

Pearson Correlation Coefficients are revealed in Table 9. There is a positive and significant relationship at 1 per cent level of significance between ICD with size of the bank ($r = 0.488$), with human capital ($r = 0.503$), with structural complexity ($r = 0.604$).

Table 9: Pearson Correlation Coefficient among Variables

	ICDS	*Size*	*Risk*	*Eff*	*Age*	*Hcap*	*Opat*	*Lev*	*Scom*	*Bcomp*
ICDS	1.000									
Size	0.488**	1.000								
Risk	−0.077	−0.072	1.000							
Eff	0.386*	0.478**	−0.331*	1.000						
Age	−0.334*	−0.439**	0.309	−0.317*	1.000					
Hcap	0.503**	0.771**	0.268	0.207	−0.171	1.000				
Opat	0.085	0.231	−0.401*	0.415**	−0.384*	−0.169	1.000			
Lev	0.389*	0.391*	−0.197	0.298	−0.532**	0.133	0.373*	1.000		
Scom	0.604**	0.630**	−0.006	0.329*	−0.445**	0.528**	0.098	0.605**	1.000	
Bcomp	0.388*	0.334*	0.447**	−0.006	−0.022	0.410**	−0.455**	0.206	0.483**	1.000

Significant at: **1 percent and *5 percent level.

There is a positive and significant relationship at 5 per cent level of significance between ICD with Efficiency of the bank ($r = 0.386$), with Board composition ($r = 0.388$), and with leverage ($r = 0.389$). There is a negative and significant relationship at 5 per cent level of significance between ICD with the age of the bank ($r = -0.334$).

Multiple Regression Analysis Results

Table 10(a) presents the results of the multiple regression analysis. Table 10(b) reveals the summary of the regression model. The adjusted R^2 is 0.408; it means this model explains 40.8 per cent of the association between ICD and independent variables. Table 10 shows that the overall regression model is significant ($F > F$ critical; $F = 3.985$ and F critical $= 0.001975$)

Analysis of Variance (ANOVA) assesses the overall significance of the model. As $p < 0.05$ model is significant and shows that the variables are significantly related to the overall intellectual capital disclosure (Table 10).

Table 10(a) reveals that four variables, namely Size, Risk, Human capital, and Board composition have association with ICD, thus rejecting the rest of five variables, namely Efficiency, Age, Ownership pattern, Leverage, and Structural complexity.

H1 *Size:* The results indicate that all the variables have coefficients of the expected sign except for Size in which the association is in the opposite direction and this association is statistically significant at 10 per cent level ($t = -1.927$). This is in contrast with the result of a study conducted by White et al. (2007) which revealed that bigger the size of the organization, more will be ICD. This can be due to environment, capital market expectations, and disclosure practices. Smaller banks may be disclosing more because they want to be assessed positively by analysts and investors.

H2 *Risk:* Risk is influencing ICD at 10 per cent level (t = −1.699). Lower the risk, higher is the ICD as revealed by the regression result. This is consistent with the result of a study conducted by Hossain (2008). Banks with high NPAs will not disclose more voluntarily.

H5 *Human Capital:* The result of linear regression analysis between Intellectual capital disclosure score and the independent variables indicate that coefficient for Human capital is significant at 5 per cent level (t = 2.630). Among all the variables, the number of employees has most significant result. This finding is consistent with the notion that banks with a larger number of employees have a positive impact on the IPO disclosure (Cordazzo, 2007).

H9 *Board Composition:* Board Composition is also significant at 10 per cent level (t = 1.990); this implies that larger the proportion of executive directors more will be ICD (Hossain, 2008). The results are also similar to the studies by Chen and Jaggi (2000) and Eng and Mak (2003).

Table 10(a): Regression Results

Coefficients[a]							
Model	*Unstandardized Coefficients*		*Standardized Coefficients*	*T*	*Sig. (p value)*	*Collinearity Statistics*	
	B	*Std. Error*	*Beta*			*Tolerance*	*VIF*
Size	−1.419E-6	0.000	−0.576	−1.927	0.063*	0.170	5.890
Risk	−1.978	1.164	−0.292	−1.699	0.100*	0.513	1.949
Eff	0.030	0.024	0.197	1.264	0.216	0.627	1.594
Age	0.000	0.000	−0.078	−0.488	0.629	0.587	1.704
Hcap	1.730E-6	0.000	0.713	2.630	0.013**	0.207	4.841
Opat	0.048	0.037	0.261	1.274	0.212	0.363	2.756
Lev	0.044	0.250	0.032	0.175	0.863	0.461	2.167
Scom	0.005	0.004	0.245	1.185	0.245	0.355	2.813
Bcomp	0.456	0.229	0.412	1.990	0.056*	0.355	2.819

[a] Dependent Variable: ICDS

*, ** Indicates significance at the 10 percent and 5 percent level, respectively.

Table 10(b): Regression Model Summary

R^2	0.545
Adjusted R^2	0.408
Intercept (constant)	0.065

Table 10: ANOVA for Regression

Sources of Variation	*Degrees of Freedom*	*Sum of Square*	*Mean Square*	*Computed F*	*F Critical*
Regression	9	0.169	0.018	3.984	0.0019
Residual	30	0.142	0.004		
Total	39	0.311			

CONCLUSION AND RECOMMENDATIONS

This study provides valuable insights about the extent of IC disclosure in the Indian Banking industry and the factors which influence the disclosure. Content analysis was done with a predetermined list of 44 items under three broad categories, namely Internal capital, External capital, and Human capital. The extent of IC disclosure is reflected through the mean score, which is 24 per cent. Most disclosed item of the 44 items is customer services (external capital category) which was disclosed by 39 banks out of 40 listed banks, followed by Information Technology and corporate philosophy (Internal capital category) which was disclosed by 38 and 37 banks, respectively, and employee education and training (Human capital category) which was disclosed by 36 banks.

Annual reports of the banks did not include information pertaining to patents, copyrights, and trademarks (Internal capital category); business collaboration, favourable contracts and brand development (external capital category), and work related knowledge, geographical distribution and entrepreneur spirit (human capital category). On one hand there is a bank which has a disclosure score of 43.182 per cent; on the other hand there is a bank with a score of 4.54 per cent. Highest score is by a public sector bank and the lowest score is also of a public sector bank. This reflects that there is no clear pattern of ICD practices of Indian banks in annual reports.

Findings reveal that of the nine variables, Size, Risk, Efficiency, Age, Human capital, Ownership pattern, Leverage, Structural complexity, and Board composition, ICD is influenced by Size, Risk, Human capital, and Board composition.

There are vast differences in items disclosed and overall ICD in banking industry. The RBI may like to introduce guidelines to improve the ICD as it helps in reducing information asymmetry between insiders and other stakeholders and make capital markets more efficient.

LIMITATIONS OF THE STUDY AND RECOMMENDATIONS FOR FURTHER RESEARCH

Research is a continuous process; one study leads to another. All studies have their own limitations and this study is no exception. The number of limitations of this study can be identified.

1. First, more evidence is needed on the determinants of intellectual capital disclosure before any generalization of the results can be made.
2. Second, this study considers one specific sector and covers a single year and is based in India. Future research should seek to broaden the current sample to further investigate the nature and determinants in other countries and/or sectors.
3. Third, for current research a predetermined checklist was used. Future research should seek to devise more vigorous method of making the list and assessing quality and quantity of ICD.
4. Fourth, only annual reports were considered for this study; there might be other means of ICD such as websites, initial public offering prospectus, employee handbook and brochures, etc.
5. Further study is necessary to identify whether the ICD is improving over a period of time for banks.

REFERENCES

A. Brüggen, P. Vergauwen, and M. Dao, 'Determinants of Intellectual Capital Disclosure: Evidence from Australia', *Management Decision*, vol. 47, no. 2, 2009, pp. 233–45.

A. Haji and S. Mubarak, 'The Trends of Intellectual Capital Disclosures: Evidence from the Nigerian Banking Sector', *Journal of Human Resource Costing and Accounting*, vol. 16, no. 3, 2012, pp. 184–209.

A. Helin, 'Quality and Measurement of Intellectual Capital at an Accounting Firm supplying an Intellectual Product', *Intellectual Product and Intellectual Capital*, Leon Kozminski Academy of Entrepreneurship and Management, Warschau, 2001, pp. 237–71.

A. Subbarao and D. Zeghal, 'Human Resources Information Disclosure in Annual Reports: An International Comparison', *Journal of Human Resource Costing and Accounting*, vol. 2, no. 2, 1997, pp. 53–73.

A. Yi and H. Davey, 'Intellectual Capital Disclosurein Chinese (mainland) Companies', *Journal of Intellectual Capital*, vol. 11, no. 3, 2010, pp. 326–47.

A.A. Ousama, A.H. Fatima, and A.R. Hafiz-Majdi, 'Determinants of Intellectual Capital Reporting: Evidence from Annual Reports of Malaysian listed Companies', *Journal of Accounting in Emerging Economies*, vol. 2, no. 2, 2012, pp. 119–39.

A.A. Rashid et al., 'IC Disclosures in IPO Prospectuses: Evidence from Malaysia', *Journal of Intellectual Capital*, vol. 13, no. 1, 2012, pp. 57–80.

A.L.M. Jameel and P.R. Weerathunga, 'The Empirical Investigation of the Extent of Disclosure in Annual Reports of Banking Sector in Sri Lanka', *The Empirical Investigation – PNCTM*, vol. 2, January 2013, 2013, pp. 114–19.

B. Kamath, 'Intellectual Capital Disclosure in India: Content Analysis of "TecK" Firms', *Journal of Human Resource Costing and Accounting*, vol. 12, no. 3, 2008a, pp. 213–24.

B.B. Graham and V.G. Pizzo, 'A Question of Balance: Case Studies in Strategic Knowledge Management', D.A. Klein, ed., *The Strategic Management of Intellectual Capital*, Woburn, MA: Butterworth-Heinemann, 1998.

C. Kamath, 'Intellectual Capital and Corporate Performance in Indian Pharmaceutical Industry', *Journal of Intellectual Capital*, vol. 9, Issue 4, 2008 b, pp. 684–704.

C.A. Ho and S.M. Williams, 'International Comparative Analysis of the Association between Board Structure and the Efficiency of Value added by a Firm from its Physical Capital and Intellectual Capital Resources', *The International Journal of Accounting*, vol. 38, no. 4, 2003, pp. 465–91.

C.J.P. Chen and B. Jaggi, 'Association between Independent Non-executive Directors, Family Control and Financial Disclosures in Hong Kong', *Journal of Accounting and Public Policy*, vol. 19, no. 2, 2000, pp. 285–310.

D. Campbell and M.R.A. Rahman, 'A Longitudinal Examination of Intellectual Capital Reporting in Marks & Spencer Annual Reports, 1978-2008', *The British Accounting Review*, vol. 42, no. 1, 2010, pp. 56–70.

D. O'Donnell et al., 'On the "Essential Condition of Intellectual Capital: Labour!",' *Journal of Intellectual Capital*, vol. 7, no. 1, 2006, pp. 111–28.

D. Ubha and M. Joshi, 'Financial Capital to Intellectual Capital: The Search for a new Paradigm in Accounting by an Indian Corporate Sector', *Proceedings of the International Conference on Intellectual Capital, Knowledge Management & Organizational Learning*, 2009, pp. 261–67.

D.S. Dhaliwal, G.L. Salamon, and E.D. Smith, 'The Effect of Owner versus Management Control on the Choice of Accounting Methods', *Journal of Accounting and Economics*, July 1982, pp. 77–117.

E. Garcia-Meca et al., 'The Explanatory Factors of Intellectual Capital Disclosure to Financial Analysts', *European Accounting Review*, vol. 14, no. 1, 2005, pp. 63–94.

F. Hamid, 'Corporate Social Disclosure by Banks and Finance Companies:

Malaysian Evidence', *Corporate Ownership and Control*, vol. 1, no. 4, 2004, pp. 118–30.

G. White et al., 'The Nature and Extent of Voluntary Intellectual Capital Disclosures by Australian and UK Biotechnology Companies', *Journal of Intellectual Capital*, vol. 11, no. 4, 2010, pp. 519–36.

G. White, A. Lee, and G. Tower, 'Drivers of Voluntary Intellectual Capital Disclosure in Listed Biotechnology Companies', *Journal of Intellectual Capital*, vol. 8, no. 3, pp. 517–37.

G.B. Kamath, 'The Intellectual Capital Performance of the Indian Banking Sector', *Journal of Intellectual Capital*, vol. 8, no. 1, 2007, pp. 96–123.

H.F. Xiao, Corporate Reporting of Intellectual Capital: Evidence from China', *The Business Review* (Cambridge), vol. 11, no. 1, 2008, pp. 124–29.

I. Abeysekera, 'Motivations Behind Human Capital Disclosure in Annual Reports', *Accounting Forum*, vol. 32, no. 1, 2008, pp. 16–29.

I. Abeysekera, 'The Influence of Board Size on Intellectual Capital Disclosure by Kenyan Listed Firms', *Journal of Intellectual Capital*, vol. 11, no. 4, 2010, pp. 504–18.

I. Abeysekera, 'The Project of Intellectual Capital Disclosure: Researching the Research', *Journal of Intellectual Capital*, vol. 7, no. 1, 2006, pp. 61–77.

I. Abeysekera, and J. Guthrie, 'An Empirical Investigation of Annual Reporting Trends of Intellectual Capital in Sri Lanka', *Critical Perspectives on Accounting*, vol. 16, no. 3, 2005, pp. 151–63.

J. Guthrie and R. Petty, 'Intellectual Capital: Australian Annual Reporting Practices', *Journal of Intellectual Capital*, vol. 1, no. 3, 2000, pp. 241–54.

J. Guthrie, R. Petty and F. Ricceri, 'The Voluntary Reporting of Intellectual Capital: Comparing Evidence from Hong Kong and Australia', *Journal of Intellectual Capital*, vol. 7, no. 2, 2006, pp. 254–71.

J. Li, R. Pike and R. Haniffa, 'Intellectual Capital Disclosure and Corporate Governance Structure in UK Firms', *Accounting and Business Research*, vol. 38, no. 2, 2008, pp. 137–59.

J. Mouritsen, H.T. Larsen and P.N. Bukh, 'Valuing the Future: Intellectual Capital Supplements at Skandia', *Accounting, Auditing and Accountability Journal*, vol. 14, Issue 4, 2001, pp. 399–422.

J.F. Hair, Jr. et al., *Multivariate Data Analysis*, 7th edn., Upper Saddle River, NJ: Prentice Hall, 2010.

K. Ahmed and J.K. Courtis, 'Associations between Corporate Characteristics and Disclosure Levels in Annual Reports: A Meta Analysis', *British Accounting Review*, vol. 31, 1999, pp. 35–61.

K.N. Krishnaswamy, Appa Iyer Sivakumar, and M. Mathirajan, *Management Research Methodology: Integration of Methods and Techniques*, Pearson Education India, 2009.

L. Edvinsson and P. Sullivan, 'Developing a Model for Managing Intellectual Capital', *European Management Journal*, vol. 14, no. 4, pp. 56–64.

L.L. Eng and Y.T. Mak, 'Corporate Governance and Voluntary Disclosure', *Journal of Accounting and Public Policy*, vol. 22, no. 4, 2003, pp. 325–45.

M. Abdolmohammadi, 'Intellectual Capital Disclosure and Market Capitalization', *Journal of Intellectual Capital*, vol. 6, no. 3, 2005, pp. 397–416.

M. Abrahamson, *Social Research Methods*, Englewood Cliffs, NJ: Prentice Hall, 1983.

M. Akhtaruddin, 'Corporate Mandatory Disclosure Practices in Bangladesh', *International Journal of Accounting*, vol. 40, 2005, pp. 399–422.

M. Bhatia and B. Agarwal, 'Intellectual Capital Disclosures in IPO Prospectuses of Indian Companies', Paper presented at *the India Finance Conference*, IIM Ahmedabad, India, 2013.

M. Cordazzo and P.G.M.C. Vergauwen, 'Intellectual Capital Disclosure in the UK Biotechnology IPO Prospectuses', *Journal of Human Resource Costing and Accounting*, vol. 16, no. 1, 2012, pp. 4–19.

M. Cordazzo, 'Intangibles and Italian IPO Prospectuses: A Disclosure Analysis', *Journal of Intellectual Capital*, vol. 8, no. 2, 2007, pp. 288–305.

M. El-Bannany, 'A Model to Explain Intellectual Capital Disclosure in UAE Banks', *International Journal of Learning and Intellectual Capital*, vol. 10, no. 1, 2013, pp. 35–51.

M. El-Bannany, 'A Study of Determinants of Intellectual Capital Performance in Banks: The UK Case', *Journal of Intellectual Capital*, vol. 9, no. 3, 2008, pp. 487–98.

M. El-Bannany, 'A Study of the Determinants of Social Disclosure Level in UK Banks', *Corporate Ownership and Control*, vol. 5, no. 1, 2007, pp. 120–30.

M. Haniffa and T. Cooke, 'Culture, Corporate Governance and Disclosure in Malaysian corporations', *Abacus*, vol. 38, no. 3, 2002, pp. 317–49.

M. Hossain, 'The Extent of Disclosure in Annual Reports of Banking Companies: The Case of India', *European Journal of Scientific Research*, vol. 23, no. 4, 2008, pp. 659–80.

M. Joshi, D.S. Ubha, and J. Sidhu, 'The Reporting on Intellectual Capital in Annual Reports: Evidence from the Australian Software and Information Technology Companies', *Journal of Knowledge Management Practice*, vol. 11, no. 3, 2010.

M. Sen and D. Sharma, 'Intellectual Capital Disclosure of Select Pharmaceutical and Software Companies in India', *IUP Journal Of Accounting Research & Audit Practices*, vol. 12, no. 1, 2013, pp. 47–62.

M. Suchman, 'Managing Legitimacy: Strategic and Institutional Approaches', *Academy of Management Review*, vol. 20, no. 3, 1995, pp. 571–610.

M.C. Jensen and W.H. Meckling, 'Theory of the Firm: Managerial Behavior, Agency Costs and Ownership Structure', *Journal of Financial Economics*, vol. 3, 1976, pp. 303–60.

M.H. Khan and M.M. Ali, 'An Empirical Investigation and Users' Perceptions on Intellectual Capital Reporting in Banks: Evidence from Bangladesh', *Journal of Human Resource Costing and Accounting*, vol. 14, no. 1, 2010, pp. 48–69.

M.L. Bhasin, 'Intellectual Capital Disclosure Scenario in India: An Empirical Study of IT Corporations', *Review of Economics and Finance, Academic Research Centre*, Canada, April 2011, 2: 58–68.

M.M. Speigal and N. Yamori, 'Determinants of Voluntary Bank Disclosure: Evidence from Japanese Shinkin Banks', *CESIFO Working Paper No. 1135, Category 6: Monitory Policy and International Finance*, 2004.

N. Bontis and J. Fitz-enz, 'Intellectual Capital ROI: A Causal Map of Human Capital Antecedents and Consequents', *Journal of Intellectual Capital*, vol. 3, Issue 3, 2002, pp. 223–47.

N. Bontis, 'Intellectual Capital Disclosurein Canadian Corporations', *Journal of Human Resource Costing & Accounting*, vol. 7, no. 1/2, 2003, pp. 9–20.

N. Bukh et al., 'Disclosure of Information on Intellectual Capital in Danish IPO Prospectuses', *Accounting, Auditing and Accountability Journal*, vol. 18, no. 6, 2005, pp. 713–32.

N.A. Mohd Ghazali and P. Weetman, 'Perpetuating Traditional Influences: Voluntary Disclosure in Malaysia following the economic Crisis', *Journal of International Accounting, Auditing and Taxation*, vol. 15, 2006, pp. 226–48.

N.D. Gujarati, *Basic Econometric*, 4th Edition, New Delhi: Tata McGraw-Hill Publishing Company Limited.

O.R. Holsti, 'Content Analysis', in G. Lindzey and E. Aronson, eds., *The Handbook of Social Psychology*, 2nd edn., Vol. II, New Delhi: Amerind Publishing Co., 1968, pp. 596–692.

Owusu-Ansah, 'The Impact of Corporate Attributes on the Extent of Mandatory Disclosure and Reporting by Listed Companies in Zimbabwe', *International Journal of Accounting*, vol. 33, no. 5, 1998, pp. 605–31.

P. Goh and K. Lim, 'Disclosing Intellectual Capital in Company Annual Reports: Evidence from Malaysia', *Journal of Intellectual Capital*, vol. 5, no. 3, 2004, pp. 500–10.

P. Vergauwen, L. Bollen, and E. Oirbans, 'Intellectual Capital Disclosure and Intangible Value Drivers: An Empirical Study', *Management Decision*, vol. 45, no. 7, 2007, pp. 1163–80.

P.D. Allison, *Multiple Regression – A Primer*, Thousand Oaks, CA: Pine Forge Press, 1999.

P.G.M.C. Vergauwen and F.J.C. Alem, 'Annual Report IC Disclosure in the Netherlands, France and Germany', *Journal of Intellectual Capital*, vol. 6, no. 1, 2005, pp. 89–104.

R.A. Johnson and D.W. Greening, 'The Effects of Corporate Governance and Institutional Ownership Types on Corporate Social Performance', *Academy of Management Journal*, vol. 42, Issue 5, 1999, pp. 564–76.

R.A. Said, Y.H. Zainuddin, and H. Haron, 'The Relationship between Corporate Social Responsibility Disclosure and Corporate Governance Characteristics in Malaysian Public Listed Companies', *Social Responsibility Journal*, vol. 5, no. 2, 2009, pp. 212–26.

R.H. Whiting and J. Woodcock, 'Firm Characteristics and Intellectual Capital Disclosure by Australian Companies', *Journal of Human Resource Costing & Accounting*, Vol. 15, Iss: 2, 2011, pp. 102–126.

S. Cohen, V.C. Naoum, and O. Vlismas, 'Intellectual Capital, Strategy and Financial Crisis from a SMEs Perspective', *Journal of Intellectual Capital*, vol. 15, Issue 2, 2014, pp. 294–315.

S. Ghosh, 'Macroprudential Regulation and Bank performance: Evidence from India', *RBI's working paper series*. Available at http://www.rbi.org.in/scripts/BS_PressReleaseDisplay.aspx?prid=29634, accessed on 20/09/2014

S. Singh and M. Kansal, 'Voluntary Disclosures of Intellectual Capital: An Empirical Analysis', *Journal of Intellectual Capital*, vol. 12, no. 2, 2011, pp. 301–18.

S. Vighneswara, 'Financial Instability, Uncertainty and Bank Lending Behavior', *International Journal of Banking and Finance*, vol. 9, Issue 4, Article 6, 2013, pp. 73–95.

S. Williams, 'Is Intellectual Capital Performance and Disclosure Practices Related?' *Journal of Intellectual Capital*, vol. 2, no. 3, 2001, pp. 192–203.

S.N. Vandemaele, P.G.M.C. Vergauwen and A.J. Smits, 'Intellectual Capital Disclosure in The Netherlands, Sweden and the UK: A Longitudinal and Comparative Study', *Journal of Intellectual Capital*, vol. 6, no. 3, 2005, pp. 417–26.

T. Das, 'Net Interest Margin, Financial Crisis and Bank Behavior: Experience of Indian Banks', *RBI Working Paper Series 10*, Reserve Bank of India, 2013.

T.E. Cooke, 'Disclosure in the Corporate Annual Reports of Swedish Companies', *Accounting and Business Research*, vol. 19, no. 74, 1989, pp. 113–24.

T.E. Cooke, 'Voluntary Corporate Disclosure by Swedish Companies', *Journal of International Financial Management and Accounting*, vol. 1, no. 2, 1989, pp. 171–95.

Efficiency Mapping of the Indian Banking System Using Data Envelopment

P.K. Gupta and Sandeepa Kaur

Centre for Management Studies, Jamia Millia Islamia, New Delhi
e-mail: pkgfms@gmail.com; sandeepakaur@gmail.com

ABSTRACT

The present paper traces the trends in the development of the Indian banking system, focusing on the dynamics of bank efficiency. Enticed by the reform of the Indian banking sector in the early 1990s and further slowdown in the economy as a result of global financial crisis in late 2000s, the current study analyses the performance of Indian banks using Data Envelopment analysis. The performance is measured in terms of technical efficiency, returns-to-scale, and Malmquist Productivity Index for a sample of 33 banks, consisting of 19 public sector and 14 private sector banks during the period spanning 1995–96 to 2012–13. The Jackknifing analysis, followed by the dummy variable regression model is used to identify the outlier and its possible impact on overall efficiency trends.

Keywords: Data Envelopment Analysis, Bank Efficiency, Indian Banking System, Global Financial Crisis, Economic Reforms, Technical Efficiency, Returns-to-Scale, Malmquist Productivity Index, Jackknifing Analysis

INTRODUCTION

A sound financial system is crucial for an indispensable and vibrant economy. The performance of any economy to a large extent is dependent on the performance of the banking sector, it being the predominant component of the financial service industry. The Indian banking sector went through structural changes since its independence in view of its financial linkages with the rest of the economy and to meet the social and economic objectives of development (Kumbhakar and Sarkar, 2005). Consequently, the sector was initially following strict controls on interest rates, as well as stringent regulations relating to branch licensing, directed credit programmes, and mergers. However, the closed and strict regulated environment started showing adverse effects on the sector, resulting in under-performance of the banks over the years. As a result, the Indian banking sector underwent a sea of changes through its liberalization policy in the early 1990s with the implementation of a series of reforms with an objective to make the banking sector more productive and efficient by limiting the state intervention and enhancing the role of market forces.

The India banking sector, like other developing nations, does have the different groups of ownership, comprising public and private (domestic and foreign). In several phases, the Indian Public Sector banks (PSBs) came into existence. In 1955, the Government of India took over the ownership of the Imperial Bank of India and reconstituted it as State Bank of India (SBI) under the State Bank of India Act of 1955. Later, the State Bank of India (subsidiary banks) Act was passed in 1959 allowing SBI to take over seven banks of large states as its associate banks. However, in spite of the progress of SBI and its subsidiaries in terms of geographic coverage and credit expansion, it was felt that bank credits were flowing mainly to the large and well-established business firms and primary sector, and agriculture and small-scale industries were almost neglected. This resulted in an announcement of a policy of social control over banks in 1969 and consequently 14 largest private banks were nationalized under the Nationalization Act, 1969. In the second phase of nationalization, another six private banks were nationalized in 1980. The private and foreign banks were operating side-by-side, but on a relatively small scale and their activities were restricted through entry regulation and strict branch licensing policies.

During the period of 1969–91, the number of banks increased slightly, but savings were successfully mobilized in part because the branches held by PSBs were encouraged to expand rapidly. Further, relatively low inflation kept negative real deposit interest rates at a mild level, which in turn helped the banks to increase deposits. However, many banks remained unprofitable, inefficient, and unsound owing to their poor lending strategy and lack of internal risk management under government ownership. The prolonged presence of excessively large PSBs resulted in inefficient resource allocation and concentration of power in a few banks.

Facing major economic crisis, the Reserve bank of India (RBI) launched major banking sector reforms in 1991 aimed at creating a more profitable, efficient, and sound banking system, based on the recommendations of the first Narasimham committee on financial sector reforms. The reforms sought to improve bank efficiency through entry regulation, branch delicensing, deregulation of interest rate, and diversifying ownership of PSBs by enabling the state-owned banks to rise up to 49 per cent of their capital from the market. The reforms also targeted at improving bank profitability through the gradual reduction of the Cash Reserve Ratio (CRR) and the Statutory Liquidity Ratio (SLR), and to strengthen the banking system by introducing the micro prudential measures (see Bhide et al., 2001; Reddy, 2006; Prasad and Ghosh, 2007; Kumar and Charles, 2011 for extensive review of the recent banking sector reform). These reforms are expected to have an impact on the operations of banks. With reduced statutory requirements banks will have more funds at their disposal for commercial lending and the interest rate liberalization is expected to bring flexibility and competition into the banking system. Opening up the banking sector for the private and foreign banks further infuses the competition. Along with these flexibilities, certain regulatory reforms are also introduced, which are meant to equip the banks to face fluctuations in the economy.

However, the turmoil in the international financial markets of advanced economies that started around mid-2007 has exacerbated substantially since August 2008. The first hint of the trouble came from the collapse of two Bear Stearns hedge funds in early 2007 (Prasad and Reddy, 2009). Subsequently, a number of other banks and financial institutions also began to show signs of distress. Matters really came to the force with the bankruptcy of Lehman Brothers, a big investment bank, in September 2008. In spite of the fact that the Indian banking system is not directly exposed to the sub-prime mortgage assets, the shock has been felt in the Indian financial market as well, since India is far more exposed to international markets after the macro-economic reforms of 1991. The financial sector, especially banks, is subject to prudential regulations, both in regard to capital and liquidity.

As the current global financial crisis has shown, liquidity risks can increase manifold during a crisis and can pose serious downside risks to macroeconomic and financial stability (Mohan, 2008). The RBI's policy response aimed at containing the contagion from the outside in order to keep the domestic money and credit markets functioning normally and see that the liquidity stress does not trigger solvency cascades (Subbarao, 2009).

In particular, three objectives were targeted – first, to maintain a comfortable rupee liquidity position; second, to augment foreign exchange liquidity; and third, to maintain a policy framework that would keep credit delivery on track so as to arrest the moderation in growth.

The present paper examines the issues – (1) how far the reform measures have been successful in their objective of improving the performance of the Indian banks during the post liberalization period; and (2) whether the global financial crisis had any impact on the performance of the Indian banking sector. The non-parametric liner programming based Data Envelopment Analysis (DEA) approach is used to examine the performance of the Indian banking sector and two major ownership structure within it in terms of technical efficiency for the entire 18 years of post-liberalization period, as well as two sub-periods – (1) pre global financial crisis period (1996–2007); and (2) global financial crisis period (2008–10).

Further, there is growing tendency of PSBs operating under Increasing-Returns-to-Scale (IRS), implying that substantial gains could be obtained from altering scale via either internal growth or consolidation in the sector. Lastly, in the total factor productivity (TFP) change, PSBs outperform private sector banks as a result of significant differences in technological change in Sub-period I. However, there is evidence of a shrink in the market and negative growth in TFP in both the sectors in Sub-period II, providing a gesture of adverse effect of global financial crisis on the Indian banking sector.

LITERATURE REVIEW

A number of attempts have been made to study the efficiency and productivity of the banking sector in developed countries (Berger and Humphrey, 1997; Berger et al., 1999; Isik and Hassan, 2002 a, b; Yildirim and Philippatos, 2007). However, studies analysing the efficiency of banks in developing countries, including India, are relatively modest. Apart from the standard accounting measures, RBI has also been using Data Envelopment Analysis (DEA) to determine the efficiency of the banking sector.

In an extensive international literature survey, Berger and Humphrey (1997) noted that the vast majority of the efficiency literature focuses on the banking markets of well-developed countries with particular emphasis on the US markets. An early study that compares alternative frontier techniques is that by Ferrier and Lovell (1990). They analyse the cost structure of 575 US banks for the year 1984 using both the **Stochastic Frontier Analysis** (SFA) and

DEA methodologies. They find higher efficiency scores with DEA compared to SFA, namely 80 per cent and 74 per cent, respectively. They conclude that DEA is sufficiently flexible to envelop the data more closely than the translog cost frontier. However, efficiency scores are not significantly correlated, thus indicating that other factors not controlled for the study may drive the obtained wedge between the two measures.

However, the European evidence has been provided by Sheldon (1994). He analyses the cost efficiency of Swiss banks with SFA and DEA in the period from 1987 to 1991. While results from DEA indicate that the average degree of cost efficiency is about 56 per cent, SFA yields only 3.9 per cent mean efficiency. This substantial deviation from usually obtained magnitudes of around 80 per cent obtained for US and European studies casts some doubt as to an appropriate specification of the cost function (Amel et al., 2004). Likewise, he reports insignificant rank-order correlation of 1 per cent, indicating that no relationship exists between the two groups of efficiency scores. These results, that two alternative methods to implement an identical theoretical cost minimization problem should not be correlated, are remarkable.

The literature on bank efficiency reveals mixed experiences of liberalization policies undertaken in various countries. A number of studies report the existence of efficiency gains due to liberalization programmes undertaken in various emerging and transition countries, including Turkey (Zaim, 1995; Isik and Hassan, 2003), Thailand (Leightner and Lovell, 1998), Hungary (Hasan and Marton, 2003), the Central and Eastern European (CEE) transition countries (Brissimis et al., 2008), Pakistan (Ataullah and Le, 2006), and Egypt (Fethi et al., 2011). However, there are few studies which show no improvement in bank efficiency over the transition period such as, Havrylchyk (2006) for Polish, Kasman and Yildirim (2006) for the CEE transition countries, and Fu and Heffernan (2009) for China. Moreover, a number of studies (Burki and Niazi, 2009; Hsiao et al., 2010) illustrate that the efficiency impact of the reform process may not be immediately visible or uniform over time. The efficiency may go down at first due to the initial costs of adjustment prior to improving later. Burki and Niazi (2010), for example, show that efficiency fell during the initial reform period in Pakistan due to the adjustment process before increasing in the later stages of the reform process. Similarly, Hsiao et al. (2010) find that the efficiency of Taiwanese banks was lower during the restructuring reform period than the pre-reform period, while being higher in the post-reform period.

In the Indian context, there are few studies which especially focused on the efficiency measurement of PSBs using DEA. For example, Das (1997) studied the technical, allocative, and scale efficiency of different PSBs for the period 1990–96 using the DEA approach. The study found a decline in the overall efficiency over time, and a decline in technical efficiency with slight improvement in allocative efficiency. The SBI was found to be more efficient than other PSBs. Saha and Ravisankar (2000) analysed the performance of Indian banks using the DEA approach for a sample of 25 PSBs banks over the period of 1992–95. Their findings reveal that, barring few exceptions, the PSBs have in general improved their efficiency over the years.

The Bauer et al. (1998) study is significant among all the studies. This study gave the application of four approaches – SFA, DEA, Thick Frontier Analysis (TFA) and Distribution Free Analysis (DFA) on a data set of 683 US banks over the period 1977–88. This study suggests six consistency conditions to analyse the robustness of frontier efficiency measures. Other group of studies, which focused on the comparison of various categories of banks based on ownership, includes Bhattacharya et al. (1997), Sathye (2003), Sahoo et al. (2007), Sinha (2008), Mahesh and Rajeev (2009), and Kumar and Charles (2011).

Bhattacharya et al. (1997) used DEA to measure the productive efficiency of Indian commercial banks in the late 1980s to early 1990s and to study the impact of the liberalizing measures taken in 1980s on the performance of various categories of banks. They found that the Indian PSBs were the best performing banks, as the banking sector was overwhelmingly dominated by the PSBs, while the new private sector banks were yet to emerge fully in the Indian banking scenario. Sathye (2003) measured the productive efficiency of 94 banks in India for the year 1996–1997 by using DEA, wherein they found that the PSBs were, on an average, more efficient than foreign banks, which in turn were more efficient than private banks. Similarly, Gupta et al. (2008) found that the SBI and its group have the highest efficiency, whereas the other private and nationalized banks are behind SBI in terms of efficiency for the period of 1999–2003. The results are consistent over the period, but efficiency differences diminish over a period of time. Mahesh and Rajeev (2009) examined the changes in productive efficiency of Indian commercial banks for the post reform period, that is, 1985–2004. They found that deregulation has significant impacts on all three types of efficiency measures. The PSBs, as a group, rank first in all the three efficiency measures showing that, as opposed to the general perception, these banks are doing better than their private counterparts. Private banks, however, have shown marked improvement during the post-liberalization period in terms of all three types of efficiency measures.

Contrary to the above stated studies, Sahoo et al. (2007), who examined the efficiency trends of the Indian commercial banks during the period 1997–98 to 2004–05, observed that foreign banks are seen outperforming both the nationalized banks and private banks, and private and foreign banks as a group outperforming the nationalized banks. Similarly, Sinha (2008) observed that the private sector commercial banks have a higher mean technical efficiency score when compared to the public sector commercial banks and most of the commercial banks experienced Decreasing-Returns-to-Scale (DRS) during the study period spanning from 2002–03 to 2004–05. Dwivedi and Charyulu (2011) determined the impact of various market and regulatory initiatives on efficiency improvements of Indian banks. With the DEA they identified banks that are on the output frontier, given the various inputs at their disposal. This study was confined only to the Constant-Return-to-Scale (CRS) assumption of Decision-Making Units (DMUs).

While most of the studies provided the evidence of the PSBs performing better than their counterparts, private and foreign banks, few other studies have found the PSBs as underperforming compared to other group of banks. The differences in the findings of various studies in the Indian context are attributed to many factors, including the selection of time period, sample size, selection of inputs and outputs variables, and the orientation of efficiency measurement.

However, one of the major limitations of all the above studies is that they focused on only one aspect of performance measurement, that is, efficiency. Controversy is not only concerned with whether deregulation stimulates efficiency, but also on different sources of productivity growth. While some studies attribute the growth of productivity to technological progress (Avkiran, 2000; Alam, 2001; Mukherjee et al., 2001; Canhoto and Dermine, 2003; Kumbhakar et al., 2001; Sturm and Williams, 2004), others are in favour of efficiency improvement (Berg et al., 1992; Gilbert and Wilson, 1998; Isik and Hassan, 2003). Compared to efficiency analysis, the literature on the issue of TFP growth in the Indian banking sector is very limited. Galagedera and Edirisuriya (2005) investigated the efficiency and productivity for a sample of Indian commercial banks over the period 1995–2002 by using the technique of DEA. The results reveal that there has been no significant growth in productivity during the study period. When analysed separately, the PSBs reveal a modest growth in productivity that appears to have been brought about by technological change. The private sector banks indicate no growth. Zhao et al. (2008) used a balanced panel data set covering the period 1992–2004 to measure the DEA-based Malmquist index of TFP change in the Indian banking sector. The results revealed that after an initial adjustment phase of deregulation period, the Indian banking sector experienced sustained productivity growth, driven mainly by technological progress. Banks' ownership structure seems to have an impact on bank efficiency, but doesn't appear to have an influence of TFP change. Kumar et al. (2010) observed that TFP growth for Indian banking sector for the period of 1995–2006 was driven mainly by technological progress as compared to efficiency change.

The current study contributes to the literature significantly in many ways. Most of the literature in the Indian banking sector focused on measurement of efficiency (Das, 1997; Saha and Ravishankar, 2000; Sathye, 2003; Ram Mohan and Ray, 2003; Sahoo et al., 2007) and a few studies on benchmarking (Gupta et al., 2008; Kumar and Charles, 2011). A detailed systematic study on the measurement of productivity change in the Indian banking sector is comparatively limited. Along with the issue of efficiency and returns-to-scale, we also use a broad dynamic indicator, TFP change index, as the measure of performance. It is an important tool for reviewing past growth patterns and for assessing the potential for future growth. Ahluwalia and Shanker (1985) pointed out that one needs to look at the concept of TFP to evaluate the performance of the service sector in India, which not merely reflects productive efficiency of inputs, but also the capacity of the management to combine these and other factors to enhance the outputs of the firm.

Secondly, in comparison to previous studies (Galagedera and Edirisuriya, 2005; Sinha, 2008; Zhao et al., 2008), the present study considers more recent data for a relatively longer period of 15 years of post-liberalization which includes 3 years of the global financial crisis period. There has been debate among the policy makers, bankers, and researchers since the mid of 2007 whether the global financial crisis had any impact on the performance of the Indian banking sector. However, no attempt has been made till date to empirically resolve this debate. The current paper compares the performance of Indian banks before and after the global financial crisis.

Thirdly, most of the previous studies in the Indian context decompose the Malmquist Productivity Index into its different components by using the extended decomposition model proposed by Fare et al. (1994). The extended model of Fare et al. (1994) assumes Constant-Returns-to-Scale (CRS) at the stage of measuring technological change, but subsequently switches to Variable-Returns-to-Scale (VRS) to separate the scale effect component, which is not internally consistent. Hence, the current study uses the Decomposition model developed by Ray and Desli (1997) that assumes VRS to measure each and every component of Malmquist Productivity Index.

Summing up, more recent studies find that SFA efficiency scores are generally higher compared to DEA scores. This may reflect the different treatment of stochastic noise and the ability to control for heterogeneity. At the same time, studies that investigate the differences across methods more systematically show that efficiency measures differ not only in terms of mean industry efficiency. Efficiency rankings, their stability over time, and the consistency with traditionally employed performance measures contain important additional information for policy-making purposes. Finally, it is noteworthy that with the exception of Bauer et al. (1998), none of these crosschecking exercises quantifies differences for a banking system as a whole, but focus on distinct time intervals and/or particular groups of banks in the system, such as large, stock-listed institutes. In fact, smaller samples that compare only a fraction of the market may even underestimate the differences of DEA and SFA measures since they are likely to sample already more akin banks.

Finally, DEA is a computationally convenient way to measure efficiency that does not require an explicit functional relationship between inputs and outputs. However, because the frontier is constructed using extreme observations, DEA can be sensitive to extreme points, especially when data may be contaminated by measurement error. In such settings, the technical efficiency scores calculated from datasets that include outliers can be misleading. In spite of this limitation, most of previous studies did not give much attention to verify the robustness of the DEA efficiency scores. The current paper diagnoses the robustness of efficiency scores obtained through DEA by using Jackknifing analysis. Further, the sensitivity of outlier on overall efficiency trends is tested through dummy variable regression models.

DATA ENVELOPMENT ANALYSIS

Data Envelopment Analysis is a specific methodology for analysis of the relative efficiency for multiple inputs and outputs by evaluation of all DMUs and measurement of their performance in respect to the best practice banks, which determine the efficient frontier. The most important advantage of DEA is that it does not require, in advance, assumptions about the production function's analytical form. At the same time, like the rest of the models, DEA also has some disadvantages. First, it is sensitive to extreme observations, and second, it does not decompose the bank's deviation from the efficient production frontier into inefficiency and random error components.

The present study was conducted with the DEA, returns-to-scale, and TFP approach to bank efficiency in order to obtain a more complete and clear picture of bank performance and efficiency. Both methods have important advantages. The traditional accounting approach provides opportunities for better comparison of the tendencies and measures the performance of the bank in terms of profitability. In its turn, the DEA approach enables for the determination of multiple outputs and multiple inputs in efficiency score calculation, and measures the technical efficiency of the banking institutions. At the same time, the DEA treats the bank as an enterprise with a specific production process, taking into account the particular production factors and allowing for optimal decision making.

The DEA is a more complex and sophisticated method than the traditional ones because it is a deterministic non-parametric approach, using multiple inputs and outputs. At the same time, unlike the parametric approaches (SFA, DFA, and TFA), it doesn't need too long time-series.

There are various models of DEA. The most frequently used ones – CCR-model and BCC-model were chosen for the study. The CCR-model was developed by Charnes, Cooper and Rhodes (Charnes et al., 1978). Its specific assumption is that the DMU operates under CRS. The BCC-model was defined by Banker, Charnes, and Cooper (Banker et al., 1984). It estimates the efficiency under the assumption of VRS. The BCC-model compares DMUs with the DMUs operating in the same region of returns-to-scale, while the CCR-model compares DMUs in the whole sample. To perform the efficiency scores calculation the software DEA Frontier, developed by Joe Zhu, was used.

CCR AND BCC MODEL

As shown in Figure 1, DEA is concerned with the efficiency of the individual unit, which can be defined as the Unit of Assessment (Thanassoulis, 2001) or the DMU (Charnes et al., 1978) that is responsible for controlling the process of production and making decisions at various levels, including daily operation, short-term tactics, and long-term strategy.

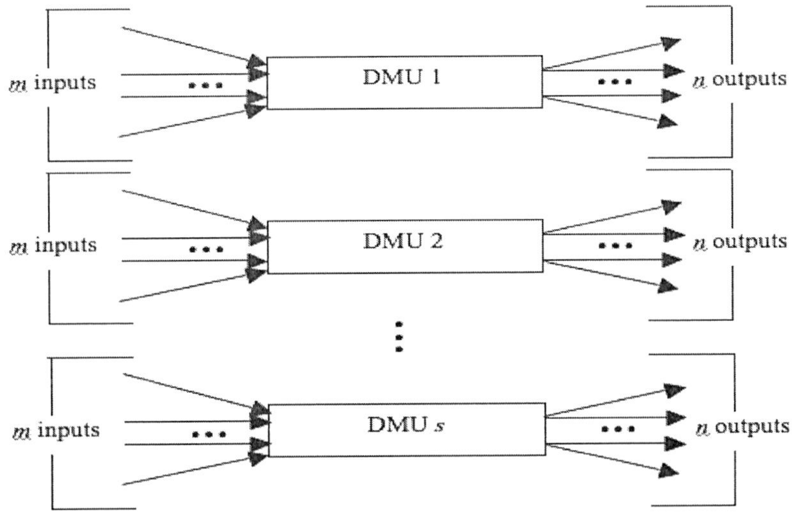

Figure 1: DMU and homogenous units

$$X = \begin{pmatrix} x_{11} & x_{12} & \ldots x_{1s} \\ x_{21} & x_{22} & \ldots x_{2s} \\ \vdots & & \\ x_{m1} & x_{m2} & \ldots x_{ms} \end{pmatrix} \quad \ldots(1)$$

$$Y = \begin{pmatrix} y_{11} & y_{12} & \ldots y_{1s} \\ y_{21} & y_{22} & \ldots y_{2s} \\ \vdots & & \\ y_{n1} & x_{n2} & \ldots y_{ns} \end{pmatrix} \quad \ldots(2)$$

The DEA is used to measure the relative productivity of a DMU by comparing it with other homogeneous units transforming the same group of measurable positive inputs into the same types of measurable positive outputs. The input and output data for Figure 1 can be expressed by matrixes X and Y in equations (1) and (2), where x_{ij} refers to the ith input data of DMU j, whereas, y_{ij} is the ith output of DMU j. A more scientific approach to measuring the efficiencies of DMUs with multiple inputs and outputs is the CCR-model (Charnes et al., 1978).

The CCR-model for the example of Figure 2 can be expressed by equations (3) to (6):

$$(FP_o) Max\ \theta = \frac{u_1 y_{1o} + u_2 y_{2o} + \cdots + u_n y_{no}}{v_1 x_{1o} + v_2 x_{2o} + \cdots + v_m x_{mo}} \quad \ldots(3)$$

Subject to

$$\frac{u_1 y_{1j} + u_2 y_{2j} + \cdots + u_n y_{nj}}{v_1 x_{1j} + v_2 x_{2j} + \cdots + v_m x_{mj}} \leq 1 \quad (j = 1, \cdots, s) \qquad \ldots(4)$$

$$v_1, v_2, \ldots, v_m \geq 0 \qquad \ldots(5)$$

$$u_1, u_2, \ldots, u_n \geq 0 \qquad \ldots(6)$$

Given the data X and Y in equations (1) and (2), the CCR-model measures the maximum efficiency of each DMU by solving the Fractional Programming (FP) problem in Equation (3) where the input weights $v_1, v_2, \ldots v_m$ and output weights $u_1, u_2, \ldots u_n$ are variables to be obtained. o in Equation (3) varies from 1 to s which means s optimizations for all s DMUs. Equation (4) reveals that the ratio of 'virtual output' ($u_1 y_{1o} + u_2 y_{2o} + \ldots + u_n y_{no}$) to 'virtual input' ($v_1 x_{1o} + v_2 x_{2o} + \ldots + v_m x_{mo}$) cannot exceed 1 for each DMU, which conforms to the economic assumption that the output cannot be more than the input in production.

The above FP equations (3) to (6) are equivalent to the following Linear Programming (LP) formulation given in equations (7) to (11) (see e.g. Cooper et al., 2000):

$$(LP_o) \text{ Max } q = u_1 y_{1o} + u_2 y_{2o} + \ldots + u_n y_{no} \qquad \ldots(7)$$

Subject to:

$$v_1 x_{1o} + v_2 x_{2o} + \ldots + v_m x_{mo} = 1 \qquad \ldots(8)$$

$$u_1 y_{1j} + u_2 y_{2j} + \ldots + u_n y_{nj} \leq v_1 x_{1j} + v_2 x_{2j} + \ldots + v_m x_{mj} \quad (j = 1, \ldots, s) \qquad \ldots(9)$$

$$v_1, v_2, \ldots, v_m \geq 0 \qquad \ldots(10)$$

$$u_1, u_2, \ldots, u_n \geq 0 \qquad \ldots(11)$$

The main difference between these two models and the CCR-model is that the former allows VRS to be assumed, while the latter is limited solely to a CRS assumption. Accordingly, the production frontiers in these models are different.

METHODOLOGY

The stochastic frontier (parametric) model and DEA (non-parametric) model has been used in this study. The choice of a non-parametric approach in the current study is based on several considerations. Firstly, when using panel data parametric approaches often use a time trend, which smoothes the variation of productivity changes over time. By contrast, non-parametric approaches allow for substantial variations embedded in data to be revealed. Secondly, in the parametric approach, the decomposition of error term into two parts, one representing stochastic error and the other inefficiency is not useful for the data sets of fewer than one hundred observations. In contrast, DEA works well with a small sample size.

Further, DEA readily incorporates the existence of multiple outputs. However, a major drawback of DEA is its inability to detect measurement error. Thus, an exceptionally well performing unit (outlier) may seriously compromise the analysis. This section deals with selection of inputs, outputs, purification of the data and the sample size to be taken up in order to generate proper results.

Selection of Inputs and Outputs and Purification of Data

There is on-going discussion in the banking literature regarding the proper definition of inputs and outputs (Fethi and Pasiouras, 2010). Till today, there is no all-encompassing theory of the banking firm and no agreement on the explicit definition and measurement of banks' inputs and outputs (Casu, 2002; Sathye, 2003). Two different approaches appear in the literature regarding the measurement of inputs and outputs of a bank, popularly known as Production Approach and Intermediation Approach (Humphrey, 1985). The Production Approach views banks as using purchased inputs to produce deposits and various categories of bank assets. Both, loans and deposits are, therefore, treated as outputs and measured in terms of the number of accounts. This approach considers only operating costs and excludes the interest expenses paid on deposits since deposits are viewed as outputs. The Intermediation Approach on the other hand considers banks as financial intermediaries and uses the volume of deposits, loans, and other variables as inputs and outputs. It views the banks as using deposits together with purchased inputs to produce various categories of bank assets. Outputs are measured in monetary values and total costs include all operating and interest expenses.

Following Berger and Humphrey (1997), the Intermediation Approach was used in the present study with restricted choice of variables. As the number of variables increases in DEA analysis, the ability of the model to discriminate among the DMUs decreases. More the variables added, the greater becomes the chance that some inefficient unit dominates in the added dimension and becomes efficient (Smith, 1997). In order to preserve the discriminatory power of DEA, the number of inputs and outputs should be kept at a reasonable level. The choice of the inputs and outputs are guided by the choices made in previous studies and also on the data availability. In the current study, two inputs have been used – total cost and total deposits.

The input total cost is measured as the sum of total interest expenses and non-interest expenses including personal expenses. Non-interest expenses include service charges and commissions, expenses of general management affairs, salaries, and other expenses (including health insurance and securities portfolios). Some researchers (Yeh, 1996; Sathye, 2003; Ram Mohan and Ray, 2004; Kao and Liu, 2004) have treated interest expenses and non-interest expenses as two different inputs along with other inputs. However, following Casu and Molyneux (2003) and Sealey and Lindley (1977), both have been treated as a single input as total cost. This kind of treatment is mainly due to the well-known dimensionality problem associated with DEA, particularly with a limited sample size – a high number of variables relative to the number of observations cause more units to be wrongly identified as efficient (Zhao et al., 2008). The input, total deposit, is taken as the sum of demand and savings' deposits held by bank and non-bank depositors.

The above two inputs are used to produce two outputs namely, total loans and other earning assets. The output, total loan, is measured as the sum of all loan accounts intermediated by banks and the output; other earning assets are measured as the sum of total securities (treasury bills, government bonds and other securities), deposits with banks and equity investments.

To ensure the validity of the DEA model specification, the isotonicity test (Avkiran, 1999) was conducted, which involves the calculation of all inter-correlations between inputs and outputs for identifying whether increasing amounts of inputs lead to greater outputs. The inter-correlation between inputs and outputs were observed positive (Pearson correlations > 0.80; $\alpha = 0.01$), the isotonicity test was passed and the inclusion of inputs/outputs was justified. The summary statistics of inputs and outputs is available from the author on request.

Sample Size

Nunamaker (1985) and Raab and Lichty (2002) suggested a rule of thumb on deciding the minimum size of the sample in any DEA study. The sample size should be at least three times larger than the sum of the number of inputs and outputs. In the present study, with a total of two inputs and two outputs, a reasonably good sample size of 33 banks (see Appendix) consisting of 19 public banks and 14 private banks, was used. All the public sector banks in the sample are nationalized banks. In May 2008, Centurion Bank of Punjab Limited (CBPL) merged with HDFC Bank Ltd. (HDFCBL). As a result, the sample for period 2007–08 to 2009–10 is confined to 32 banks with 19 public banks and 13 private banks. And as per the inconsistency of the data related to Centurion Bank of Punjab Limited, it has not been considered in the pre-liberalization period.

RESULTS

Though the commercial banks are homogeneous with respect to their organizational structure, goals and objectives, they differ significantly in size and production level. So, the scale of banks plays a vital role in their relative efficiency. The CCR measures of technical efficiency captures not only the productive inefficiency of a bank at its actual scale size, but also some inefficiency resulting from its actual scale size being different from the most productive scale size (Banker et al., 1984). If a DMU is scale efficient, it implies that it operates under the most productive scale size and thus, maximizes its average productivity. As the productivity growth could be achievable solely through reduction in wastefulness or through the change in scale of operation, without resort to new technology, the issue of efficiency and scale of production in the Indian banking sector is dealt with first.

Productive Efficiency of Indian Banking Sector

Table 1 provides the summary statistics of technical efficiency and its components in the Indian banking sector during the period 1995–96 to 2012–13 along with their average trends.

Out of a total of 33 banks in the sample the number of efficient banks varies from three to eight with average technical efficiency score varying from 0.859 to 0.946 during the period of study. The percentage of banks found to be technically efficient in the private sector is more than that in public sector throughout the period, except during the year 2007–08. The average technical efficiency of PSBs varies from 0.828 to 0.955 and that of private sector banks varies from 0.877 to 0.940.

However, the difference in the average technical efficiency scores between the private and public sector banks is found to be insignificant except during the year 1998–99. The findings of this study reinforce those of Kumar and Charles (2011) for the period 1996—2007 and Ram Mohan and Ray (2003, 2004) for the period 1992–2000. They failed to uncover any significant differences between public and private sector banks using financial measures of performance. It can be observed that the private sector banks are performing faintly better than the PSBs during 1995–96 to 2003–04, except in the years 1997–98 and 2002–03.

However, the PSBs are continuously performing better than private sector banks since 2004–05 onwards. The Coefficient of Variations (CV) measures the consistency in technical efficiency across the banks in each year. It can be observed that the variations in efficiency across the private sector banks are relatively high throughout the study period as it is evident from the relatively high value of CV in private sector banks than that of its counter sector banks.

Table 1: Summary Statistics of Technical Efficiency and its Components in Indian Banking Sector

Technical Efficiency	**1996**	**1997**	**1998**	**1999**	**2000**	**2001**	**2002**	**2003**	**2004**	**2005**	**2006**	**2007**	**2008**	**2009**	**2010**	**2011**	**2012**	**2013**
Average (All Banks)	0.93	0.889	0.907	0.859	0.908	0.931	0.92	0.915	0.88	0.884	0.922	0.937	0.935	0.944	0.946	0.943	0.825	0.983
Coefficient of Variation (%)	6.01	8.51	8.93	10.37	6.87	5.19	5.2	6.22	7.05	8.16	6.92	5.23	5.56	4.69	4.96	4.89	5.15	5.35
Efficient Banks (in %)	24.2	9.09	12.1	12.1	9.09	15.2	12.1	15.2	9.09	9.09	9.09	18.2	18.8	21.9	-	20.9	19.8	18.7
Average (Public Banks)	0.92	0.882	0.92	0.828	0.892	0.92	0.92	0.922	0.87	0.889	0.933	0.941	0.945	0.95	0.955	0.942	0.913	0.925
CV (%)	5.64	5.75	6.34	9.07	6.08	4.63	4.63	4.45	5.4	7.3	4.68	3.73	4.81	4.16	3.55	4.65	4.21	4.12
Efficient Public Banks (in %)	21.1	0	5.3	5.3	5.3	10.5	10.5	10.5	0	5.26	5.26	10.5	26.3	21.1	15.8	23.2	24.7	26.9
Average (Private Banks)	0.93	0.897	0.889	0.901	0.929	0.94	0.92	0.907	0.89	0.907	0.907	0.931	0.919	0.936	0.933	0.983	0.973	0.921
CV (%)	6.66	11.35	11.7	10.18	7.34	5.93	6.08	8.19	8.91	9.21	9.21	6.92	6.38	5.45	6.47	6.59	6.89	6.789
Efficient Private Banks (in %)	28.6	21.4	21.4	21.4	14.3	21.4	14.3	21.4	21.4	14.3	14.3	28.6	7.69	23.1	23.1	22.5	24.7	24.1
Pure Technical Efficiency	**1996**	**1997**	**1998+**	**1999**	**2000**	**2001**	**2002**	**2003**	**2004**	**2005**	**2006**	**2007**	**2008**	**2009**	**2010**	**2011**	**2012**	**2013**
Average (All banks)	0.95	0.958	0.949	0.94	0.944	0.953	0.94	0.939	0.92	0.917	0.942	0.957	0.96	0.961	0.961	0.965	0.971	0.998
CV (%)	5.58	5.39	7.18	7.88	6.21	4.65	5.06	5.83	7.56	7.97	6.88	4.28	4.3	4.17	4.06	4.07	4.12	4.46
Pure Efficient banks (in %)	36.4	48.5	42.4	42.4	27.3	30.3	21.2	27.3	24.2	24.2	30.3	36.4	43.8	34.4	25	28.9	32.1	32.7
Average (Public banks)	0.95	0.965	0.97	0.949	0.944	0.949	0.94	0.939	0.91	0.909	0.948	0.948	0.95	0.956	0.961	0.927	0.941	0.928
CV (%)	5.53	4.55	4.46	5.74	5.45	3.69	4.5	4.61	6.91	6.47	4.81	3.58	4.67	4.04	3.48	3.26	3.11	4.83
Pure Efficient public banks (in %)	36.8	47.4	47.4	42.1	21.1	21.1	15.8	15.8	15.8	10.5	26.3	15.8	36.8	21.1	15.8	25.9	36.1	43.9
Average (Private banks)	0.94	0.948	0.92	0.928	0.944	0.959	0.95	0.939	0.94	0.928	0.934	0.968	0.976	0.969	0.962	0.971	0.956	0.978
CV (%)	5.84	6.43	9.29	10.29	7.34	5.79	5.79	7.36	8.22	9.72	9.18	4.95	3.27	4.37	4.95	6.38	6.59	6.83
Pure Efficient private banks (in %)	35.7	50	35.7	42.9	35.7	42.9	28.6	42.9	35.7	42.9	35.7	64.3	53.8	53.8	38.5	47.6	53.9	65.2
Scale Efficiency	**1996**	**1997**	**1998**	**1999***	**2000***	**2001**	**2002**	**2003**	**2004**	**2005+**	**2006**	**2007+**	**2008**	**2009**	**2010**	**2011**	**2012**	**2013**
Average (All banks)	0.98	0.929	0.955	0.915	0.962	0.976	0.98	0.975	0.96	0.964	0.979	0.979	0.974	0.982	0.984	0.973	0.981	0.993
CV (%)	2.84	8.09	4.48	8.32	3.65	2.3	2.46	3.29	4.88	4.29	3.25	3.82	4.7	2.91	2.91	3.89	4.37	4.72
Scale Efficient banks (in %)	24.2	9.09	12.1	12.1	9.09	15.2	12.1	15.2	9.09	9.09	9.09	18.2	18.8	25	18.8	20.4	22.9	27.5
Average (Public banks)	0.97	0.914	0.948	0.874	0.945	0.973	0.98	0.981	0.97	0.977	0.985	0.992	0.996	0.994	0.994	0.983	0.991	0.977
CV (%)	3.39	4.38	3.87	7.96	3.85	2.26	1.76	2.69	4.27	2.5	1.94	0.9	0.45	0.74	0.67	0.62	0.59	0.69
Scale Efficient public banks (in %)	21.1	0	5.26	5.26	5.26	10.5	10.5	10.5	0	5.26	5.26	10.5	26.3	26.3	15.8	15.8	22.8	27.5
Average (Private banks)	0.99	0.948	0.965	0.972	0.984	0.98	0.97	0.966	0.95	0.947	0.972	0.962	0.942	0.966	0.97	0.976	0.98	0.985
CV (%)	1.71	11.04	5.16	4.11	1.69	2.37	3.08	3.89	5.65	5.6	4.47	5.49	6.31	4.05	4.25	4.67	4.84	4.87
Scale Efficient private banks (in %)	28.6	21.4	21.4	21.4	14.3	21.4	14.3	21.4	21.4	14.3	14.3	28.6	7.69	23.1	23.1	25.9	27.8	23.1

Note: (i) CV = coefficient of variations; (ii) * and + indicate that there is significant difference in the scale efficiency scores between public and private sector banks in the corresponding year respectively at 99% and 95% level of confidence.

In 9 out of 18 years of study period, PSBs perform relatively better than private sector banks. The findings are quite consistent with some of the past studies such as Sathye (2003) for the period 1996–1997; Sinha (2008) for the period 2002–03 to 2004–05; Mahesh and Rajeev (2009) for the period 1985–2004. The radial changes in accounting, deregulation of interest rates, close follow-up of non-performing assets, introduction of prudential norms, voluntary retirement of old generation staff, concern for customer care, and professionalism as a part of reform process have made the management of PSBs to turn to generate surpluses and make these banks self-sufficient even by approaching capital market (Ram Mohan and Ray, 2004). With these developments and by taking advantage of information technology in the banking system, the PSBs have geared up to achieve the performance as par with its counterpart in the post-reform period.

The nature of technical inefficiency may be due to ineffective implementation of the production plan of the banks in converting inputs to outputs and due to the divergence of the bank from the most productive scale size. Thus, decomposition of technical efficiency into pure efficiency and scale efficiency allows an insight into the sources of inefficiency. Larger the difference between pure efficiency and technical efficiency, more scale inefficient a bank is, which in turn, indicates the larger deviation of the bank from the most productive scale size. On the other hand, as pure efficiency approaches technical efficiency, the bank approaches the most productive scale size, and a bank becomes scale efficient as pure efficiency equals technical efficiency.

On an average, the number of pure efficient banks under VRS varies from 7 to 16 with an average pure efficiency score varying from 0.917 to 0.961. The average pure efficiency score of public and private sector banks varies from 0.905 to 0.970 and 0.920 to 0.976, respectively. The PSBs surpassed the private sector banks in terms of pure efficiency till 1998–99. However, the reverse is true since 2000–01 onwards except for the years 2002–03 and 2005–06. However, the average pure efficiency score does not differ significantly between two types of banks except for the year 1997–98.

Technical Efficiency and its Sources in Indian Banking Sector

The number of banks that are scale efficient varies from 3 to 8 out of total 33 banks in the sample with the average scale efficiency score varying from 0.915 to 0.984. The average scale efficiency score of PSBs varies from 0.914 to 0.994 and that of private sector banks varies from 0.942 to 0.988. The difference in the average scale efficiency is found to be statistically significant between public and private sector banks during 1998–99, 1999–2000, 2004–05 and 2006–07. On an average, the private sector banks are performing better than the PSBs in terms of scale efficiency till 2000–01. However, the scenario is just the reverse since 2001–02 onwards.

Table 2 reports the average technical efficiency and its sources for each individual bank for the entire post-reform period (1996–2013) as well as two sub-periods: (1) pre-global financial crisis period (1996–2007) and (2) global financial crisis period (2008–2010). The HDFC Bank Ltd. is the only bank, which is technically efficient in Sub-period I. The next most efficient bank is found to be Bank of India, followed by SBI during the entire period of study. Though they failed to become efficient throughout the Sub-period I, they are the only banks, which are technical, as well scale efficient in Sub-period II. It is worth noting that in spite of global financial crisis, both public, as well as private sector banks are performing better in terms of technical efficiency in Sub-period II and it continues to show increasing trends.

Table 2: Technical Efficiency and its Sources in Indian Banking Sector

S. No.	Bank	Pre-Global Financial Crisis (1995-96 to 2006-07)			Global Financial Crisis (2007-08 to 2009-10)			Post Liberalisation (1995-96 to 2012-13)		
		TE	PE	SE	TE	PE	SE	TE	PE	SE
1	AB	0.877	0.913	0.963	0.939	0.944	0.995	0.890	0.919	0.969
2	AnB	0.900	0.931	0.967	0.942	0.948	0.994	0.908	0.934	0.972
3	BOB	0.868	0.930	0.934	1.000	1.000	1.000	0.895	0.944	0.947
4	BOI	0.977	1.000	0.977	0.990	0.990	0.999	0.980	0.998	0.982
5	BOM	0.903	0.938	0.964	0.916	0.922	0.993	0.905	0.935	0.97
6	BORL	0.848	0.878	0.967	0.96	0.982	0.977	0.870	0.899	0.969
7	CB	0.874	0.966	0.905	0.938	0.947	0.992	0.887	0.962	0.922
8	CBOPL	0.86	0.929	0.924	-	-	-	-	-	-
9	CUBL	0.918	0.991	0.927	0.889	0.954	0.933	0.912	0.983	0.928
10	CoB	0.953	0.973	0.980	0.977	0.980	0.997	0.958	0.975	0.983
11	DB	0.924	0.940	0.984	0.909	0.920	0.988	0.921	0.936	0.985
12	DCBL	0.955	0.992	0.963	0.951	1.000	0.951	0.955	0.993	0.961
13	DBL	0.873	0.979	0.894	0.834	1.000	0.834	0.865	0.983	0.882
14	FBL	0.909	0.916	0.992	0.976	0.984	0.992	0.922	0.930	0.992
15	HDFCBL	1.000	1.000	1.000	0.98	0.986	0.994	0.996	0.997	0.999
16	INGVBL	0.905	0.919	0.984	0.974	0.982	0.992	0.919	0.932	0.986
17	IB	0.894	0.921	0.970	0.973	0.975	0.998	0.909	0.932	0.975
18	IOB	0.861	0.897	0.959	0.955	0.964	0.991	0.880	0.911	0.965
19	IBL	0.968	0.973	0.995	0.934	0.947	0.986	0.961	0.968	0.993
20	JKBL	0.902	0.916	0.985	0.891	0.908	0.981	0.900	0.915	0.984
21	KBL	0.883	0.897	0.985	0.958	0.977	0.980	0.898	0.913	0.984
22	KVBL	0.962	0.980	0.981	0.933	0.957	0.974	0.956	0.976	0.980
23	LVBL	0.878	0.923	0.951	0.906	0.992	0.914	0.883	0.936	0.944
24	OBOC	0.897	0.946	0.949	0.898	0.907	0.991	0.897	0.938	0.958
25	PNB	0.897	0.971	0.925	0.973	0.977	0.996	0.912	0.972	0.939
26	SIBL	0.877	0.887	0.989	0.895	0.927	0.965	0.881	0.895	0.985
27	SBBJ	0.938	0.952	0.985	0.968	0.977	0.991	0.944	0.957	0.986
28	SBI	0.954	1.000	0.954	1.000	1.000	1.000	0.963	1.000	0.963
29	SBM	0.936	0.944	0.992	0.985	0.996	0.989	0.946	0.954	0.991
30	SB	0.889	0.926	0.961	0.927	0.931	0.996	0.897	0.927	0.968
31	UB	0.894	0.937	0.955	0.914	0.924	0.990	0.898	0.934	0.962
32	UBI	0.875	0.929	0.942	0.952	0.953	0.999	0.890	0.934	0.953
33	VB	0.866	0.894	0.969	0.898	0.902	0.995	0.872	0.895	0.974
All Banks		**0.906**	**0.942**	**0.963**	**0.942**	**0.961**	**0.980**	**0.913**	**0.946**	**0.966**
Public Banks		**0.904**	**0.943**	**0.960**	**0.95**	**0.956**	**0.994**	**0.913**	**0.945**	**0.967**
Private Banks		**0.91**	**0.941**	**0.967**	**0.929**	**0.969**	**0.960**	**0.913**	**0.946**	**0.965**

Note: TE = Technical Efficiency, PE = Pure Efficiency, SE = Scale Efficiency

However, it will be misleading to conclude at this stage that the Indian banking sector has been operating completely under the clear sky during the global financial crisis period. It could be vital to address the issue through other performance measures such as returns-to-scale and mixed period Malmquist Productivity Index before arriving at any definite conclusion.

Robustness of Efficiency Scores: Sensitivity Analysis

To test the robustness of the DEA results with regards to outliers, the Jackknifing procedure was applied, wherein the DEA was done that drops out each efficient bank one at a time from analysis. Unlike Bonesronning and Rattso (1994) who dropped each unit once at a time, only the efficient units that construct the frontier were dropped (Mostafa, 2010; Charles et al., 2011).

The similarity of mean efficiency between the model with all the banks included and those based on dropping out each efficient bank one at a time has been tested by One-way ANOVA. The null hypothesis that 'the removal of an efficient bank from the sample of banks under study does not affect its mean efficiency' has been tested for each year under study. The results of hypotheses tests are reported in Table 3.

Table 3: Jackknifing Analysis for Robustness of Efficiency Scores: One-way ANOVA

	CRS			VRS		
	df	*F*	*Sig.*	*df*	*F*	*Sig.*
1996	(8, 280)	0.128	0.998	(12, 404)	0.274	0.993
1997	(3, 125)	3.369	0.021*	(16, 528)	0.200	1.000
1998	(4, 156)	0.142	0.966	(14, 466)	0.063	1.000
1999	(4, 156)	3.706	0.007*	(14, 466)	0.111	1.000
2000	(3, 125)	0.811	0.490	(9, 311)	0.470	0.895
2001	(5, 187)	0.918	0.470	(10, 342)	0.339	0.970
2002	(4, 156)	1.610	0.174	(6, 218)	1.052	0.392
2003	(5, 187)	1.700	0.136	(8, 280)	1.142	0.335
2004	(3, 125)	17.297	0.000*	(8, 280)	3.910	0.000*
2005	(3, 125)	8.835	0.000*	(7, 249)	3.568	0.001*
2006	(3, 125)	1.288	0.281	(9, 311)	0.548	0.839
2007	(6, 218)	0.442	0.850	(9, 311)	0.597	0.800
2008	(6, 211)	0.246	0.960	(14, 451)	0.194	0.999
2009	(7, 241)	0.355	0.927	(11, 361)	0.293	0.987
2010	(6, 211)	0.703	0.647	(8, 271)	0.590	0.786

Note: * and ** indicates that the mean difference across the groups in the corresponding year is significant at 99% and 95% level of confidence respectively.

Effect of Elimination of DMU-15 on Efficiency Trends

It can be observed that the null hypothesis is accepted in all the years except during 1997, 1999, 2004 and 2005 under CRS, and during 2004 and 2005 under VRS. Post-hoc analysis revealed that the mean efficiency score is sensitive only to DMU-15 in the above stated years. Next, how far the inclusion of DMU-15 during the above years affects the overall efficiency trends of Indian banking sector was examined. In order to test whether there is any significant difference in the slope and intercept of the trends before and after the removal of DMU-15, the following dummy variable regression model was used:

$$Y_i = \alpha + \beta X_i + \gamma D_i + \varepsilon_i$$

where, Y_i is the average efficiency score as the dependent variable, Y is time as an independent variable, and ε_i is the stochastic disturbance term which is assumed to satisfy all the usual assumptions of least square estimates. D_i = 1 for Trend I (with inclusion of DMU-15 in the sample during the sensitive years) and $D_i = 0$ for Trend II (without the inclusion of DMU-15 in the sample during the sensitive years). In the above model, α_1 and α_2 are the coefficients of Trend II and $(\alpha_1 + \alpha'_1)$ and $(\alpha_2 + \alpha'_2)$ are the coefficients of Trend I. α'_1 and α'_2 are the differential coefficients, showing the effect of DMU-15 on the trend line. In order to test the significance of coefficients of variables in Trend I, the following model was used (Table 4).

$$Y_i = \alpha + \beta_1 X_{i1} + \beta_2 X_{i2} + \gamma_2 D_{i2} + \gamma_3 D_{i3} + \varepsilon_i.$$

Table 4: Effect of Elimination of DMU-15 on Efficiency Trends: Dummy-Variable Regression Model

Dependent Variable		Trend I $\beta_k = (\alpha_k + \alpha'_k)$	Trend II $\alpha_k = (\beta_k + \beta'_k)$	Differential Effect $\alpha'_k = \beta'_k$	R^2	n
TE	*Constant*	0.9053 (0.001)	0.8900 (0.001)	-0.0152 (0.389)	0.304	30
	t	0.0027 (0.0561)	0.0029 (0.039)	0.0002 (0.903)		
PE	*Constant*	0.9460 (0.001)	0.9467 (0.001)	-0.0007 (0.958)	0.328	30
	t	0.0025 (0.021)	0.0026 (0.017)	-0.0001 (0.944)		
SE	*Constant*	0.9411 (0.001)	0.9546 (0.001)	-0.0135 (0.315)	0.133	30
	t	0.0005 (0.596)	0.0003 (0.740)	0.0002 (0.889)		

As it can be observed from Table 4, the differential coefficients, intercept, and slope of the trends are insignificant in all the three cases. This indicates that the inclusion of DMU-15 does not affect the overall trends, in spite of it being an outlier in the present context.

The Returns to Scale in Indian Banking Sector

The presence of scale inefficiency in a bank indicates that it does not operate under the optimal scale and thus, efficiency gains could be achieved by either expanding the production level for a bank operating under IRS or contracting the production level for a bank operating under DRS. Table 5 reports the summary statistics of returns-to-scale in the Indian banking sector during the period 1995–96 to 2012–13. As it appears from the Table 5, most of the banks operate at non-optimal scale (IRS or DRS). Only 9 per cent to 33 per cent banks in the sample operate under optimal scale. It is worth noting that the number of banks that operate under DRS declines over a period of time and banks that operate under IRS increases over a period of time.

The percentage of banks that operate at optimal scale is higher in the private sector than its counterpart throughout except during the year 2005–06, 2007–08 and 2008–09. Most of the banks in the public sector operate at

DRS. On the other hand, majority of the banks in the private sector operate at IRS. The finding is well supported with the study of Zhao et al. (2008), who found that a substantial proportion of PSBs remain characterized by DRS, whereas, two-third of foreign and private banks operate under IRS and optimal returns-to-scale during the period 1992–2004. It is observed that the percentage of banks operating under optimal, decreasing, and increasing returns-to-scale, respectively, during the period 1995–96 to 2009–10. One can observe from table above that: (1) the percentage of PSBs operating under DRS is substantially higher than that of private sector banks at any point of time; and (2) on an average, percentage of banks operating under DRS declines over a period of time for both the sectors. Similarly, it can also be observed from above data that: (1) the percentage of PSBs operating under IRS is substantially higher than that of private sector banks; and (2) on an average, percentage of banks operating under IRS increases over a period of time for both the sectors. There is a sharp decline (increase) in the number of banks operating under DRS (IRS) in 2007–08, possibly because of a shrink in the market as a result of global financial crisis.

Table 5: Summary Statistics of Returns to Scale in Indian Banking Sector

	Pre-Global Financial Crisis												Global Financial Crisis			Post-Global Financial Crisis		
	1996	1997	1998	1999	2000	2001	2002	2003	2004	2005	2006	2007	2008	2009	2010	2011	2012	2013
No. of Banks	33	33	33	33	33	33	33	33	33	33	33	33	32	32	32	32	32	32
Optimal Scale	11	3	4	4	3	7	4	6	4	3	5	7	6	8	6	4	3	5
DRS	20	24	24	21	23	17	16	14	17	11	14	13	1	10	5	17	10	13
IRS	2	6	5	8	7	9	13	13	12	19	14	13	25	14	21	11	19	14
No. of Public Banks	19	19	19	19	19	19	19	19	19	19	19	19	19	19	19	19	19	19
Optimal Scale	6	0	1	1	1	3	2	3	1	1	3	3	5	5	3	1	1	3
DRS	13	19	18	18	17	16	16	14	14	11	14	13	1	9	3	14	11	14
IRS	0	0	0	0	1	0	1	2	4	7	2	3	13	5	13	4	7	2
No. of Private Banks	14	14	14	14	14	14	14	14	14	14	14	14	13	13	13	13	13	13
Optimal Scale	5	3	3	3	2	4	2	3	3	2	2	4	1	3	3	1	1	1
DRS	7	5	6	3	6	1	0	0	3	0	0	0	0	1	2	3	0	0
IRS	2	6	5	8	6	9	12	11	8	12	12	10	12	9	8	8	12	12

Sources of TFP Change in Indian Banking sector

The Malmquist Productivity index includes: (1) technological change, indicating how much benchmark production frontier shifts at each bank's observed input mix (innovation or shocks); (2) pure efficiency change, indicating how much closer a bank gets to the efficient frontier; and (3) scale efficiency change, indicating how much closer the banks are moving towards the most productive scale size. Table 6 reports the summary of Malmquist Productivity Index and its components for the entire period, as well as two sub-periods and their trends over the years.

The average annual change of TFP in Indian banking sector is observed as 1.27 per cent during the post-reform period, with an average annual

Table 6: Sources of TFP Change in Indian Banking Sector

S. No.	Bank	Pre-Global Financial Crisis (1995-96 to 2006-07)				Global Financial Crisis (2007-08 to 2009-10)				Post Liberalisation (1995-96 to 2012-13)			
		TC	PEC	SEC	TFPC	TC	PEC	SEC	TFPC	TC	PEC	SEC	TFPC
1	AB	1.69	-0.14	0.02	1.61	0.46	1.68	-0.23	1.93	1.43	0.25	-0.03	1.68
2	AnB	2.61	0.24	-0.05	2.82	-1.99	0.22	-0.34	-2.08	1.63	0.24	-0.11	1.77
3	BOB	0.89	-0.36	0.6	1.11	1.32	2.04	0.17	3.54	0.98	0.15	0.51	1.63
4	BOI	2.48	0.00	0.53	3.01	-0.47	-0.98	-0.03	-1.49	1.85	-0.21	0.41	2.04
5	BOM	0.52	-0.82	0.01	-0.31	-0.34	-0.65	-0.04	-1.02	0.33	-0.79	0	-0.46
6	BORL	-1.11	0.34	-0.67	-1.43	-7.32	2.83	2.58	-1.91	-2.44	0.88	0.02	-1.53
7	CB	3.72	-0.64	0.35	3.43	-0.02	0.48	0.18	0.68	2.92	-0.4	0.31	2.84
8	CBOPL	2.44	0.01	0	2.44	-	-	-	-	2.44	0.01	0	2.44
9	CUBL	0.72	0.91	-0.29	1.34	-0.66	-3.64	-1.07	-5.41	0.43	-0.06	-0.45	-0.1
10	CoB	4.25	0.87	0	5.14	-0.58	0	0	-0.6	3.21	0.68	0	3.91
11	DB	0.59	-0.51	0.04	0.12	-0.32	0.03	-0.47	-0.81	0.39	-0.39	-0.07	-0.08
12	DCBL	0.15	0.00	-0.63	-0.45	-0.3	0	2.27	1.97	0.05	0	0	0.07
13	DBL	0.81	1.23	-1.84	0.19	-0.6	0	1.33	0.77	0.51	0.97	-1.16	0.32
14	FBL	-0.49	0.14	0.38	0.01	-0.69	1.05	-0.13	0.2	-0.54	0.34	0.27	0.05
15	HDFCBL	3.51	0.00	0	3.51	-2.86	-1.43	-0.07	-4.31	2.15	-0.31	-0.02	1.84
16	INGVBL	2.11	1.18	0.45	3.71	-0.44	0	0.01	-0.45	1.56	0.93	0.36	2.82
17	IB	-1.38	0.59	0.41	-0.39	-0.31	-0.41	-0.07	-0.82	-1.15	0.38	0.31	-0.48
18	IOB	1.63	0.54	0.06	2.2	-1.66	-0.41	0.12	-2.01	0.92	0.34	0.08	1.3
19	IBL	2.41	-1.23	-0.19	0.98	0.2	4.26	0.26	4.71	1.94	-0.05	-0.1	1.78
20	JKBL	2.78	-0.01	0	2.8	-1.84	-5.42	-0.58	-7.8	1.79	-1.17	-0.12	0.53
21	KBL	-0.62	0.16	-0.13	-0.57	-2.7	1.68	0.17	-0.91	-1.07	0.48	-0.06	-0.64
22	KVBL	1.87	0.07	0.12	2.06	-0.15	-1.96	-0.6	-2.73	1.44	-0.36	-0.03	1.04
23	LVBL	1.6	0.46	-0.63	1.42	0.26	-0.84	0.23	-0.36	1.31	0.18	-0.45	1.04
24	OBOC	2.87	-0.84	-0.05	2	0.11	-0.86	-0.17	-0.92	2.28	-0.85	-0.07	1.38
25	PNB	2.22	-0.6	0.71	2.34	-0.09	0.33	0.23	0.41	1.73	-0.4	0.6	1.93
26	SIBL	1.13	0.19	-0.08	1.28	-0.88	0.93	-1.06	-1	0.7	0.35	-0.29	0.79
27	SBBJ	1.18	0.44	-0.01	1.63	0.22	1.58	-0.47	1.28	0.97	0.68	-0.11	1.55
28	SBI	-0.68	0.00	0.01	-0.67	0.92	0	0	0.92	-0.34	0	0.01	-0.33
29	SBM	1.58	1.72	-0.01	3.28	-0.18	-0.37	-0.71	-1.29	1.2	1.27	-0.16	2.3
30	SB	3.97	-0.77	-0.2	3.02	-1.3	2.31	0.2	1.22	2.84	-0.11	-0.12	2.63
31	UB	3.18	-0.19	0.48	3.45	0.27	0.99	-0.57	0.73	2.56	0.07	0.26	2.87
32	UBI	3.86	0.87	0.35	5.09	0.69	0.24	-0.03	0.95	3.18	0.73	0.27	4.2
33	VB	2.22	-0.35	-0.02	1.82	-1.64	0.9	-0.17	-0.91	1.39	-0.09	-0.05	1.23
All Banks		1.66	0.11	-0.01	1.76	-0.72	0.14	0.03	-0.55	1.16	0.11	0	1.27
Public Banks		1.97	0	0.17	2.14	-0.26	0.37	-0.13	-0.01	1.49	0.08	0.11	1.68
Private Banks		1.24	0.25	-0.25	1.24	-1.38	-0.2	0.26	-1.33	0.7	0.15	-0.14	0.72

Note: TC, PEC, SEC and TFPC respectively indicates technological change, pure efficiency change, scale efficiency change and total factor productivity change (ii) Centurion Bank of Punjab Ltd. (CBOPL) merged with HDFC Bank Ltd. (HDFCBL) in May 2008.

change of 1.68 per cent and 0.72 per cent in public and private sector banks, respectively. The difference in the TFP change between these two types of banks is found to be statistically significant. When the contributions of different components towards TFP change are seen, it is observed that the technological change has been the dominating source of productivity growth in the Indian baking sector during the post-reform period with average annual technological change for all banks, public banks and private banks as 1.16 per cent, 1.49 per cent and 0.70 per cent, respectively. On an average, the contribution of both, pure efficiency change, as well as scale efficiency change is found to be negligible for the entire period in both the sectors. During the entire 15 years of the post-liberalization period, the bank that achieves the highest change in TFP is the Union Bank of India with an average annual change of 4.20 per cent. This is followed by Corporation Bank (3.91 per cent), Uco Bank (2.87 per cent), Canara Bank (2.84 per cent),

ING Vysya Bank Ltd. (2.82 per cent) and Syndicate Bank (2.63 per cent) just to name few. In all the above banks, technological change is found to be the dominating source of productivity change. The banks that suffer loss during the entire period of study are Karnataka Bank Ltd. (−0.64 per cent), Indian Bank (−0.48 per cent), Bank of Maharashtra (−0.46 per cent), SBI (−0.33 per cent), City Union Bank Ltd. (−0.10 per cent) and Dena Bank (−0.08 per cent). The technological regress is found to be the cause of loss in TFP in Karnataka Bank Ltd., Indian Bank, and SBI. On the other hand, the pure efficiency change in the case of Bank of Maharashtra and Dena Bank and the scale efficiency change in the case of City Union Bank Ltd. are the main cause of negative growth in their TFP.

On an average, the Indian banking sector has achieved a positive growth of 1.76 per cent in pre-global financial crisis period with an average annual growth of 2.14 per cent and 1.24 per cent, respectively, in public and private sector banks. Most of the banks experience positive average annual change in TFP except for few exceptions such as Bank of Rajasthan Ltd. (−1.43 per cent), SBI (−0.67 per cent), Karnataka Bank Ltd. (−0.57 per cent), Development Credit Bank Ltd. (−0.45 per cent), Indian Bank (−0.39 per cent), and Bank of Maharashtra (−0.31 per cent). The technological regress was observed to be the major cause of decline in TFP for Bank of Rajasthan Ltd., SBI, and Karnataka Bank Ltd. On the other hand, loss in pure efficiency in Bank of Maharashtra and negative change in scale efficiency in Development Credit Bank Ltd. was the cause of negative average annual change in their TFP.

However, the scenario in the global financial crisis period, as expected, is somewhat discouraging. On an average, banks suffer loss in TFP by 0.55 per cent with an average annual loss of 0.01 per cent and 1.33 per cent, respectively, in public and private sector banks. The banks which manage to sustain the positive change in TFP are Indusind Bank Ltd., Allahabad Bank, Canara Bank, Dhanalakshmi Bank Ltd., Federal Bank Ltd., State Bank of Bikaner & Jaipur, Syndicate Bank, Uco Bank, and Union Bank of India. The source of positive change in TFP for these banks during the global financial crisis period is basically due to pure efficiency change, except for Development Credit Bank Ltd. and Dhanalakshmi Bank Ltd., which achieve the gain in TFP through the scale efficiency change.

In contrast with the findings of Ram Mohan and Ray (2004) for the period 1992–2000 who could not ascertain the proposition that productivity is lower in PSBs relative to their peers in the private sector, the present study shows significant difference in favour of PSBs, mainly as a result of technological change. This is quite consistent with the findings of Galagedera and Edirisuriya (2005) for the period 1995–2002, Kumar et al. (2010) for the period 1995–2006, Zhao et al. (2008) for the period 1992–2004, Heffernan and Fu (2010) for the period 2000–2007, and Mahesh and Rajeev (2009) for the period 1985–2004. They observed that TFP change in the Indian banking sector is largely driven by technological progress/innovation.

CONCLUSION

In this study the performance of the Indian banking sector and different ownership structures within it during the post liberalization period were examined. The time period spans from 1996 to 2013, which also covers 3 years of global financial crisis. The technique of DEA is applied to measure efficiency, returns-to-scale and Malmquist indices of TFP change. The TFP change is further decomposed into its different components – technological change, pure efficiency change, and scale efficiency change. The results reveal that DEA efficiency scores are robust with an exception. However, inclusion of the outlier does not affect the overall efficiency trends of the Indian banking sector in the present context. The performance of PSBs is at par with the private sector banks in terms of efficiency. The PSBs are faintly doing better than the private sector banks in terms of (1) technical efficiency since 2003–04 and (2) scale efficiency from 2000–01 onwards. Contrary to our general believe, PSBs have performed better than their counterpart in terms of TFP change as a result of significant differences in technological change. The performance of PSBs in the post-reform period could be attributed to a number of factors such as import of better risk management skills from private domestic banks, intensified competition, the diversification effect, adoption of information technology, concentration towards customer care in terms of service quality, and professionalism as a part of reform process. However, there is a growing tendency of public banks operating under increasing returns-to-scale, implying that substantial gains could be obtained from altering scale via either internal growth or consolidation in the sector. The banks that experience IRS should either eliminate their scale inefficiency or be ready to become a prime target for acquiring banks, which can add value from underperforming banks by streamlining their operations and eliminating their redundancies and inefficiencies that in turn will further boost the efficiency and productivity of the Indian banking sector. The analysis for two different sub-periods reveals that in spite of the global financial crisis, Indian banks continue to show increasing trends in efficiency. However, there is evidence of a shrink in the market, resulting in the movement of the banks towards increasing returns-to-scale, as well as negative growth in TFP in both the sectors during the period of global financial crisis.

REFERENCES

A.N. Berger, W.C. Hunter, and S.G. Timme, 'The Efficiency of Financial Institutions: A Review and Preview of Research: Past, Present and Future', *Journal of Banking and Finance*, vol. 17, 1993, pp. 221–49.

A. Bhattacharyya, C.A.K. Lovell, and P. Sahay, 'The Impact of Liberalization on the Productive Efficiency of Indian Commercial Banks', *European Journal of Operational Research*, vol. 98, 1997, pp. 332–45.

A. Charnes et al., 'Foundations of Data Envelopment Analysis for Pareto-Koopmans Efficient Empirical Production Functions', *Journal of Econometrics*, vol. 30, 1985, pp. 91–107.

A. Das, 'Technical, Allocative and Scale Efficiency of Public Sector Banks in India', *Reserve Bank of India Occasional Papers*, vol. 18, no. 2-3, 1997, pp. 279–97.

A.G. Noulas and K.W. Ketkar, 'Technical and Scale Efficiency in the Indian Banking Sector', *International Journal of Development Banking*, vol. 14, no. 1, 1996, pp. 19–27.

Angadi, V.B. (1987), 'Integrated Approach to Study Banks' Profitability', *Prajnan*, 16(4): 523-538.

B. Casu and P. Molyneux, 'A Comparative Study of Efficiency in European Banking, Applied Economics', *Taylor and Francis Journals*, vol. 35, no. 17, 2003, pp. 1865–76.

B. Golany, F.Y. Phillips, and J.J. Rousseau, 'Models for Improved Effectiveness based on DEA Efficiency Results', *IIE Transactions*, vol. 25, no. 6, 1993, pp. 2–10.

C. Rangrajan and P. Mempilly, 'Economies of Scale in Indian Banking in Technical Studies for Banking Commission Report', Reserve Bank of India, Mumbai, 1972, pp. 244–68.

D. Giokas, 'Bank Branch Operating Efficiency: A Comparative Application of DEA and the Log Linear Model', *Omega*, vol. 19, no. 6, 1991, pp. 549–57.

E.J. Viitala and H. Hanninen, 'Measuring the Efficiency of Public Forestry of Organizations', *Forest Science*, vol. 44, no. 2, 1998, pp. 298–307.

G. Subramanyam, 'Productivity Growth in India's Public Sector Banks: 1979-89', *Journal of Quantitative Economics*, vol. 9, 1993, pp. 209–23.

K. Luoma et al., 'Financial Incentives and Productive Efficiency in Finish Health Centres', *Health Economics*, vol. 5, 1996, pp. 435–45.

M.G. Bhide, A. Prasad, and S. Ghosh (2001), 'Banking Sector Reforms: A Critical Overview', *Economic and Political Weekly*, Vol. 36, February–March, pp. 399–408.

M.J. Farrell, 'The Measurement of Productive Efficiency', *The Journal of Royal Statistical Society*, vol. 120, 1957, pp. 253–81.

M. Sathye, 'Efficiency of Banks in a Developing Economy: The Case of India', *European Journal of Operational Research*, vol. 148, no. 3, 2003, pp. 662–971.

M. Tyagrajan, 'Expansion of Commercial Banking, An Assessment', *Economic and Political Weekly*, vol. 10, 1975, pp. 1819–24.

P. Allen, *Reengineering the Bank*, Chicago, Illinois: Probus Publishing, 1994.

P. Brockett and B. Golany, 'Using Rank Statistics for Determining Programmatic Efficiency Differences in Data Envelopment Analysis', *Management Science*, vol. 42, no. 3, 1996, pp. 466–72.

P. Byrnes, 'The Effect of Ownership on Efficiency: A Nonparametric Programming Approach', PhD dissertation, Southern Illinois University, Carbondale, Illinois, 1985.

P.C. Sarkar and A. Das, 'Development of Composite Index of Banking Efficiency: The Indian Case', *Reserve Bank of India Occasional Papers*, vol. 18, no. 1, 1997, pp. 679–707.

P.K. De, 'Technical Efficiency, Ownership, and Reforms: An Econometric Study of Indian Banking Industry', *Indian Economic Review*, vol. 39, no. 1, 2004, pp. 261–94.

P. Mackay, 'Real Flexibility of Financial Structure: An Empirical Analysis', *The Review of Financial Studies*, vol. 16, no. 4, 2003, pp. 1131–65.

Reserve Bank of India, 'Report of the Productivity, Efficiency and Profitability Committee on Banking', (Luther committee), Mumbai, 1977.

R.D. Banker, A. Charnes, and W.W. Cooper, 'Some Models for Estimating Technical and Scale Inefficiencies in Data Envelopment Analysis', *Management Science*, vol. 30, no. 9, 1984, pp. 1370–82.

R. Colwell and E. Davis, 'Output and Productivity in Banking', *Scandinavian Journal of Economics*, vol. 94 (Supplement), 1992, pp. 111–29.

S.C. Kumbhakar, and S. Sarkar, (2005). 'Deregulation, ownership and efficiency change in Indian banking: an application of stochastic frontier analysis', in Ghosh R. and Neogi C. (Eds.), *Theory and Application of Productivity and Efficiency: Econometric and DEA Approach*, Macmillan, India.

S.K. Hansda and T.R. Venkatachalam, 'Performance Variability of Public Sector Banks: Need for Strategic Planning', *Reserve Bank of India Occasional Papers*, vol. 16, no. 4, 1995, pp. 313–27.

T.T. Ram Mohan and S.C. Ray, 'Productivity and Efficiency at Public and Private Sector Banks in India', Working Paper, Indian Institute of Management, Ahmedabad, 2003.

V.V. Divatia and T.R. Venkatachalam, 'Operational Efficiency and Profitability of Public Sector Banks', *Reserve Bank of India Occasional Papers*, vol. 3, no. 1, 1978, pp. 1–16.

V.B. Angadi, 'Measurement of Efficiency in Banking Industry', *Reserve Bank of India Occasional Papers*, vol. 4, no. 1 , 1983, pp. 110–17.

APPENDIX

List of Banks

S. No.	*Abbreviation*	*Name of the Bank*	*S. No.*	*Abbreviation*	*Name of the Bank*
1	AB	Allahabad Bank[1]	18	IOB	Indian Overseas Bank[1]
2	AnB	Andhra Bank[1]	19	IBL	IndusInd Bank Ltd.[2]
3	BOB	Bank of Baroda[1]	20	JKBL	Jammu & Kashmir Bank Ltd.[2]
4	BOI	Bank of India[1]	21	KBL	Karnataka Bank Ltd.[2]
5	BOM	Bank of Maharashtra[1]	22	KVBL	Karur Vysya Bank Ltd.[2]
6	BORL	Bank of Rajasthan Ltd.[2]	23	LVBL	Lakshmi Vilas Bank Ltd.[2]
7	CB	Canara Bank[1]	24	OBOC	Oriental Bank of Commerce[1]
8	CBOPL	Centurion Bank of Punjab Ltd.[2]	25	PNB	Punjab National Bank[1]
9	CUBL	City Union Bank Ltd.[2]	26	SIBL	South Indian Bank Ltd.[2]
10	CoB	Corporation Bank[1]	27	SBBJ	State Bank of Bikaner & Jaipur[1]
11	DB	Dena Bank[1]	28	SBI	State Bank of India[1]
12	DCBL	Development Credit Bank Ltd.[2]	29	SBM	State Bank of Mysore[1]
13	DBL	Dhanalakshmi Bank Ltd.[2]	30	SB	Syndicate Bank[1]
14	FBL	Federal Bank Ltd.[2]	31	UB	Uco Bank[1]
15	HDFCBL	HDFC Bank Ltd.[2]	32	UBI	Union Bank of India[1]
16	INGVBL	ING Vysya Bank Ltd.[2]	33	VB	Vijaya Bank[1]
17	IB	Indian Bank[1]			

Note: [1] and [2] respectively indicate that the corresponding bank is public and private bank.

Low Risk Anomaly

Evidence from India

Nehal Joshipura
Durgadevi Saraf Institute of Management Studies, Mumbai
e-mail: nehal.joshipura@gmail.com

ABSTRACT

This study aims to investigate the presence of the low risk anomaly in the Indian stock market. Finance theory suggests that a higher return comes with higher risk. However, several studies have reported evidence of low risk anomaly in the US and other global markets, where the portfolio of low volatility stocks delivers superior risk adjusted returns compared to the market index and high volatility stocks' portfolio. The study uses all constituent stocks of CNX 200 index of the National Stock Exchange (NSE). The CNX 200 Index represents about 89 per cent of the free float market capitalization of the stocks listed on NSE as on 31 August 2014. Data from January 2004 to September 2014 is used for the study. The present paper is based on construction of low and high volatility portfolios using volatility of historical monthly returns of stocks and holding portfolios for the next period on iterative basis. The results of the study are consistent with (Blitz and Vliet, 2007) wherein the portfolio of low volatility stocks outperforms both high volatility and market portfolio by a margin, both on absolute and risk adjusted basis.

Keywords: Market Efficiency, Anomaly, Sharpe Ratio, Composite Index

INTRODUCTION

According to the Markowitz's 'Modern Portfolio Theory' (Markowitz, 1952) and Capital Asset Pricing Model (Sharpe, 1964), there is a direct relationship between risk and the expected return. Higher required return comes with higher risk. In an efficient market, investors realize above average returns only by taking above average risks. It is believed that the so-called market portfolio is on the efficient frontier of risky portfolios offering highest possible return at a given level of risk.

It is also believed that market portfolio gives highest excess return at a given level of risk as measured by Sharpe Ratio. However, recently found Low Volatility (LV) and Minimum Variance (MV) investment strategies show that portfolios with low volatility generate higher risk-adjusted returns. Now the next question which immediately comes to mind is that is it possible to have portfolios which give returns greater than High Volatility (HV) portfolio and market portfolio with lesser risk? Is it possible to have a portfolio, which lies above the Capital Allocation Line? This is the basic premise behind 'exploring for low risk anomaly in stock markets!'

There are two ways to test and exploit risk anomaly – (1) LV portfolio, and (2) MV portfolio. Many studies in developed markets report superior returns associated with low volatility portfolios over the market portfolio, as well as the portfolios with higher risk, the risk being measured either by standard deviation of returns or by beta of the stock returns.

Here is the brief explanation of the LV and MV investment strategies:

1. *Low volatility investing* (Blitz and Vliet, 2007): This strategy sorts all the stocks by their volatility and/or beta and then takes a subset of these stocks, comprising those with the lowest beta and/or volatility.
2. *Minimum variance investing* (Clarke et al., Exploring the Risk Anomaly in the Equity Market, 2006): It relies on observations and/or estimates of correlations of individual stocks. Individual stocks have higher risk, but a well-diversified portfolio when optimized for minimum risk is identified as the MV portfolio.

These investment strategies have been noteworthy in the sense that they have been able to deliver higher absolute returns, as well as risk-adjusted returns over time. Both, MV, and LV portfolios reduce volatility and are least hit during the drawdowns.

REVIEW OF LITERATURE

It has long been documented that relationship between risk and return is much more flat than provided by the Capital Asset Pricing Model (CAPM) in many studies (Black, 1972; Haugen and Heins, 1975). Haugen and Heins pointed out that the relationship was not merely flat in their sample period, but was actually inverted. Extending their analysis through the 1990s, Fama and French (1992) also reported that the relationship was flat or even negative, prompting many to conclude that beta was dead.

Minimum variance investing or low volatility investing has been inspired by early works from Haugen & Baker, 1991. For the period covering the years 1972 to 1989, the authors found that repeatedly investing into a stock portfolio constructed to expose investors to minimum risk (as measured by variance) would outperform the Wilshire 5000 index (provide a higher Sharpe ratio). After this, many studies in the US market (Chan et al., 1999; Schawartz, 2000; Jagannathan and Ma, 2003) reported both higher returns and lower realized risks for the Minimum Variance Portfolio (MVP) versus a capitalization weighted benchmark (MWP).

More recently, the following results, showing evidence for low risk anomaly, its sustainability and possible explanations were found:

Anget et al. (2006) report that US stocks with high volatility earned abysmally low returns over the 1963–2000 period.

Frazzini and Pedersen (2010) document that low-risk securities have high risk-adjusted returns in global stock, treasury, credit and futures market.

Clarke et al. (2006) focused on the characteristics of MV portfolios. Their study reports that MV portfolios, based on the 1,000 largest US stocks over the period of 1968–2005, achieved a volatility reduction of about 25 per cent while delivering comparable or even higher average returns than the market portfolio. This means that the MV portfolios had around 75 per cent of the risk of the market portfolio, with returns comparable to those of the broad market. The MV portfolios gave, an average 6.5 per cent excess return above T-Bills with a volatility of 11.7 per cent, whereas, the market index gave an average excess return of 5.6 per cent with a volatility of 15.4 per cent.

Blitz and Vliet (2007) report that low volatility stocks have superior risk-adjusted returns relative to the FTSE World Development Index. The study also reports that low beta stocks had higher returns than predicted, while the reverse held for high beta stocks. They also provide a detailed analysis of the volatility anomaly and demonstrated its robustness across regions and to controls for size, value, and momentum effects. They show outperformance associated with low historical volatility stocks, both in terms of higher Sharpe ratio and higher positive CAPM alpha. They attribute such sustainable outperformance to restricted borrowing as reported by Fisher (1972), decentralized investment approach, and behavioural biases, such as preference for lotteries. Further details on explanations are given in possible explanations section of this document.

Choueifaty and Coignard (2008), proposed maximizing a diversification ratio, the weighted average of the stocks' volatilities divided by the portfolio volatility, as a way to achieve risk-adjusted returns superior to those of the market cap-weighted portfolios. Based on the results on the universe of US and Euro zone securities, the authors concluded that if all of the stocks in the study's universe possessed the same volatility, then the maximum diversification portfolio was equal to the global minimum-variance portfolio.

Managed Volatility: A New Approach in Equity Investing (2009) used the monthly returns for Russell 3000 Universe from December 1986 to October 2007 to note that low beta stocks outperform high beta stocks. According to this study, lowest beta stocks don't necessarily produce the highest returns, thus attributing some success to portfolio construction.

Poullaouec (2010) reports that MSCI MV Index has outperformed the MSCI World Index by +0.5 per cent per annum over the long period of June 1988 to June 2010. However, a large component of the outperformance was concentrated in the June 2000 to June 2003 period. Strong underperformance occurred at the height of the tech bubble, with superior performance in the extended downturn that followed. That leads to a possible conclusion that low volatility strategy tends to work better in a bearish market.

Baker et al. (2011) report that contrary to basic finance principles, high-beta and high-volatility stocks long underperformed low-beta and low-volatility stocks.

Jason and Karceski (2002), provide behavioural explanation to low risk anomaly. According to them, mutual funds investors tend to chase returns over the time and across the funds, possibly because of an extrapolation bias. These forces make fund managers care more about outperforming in bull markets rather than underperforming in bear markets, and therefore increase their demand for high beta stocks and reduce required rate of returns.

Baker et al. (2011) and Baker et al. (2013), provide some explanation for the presence and sustainability of low risk anomaly. According to that, the typical institutional investor's mandate to outperform a fixed benchmark discourages arbitrage activity in high-alpha, low-beta stocks, and low-alpha, high-beta stocks. They replicated the Pettengill et al. (1995) study, which reports higher (lower) total return associated with high beta stock in months where markets report above (below) median return compared to their low beta counterparts. The results are similar. However, on CAPM adjusted basis, low beta stocks still outperform in bull, as well as bear markets and provide evidence for the presence of low risk anomaly over market cycles.

According to Scherer (2011), the MV portfolio tends to invest in two identified anomalies, capturing the return inefficiency of low risk and low beta stocks:

1. 83 per cent of MV excess returns compared to the index can be attributed to the Fama-French factors and the two anomalies of low volatility and low beta.
2. Anomalies explain a sizeable 73 per cent of the excess performance of the MV portfolio and nearly crowd out the Fama-French factors.
3. Investors should decide the degree to which they invest in these two anomalies.

Soe (2012), tested the low-risk anomaly in different markets and across various market cap stocks to find that the low-volatility effect is not unique to the US equity markets; it is present on a global scale.

Carvalho et al. (2012), proposed that a rankings- or quintile-based low volatility construction approach could be considered as an equal risk budget strategy that does not account for the impact of correlations between stocks.

RESEARCH METHODOLOGY

Focus of research is two-fold – exploring and exploiting low risk anomaly and looking for explanations (behavioural and others) for its persistence.

The study is primarily drawing its methodology from Blitz and Vliet (2007) where they test the LV portfolio created, based on ranking using standard deviation of 36 months estimation period and tested for 1 month holding period. Second one is the methodology of Blitz et al. (2012), who conducted their study based on beta and volatility as a measure of risk.

The present study takes beta as a measure of risk.

Data

The data consists of the present and past constituent stocks from CNX 200, for which adjusted monthly price data for the period from the inception of the index to September 2014 is available. The CNX 200 Index represents about 89 per cent of the free float market capitalization of the stocks listed on the National Stock Exchange (NSE) as on 31 July 2014.

Many return anomalies are known to disappear or become less pronounced when the universe is restricted to large-caps, which is the reason behind the choice of universe. And by taking all constituents of the benchmark CNX 200, an attempt is made to avoid survivorship bias.

Out of the total available list of companies of the market-capitalization weighted index, companies with entire or significant non-availability of trading data, either for price or volume for past 36 months, are not used for this study.

This filtering helped the authors to avoid illiquid stocks or those stocks that stopped trading during the study period and may have contaminated results as they may have exhibited high volatility and poor returns. So, effort were made to avoid the size effect as mentioned by Merton (1987) and Banz (1981).

Data Source

The capital market on-line database, Capitaline is the data source of the constituents and adjusted monthly closing prices for CNX 200.

Data Collection Period

The data collection period is from the inception of CNX 200, that is, January 2004 to September 2014. The period is long enough so that it includes both, bullish, and bearish period. The iterations start after 36 months, that is, if base date is 1 January 2004, then the first iteration starts from February 2007 using monthly returns data from February 2004 to January 2007.

PORTFOLIO FORMATION AND TESTING

Formation period is of 36 months, which is followed by testing period or portfolio holding period of 1 month. Stock returns are to be measured monthly on adjusted monthly closing prices of the companies by using the formula $\ln(P_1/P_0)$, where P_1 is the current month's adjusted closing stock price, P0 is previous month's adjusted closing stock price. This period of 36 months is called the formation period. The stocks with more than 36 months data are considered for the estimation and are called eligible stocks. The portfolio with all the eligible stocks of the iterations is called universe portfolio (Equally Weighted Index – EWI). The stocks are selected for the portfolios depending on their riskiness, which is represented by beta.

The methodology consists of creating, at the end of every month, equally-weighted portfolios of the 10 per cent (decile) of the eligible stocks based on ranking stocks on their past volatility as measured by trailing 36 months beta. Thus, the Portfolio 1 (Decile 1) has the top decile volatile stocks (most volatile stocks) and the Portfolio 10 (Decile 10) will have the bottom decile volatile stocks (least volatile stocks). The bottom decile portfolio is known as LV portfolio and top decile portfolio is called HV portfolio. The performance of these decile portfolios is measured as the simple average of log returns of all the stocks in the portfolios.

Hypotheses

- H_{00}: There is no significant difference between the Sharpe ratios of low volatility portfolio and universe portfolio.
- H_{01}: Sharpe ratio of low volatility portfolio is significantly higher than universe portfolio.
- H_{10}: There is no significant difference between the Sharpe ratios of low volatility portfolio and high volatility portfolio.
- H_{11}: Sharpe ratio of low volatility portfolio is significantly higher than high volatility portfolio.
- H_{20}: Ex-post alpha for low volatility portfolio is not significantly different than zero.
- H_{21}: Ex-post alpha for low volatility portfolio is significantly higher than zero.
- H_{30}: Ex-post alpha for high volatility portfolio is not significantly different than zero.
- H_{31}: Ex-post alpha for high volatility portfolio is significantly lower than zero.
- H_{40}: There is no significant difference between the variance of returns of low volatility portfolio and universe portfolio.
- H_{41}: Variance of returns of low volatility portfolios is significantly lower than the universe portfolio.
- H_{50}: There is no significant difference between the variance of returns of low volatility portfolio and high volatility portfolio.
- H_{51}: Variance of returns of low volatility portfolios significantly lower than high volatility portfolio.

Statistical Testing – Test of Significance

1. Comparison of Sharpe ratio for LV, HV, Index portfolio and the present study's index, EWI – equally weighted portfolio of all candidate stocks. To test for the statistical significance of the difference between Sharpe ratios, the study applies the (Jobson & Korkie, 1981) test with the (Memmel, 2003)correction. This test statistic is calculated according to the formula below and asymptotically follows a standard normal distribution.

$$z = \frac{SR_1 - SR_2}{\sqrt{\frac{1}{T}\left[2(1-\rho_{1,2}) + \frac{1}{2}(SR_1^{\,2} + SR_2^{\,2} - SR_1 SR_2(1+\rho_{1,2}^{\,2}))\right]}}$$

Here SR_i is the Sharpe ratio of portfolio i, $\rho_{i,j}$ is the correlation between portfolios i and j, and T is the number of observations.

2. For testing significance of ex-post alpha for LV and HV portfolios, study will employ one sample t-test.

$$t = \frac{\overline{x} - \mu_0}{s / \sqrt{n}}$$

3. F test – for testing the significance of variance between the two samples
   (a) LV and EWI (universe)
   (b) LV and HV portfolios
   Test statistic $= s_1^2 / s_2^2$

RESULTS AND DISCUSSION

Table 1 summarizes the results for LV investment strategy. LV portfolio delivers an excess annualized return of 2.84 per cent over risk-free return with standard deviation of 18.93 per cent per annum. That results in Sharpe ratio of 0.15. Whereas, HV portfolio delivers a massive negative excess return of –12.99 per cent over risk-free return with a standard deviation of a whopping 52.81 per cent per annum and a Sharpe ratio of –0.25. EWI (Universe) portfolio delivers an excess return of –1.14 per cent per annum with standard deviation of 32.19 per cent and a Sharpe ratio of –0.04. The difference between the Sharpe ratio of LV and universe portfolio is highly significant with t-stat of 2.48 using (Jobson and Korkie, 1981) test with (Memmel, 2003) correction for testing the difference between Sharpe ratios. The corresponding statistics is –6.25 for the difference between Sharpe ratio of HV and universe portfolio. This shows that LV portfolio delivers a significantly higher reward to risk ratio compared to both universe and HV portfolio and we reject both H_{00} and H_{10} null hypotheses.

While ex-post alpha is positive with an annualized value of 3.34 per cent, it has a corresponding t-stat of 0.75 and hence statistically not significant. We therefore do not reject H_{20}. However, alpha for HV portfolio is –11.99 per cent on an annualized basis and it is highly significant with t-stat of –3.17. We reject H_{30}. Ex-post beta for LV portfolio is 0.44 and 1.51 for HV portfolio. This shows that while LV portfolio delivers comparable returns to universe portfolio, but at a much lower risk, and therefore contributes to higher risk adjusted returns. Surprisingly, LV portfolio outperforms HV portfolio, both in terms of absolute, as well as risk adjusted return basis.

Table 1: Main Results (Annualized) for LV, HV and Universe Portfolios based on Historical Volatility

	LV (%)	*HV (%)*	*LV-HV (%)*	*EWI (universe) (%)*
Excess Return (Annualized)	2.84	–12.99	15.82	–1.14
Standard Deviation	18.93	52.81	44.20	32.19
Sharpe ratio	0.15	–0.25	0.36	–0.04
(t-value for difference over universe)	2.48	–6.25		
Beta	0.44	1.51		1
Alpha (Annualized)	3.34	–11.19		
(t-value)	0.75	–3.17		

Table 2 provides an additional test of ex-post variance of both, LV, and EWI, as well as LV and HV portfolios to test whether portfolio consisting of low beta stocks continues to exhibit low volatility and whether its volatility remains significantly lower compared to both, universe, and HV portfolio. F-stat for test of two sample variance between LV and universe portfolio, at 2.89 shows that universe portfolio has a much higher volatility. The corresponding number for LV and HV portfolio is 7.78, which shows that the volatility of HV portfolio is highly significant compared to its LV counterpart. We reject both H_{40} and H_{50}.

Table 2: F Test for Two Sample Variance for EWI and LV, and HV and LV Portfolios

	EWI	*LV*	*HV*	*LV*
Mean	0.005548342	0.008864123	–0.00432181	0.008864123
Variance	0.008634914	0.002986428	0.02323842	0.002986428
Observations	92	92	92	92
df	91	91	91	91
F	2.89138496		7.78134102	
P(F<=f) one-tail	3.92733E-07		6.3388E-20	
F Critical one-tail	1.414340633		1.41434063	

The above results show that while LV portfolio may or may not outperform universe portfolio on absolute return basis, it definitely outperforms based on risk adjusted basis.

Figure 1 shows the composite index of LV, HV and EWI portfolios with base value of 100 in the beginning of the year 2007. INR 100 invested in each LV, HV and EWI portfolios is worth INR 226.03, INR 166.60, and INR 67.19, respectively. This shows a real significant difference and benefit associated with low volatility investments that may not be captured in average returns and alpha value. The biggest benefit associated with the LV portfolio compared to HV and EWI is that it has the lowest drawdown when the market starts sliding from its top. When it comes to falling markets, LV portfolio outperforms both universe and HV portfolio by a huge margin and hence, even if it underperforms both universe and HV portfolio in rising market, net-net it delivers not only risk adjusted, but superior absolute returns compared to both universe and HV portfolios.

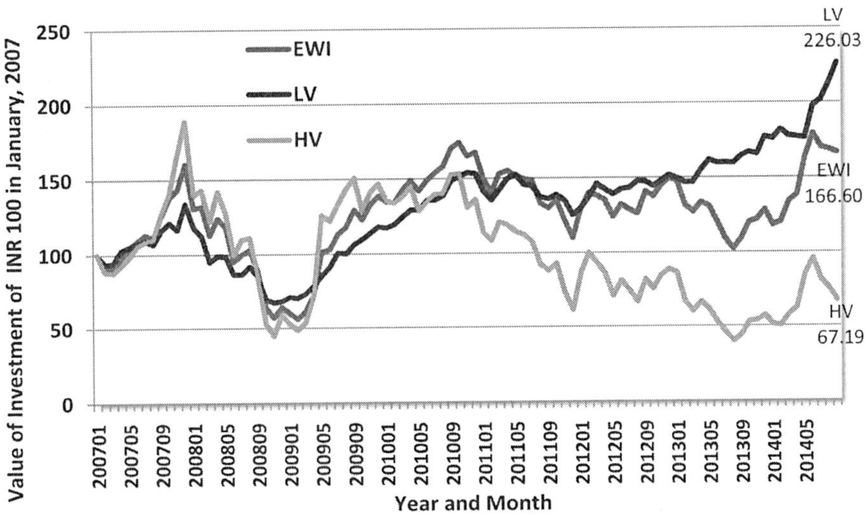

Figure 1: Composite Wealth Index of LV, HV, EWI (universe) Portfolios

Possible Explanations

While it is difficult to explain the presence of such low risk anomaly and its sustainability using the traditional Finance theory and models such as the Capital Asset Pricing Model (CAPM) and the Markowitz Modern Portfolio Theory (MPT), there are some plausible explanations to explain such consistent outperformance of low volatility investment strategies.

Following three behavioural biases can explain investors' preference for high volatility stocks that, in turn, make those stocks overvalued and subsequently deliver lower returns.

1. *Preference for Lottery:* The general assumption is that investors are risk averse and that is true under normal circumstances. A layman tends to reject a bet with 50 per cent probability of winning INR 110 and 50 per cent probability of losing INR 100 despite positive expected payoff associated with this bet Kahneman and Tversky

(1979) explain such behaviour as 'loss aversion'. However, something strange happens with individuals when probability shifts. If the same individual who rejected the bet with positive expected payoff of INR 5 earlier is now offered a bet with an almost certain loss of INR 1 and a small chance (probability is 0.15 per cent) of getting INR 5,000 is willing to accept the bet despite the negative accepted payoff associated with it. That's the very reason people buy lottery! This has something to do with positive skewness of payoffs and not volatility. However, Mitton and Vorkink (2007) highlighted that high volatility individual stocks with limited liability are also positively skewed. Buying a high volatility, low priced stock is like buying a lottery – high probability of losing money vs. a small chance of doubling or tripling money in short-term. Kumar (2009) shows that individual investors show clear preference for stocks with lottery like payoff measured as idiosyncratic volatility or skewness. Boyer et al. (2010), argued that volatility is a proxy for expected skewness.

2. *Representativeness:* Hazards of ignoring representativeness bias were explained by Kahneman and Tverskey (1983). Due to this behavioural bias, a layman and quant look at characteristics of 'a great investment' from two completely different perspectives. For a layman, Microsoft represents a success story and therefore buying new technology stocks at the time of IPO makes great sense. However, the question is whether all new technology stocks will become Microsoft and whether Microsoft represents the entire universe of new technology stocks? A quant based model will favour high risk investments such as Microsoft at the time of IPO only if it can separate Microsoft from similar other risky technology companies and therefore generally avoid high risk stocks.
3. *Overconfidence:* Overconfidence leads to a tendency to precisely forecast uncertain outcomes and sticks to that. Miller (1977) reports that the market is dominated by optimistic investors, as generally pessimistic individual or even institutional investors are averse to short selling and therefore markets are dominated by optimistic overconfident investors who push the price of highly volatile stocks upwards and make them overvalued, leading to lower returns.
4. *Limits to Arbitrage:* The other explanation for persistence of low risk anomaly is limits to arbitrage as explained by Baker et al. (2011). Most of the institutional investors are working for beating some benchmark and in order to do that they tend to go for high

beta stocks. They can achieve the same result by investing in low beta stocks using leverage, but restrictions on borrowing including longonly mandate, i.e. mandate to buy the stocks and not allowed to short-sell, leads to the elimination of the possibility of exploiting arbitrage opportunity between low beta-high alpha and high beta-low alpha stock.

CONCLUSION

The findings of the study are consistent with global markets and it shows an evidence for the presence of low risk anomaly, and that low volatility portfolio outperforms both high volatility portfolio and market portfolio on risk adjusted basis. While LV portfolio delivers higher absolute return over both HV and market portfolios, it is statistically not significant. However, when it comes to the variance of returns, LV portfolio has much lower variance than both HV and market portfolio and it is highly significant statistically. In addition, LV portfolio suffers much smaller drawdown compared to their HV counterpart. Thus, it can be taken as a very good strategy when the markets don't have any specific direction and the volatility in general is very high. In such situations it warrants minimum erosion of wealth, but ensures that an investor doesn't miss out on the upside returns totally. Finally, this study confirms that the behaviour of emerging markets like the Indian stock market is similar to a mature US market and that similar anomalies exist in both these markets. This opens new doors for the Indian markets to the investment strategies which have been successful in developed markets.

REFERENCES

Ang, A., Hodrick, R.J., Xing, Y., & Zhang, X. (2006). The Cross Section of Volatility and Expected Return. *Journal of Finance*, 61(1), 259-299.

Baker, M., Bradley, B., & Taliaferro, R. (2014, January 23). The Low Risk Anomaly: A Decomposition into Micro and Macro Effects. *Financial Analysts Journal*, 70(2), 43-58.

Baker, M., Bradley, B., & Wurgler, J. (2011, January). Benchmarks as Limits to Arbitrage: Understanding the Low-Volatility Anomaly. *Financial Analysts Journal*, 67(1), 40-54.

Banz, R. (1981). The Relationship Between Return and Market Values of Common Stock. *Journal cif Finandal Economics*, 9, 3-18.

Black, F. (1972 йил July). Capital Market Equilibrium with Restricted Borrowing. *Journal of Business*, 4(3), 444-455.

Blitz, D.C., & Vliet, P.V. (2007). The Volatility Effect. *The Journal of Portfolio Management, 34*(Fall), 102-113.

Blitz, D.C., Pang, J., & Vliet, P.V. (2013). The Volatility Effect in Emerging Markets. *Emerging Markets Review*, 16, 31-45.

Boyer, B., Mitton, T., & Vorkink, K. (2010, January). Expected Idiosyncreatic Skewness. *Review of Financial Studies*, 23(1).

Carvalho, Raul Leote de, Xiao Lu, Pierre Moulin. (2012). Demystifying Equity Risk-Based Strategies: A Simple Alpha plus Beta Description. *Journal of Portfolio Management*, 38(3).

Chan, L., Karceski, J., & Lakonishok, J. (1999). Portfolio Optimisation: Forecasting Covariances and Choosing the Risk Model. *Review of Financial Studies*, 12, 937-974.

Choueifaty, Y., & Coignard, Y. (2008). Toward Maximum Diversification. *Journal of Portfolio Managemen*, 35(1).

Clarke, R., deSilva, H., & Thorley, S. (2006 йил December). Exploring the Risk Anomaly in the Equity Market. *Economics and Porfolio Strategy*.

Clarke, R., Silva, H.D., & Thorley, S. (2006 йил December). Exploring the Risk Anomaly in the Equity Market. *Economics and Porfolio Strategy*.

Fama, E., & French, K. (1992). The Cross-Section of Expected Stock Returns. *Journal of Finance*, 47, 427-465.

Frazzini, A., & Pedersen, L. H. (2010 йил October). Betting against Beta. *Working paper*, New York University.

Haugen, R.A., & Baker, N.L. (1991, Spring). The efficient market inefficiency of capitalization – weighted stock portfolios. *The Journal of Portfolio Management*, 17(3), 35-40.

Haugen, R.A., & Heins, A.J. (1975, December). Risk and the Rate of Return on Financial Assets: Some Old Wine in New Bottles. *Journal of Financial and Quantitative Analysis*, 10(5), 775-784.

Jagannathan, R., & Ma, T. (2003). Risk Reduction in large portfolios: Why imposing the wrong constraints helps. *The Journal of Finance*, 58(4), 1651-1684.

Jobson, & Korkie. (1981). Performance Hypothesis Testing with the Sharpe and Treynor Measures. *Journal of Finance*, 36, 889-908.

Kahneman, D., & Tverskey, A. (1983, October). Extensional verseus Intitutive Reasoning: The conjuction Fallacy in Probability Judgement. *Psychological Review*, 90(4), 293-315.

Kahneman, D., & Tversky, A. (1979, March). Prospect Theory: An Analysis of Decision under Risk. *Econometrica*, 47(2), 263-291.

Karceski, J. (2002, December). Returns-Chasing Behavior, Mutual Funds, and Beta's Death. *Journal of Financial and Quantitative Analysis*, 37(4), 559-594.

Kumar, A. (2009, August). Who Gambles in the Stock Market? *Journal of Finance*, 64(4), 1889-1933.

Managed Volatility: A New Approach in Equity Investing (2009). *State Street.*

Markowitz H. (1952). Portfolio Selection. *Journal of Finance*, 7(1), 77-91.

Memmel, C. (2003). Performance Hypothesis Testing with the Sharpe Ratio. *Finance Letters*, 1(1), 21-23.

Merton, R.C. (1987). On the Current State of the Stock Market Rationality Hypotheses. Rudiger Dornbusch, Stanley Fischer, and John Bossons, eds., *Macroeconomics and Finance Essays in Honor of Franco Modigliani*. Cambridge, MA: MIT Press, 93-124.

Miller, E.M. (1977, September). Risk, Uncertainty, and Divergence of Opinion. *Journal of Finance*, 32(4), 1151-1168.

Mitton, T., & Vorkink, K. (2007, July). Equillibrium Underdiversification and the Preference for Skewness. *Review of Financial Studies*, 20(4), 1255-1288.

Pettengill, G.N., Sundaram, S., & Mathur, I. (1995, March). The conditional Relation between Beta and Return. *Journal of Financial and Quantitative Analysis*, 30(1), 101-116.

Poullaouec T. (2010). *Things to Consider When Investing in Minimum Volatility Strategies.* State Street Global Advisors Asset Allocation Research.

Schawartz, T. (2000). How to beat the S&P 500 with portfolio optimization. *Working paper*, DePauls University.

Scherer, B. (2011). A Note on the Returns from Minimum Variance Investing. *Journal of Empirical Finance*, 18(4), 652-660.

Sharpe, W.F. (1964 йил September). Capital Asset Prices: A Theory of Market Equilibrium under Conditions of Risk. *The Journal of Finance*, XVIII, 425-442.

Soe, A.M. (2012, August 1). The Low Volatility Effect: A Comprehensive Look. *S&P DOW JONES Indices Paper.*

Basel-III
Implications for Indian Banks

Siddharth Shukla
School of Petroleum Management, Pandit Deendayal Petroleum University, Gandhi Nagar, Gujarat
e-mail: siddharth_elect@yahoo.co.in

ABSTRACT

Banks and credit institutions are of utmost importance while considering the economic growth and social welfare. To ensure viability of banking sector and prevent bank failures the banking sector is subjected to many regulations and is continuously under supervision of the concerned authorities of respective countries across the globe. The Basel Committee on Banking Supervision is the central body that develops and standardizes banking regulation globally. However, the recent financial crisis in the late 2000s demonstrated that the Basel Accords II were not robust enough to assess the risks that banks faced. Many financial institutions drove innovation to avoid legislative capital requirements and to take on more risk. As per the Basel Committee the reason for financial crises was built up of excessive on and off balance sheet leverage, and when the financial market forced banks to cut leverage it resulted into the downfall of asset prices exacerbated by losses, falling bank capital, and non-availability of credit. In response to the financial crises Basel-III regulations were suggested by the Basel Committee. The aim of the Basel-III Accord is to make the banking system more resilient to financial crisis and provide stability. Nevertheless, the new regulations have stricter capital requirement. It has also prescribed the framework with specific liquidity requirement. This paper discusses the suitability, compliance, and the possible impacts of implementation of Basel-III regulations on Indian Banks. The opening part in this paper discusses the requirement and suitability of Basel-III regulations for Indian banks, the middle part emphasis on the compliance process of Basel-III for Indian banks, and the final part discusses the possible impacts on a bank's capital, growth, and liquidity. The issues and challenges faced by Indian banks are placed in the conclusive part.

Keywords: Banking Regulations, Basel-III, Leverage, Capital Requirement

INTRODUCTION

The financial sector in India went through the limited growth till early 1990s where the Government policies were the only major factor which decided the direction and quantum of growth. The fundamental changes brought in the financial system in 1991 not only improved the balance of payment situation of the country, but also provided a suitable environment for a positive and balanced growth for the entire economy.

Among the various financial institutions in the economy, banks are considered to be of utmost importance because of their central role in the payments system. Besides this, banking being a highly leveraged business with short-term liabilities in terms of deposits and broader customer base, the protection of depositors is also equally important. Considering these facts the banks are subject to various regulations.

The primary goal of banking regulation is the stability of the banking system. Bank failures are considered to have enormous undesirable effects on the economy because of their cascading effect. This constitutes the fundamental rational for the need of a safety net arrangement for the stability of the banking system (Vighneshwara Swamy, 2013). At the same time it needs to be ensured that the financial system operates efficiently; so the banks are expected to take an acceptable level of risk considering the fact it must not hamper their stability.

Like any other business, the capital facilitates as a buffer in banking too against the losses and hence failure. However, there are various views on this issue as one logic can be that raising the capital requirement for banks will escalate the banks' risk-taking behaviour, whereas, in the absence of such regulations banks may end up becoming victims of economic downfall, resulting in a very intense effect on the entire financial sector. Besides this the inter-connection among the banks for extending credit, particularly at the times of economic boom, and the possibility that one bank not being able to meet its commitment to the other bank due to prolonged liquidity crunch exposes banks to systematic risk. Thus, addressing the excessive asset growth during a period of boom will help in the mitigation of systemic risk because of the cross-exposures across the banks.

Basel Committee on Banking Supervision (BCBS) since its formation has been instrumental in standardizing the banking regulations across the globe by following a thorough consultative approach. The BCBS formulated the first accord on bank regulation by developing a risk-based capital adequacy standard. The Basel-I Accord introduced in 1988 primarily focused on the credit risk of banks. Basel-I Accord can be divided into a four-pillar framework. While the first pillar is about the constituents of capital, the second is about the risk weighting system. The third pillar deals with target standard ratio and the fourth pillar pertains with transitional and implementation arrangements.

Basel-I Accord failed to pick important differences between risk exposures of different banks and it also failed to keep pace with innovations in the banking industry which rendered it to be obsolete. It did not differentiate between different levels of risk, thus creating opportunities for regulatory capital arbitrage which is a process through which banks can switch to high-risk, high-return portfolios without altering their capital-to-asset ratio (Tanaka, 2003). Basel-I was centred around credit risk ignoring other important risks, viz., operation risk and market risk, that resulted in inadequate capital adequacy for the banks in meeting risks. Hence, the failure of the 'one-size-fits-all' approach under Basel-I to risk management did not provide enough incentive for banks to improve their risk management functions.

Basel-II Accord presented in 2004 was intended to address most of the shortcomings of Basel-I. Besides imposing minimum capital requirements in line with technological advancement in the financial industry, Basel-II was expected to incorporate a more enhanced supervisory review process and greater transparency by requiring public disclosure as part of market discipline. Basel-II was intended to provide a more risk-sensitive approach while maintaining the overall level of regulatory capital within the financial system. It provided room for banks to adequately emphasize their own internal risk management methodologies and provided more incentives for their efficiency in risk management, thereby increasing the flexibility of their systems. Basel-II was envisioned to align regulatory capital requirements with the existent risk associated with banks' assets, computed with latest risk management techniques. It was introduced with a purpose to increase the regulatory capital for lower rating classes and, as a result, several observers expressed their concern that bank lending to emerging markets would decline (Reisen, 2001 Griffith-Jones, 2003)

The three pillars of Basel-II, namely (1) Minimum capital requirement, (2) Supervisory review, and (3) Market discipline took care of the capital requirement for credit risk, banks' internal procedure for capital determination with respect to risk profile, and encouraged greater transparency of banks' holdings, in the interest of all the stakeholders and to bring in accountability. Thus, Basel-II took care of most of the shortcomings of Basel-I, but still financial crises that hit the entire system in the late 2000s proved that Basel-II too was not so full proof against the economical stress and emphasized on the requirement of better and improved regulations to keep the banking system immune from the economic shocks.

If we have a closer look at Basel-II Accord we can see that the risk sensitivity, which was at the centre of this accord, made it procyclical (M. Jayadev, 2013). During the economic boom when the market was doing well and investors were willing to put capital with banks it did not impose any significant additional capital requirement, whereas, in times of stress, when banks required additional capital, when market was not in position to supply this additional capital, Basel-II required to bring in more of it. As we saw during the crises in 2008, it was the failure to bring additional capital when under pressure that forced major international banks into a vicious cycle of deleveraging and thereby hurting the global financial market and economies around the world.

Besides this, the widely promoted capital regulation under Basel-II were more risk sensitive, but it didn't bring corresponding changes in the definition and composition of the regulatory capital as per the changing market scenario. Thus, the market risk models failed to derive the quantum or risk from the complex derivative products which were introduced in the market in a big way. The less capital requirement against the trading book exposures on the assumption that the trading book position can easily be squared-off without much hit, encouraged banks to park funds into these toxic assets and their securitized derivatives which became the centre of crises.

One of the other major concerns about Basel-II is that there is no explicit control over leverage. It was assumed that risk based capital requirement would automatically take care of the risk of excessive leverage (Carmassi and Micossi, 2012), which was not held well during crises. The lack of paying attention to systematic risk, which arises from the interconnections among financial institutions, resulted into the spread of risk across the financial markets.

In response to the economic crises encountered, the Basel-III Accord was introduced in December 2010 with the purpose of strengthening global capital and liquidity rules for promoting a more resilient banking sector. The objective of the reforms is to improve the banking sector's ability to absorb shocks arising from financial and economic thrust, thus reducing the risk of spill-over from the financial sector to the real economy.

The goal of the introduction of Basel-III is to enhance the quality and quantity of a bank's capital. Increased Tier-I capital requirement, capital buffers, liquidity requirements and overall leverage restrictions are the prime issues which are addressed under Basel-III as mentioned below:

1. *Tier-I Capital:* The loss absorbing component, that is, common equity and retained earnings are declared as the predominant form of Tier-I capital and have been stipulated to be maintained at 4.5 per cent of risk weighted assets.
2. *Capital Conservation Buffer:* Over and above the minimum capital requirements to the extent of 2.5 per cent of risk weighted assets, capital buffer in the form of Tier-I common equity is to be maintained.
3. *Counter-Cyclic Buffer:* Capital buffer to control excessive growth during economic upturn up to 2.5 per cent of risk weighted assets in the form of equity capital.

The other major features of Basel-III are global standards for banks' liquidity with the introduction of Liquidity Coverage Ratio (LCR) and Net Stable Funding Ratio (NSFR) to ensure short-term and long-term liquidity in the system.

STEPS FOR INDIAN BANKS TO COMPLY WITH BASEL-III

Basel-III represents an effort to bridge the gap and lacunae in Basel-II which came to the light during the crises; thus it is an enhancement over Basel-II. This enhancement is majorly in four areas which need to be taken care of to comply with Basel-III.

1. *Higher Capital Requirements:* However, minimum capital requirement is still 8 per cent of Risk Weighted Assets (RWAs), as, per Basel-III, banks are required to maintain an additional 2.5 per cent of RWA in the form of capital conservation buffer. This additional capital requirement is to provide a shock absorbing capacity to banks without effecting the minimum capital requirement and to provide the ability to banks to carry on their business even during economic downturn. Besides this, the additional capital requirement in the form of counter cyclical buffer is introduced to trap the excessive growth during the economic boom.
2. *Liquidity Standards:* To mitigate the risk of excessive leverage as happened under Basel- II, banks are required to maintain a minimum Tier-I leverage ratio of 3 percentages. Basel-II failed to demand an adequate loss absorbing capital to cover market risk. This issue has been taken care of in Basel-III by the use of stressed input parameters to determine capital requirement under counterparty default risk.

Moreover, the new capital requirement in the form of Capital Valuation Adjustment (CVA) risk capital charge for Over The Counter (OTC) derivatives is introduced for taking care of the decline in the credit quality of counterparty. Further, to address the short-term liquidity requirement Liquidity Coverage Ratio (LCR) and long-term liquidity requirement NSFR are introduced. Under LCR banks are required to maintain sufficient high quality unencumbered liquid assets to withstand any stressed funding scenario over a period of 30 days, and under NSFR banks are required to maintain a minimum amount of stable sources of funding relative to the liquidity profile of assets. Thus, the long-term liquidity mismatch issue is addressed by NSFR which emphasizes on stable sources of funding.

3. *Provisioning Norms:* The Basel committee is supporting the proposal for the adoption of an 'expected loss' based measure of provisioning which captures the actual losses more transparently in place of an 'incurred loss' approach. This gives a better picture of the financial health of bank to all stakeholders, including regulators and supervisors.
4. *Disclosure Requirements:* The disclosures made by banks are very crucial for market participants for making informed decisions. One of the observations during analysis of financial crises of the late 2000s was that disclosures made by banks on their risky exposures and on regulatory capital were neither appropriate nor sufficiently transparent.

To comply with stipulated Basel-III norms banks will have to consider the following issues and decide accordingly in areas, namely capital management, liquidity management, and general capital management planning as discussed below:

1. *Capital Management:* The optimum use of capital and rewarding the efforts taken in that direction will be fruitful. Banks need to carry on a scenario analysis (Pokutta, Sebastian and Schmaltz Christian, 2012), to develop the strategy for optimum use of capital. Besides this, they need to re-check which business/product is more in line with Basel-III and which business is worth exiting without affecting the overall profitability. To create awareness among the down-the-line staff and apply consistent and quantified capital objectives throughout the group will be needed as well. Reviewing the plan at regular intervals will also serve the need of cross checking and give the banks a chance to make necessary changes accordingly, if needed.

2. *Liquidity Management:* Analysis of current liquidity position of the banks and finding out the current stressed points is the prime necessity. Considering the effect of new liquidity regulations on profitability and, whether it is implemented into the business process and pricing, needs to be changed. Banks need to decide an appropriate set of liquidity stress tests and how these would change over a period of time. Further, checking the bank's liquidity management strategy as per stipulated regulations and regulatory structure will be a necessary issue here.
3. *General Capital Planning:* It needs to ensure that RWAs are properly supported by the capital. For any new business the Basel-III capital regulations should be taken into account, and to decide how non-core businesses, like insurance or subsidiaries, etc., can be restructured. Evaluate the performance of existing assessment methodologies (i.e. IRB Models). Review the strategies implemented and make necessary changes, if needed, accordingly.

PROBABLE EFFECT OF BASEL-III IMPLEMENTATION

With the introduction of capital and liquidity buffers, the Basel-III framework will help in the better management of the risk arising from counterparty default and liquidity stress. The stricter norms for inter-bank liability limits will reduce the interdependence of banks, and thus will save banks from contagion risk during the crises. Thus Basel-III implementation will improve the shock absorbing capacity of Indian banks and reduce the risk of effects of financial crises being spread to the entire economy.

The weaker banks may find it difficult to meet the additional capital requirement further. If the condition worsens, the regulatory capital requirement will become much stricter and the weaker banks will find it even more difficult to raise the required capital. However the study conducted by S. Stolz and M. Wedow for period 1993–2003 suggests that during business downturn the low-capitalized banks do not decrease the risk-weighted assets if the said theory holds good, survival may become difficult for these banks and may result into takeover by big players.

Increased supervisory control on banking activities in term of LCR and NSFR may result into very limited growth for the banking sector. With the introduction of NSFR, banks will have to invest in high quality assets and dispose off the low to medium quality assets adversely affecting the Net Interest Margin (NIM), necessitating greater focus on Asset Liability Management and strategies to make-up for NIM degradation.

The requirement to maintain capital conservation buffer and counter cyclical buffer will force banks to keep higher amount of capital aside and will leave banks with less leverage to lend money; so to maintain profitability banks will be compelled to raise the lending interest rates which may have an adverse effect on the scale of their business (B. Mahapatra, 2012). Further, during times of excessive economic growth, non-aggressive banks will also be subject to counter cyclical buffer which will result in pressure on these banks to increase growth.

The introduction of counter cyclical buffer will ensure a forced slow-down to the excessive economical growth by making the cost of credit comparatively higher. This forced slow-down may have adverse effect on planning and business at large, which are at expansion stage. Such regulatory slow-down will affect not only the demand of credit, but also on the consumption of credit. Thus, the effort to avoid possibility of funding to potentially risky projects during excessive economic growth may accentuate the risk of turning viable projects into Non-Performing Assets (NPAs), as subsequent credit will be costlier during such times to already funded, even viable projects.

Although Indian Banks already meet the minimum capital requirement stipulated under Basel-III at an aggregate level, some individual banks may have to put some capital. But capital adequacy today can't guarantee capital adequacy tomorrow. Considering the structural changes in the Indian economy and favourable steps taken for the industrial sector to maintain the momentum of growth, the bank credit to the gross Domestic Product (GDP) ratio must go up. Which means Indian banks will have to raise additional capital anyhow. The quantum of additional capital required post Basel-III implementation as per the estimation made by the Reserve Bank of India (RBI) is INR 5 trillion, of which the non-equity base will be INR 3.25 trillion and equity base INR 1.75 trillion. Out of the total new equity base requirement about 85 per cent is in the Public Sector Undertaking (PSU) Banks (Subbarao Duvvuri, 2012). Considering the fact if the Government decides to maintain its shareholding at the current level, the recapitalization amount it will have to provide is of the order of INR 900 billion, whereas, the market can provide INR 700 to 1,000 billion based upon the experience that over the last 5 years banks in India have raised the equity capital of INR 520 billion through primary market. The possible options for the Government may be to issue the recapitalization bonds against common equity infusion or reducing the Government stake below 51 percentages in Public Sector Banks (PSBs).

One of the other major concerns is the effect of implementation of Basel-III on the profitability of Indian banks. As Basel-III requires higher and better quality of capital, that is, equity, which is costly. It is also likely that the loss absorbency requirement of non-equity regulatory capital will increase the cost. However, it is likely that the implementation of Basel-III may result into a decline of return on equity (ROE) in short-term, but the likely benefits resulting from the more stable and stronger banking system will largely offset the negative impacts of lower return on equity. It is also fair to consider the fact that investors may perceive the benefits of less risky and more stable banks; so be ready to trade off the higher returns for lower risk. Further, banks will also have to consider the option of reducing the NIM, which is as high as 3 per cent and consider suitable reduction in the cost of intermediation so that the optimum level of return can be maintained.

On macroeconomic prospective, higher capital requirements in PSBs may result into increased Government borrowings, fiscal deficit and pressure on GDP. A lower GDP may affect investment, credit line, and bank's profitability. As per the research carried out by CARE on banking industry, for 1 per cent increase in the core equity, the ratio is expected to be met by a fall of ROE by 80–100 basis points, which show how much the profitability is expected to be affected.

However, as of now most of Indian banks are better positioned to implement the guidelines under Basel-III (Dr K.C. Chakrabarty, 2012), but going forward to maintain the same level of performance may present newer challenges and banks will have to focus more on quality and profitable business sourcing.

CONCLUSION

However, as the Capital Adequacy Ratio (CAR) prescribed by the BCBS was as 8 per cent, the RBI had already taken the precautionary measure by raising it to 9 per cent for banks in India which has placed Indian banks in a better position as compared to many other international banks to implement Basel-III. Yet, the real concern towards implementation of Basel-III is raising additional capital to make provision for capital conservation buffer and counter cyclical buffer, that also in situations where investors are well aware that they will have to trade off between return and safety of investment, and the returns may even go lower when coupled with the higher inflation prevailing. The important questions to be addressed here are: Can individual banks access the capital market to raise this capital? How do current ownership structures and valuations impact a bank's capital raising proposals? Should the Government retain majority ownership? How should the Government capitalise the PSBs? What are the options before the Government?

The counter cyclical buffer as mentioned above mandates banks to build up capital in good times, which could be run down during economic contraction, keeping in view safety and soundness consideration. The critical issue here is to decide trigger points during an economic cycle at which the capital should be released. Tightening too early or tightening too late can be too costly on macroeconomic perspective and accordingly will result into liquidity crunch (T. Gopinath and A.K. Chowdhary, 2012). One of the good economic indicators to decide the trigger point is credit/GDP ratio, but because banks in India have started to finance various sectors, like retail estate, housing, micro finance, and consumer credit in big way in the last two decades only there is limited data on these sectors. Moreover, the risk built up in these sectors can't be appropriately captured by aggregating them, so the regulator needs to take a broad range of various simple indicators and make a country specific decision.

Non-Performing Asset management is another major and critical issue for Indian banks. The gap between reported NPA and actual NPA needs to be bridged and its challenge to provide incentive to the banks which recognize losses on account of NPA as per the Basel norms, because NPA recognition changes the capital requirement and in many cases it means considerable additional capital requirement. The lack of transparency and credibility in banks' balance sheet makes the situation even worse and may be discouraging for investors.

There is an imminent need for capacity building within banks and on the part of RBI for effective implementation of Basel-III. Therefore, there must be a radical change in a bank's approach to risk management. Indian banks are currently operating on the Standardized Approach of Basel-II. The larger banks need to migrate to the Advanced Approaches considering their overseas expansion. The adoption of advance approach will enable banks to manage their capital more efficiently and improve their profitability. However, to move to Advance Approach banks have to bring three major changes – first, to look upon capital framework as a pre-requisite rather than merely a compliance function to keep bank sound and stable financially; second, as deeper and more broad-based capacity in risk management; and third as adequate and good quality data.

Similar to the Globally Systematically Important banks (G-SIBs), the Basel committee is working on establishing a minimum set of principles for

Domestic Systematically Important Banks D-SIBs) and these banks will be prescribed Higher Loss Absorbency (HLA) capital standards.

Besides this, it is also a challenging task to evolve a sound resolution mechanism for D-SIBs.

The pressure to implement Basel-III at a faster pace for Indian banks may force the Government to make a choice between reducing its stake in PSBs or fuel more capital, resulting in an increased fiscal deficit. A tempting option for the Government may be issuing the recapitalization Bonds against common equity infusion, but this will go contrary to fiscal transparency. Thus, it is a question of time to wait for the wise decision of the Government.

It is worth consideration that in Indian context, new and private banks, with their better capital adequacy ratios, greater proportion of common equity, and well equipped IT and technically well qualified manpower, are well placed to comply with Basel-III norms in general, whereas, PSU banks, although holding a sizable amount of market share, may take more time to face more challenges in the implementation of Basel-III guidelines.

REFERENCES

B. Mahapatra, *Implications of Basel-III for Capital, Liquidity and Profitability of Banks*, Address by Executive Director, Reserve Bank of India, Bank for International Settlements, publications, 05 March 2012.

Basel Committee on Banking Supervision, *A Brief History of Basel Committee,* Bank for International Settlements, publications, July 2013, pp. 2–6.

Basel Committee for Banking Supervision, *A Global Regulatory Framework for More Resilient Banks and Banking Systems*, Bank for International Settlements, publications, June 2011.

Basel Committee on Banking Supervision, *Basel-III: The Liquidity Coverage Ratio and Liquidity Risk Monitoring Tools*, Bank for International Settlements, publications, January 2013.

Basel Committee on Banking Supervision, *Operational Risk – Supervisory Guidelines for the Advanced Measurement Approaches*, Bank for International Settlements, publications, June 2011, p. 3.

Canadian Bankers Association (CBA), Basel Committee's Consultative Document, *'Strengthening the Resilience of Banking Sector'*, Bank for International Settlements, publications, 16 April 2010, p. 3.

Carmassi and Micossi, *Time to Set Banking Regulation Right,* Brussels: Centre for European Policy Studies, EPS, March 2012, pp. 32–45.

Duvvuri Subbarao, 'Basel-III in International and Indian Contexts: Ten Questions We Should Know the Answers for', Inaugural Address by Governor, Reserve

Bank of India at the Annual FICCI-IBA Banking Conference, Mumbai, 4 September 2012.

Griffith-Jones, S., *How to Prevent the New Basel Capital Accord Harming Developing Countries*', paper presented at the IMF-World Bank Annual Meetings, IMF annual meeting journal, September 2003.

K.C. Chakrabarty, *Indian Banking Sector Towards Next Orbit*, Inaugural address delivered by Deputy Governor, Reserve Bank of India, 9th Advanced Management Programme, IMI, Delhi, RBI Monthly bulletin, March 2012.

M. Jayadev, 'Round Table Basel-III Implementation: Issues and Challenges for Indian Banks', Peer – review, *IIM Banglore Management Review*, vol. 25, May 2013, pp. 115–30.

Pokutta Sebastian and Schmaltz Christian, 'Optimal Bank Planning under Basel-III Regulations', *Journal of Financial Transformations*, vol. 34, June 2012, pp. 165–74.

Reisen, H., *Will Basel-II Contribute to Convergence in International Capital Flows*?, Paper prepared for Osterreichische National Bank, 29th Economics Conference, OECD Development Centre-Paris, publications, 2001.

S. Stolz and M. Wedow, 'Banks' Regulatory Buffer and Business Cycle: Evidence for Germany', *Journal of Financial Stability*, vol. 7, no. 2, June 2011, pp. 98–110.

T. Gopinath and A.K. Choudhary, *Counter Cyclical Buffer Guidance for India*, RBI working paper series WPS (DEPR) # 12/2012, June 2012, pp. 4–9.

Tanaka, M., *The Macroeconomic Implications of the New Basel Accord*, CESIFO Economics Studies, 49(2): 217-232. IFO Institute for Economic Research-Munich, publications, 2003.

Vighneswara Swamy, *Basel-III Implications for Indian Banking*, Research Report published by Indian Institute of Banking and Finance, Mumbai, October 2013.

Impact of Risk Management Capabilities on Profitability of Banks in India in Post-Reform Era

Shalu Mahajan and Madhu Vij[1]
Acharya Narendra Dev College, University of Delhi, Delhi
[1] Faculty of Management Studies, University of Delhi, Delhi
e-mail: shalu3a@gmail.com; madhuvij@hotmail.com; madhufms@gmail.com

ABSTRACT

Risk Management is considered to be an important aspect of all financial institutions from the aspect of value creation for shareholders and the various customers. It puts an onus on these institutions to follow such practices. Risk Management has been able to directly influence the financial performance of the banks. With this aim, the current paper attempts to assess the impact of Risk Management capabilities on profitability amongst different banks of India in the post-reform era. Profitability is measured in terms of Return on Assets (ROA). The present research is exploratory in nature and considers secondary data for the quantitative analysis. A panel regression is run to investigate the impact of Risk Management capabilities on profitability of banks in India. The profitability for the period 1999–2012 in terms of ROA is regressed on Risk management capabilities of banks, which comprises Interest Rate Risk Management (NETIM), Natural Hedging (NOTIM), Credit Risk Management (PROV), and Solvency Risk Management (CAR). The results indicate that NETIM, NOTIM and PROV are significant predictors of ROA, while CAR is not. It was suggested through these results that risk awareness amongst the banks increased during the given sample period. These findings will hold importance for the bank managers, investors, and policy makers in the current era of banking in India. Even the regulators would be able to develop quantitative indicators for the increased efficiency of the banking system. The study is conducted specifically within the Indian banking system and will be useful for policy making within different categories like public, private, and foreign banks separately.

Keywords: Risk Management Capabilities, Return on Assets, Commercial Banks, Panel Data

INTRODUCTION

Every business needs money for its operations, be it the manufacturing sector or any service provider. There emerges the need of the financial sector that can provide them with the much needed money. Thus, the financial sector forms the backbone of any economy. It ensures the mobilization of savings, allocation of resources, and provision of adequate financial services to the deserving. Hence, a strong financial system would ensure growth and an increase in the financial stability.

An important part of the financial sector of a country is its banking segment. A competitive banking system will promote efficiency. It will force the players to be more competent and adopt the best strategies possible for managing their operations and risks. The banks face multitude of risks and if properly dealt, can provide a lot of opportunities to exploit and gain from them. Risk Management, as identified by many, is an integral part of commercial banking. In Risk Management a financial institution takes the risk and distributes it among the various players. This importance of Risk Management also makes it relevant in determining the performance of the banking sector. Today, it has become an eminent component of the planning process of any organization. It is known universally that higher the risk, higher will be the profit. Thus, it becomes absolutely necessary to maintain a trade-off between them.

The banking sector, which was subject to strict rules before the liberalization of the Indian economy in 1991, has now been brought under a deregulated regime. The reforms, introduced as a result of liberalization, made the banking system more resilient and lucrative. In 1998 a second phase of reforms was introduced which emphasized on Risk Management. Post-1998 the Reserve Bank of India (RBI) also introduced a certain set of measures to implement Risk Management systems. The BASEL Committee on Banking Supervision (BCBS) was formed to maintain the international system of banking by introducing measures that are safe and assure stability. The BASEL I framework was introduced in 1988 and emphasized on both, the credit risk, as well as minimum capital requirement. An amendment was introduced in 1996 to regulate the market risk (BIS, 2013). It recognized the short-term subordinated debts as capital instruments (Balthazar, 2006; Elizalde, 2007). With an objective of promoting more stringent practices for Risk Management, BASEL II was introduced. It was built on three pillars namely minimum capital requirements, supervisory review, and internal assessment and market discipline. The internal models introduced in BASEL II lead to the speculations of the introduction of full grown internal models which gave way to the BASEL III accord (Balthazar, 2006; Elizalde, 2007). The BASEL III accord introduced a new and stronger definition of capital which would be fully accepted by 2017.

The emphasis being laid on Risk Management at the international level makes it evident that it helps the advanced institutions to maintain a low risk profile and thus affects their performance. So, this necessitates the evaluation of the impact of Risk Management on the performance by employing the financial ratio method in the Indian banking sector in the post-reform era.

LITERATURE REVIEW

Various studies have been conducted in the foreign and Indian context, addressing the issue of studying the effects of Risk Management techniques on performance of banks.

Hosna et al. (2009) have studied the impact of Credit Risk Management on the profitability of four commercial banks of Sweden using Return on Equity (ROE) as a measure for profitability. In all it was found that Credit Risk Management had a fair amount of influence on the profitability. On the other hand, Williams and Prather (2010) studied the effect of another type of Risk Management technique based on banks in Australia. They suggested that an increased exposure to non-interest bearing income would diversify the portfolio and improve the risk-return tradeoff. This is supported by Baele et al. (2007), but it differs on the point of diversification. It states that diversification on the one hand increases the systematic risk, and on the other hand reduces the idiosyncratic risk.

Drehmann et al. (2010) analysed the impact by taking into account the characteristics of factors like assets, liabilities, and off-balance sheet items. They further assessed the banks' economic value and capital adequacy affected by these risks. To study the impact two criterions have been used. The first being the economic value condition and second is capital adequacy condition. The results obtained displayed that both the interest and credit risk are measured together. It was found that interaction between both the risks had high quantitative significance.

A third type of risk has been discussed by Memmel (2011). It uses data on German banks to see the impact of interest rate risk and term transformation on the income. Term transformation and the regulatory effects of banks are both seen to affect the earnings. The importance of these factors differed within different types of banks. A similar study has also been done on the German stock market that also reported a positive impact (Czaja et al., 2010).

In the Indian context, Chipalkatti and Rishi (2007) analysed the performance of Indian banks on the basis of bank profitability and risk in accordance with the market-oriented reforms in 1991. To raise the quality of the disclosures a bank transparency indicator was also established and its assessment displayed decreasing profitability, increased risk exposure, and insufficient transparency of the accounting disclosures. The study further called for the need of improved risk Management systems.

Another study by Vyas et al. (2008) uses panel data to investigate the impact of capital adequacy requirements on the performance of scheduled commercial banks in India for the period 1997–2007. The results indicate that there is a significant positive impact on performance.

Sensarma and Jayadev (2009) studied the data on Indian banks and measured the effect of Risk Management capabilities on the performance of the bank stocks. The results suggest that bank stocks are sensitive to Risk Management.

Ghosh (2010) studied the relation between credit growth, the soundness of the bank, and the financial fragility for Indian banks for the time period 1996–2008. Through the modelling of the three factors with respect to each other and other bank specific factors, it was concluded that, whereas, soundness of a bank leads to credit growth, the latter in turn leads to increased fragility.

RESEARCH METHODOLOGY

The section elaborates on the research methodology used for finding the impact of Risk management capabilities on the profitability of banks in India. An effort has been made to enumerate the theoretical framework, econometric model, selection of variables, and various statistical tools used in the study. A three-stage analysis comprising descriptive analysis, correlation analysis, and regression analysis is carried out. Before a detailed discussion on the methodology used for the study, the basic theoretical framework, which is used to derive the Risk Management capability indicators is discussed in the following section:

Theoretical Framework

The standard DuPont identity is used to decompose a bank's Return on Equity (ROE) into operating efficiency (profit margin), asset-use efficiency (asset turnover), and financial leverage (equity multiplier) (Sensarma and Jayadev, 2009). The product of operating efficiency and asset turnover can be expressed as Return on Assets (ROA) (Sensarma and Jayadev, 2009). Therefore,

ROE = (PAT / TA) × (TA / Equity) ...(1)

where, ROA is profit after tax to total assets and equity multiplier is total assets to equity.

ROA is further decomposed as below:

ROA = (II – IE) / TA + (NII – NIE) / TA – (Provisions / TA) ...(2)

where, II – Interest Income, IE – Interest Expense, NII – Non Interest Income, NIE – Non Interest Expense, and TA – Total Assets.

Equation 2 can be re-written as:

ROA = Net interest margin + Non interest margin – Provisions ...(3)

Substituting Equation (3) in Equation (1), we obtain

ROE = (NETIM + NOTIM – PROV) × (EM) ...(4)

Each of these four factors represents a bank's capability of managing various risks. The banks shall attempt to maximize either NETIM or NOTIM or equity-to-assets ratio while minimize PROV in order to increase its returns (Sensarma and Jayadev, 2009). Based on the premise of Risk Management capabilities impacting the profitability of the banks, the current study has been designed to test the following hypothesis:

H0: There is no significant impact of Risk Management capability on ROA.

Sample and Period of the Study

The data has been collected from statistical tables relating to banks in India (RBI) for the period 1999–2012. The study is based on a balanced panel of 70 banks that survived throughout the period of the study. A total of 26 public sector banks, 18 private sector banks, and 26 foreign sector banks were considered for the study. During the period of the study, the banking sector witnessed mergers of various banks. So, an attempt is made to combine the ratios of the merging banks by finding a weighted average of the ratios. The period after 1998 gives a suitable set- up for the analysis of Risk management capabilities of banks as RBI introduced prudential norms along with guidelines for Asset-Liability Management and Risk Management. The empirical study was carried out by using STATA 11.0 software.

Model Specification

The study uses fixed effect panel regression to evaluate the impact of Risk Management capabilities on profitability of a balanced panel of 70 banks. Thus, in accordance with the variables the following model has been developed for the current study.

$$ROA_{it} = \alpha + \beta 1NETIM_{it} + \beta 2NOTIM_{it} + \beta 3PROV_{it} + \beta 4CAR_{it} + \varepsilon_{it} \quad ...(5)$$

where, i stand for bank and t for year, ROA denotes profitability. CAR is Solvency Risk Management, NETIM is Interest Rate Risk Management, NOTIM is Natural Hedging strategy, PROV is Credit Risk Management, and ε_{it} random error.

Dependent Variable

For the performance evaluation we have used the concept of ROA. It measures the ability of the management to convert the assets of bank into net earnings (Vyas et al., 2008; Sarkar et al., 1998). It is calculated as:

ROA = Net profit after tax/Total assets

Independent Variables

The independent variables used in the study have been discussed as follows:

1. **Interest Rate Risk Management (NETIM):** Interest rate risk is one of the important forms of financial risk in which bank's income and/or market value will be adversely affected due to interest rate movements. Movement of interest rates would affect a bank's Net Interest Margin and therefore ROA. Banks in India have adopted Asset-Liability Management systems, duration gap analysis, and risk control measures that are based on value at risk techniques to manage interest rate risk (Sensarma and Jayadev, 2009). The study uses NETIM as a proxy for Interest Rate Risk Management capabilities of a bank. It is calculated as follows:

   NETIM = (Net interest income/Total assets) × 100.
2. **Natural Hedging (NOTIM):** A bank faces many other risks apart from the interest rate risk, solvency risk and credit risk. So, banks adopt a strategy of NOTIM against all other risks by increasing the proportion of non-interest income from total income. Non-interest income is generated from various activities, namely transfer of funds or other payment services, letters of credit, usage of derivative contracts such as forwards, futures, swaps, etc. It increases ROA without elevation of any corresponding risks. It is calculated as follows:

   NOTIM = (Net non-interest income/Total assets) × 100.
3. **Credit Risk management (PROV):** In order to manage credit risk, banks make provisions for all anticipated loan losses. Though provisioning reduces the bank profitability, but at the same time it tries to mitigate credit risk. In this study the ratio of Provisions to Total Assets (PROV) is used as a proxy for Credit Risk Management capabilities of banks. It is calculated as follows:

   PROV = (Provisions/Total assets) × 100.

4. **Solvency Risk Management (CAR)**: It ensures the maintenance of resources enough to safeguard one from facing the dreads of financial insolvency. The shareholders who aim for long-term sustainability of a bank and continued distribution of profits may try for minimization of solvency risk. It is calculated as follows:

   CAR = regulatory capital adequacy ratio.

RESULTS AND DISCUSSION

Initially, descriptive analysis and correlation analysis were conducted in order to understand the characteristics and magnitude of relationship between the variables. After this a panel regression is run to find the impact of various Risk Management capabilities. A detailed discussion on the empirical results is presented below:

Descriptive Analysis

The descriptive statistics of Risk Management variables are presented in Table 1. A high mean of ROA of foreign banks show that they are able to efficiently convert their assets into earnings. The mean value of NETIM for the overall sample is 2.85, while its standard deviation is 1.13. A comparison amongst banks shows that foreign banks are better off in NETIM. They are able to maintain a higher spread which further improves the profitability of a bank.

In case of NOTIM foreign banks are better than public sector and private banks. The mean value of PROV for public sector banks is 1.06 which is lower than that for private and foreign banks. The provisions are created in order to cover non-performing assets and thus are a measure of asset quality. So, the creation of less provision indicates that public banks have less probability of defaults and they are able to manage asset quality well. In terms of CAR,

Table 1: Descriptive Statistics

Variable	*PSB*	*PB*	*FB*	*Pooled*
ROA	0.88 (0.39)	0.98 (0.66)	1.64 (2.41)	1.19 (1.56)
NETIM	2.63 (0.59)	2.61 (0.69)	3.24 (1.59)	2.85 (1.13)
NOTIM	−0.80 (0.56)	−0.62 (0.77)	0.07 (2.75)	−0.43 (1.80)
PROV	1.06 (0.42)	1.11 (0.50)	2.11 (1.65)	1.46 (1.18)
CAR	12.24 (2.05)	13.82 (5.20)	24.11 (17.62)	17.05 12.38)
OBS	364	252	364	980

PSB: Public sector banks; PB: Private banks; FB: Foreign banks, Standard Deviation in Parenthesis foreign banks have a mean value of 24.11 which is quite high. This signifies that foreign banks are well capitalised which shows that they are better risk managers. However, the standard deviation is high in case of foreign banks in all the Risk Management variables.

Correlation Analysis

Table 2 depicts the correlation coefficients between the variables. A correlation matrix is prepared to find the degree of association between Risk Management variables. The result shows that there is low to medium correlation between the variables. So, there is no problem of multi-collinearity among the explanatory variables.

Table 2: Correlation Matrix

	NETIM	*NOTIM*	*PROV*	*CAR*
NETIM	1.0000	–	–	–
NOTIM	–0.1230*	1.0000	–	–
PROV	0.3549*	0.0716*	1.0000	–
CAR	0.1771*	0.1871*	0.2368*	1.0000

* Significant at 0.05 level.

Regression Analysis

The results for panel data regression are presented in Table 3. To begin with, Fisher-type tests based on Augmented Dickey Fuller (ADF) is applied to examine the presence of unit root in the variables. The results show that all the variables are stationary. To select an appropriate model for empirical analysis, Hausman specification test was conducted. The results are in favour of fixed effects model for identifying the impact of Risk Management on ROA. The tests reject presence of autocorrelation and hetroskedasticity.

Table 3: Regression Results for the Impact of Risk Management on Profitability

Independent Variables	*Coefficient (p-value)*
NETIM	0.621***(0.000)
NOTIM	0.547***(0.000)
PROV	−0.283***(0.000)
CAR	−0.001 (0.844)
Constant	0.076 (0.601)
R-square overall	0.5280
Hausman Test	17.81(0.0013)
Breusch Pagan test	4246.45(0.000)

***Significant at 0.01 level.

The results indicate that there is a positive and highly significant impact of NETIM on ROA which shows an improvement in the Asset-Liability Management of banks. The banks are able to generate sufficient funds from interest income to finance its expenses. The result is consistent with the findings of Vyas et al. (2008) and Jha and Hui (2012).

There is a highly significant (at 1 per cent level) and positive impact of natural hedging strategy (NOTIM) on ROA. It shows that profitability of banks in India has improved by diversifying into new products and services. The result suggests that during the sample period, risk awareness among banks has increased. It is reflected from reliance of banks on off balance sheet portfolio and fee based services apart from increased spread. The result is consistent with the results of Vyas et al. (2008).

Further, it is found that Credit Risk Management (PROV) has a negative and highly significant impact on the profitability of a bank. It shows that banks in India have to strengthen Credit Risk Management and take required steps to control non-performing assets. This will help in increasing the profitability of banks. The results confirm the findings of existing literature Jha and Hui (2012).

There is a negative but insignificant impact of CAR on profitability. This result is different from the findings of Vyas et al. (2008) and Sensarma and Jayadev (2009). It indicates that banks did not focus on increasing capital adequacy. The banks have viewed it as a matter of regulatory compliance instead of a step towards better Risk Management practice.

Thus, from the above analysis it is concluded that when a panel regression was run to find the impact on profitability in terms of ROA from NETIM, NOTIM, PROV and CAR, these factors were able to impact ROA partially $p < 0.05$, $R^2 = 0.5280$. The significant predictors were NETIM ($\beta = -0.621$, $p = 0.000$), NOTIM ($\beta = 0.547$, $p = 0.000$), and PROV ($\beta = -0.283$, $p = 0.000$), whereas, the insignificant predictor was CAR ($\beta = -0.001$, $p = 0.844$). Hence, with respect to ROA (profitability), null hypothesis is rejected. The results indicate that Risk Management capabilities have a significant impact on the profitability of banks.

CONCLUSION AND IMPLICATION OF THE STUDY

The study uses a framework where profitability is decomposed in Risk Management capability variables. An attempt is made to find the impact of Risk Management capabilities on the profitability of banks. It has been found that the profitability of banks is significantly determined by Interest Rate Risk

Management, Natural Hedging Strategy and Credit Risk Management in the sample period. So, it can be said that banks that focus on Risk Management are able to enhance profitability.

As a matter of implications, the following conclusions can be drawn from the results of the study for different stake-holders like bank managers, policy makers, and investors.

The managers of banks take various measures to increase the profitability of their banks. The results show a positive significant link between the profitability of the bank and both, Asset-Liability management, as well as diversification of business. So, managerial compensation schemes encouraging achievement of performance targets should be formulated to further strengthen the process of Risk Management.

The managers shall also focus on improving the quality of assets which will reduce the need for provisions. This will help in increasing profitability. It is found that there is a negative, but insignificant impact of regulatory CAR on profitability. The banks shall try and increase capital to risk weighted asset ratio in order to manage solvency risk.

Profitability of banks is important for policy makers as well. They can implement existing policies, frame new policies, and thereby improve the financial position of banks. As per the guidelines, banks whose non-performing assets level is 5 per cent or more are required to take permission from the RBI to declare dividend (Reddy, 2014) There is a need to formulate policies which reduce the share of non-performing assets, thereby reduce its credit risk. The regulators shall also try to improve the transparency in the financial system so that credit risk is evaluated and thus associated exposures may be avoided. Efforts shall be made to increase the capital adequacy ratio further in view of an increase in the risk weighted assets. There shall be provision for heavy penalties in case of non-compliance with Risk Management policies.

Better Risk Management strategies have a positive impact on investors as they get good returns and their investment remains safe. The Management Information System of the banks shall facilitate sharing of relevant information which assists them in taking crucial decisions regarding their investment.

REFERENCES

A. Elizalde, *From Basel I to Basel-II: An Analysis of the Three pillars,* No.wp2007_0704), 2007. Available on http://ideas.repec.org/p/cmf/wpaper/wp2007_0704.html. Accessed on 29 September 2014.

A. Hosna, B. Manzura, and S. Juanjuan, 'Credit Risk Management and Profitability in Commercial Banks in Sweden', Master's thesis, School of Business, Economics and Law, Goteburg University, 2009.

B. Williams and L. Prather, 'Bank Risk and Return: The Impact of Bank Non-interest Income', *International Journal of Managerial Finance*, vol. 6, no. 3, 2010, pp. 220–44.

BIS, *A Brief History of Basel Committee, Bank for International Settlements*, 2013. Available on www.bis.org/bcbs/history.pdf. Accessed on 29 September 2014.

C. Memmel, 'Banks' Exposure to Interest Rate Risk, Their Earnings from Term Transformation, and the Dynamics of the Term Structure', *Journal of Banking & Finance*, vol. 35, no. 2, pp. 282–89.

J. Sarkar, S. Sarkar, S. Bhaumik, 'Does Ownership Always Matter? Evidence from the Indian Banking Industry', *Journal of Comparative Economics*, vol. 26, 1998, pp. 262–81.

L. Baele, O. De Jonghe, and R. Vander Vennet, 'Does the Stock Market Value Bank Diversification?' *Journal of Banking & Finance*, vol. 31, no. 7, 2007, pp. 1999–2023.

Laurent Balthazar, *From Basel 1 to Basel 3,* Palgrave Macmillan, Houndmills, Basingstoke, Hampshire RG21 6XS 2006.

Mathias Drehmann, Steffen Sorensen, and Marco Stringa, 'The Integrated Impact of Credit and Interest Rate Risk on *Banks*: A Dynamic Framework and Stress Testing Application', *Journal of Banking and Finance*, vol. 34, 2010, pp. 713–29.

M.G. Czaja, H. Scholz, and M. Wilkens, 'Interest Rate Risk Rewards in Stock Returns of Financial Corporations: Evidence from Germany', *European Financial Management*, vol. 16, no. 1, 2010, pp. 124–54.

N. Chipalkatti and M. Rishi, 'A Post-reform Assessment of the Indian Banking Sector: Profitability, Risk and Transparency', *International Journal of Financial Services Management*, vol. 2, no. 1/2, 2007, pp. 159–74.

N.S.N. Reddy, 'Non-Performing Assets Impact on Bank Balance Sheet, All Banking Solutions', 2014, Available on http://www.allbankingsolutions.com/Articles/NPA-impact-on-Balance-Sheet.htm. Accessed on 1 October 2014.

R. Sensarma and M. Jayadev, 'Are Bank Stocks Sensitive to Risk Management?' *Journal of Risk Finance,* vol. 10, no. 1, 2009, pp. 7–22.

R.K. Vyas, M. Singh, and R. Yadav, 'The Impact of Capital Adequacy Requirements on Performance of Scheduled Commercial Banks', *Asia Pacific Business Review,* vol. 4, no. 2, 2008, pp. 74–81.

S. Ghosh, 'Credit Growth, Bank Soundness and Financial Fragility Evidence from Indian Banking Sector', *South Asia Economic Journal*, vol. 11, no. 1, 2010, pp. 69–98.

Suvita Jha and Xiaofeng Hui, *African Journal of Business Management,* vol. 6, no. 25, 2012, pp. 7601–11.

Basel-III Norms Implementation in Indian Banking Sector

A Critical Analysis

Neelam Tandon and Deepak Tandon[1]

Bhartiya Vidya Bhavan's Usha Lakshmi Mittal Institute of Management, New Delhi

[1] International Management Institute (IMI), New Delhi

e-mail: neelam.tandon@bulmim.ac.in; deepaktandon@imi.edu

ABSTRACT

Basel I, II and III present the Basel Committee's reforms to strengthen global capital and liquidity rules of a country with the goal of promoting a more resilient banking sector. The objective of Basel III is to improve the banking sector's ability to absorb shocks if any in the future, greater transparency and disclosures, improve – governance and Risk Management. A strong and resilient banking system is the foundation for sustainable economic growth. Post Basel II norms and non-adherence in Operational Risk Management, the Indian Banks have learnt to be reliable, robust and resilient through – Capital, Leverage, and Liquidity maintenance. Thus they would gear themselves for Basel III- implementation by 2019. With the surge of Non-Performing Assets (NPAs) in the Indian banking sector in the past few years and the average NPA ratio being 3.9 percent as on March 2014, risk identification and mitigation has become all the more important. The authors have emphasized the need for regulatory compliance and proactive actions by Indian Banks to assess their business lines, level of risk profiles, economizing Capital and drawing up strategies to raise further capital amidst dynamic Risk Management divisions in the Indian Banks in the light of implementation of Basel III norms. The exposure of the private sector Indian banks is more extreme with high exposure in only the infrastructure industry which is a stressed sector. On the other hand, the exposure of public sector Indian banks is high for Infrastructure, Textiles and Metal and Metal products. The exposure is also more diversified in case of public sector Indian banks. The paper also shows how recent growth in NPAs is higher in the private sector than the public sector banks. Finally, all the banks have been able to achieve the Basel III requirement for 2014. However, private sector Indian banks have overachieved in this regard which suggests the private bank's' greater ability to absorb shocks than their public counterparts.

Keywords: CCB – Counter Cyclical Buffer, LCR – Liquidity Coverage Ratio, NSFR – Net Stable Funding Ratio, RWA – Risk Weighted Average, BCBS – Basel Committee on Bank Supervision, RM – Risk Management, CAR – Capital-Adequacy Ratio, Tier-I, Tier II.

INTRODUCTION

The banking sector by its very nature entails risk. Risk for banks is defined as an unplanned event that results in financial loss or reduced earnings. With greater competition in the banking sector, banks often have the incentive of taking on more risk by easing their credit standards. For financial institutions, the risk they bear can be categorized as market, credit, and operational risk. Similarly, any risky proposition that can either have potential gains or looming losses needs proper risk assessing and management.[1]

Risk

Risk for the banks can be classified as follows, where both credit and market risk fall under the purview of financial risk (Figure 1).

With the breakdown of the Bretton woods system of managed exchanged rates in 1973, banks suffered huge foreign exchange losses with many also closing their doors. In response to this and other disruptions in the financial markets, the central bankers of the G10 countries established a committee on Banking Regulations and Supervisory practices which was later renamed as Basel Committee on Banking Supervision (BCBS).[2]

Basel I

The capital regulations that came under Basel I in 1992 required banks to maintain a minimum capital to cushion losses without causing systematic losses, and also to provide a level playing field internationally. A minimum capital ratio of capital to risk weighted assets (CRAR) (Tier I capital) of 8 per cent was required to be maintained.

---

[1] *Source:* http://www.allbankingsolutions.com/Banking-Tutor/risk-management.shtml

[2] *Source:* http://www.bis.org/bcbs/history.pdf

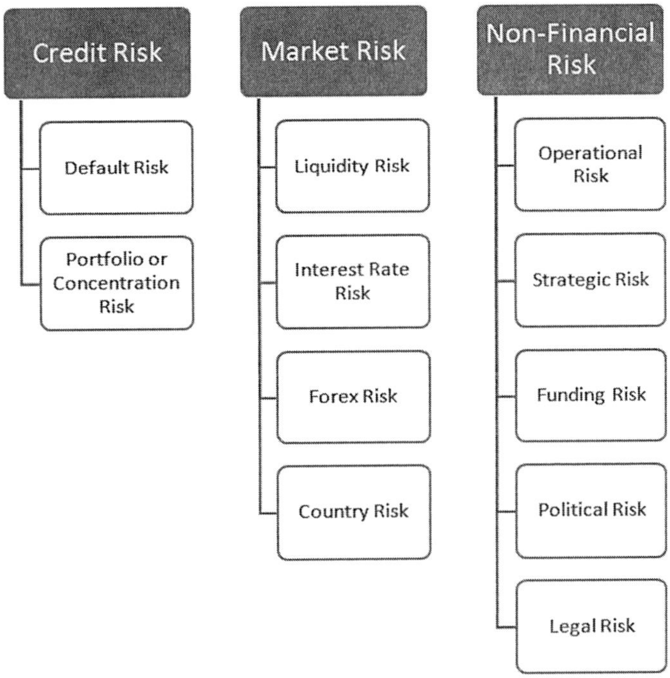

Figure 1

Basel II

Under BASEL II implemented in 2004, the new framework comprised three pillars, namely:

1. Minimum capital requirements;
2. Supervisory review of an institutions capital adequacy; and
3. Effective use of market disclosure to strengthen market discipline.

But BASEL II also had many problems which were highlighted during the global financial crisis. It was mainly due to banks' involvement in capital market activities for which they had adequate capital. Thus, the failure of Lehman Brothers and AIG were partly traced to counterparty risks, which were not fully traced under Basel II.

Basel III

In response to this, the BCBS came up with Basel III norms. This was done with an aim to improve the quality, consistency, and transparency of the capital base of the banks by introducing stricter eligibility rules on instruments included in Tier I capital (core capital). It also included introduction of capital buffers with two components, namely Capital Conservation Buffer

Table 1: Components of Tier I and Tier II Capital

Tier I	*Tier II*
• Paid-up Capital, Statutory reserves, other disclosed free reserves • Capital reserves representing surplus arising out of sale proceeds of assets • Innovative Perpetual Debt Instruments • Perpetual Non-Cumulative Preference Shares • Minus • Equity investments in subsidiaries, • Intangible assets, and • Losses in the current period and those brought forward from previous periods.	• Revaluation Reserves (to be taken at a discount of 55% of their amount) • General Provisions and Loss Reserves up to a maximum of 1.25% of RWA. (These include Floating Provision, Standard Asset Provision, Country Exposure Provision, Investment Reserve Account and excess provision for sale of NPA). • Hybrid debt Capital Instruments such as: (i) Redeemable Cumulative Preference Shares; (ii) Redeemable Non-Cumulative Preference Shares; (iii) Perpetual Cumulative Preference Shares. • Sub-ordinated debt (max 50% of Tier I) not less than initial maturity of 5 years or a residual maturity of not less than one year.

Source: www.rbi.org .in

Table 2: Risk Weighted Assets

Fund Based	*Non-Funded (Off-Balance Sheet) Items*
Cash, loans, investments and other assets, to which the degree of risk expressed as % age weights has been assigned by RBI, under Standardized Approach.	Includes LC, Bank Guarantees, etc. The credit risk attached to these items is first calculated by multiplying the face amount of each off-balance sheet items by the Credit Conversion Factor. This will be again multiplied by the relevant risk weight age to calculate the risk value.

and Counter Cyclical Buffer (CCB) to absorb shocks. For liquidity Ratios, Net Stable Funding Ratio (NSFR) and Liquidity Coverage Ratio (LCR) have also been introduced which will be put in effect by 2015 and 2019, respectively, in the Indian banking sector.[3] A leverage ratio of 3 per cent of Tier I capital will also become mandatory by 2018. Apart from this, systematically important financial institutions are expected to have a loss absorbing capacity which is beyond BASEL III norms.

[3] *Source:* http: / / www.scorto.com / basel-3.htm

LITERATURE REVIEW

A lot of work has been done in the field of Banking and Risk Management (RM) and Basel norms in particular. With the introduction of Basel III accord after the financial crisis of 2008–09, the Basel committee has laid out the guidelines for the implementation of the regulatory norms with a deadline of

Table 3: Regulatory Capital as % to Risk Weighted Average (RWA)

The BIS guidelines are implemented by the Indian Banks: Regulatory Capital as % to RWAs	*Indian Banks**	*BCBS*
(1) Minimum Common Equity Tier I ratio (Credit + Market + Operational Risk)	5.5	4.5
(2i) Capital conservation buffer (comprising Common Equity)	2.5	2.5
(3) Minimum Common Equity Tier I ratio plus Capital conservation buffer [(1)+(2)]	8.0	7.0
(4) Additional Tier I Capital 1.5	1.5	1.5
(5) Minimum Tier I capital ratio [(1) +(4)]	7.0	6.0
(6) Tier II capital 2.0	2.0	2.0
(7) Minimum Total Capital Ratio (MTC) [(5)+(6)]	9.0	8.0
(8) Minimum Total Capital Ratio plus capital conservation buffer [(7)+(2)]	11.5	10.5

* For all Scheduled Banks excluding RRBs and LABs

Table 4: Comparison of Capital Requirements under Basel II and Basel III

The Basel II failed and thus the Basel III was required to be introduced. Comparison can be made:

Requirements	*Under Basel II (%)*	*Under Basel III (%)*
Minimum Ratio of Total Capital To RWAs	8	10.50%
Minimum Ratio of Common Equity to RWAs	2	4.50–7.00%
Tier I capital to RWAs	4	6.00%
Core Tier I capital to RWAs	2	5.00%
Capital Conservation Buffers to RWAs	None	2.50%
Leverage Ratio	None	3.00%
Counter cyclical Buffer	None	0–2.50%
Minimum Liquidity Coverage Ratio	None	TBD (2015)
Minimum Net Stable Funding Ratio	None	TBD (2018)
Systemically Important Financial Institutions Charge	None	TBD (2011)

2019. The *Basel III Monitoring Report* (2014) shows progress of implementation of the guidelines where most of the banks are on track. All the internationally active banks now meet the minimum capital requirements and the capital shortfalls have been further reduced from the target level. The Reserve Bank of India (RBI), through its publication on Guidelines for Implementation of Basel III (2012), has clearly laid out the timeframe for Indian banks to achieve these goals. Work on RM in banking sector by Kanchu T, Sunitha R (2013) show how banks face different types of risk, and the need to identify and mitigate them. Apart from this, there are many books written on RM in the banking sector, for example, *Credit Risk Management for Indian Banks* by K. Vaidyanathan (2013) and other articles published.

With regards to implementation of Basel III and its importance for the Indian banking sector, M. Jayadev (2013) in the *IIM Bangalore Review* (2013) has shown the challenges and issues faced by banks in following this phased implementation of Basel III norms. Also, Vighneswara Swamy, in his paper, talks about the evolution of Basel III, its implementation, and the effectiveness of the timeline set for the Indian banks. Bank of Ghana, in its working group report on whether Basel III was necessary and will bring prudent RM in banking (2011) shows that though the introduction of Basel III will improve stability, it did not address many issues like account manipulation, corporate governance, and full disclosures. Also, it shows that the risk weighted system suffers from portfolio invariance. Apart from Basel III and its impact not much work has been done for the Indian banks to study their progress made towards the implementation of major capital requirements under Basel III. Only RBI keeps a check on whether the banks are on track and in sync with the timeframe for implementation. Besides this, many articles have been published in newspapers where Iron and Steel, Mining, Aviation, Infrastructure, and Textiles have been identified as the stressed sectors.[4] Also, Power is one sector which has now become a risky asset for Indian banks.[5] However, no comparative analysis has been done till now on the basis of regulatory disclosures made by banks in order to study their exposure to different sectors. Thus, the present paper aims to do a comparative analysis of the progress made by the Indian public and private sector banks towards implementation of Basel III norms. It also shows the exposure of different public and private sector banks based on their regulatory disclosure. As part

[4] *Source:* http://www.business-standard.com/article/finance/private-banks-cut-exposure-to-stressed-sectors-114062301069_1.html

[5] *Source:* http://www.thehindubusinessline.com/economy/macro-economy/power-sector-a-risky-asset-for-indian-banks/article6127005.ece

of RM, the paper also aims to analyse the Non-Performing Assets (NPAs) across the banking sector and then link the results with the exposure the banks have in different sectors.

OBJECTIVES

The main objectives of the present work are:

1. To study the risk exposure of Indian banks after the introduction of Basel III norms.
2. To critically analyze the NPAs in the banking sector among different Indian banks – both public and private sector banks.
3. To study the implementation of Basel III capital requirement ratios as per RBI Guidelines across various public and private sector banks.

RESEARCH DESIGN AND METHODOLOGY

The implementation of Basel III norms in India has become a challenge as the industry is burdened by bad loans and slower economic growth. The RBI, in March 2014 extended the deadline for full implementation of Basel III by a year to March 2019, offering relief to the banking sector. Of late, there have been concerns about rising risk in banks in terms of asset quality and its impact on profitability. Thus, risk identification and management, along with implementation of Basel III standards, is now the prime agenda for banks in India.

Phase I

A secondary research from sources like journals, articles, and government publications including both from BCBS and RBI was done in order to get a basic understanding of Basel III norms and the time frame for implementation of these requirements in India.

Phase II

This stage involved collection of data from different Indian private and public sector banks. Data collected includes financial disclosures regarding NPAs, Total Capital ratio (along with Tier I and Tier II capital), exposure of banks in different industries and other regulatory disclosures made under Basel II and Basel III.

Sample Size

Public Sector Indian Banks – 17
Private Sector Indian Banks – 16

Phase III

In the final stage, statistical analysis of the data was done to study the objectives of the paper, and find out key findings and provide recommendations based on the findings.

EXPOSURE OF INDIAN BANKS ACROSS DIFFERENT SECTORS

H0: Exposure to a particular industry is equal to 3 per cent of total loans and advances.

H1: Exposure to a particular industry is not equal to 3 per cent of total loans and advances.

Source: Authors' compilation.

The Exposure in Banking Industry is as follows:

Table 5: Exposure of Banking Industry

	Test value = 0.03		
	t	*df*	*Sig. (2-tailed)*
Chemicals and chemical products	−0.469	31	0.643
Construction	−0.867	31	0.393
Engineering	1.992	31	0.055
Food, Beverages &Tobacco	1.445	31	0.158
Infrastructure	6.724	31	0.000
Metal and metal products	4.863	31	0.000
NBFCs	−2.003	31	0.054
Real estate	−1.451	31	0.157
Textiles	2.354	31	0.025

The overall exposure of banks in different sectors has generally been less than or equal to 3 per cent of total loans and advances (including both fund-based and non-fund based) except for two industries namely, Infrastructure, and Metal and Metal products. Through two-tailed t-test it was found that for six industries the overall exposure of the banking sector (Indian banks) is at 3 per cent of total advances including loans. These industries are Chemical and Chemical products, Construction, Food Beverages & Tobacco, Engineering, Real estate, and NBFCs. There are three more industries which have an exposure of more than 3 per cent of total advances. These industries are Infrastructure, Metal and Metal products, and Textiles. All the other sectors have an exposure of less than 3 per cent of total advances. Among these it is consumer durables that have the least exposure followed by Renting of equipment, Glass and Glassware, Entertainment and Media, Leather and Leather products, Computer Software and Hardware, and Travel and Tourism.

By doing a comparative analysis of both public and private sector banks it was found that for private banks it is only Infrastructure sector which has an exposure upwards of 3 per cent. On the other hand, for public sector Indian banks Infrastructure, Metal and Metal products, and Textiles have an exposure of more than 3 per cent. Also, a lot of industries in case of private sector Indian banks have an average exposure of around 3 per cent of total assets. This shows that for a lot of sectors, these banks have cautiously maintained their exposure and not allowed to increase it beyond a certain measure.

Exposure of Private Banks is summarized as follows:

Table 6: Exposure of Private Banks

	Test value = 0.03		
	t	*Df*	*Sig. (2-tailed)*
Agriculture	−1.810	15	0.090
Banking and Finance	−0.862	15	0.402
Chemicals & Chemical products	−1.072	15	0.301
Construction	−0.955	15	0.355
Engineering	0.700	15	0.495
Food, Beverages & Tobacco	0.766	15	0.456
Infrastructure	3.135	15	0.007
Metal and metal products	1.658	15	0.118
Professional services	−1.353	15	0.196
Real estate	0.405	15	0.692
Textiles	1.324	15	0.205
Trade	0.023	15	0.982

Source: Authors' compilation.

The t-test statistic shows that public sector banks have eight industries with an exposure of greater than or equal to 3 per cent of total loans and advances. These industries are Infrastructure, Metal and Metal products, Textiles, Chemical and Chemical products, Construction, Engineering, Food Beverages & Tobacco, and NBFCs.

Clearly, we can see that the sectors with an exposure of more than or equal to 3 per cent of total loans and advances is more in case of private sector Indian banks. They also have a higher number of low exposure industries. In total, in seven industries these banks have an exposure of less

Table 7: Exposure of Public Sector Banks

			Test value = 0.03
	t	*Df*	*Sig. (2-tailed)*
Chemicals & chemical products	0.176	15	0.863
Construction	−0.247	15	0.808
Engineering	2.082	15	0.055
Food, Beverages & Tobacco	1.376	15	0.189
Infrastructure	7.881	15	0.000
Metal & Metal products	6.131	15	0.000
NBFCs	−0.776	15	0.450
Textiles	2.209	15	0.043

Source: Authors' compilation.

than 0.3 per cent. These sectors are Glass and Glassware, Computer Software and Hardware, Leather and Leather products, Entertainment and Media, Consumer durables, Renting of equipment, and Travel and Tourism. For public sector banks, the same low exposure industries are very few. These are Computer Software and Hardware, Glass and Glassware, and Leather and leather products where the exposure is less than 0.2 per cent.

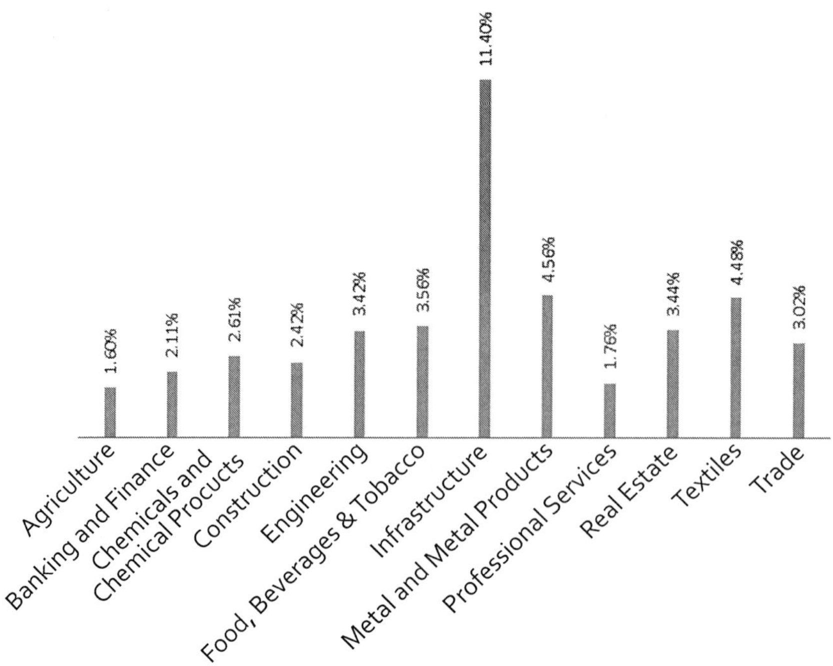

Figure 2: Exposure Percentage of Private Banks

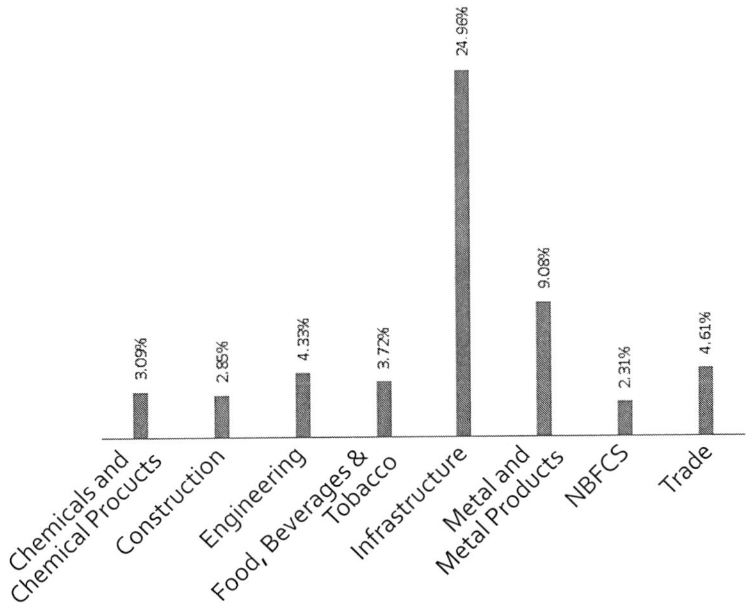

Figure 3: Exposure Percentage of Public Sector Banks

Hence, the analysis of the exposure of banks to different sectors shows that private sector banks have been following a very extreme approach, where many sectors either have high exposure of more than or equal to 3 per cent, or a very exposure of less than 0.3 per cent of total loans and advances. Thus, private sector banks have not followed a diversified approach while lending to different industries. On the other hand, public sector Indian banks have not followed a very extreme approach and have many industries with an exposure of around 1–2 per cent of total loans and advances.

Analysis on NPAs Among Different Public and Private Sector Banks

The rise in NPAs has become a serious issue in the banking sector where average NPAs as on March 2014 stood at 3.9 per cent. Gross NPAs for public sector banks is much higher as compared to the private counterpart. As per the RBI report, the Gross NPAs in the public sector banks till the year 2013 was INR 1558.90 billion. This is 3.84 per cent of the total assets. For private sector, the Gross NPAs as on 2013 was INR 199.92 billion. Thus, the total NPAs for the public sector banks have been much higher.[6]

---

[6] *Source:* http://www.rbi.org.in/scripts/PublicationsView.aspx?id=15501.

On the basis of statistical analysis of the sample data, the Gross NPAs in the public sector Indian banks as on FY 2014–15 Q1 disclosure was 4.8 per cent. For the same period, for private sector Indian banks this value was 2.2 per cent. The striking point in the analysis was the difference in the growth rate of Gross NPAs between public and private sector Indian banks. While public sector has a higher value of absolute NPAs, the growth rate for the Quarter Q1 of the Financial Year 2014–15 has been 8.11 per cent. The same value for the private sector Indian banks is almost double at 16.25 per cent. This shows that the NPAs across private sector Indian banks are rising at a much higher growth rate, vis-à-vis their public counterpart. Hence, it is a serious cause of concern for the banks in the private sector.

H0: There is no association between the sector to which the bank belongs and the level of NPAs in that bank.

H1: There is an association between the sector to which the bank belongs and the level of NPAs in that bank.

Based on the Chi-square test, we found that there is an association between the sector to which the bank belongs and the level of percentage of Gross and Net NPAs in that bank. Hence, it has been statistically proven that the percentage of Gross NPAs is different among public and private sector Indian banks where the value for public sector is much higher as compared to their private counterpart.

Along with the growth rate of NPAs, as per the statistical analysis done for the sample, the percentage of loss to Gross NPAs is also higher for private

Table 8: Chi-Square (Gross NPA)

	14.00	2.00	4.00	13.00
Ei	9.00	7.00	9.00	8.00
|Oi-Ei|–0.5	4.50	4.50	4.50	4.50
(|Oi-Ei|–0.5)^2	20.25	20.25	20.25	20.25
(|Oi-Ei|–0.5)^2/Ei	2.25	2.89	2.25	2.53
Chi-square	9.92	Critical Value		3.84

Table 9: Chi-Square (Net NPA)

Oi	13.00	3.00	2.00	15.00
Ei	7.00	9.00	8.00	9.00
|Oi-Ei|-0.5	5.50	5.50	5.50	5.50
(|Oi-Ei|-0.5)^2	30.25	30.25	30.25	30.25
(|Oi-Ei|-0.5)^2/Ei	4.32	3.36	3.78	3.36
Chi-square	14.82	Critical Value		3.84

Table 10: NPA Break-up

	Private Banks	*Public Banks*
% Change in NPA since 31.03.2014	17.45	7.69
% of Substandard NPAs to Gross NPAs	49.00	49.08
% of Doubtful 1 to Gross NPAs	23.75	24.20
% of Doubtful 2 to Gross NPAs	16.10	20.16
% of Doubtful 3 to Gross NPAs	4.04	2.70
% of Loss to Gross NPAs	7.11	3.87

Source: Authors' compilation.

sector Indian banks at 10 per cent which is much lesser at 3 per cent for the public sector Indian banks. The percentage of Doubtful 2 to Gross NPAs for the private sector Indian banks is lower at 15 per cent which is 20 per cent for the public sector Indian banks. However, the percentage of Doubtful 3 to Gross NPAs for the private sector is 5 per cent which is marginally lower for the public counterpart at 3 per cent. This shows that along with the growth rate of the NPAs the percentage of loss to NPAs and the percentage of Doubtful 3 to Gross NPAs is also higher than the public sector banks.

Another difference that emerged during the analysis of the sample was in case of provisioning for NPAs that is done by Indian banks across the private and public sector. This is another aspect of managing the non-performing loans where, even before the asset becomes non-performing, a provision is made for it. Thus, if the provisioning equals the actual amount of NPAs for a particular period, the Net NPA ratio for that period will be zero. Thus, through the statistical analysis, we found that on an average the provisioning done by private sector is 50.76 per cent which, in case of the public sector Indian banks, is 35.48 per cent. Hence, a prudent practice is being followed by private sector Indian banks where, in order to handle the higher growth rate of Gross NPAs, the banks are also making more provisions for NPAs. Nevertheless, the growth rate of Gross NPAs in Q1 of FY 2014–15 is still a cause for concern for the private sector.

CURRENT PROGRESS ON IMPLEMENTATION OF BASEL III CAPITAL REQUIREMENTS ACROSS PUBLIC AND PRIVATE SECTOR INDIAN BANKS

As per the schedule provided by RBI for implementation of Basel III norms, the Indian banking sector will fully align itself with the Basel standards by March, 2019. This is after extending the deadline by one year. The schedule for implementation is given in Table 11.

Table 11: Transitional Arrangements – Scheduled Commercial Banks (excluding LABs and RRBs)

(% of RWAs)

Minimum Capital Ratios	*April 1, 2013*	*March 31, 2014*	*March 31, 2015*	*March 31, 2016*	*March 31, 2017*	*March 31, 2018*	*March 31, 2019*
Minimum Common Equity Tier 1 (CET1)	4.5	5	5.5	5.5	5.5	5.5	5.5
Capital Conservation Buffer (CCB)	–	–	–	0.625	1.25	1.875	2.5
Minimum CET1+CCB	4.5	5	5.5	6.125	6.75	7.375	8
Minimum Tier 1 Capital	6	6.5	7	7	7	7	7
Minimum Total Capital*	9	9	9	9	9	9	9
Minimum Total Capital + CCB	9	9	9	9.626	10.25	10.875	11.5
Phase-in of All Deductions from CET1 (in %)#	20	40	60	80	100	100	100

*The difference between the minimum total capital requirement of 9% and the Tier 1 requirement can be met with Tier 2 and higher forms of capital;

#The same transition approach will apply to deductions from Additional Tier 1 and Tier 2 capital.

As per the schedule all the banks have achieved the target for March 2014 where banks had to create 9 per cent of total CRAR reserve.

H0: Total CRAR in the banking industry is equal to 12.5%

H1: Total CRAR in the banking industry is not equal to 12.5%

For the sample including both public and private sector Indian banks, the one sample t-test shows that average total CRAR is 12.5 per cent. The test is statistically insignificant and the null hypothesis is true. Hence, the average total CRAR for the banking sector is 12.5 per cent only.

Table 12: Mean Total CRAR %

	N	*Mean*
Total CRAR (%)	32	0.125447

Source: Authors' compilation.

Table 13: T-Test for CRAR %

	t	*df*	*Sig. (2-tailed)*
Total CRAR (%)	0.100	31	0.921

Source: Authors' compilation.

Coming to the individual analysis of the implementation of Basel norms in the private sector Indian banks, the average total CRAR is 14.28 per cent. Through one sample t-test, we have shown that the null hypothesis is not accepted and the average CRAR is much higher than 12.5 per cent, which is the average for both the sectors.

Table 14: Private Banks

	N	*Mean*
Total CRAR (%)	15	0.14362

Source: Authors' compilation.

Table 15

	t	*df*	*Sig. (2-tailed)*
Total CRAR (%)	2.804	14	0.014

Source: Authors' compilation.

On the other hand, for public sector Indian banks, the average value of total CRAR is 10.95 per cent. Through one sample t-test we found that the null hypothesis is rejected and the total CRAR is much lesser than the average of the two sectors. This is also shown by the average calculated for the sector.

Table 16: Public Sector Banks

	N	*Mean*
Total CRAR (%)	17	.109412

Source: Authors' compilation.

Table 17

	t	*df*	*Sig. (2-tailed)*
Total CRAR (%)	−7.624	16	0.000

Source: Authors' compilation.

Thus, banks in both the sectors have been able to achieve the minimum requirement of 9 per cent of the Total Capital, but it is the private sector Indian banks which have outperformed the public counterpart with a much higher reserve for Total Capital. This shows that the private banks are better prepared for implementation of Basel III and are in a better position to absorb shocks as they have over- achieved the capital requirement which is much higher than the requirement as per the RBI timeframe, that is, 9 per cent.

CONCLUSIONS

The paper has analysed the exposure of banks in different industries. As we know, NPAs in the banking sector have been rising; it is essential for banks to identify different risks and then work on mitigating them. As per Pillar 3 of Basel III, it is now mandatory for banks to disclose their exposure to different sectors. The five stressed sectors for banks today are Infrastructure, Iron and Steel, Mining, Textiles and Aviation. Through the analysis, it was found that the Infrastructure sector had high exposure in both public and private sector Indian banks which was greater than 3 per cent of total loans and advances. It was also found that private sector banks follow a very extreme approach while deciding on the sectors to target. There are many industries with high and also low exposure. On the other hand, public sector Indian banks have a more diversified exposure to different industries, with very few sectors having exposure of more than or equal to 3 per cent, though they have more high exposure industries which are Infrastructure, Metal and Metal products, and Textiles.

The higher absolute value of NPAs in the public sector banks can now be linked to the high exposure industries for these banks. All the said industries have been identified as stressed sectors for the banks which can be a big reason for a higher absolute amount of NPAs in public sector banks. On the other hand, private banks have only one stressed sector, viz., Infrastructure with exposure greater than 3 per cent.

The analysis also showed that the growth of NPAs is has been higher for Q1 of FY 2014–15 in case of private sector banks. This high growth of NPAs can be linked to the fact that private sector banks have not diversified their exposure. These are two major areas of risk that have been identified for private sector banks, which need to be mitigated.

As we know that Basel III norms have been introduced after the financial crisis of 2008–09, it is also important to study how banks have performed in adopting the Basel guidelines. Though there is a minimum requirement of 9 per cent, both public and private sector Indian banks have achieved this target. But the performance of private banks in this regard has been commendable. On an average, the Total CRAR for private sectors stands at 14.28 per cent as opposed to the minimum capital requirement of 9 per cent of Total CRAR. Thus, private sector banks are better prepared for the implementation of Basel III and have a greater shock absorbing capacity where the Total CRAR percentage is much higher from the stipulated value. Also, the performance of public sector Indian banks in this regard is good, but the Total CRAR reserve is lesser as compared to the private sector Indian banks.

REFERENCES

Allahabad Bank Ltd. (2014), Pillar III Disclosure under Basel-III Framework for the year ended 30th June, 2014, downloaded from: https://www.allahabadbank.in/pdf/Pillar_III_Disclosure_as_on_30_06_2014.pdf

Andhra Bank Ltd. (2014), Disclosures under Basel III Capital Regulations (Pillar III) as on 30.06.2014, downloaded from: http://andhrabank.in/UserFiles/File/June_2014_Disclosures_latest.pdf

Axis Bank Limited (2014), Disclosures under Basel III Capital Regulations (Consolidated)For the Quarter Ended 30th June 2014, downloaded from: http://www.axisbank.com/download/BaselIII/BaselIII-Disclosures-for-the-quarter-ended-30th-June-2014.pdf.

Bank of Baroda Ltd. (2014), Quarterly Disclosures (on solo basis) under Pillar 3 in terms of New Capital Adequacy Framework (Basel III) of Reserve Bank of India as on 30.06.2014, downloaded from: http://www.bankofbaroda.co.in/download/Basel_III_Pillar_III_Disclosure_for_June_2014.pdf

Bank of India Ltd. (2014), Basel III (Pillar 3) - Disclosures (Consolidated) June 2014, downloaded from: http://www.bankofindia.co.in/pdf/Pillar_III_disclosure_under_Basel_3_for_June_2014.pdf

Bank of Maharashtra Ltd. (2014), Basel III – Pillar 3 Disclosures as on 30.06.2014, downloaded from: http://www.bankofmaharashtra.in/downdocs/Basel-III-Pillar-3-disclosures-at-June-30-2014.pdf

Basel III Monitoring Report (2014) – Bank for InternationalSettlements*www.bis.org/publ/bcbs289.pdf*

Business Standard, 'Private Banks to Cut Exposure to Stressed Sectors', 2014. Available at: http://www.business-standard.com, accessed on 24 June 2014.

Canara Bank Ltd. (2014), Basel III Pillar 3 Disclosure as on 30.06.2014, downloaded from: http://canarabank.com/upload/english/content/Basel%20III%20Disclosures%20as%20on%2030.06.14.pdf

Catholic Syrian Bank Ltd. (2014), Basel III Pillar 3 Disclosures for the Quarter Ended 30th June 2014, downloaded from: http://www.csb.co.in/uploadedfiles/customimages/pillar3%2030.06.2014.pdf.

Central Bank of India Ltd. (2014), Pillar 3 (Basel III) Disclosures as on 30.06.2014, downloaded from: https://www.centralbankofindia.co.in/upload/BASEL%20III%20Disclosures%20as%20on%2030.06.2014.pdf

City Union Bank Ltd. (2014), Pillar 3 Disclosure (Quarterly) Requirements as on 30.06.2014, downloaded from: http://www.cityunionbank.com/PageMenuDocs/basel/Quarterly_Disclosures_30.06.2014.pdf.

Corporation Bank Ltd. (2014), DF-3 Capital Adequacy – Qualitative Disclosure as on 30th June 2014, downloaded from: http://www.corpbank.com/sites/default/files/Disclosure%20june%202014.pdf

DCB Bank Ltd. (2014), Pillar 3 Disclosures under the New Capital Adequacy Framework (Basel III) for the Quarter Ended 30th June 2014, downloaded from: http://www.dcbbank.com/pdfs/Basel-III-Pillar-III-disclosure-June-30-2014.pdf

Dhanlakshmi Bank Ltd. (2014), Pillar III Disclosure Requirements for the Quarter Ended 30th June 2014, downloaded from: http://www.dhanbank.com/pdf/Pillar_III_disclosure-30.06.2014.pdf

Federal Bank Ltd. (2014), Basel III – Pillar 3 Disclosures Of The Federal Bank Limited as on 30th June 2014, downloaded from: http://www.federalbank.co.in/documents/10180/50555/BASEL+III+DISCLOSURES+as+on+30th+June+2014/43f9f50e-b557-4a18-bd11-bab0c9ef1a0d

HDFC Bank Ltd. (2014), Basel III – Pillar 3 Disclosures for the Quarter Ended 30th June 2014, downloaded from: http://www.hdfcbank.com/htdocs/common/pdf/Basel_III_Pillar3_Jun14.pdf

ICICI Bank Ltd. (2014), Basel – Pillar 3 Disclosures (Consolidated) At June 30, 2014, downloaded from: http://www.icicibank.com/managed-assets/docs/investor/basel-investor-disclosure/basel3-pillar3-jun2014.pdf

IDBI Bank Ltd. (2014), Consolidated Pillar III Disclosures (June 30, 2014), downloaded from: http://www.idbi.com/pdf/basel/Final-Consolidated-Pillar-III-Discosures-June-2014.pdf

IndusInd bank Ltd. (2014), Disclosures under Basel III Capital Regulations – 30th June 2014, downloaded from: http://www.indusind.com/content/dam/indusind/PDF/Basel-III-Disclosure-June2014.pdf

ING Vysya Bank Ltd. (2014), Basel III Pillar 3 Disclosures for Period Ending 30 June 2014, downloaded from: http://www.ingvysyabank.com/IngBlog/Media/PDF/Basel-III-Disclosures-for-the-Period-ended-30th-June-2014.pdf

Karnataka Bank Ltd. (2014), Disclosure under Pillar III of Basel III Accord for Period Ending 30 June 2014, downloaded from: http://www.karnatakabank.com/ktk/BaselDisclosures.jsp

Karur Vysya Bank Ltd. (2014), Pillar III Disclosures under the New Capital Adequacy Framework (Basel III) for Period Ending 30 June 2014, downloaded from: http://www.kvb.co.in/pdf/Disclosures/PILLAR%20III%20Disclosure_June%202014.pdf

Kotak Mahindra Bank Ltd. (2014), Disclosures under BASEL III Capital Regulations for the quarter ended 30th June, 2014, downloaded from: http://ir.kotak.com/downloads/pillar3_disclosures_june_14.pdf

M. Jayadev, 'Basel III Implementation - Issues and Challenges for Indian Banks', *IIMB Management Review*, vol. 25, Issue 2, June 2013, pp. 115–30.

M. Shah, 'Basel-3 and its Impact on Indian Banking Sector', *Journal of India Research*, vol. 1, no. 1, pp. 53–8.

Oriental Bank of Commerce Ltd. (2014), Disclosure under Basel III (Pillar 3) in terms of Revised Capital Adequacy Framework as on 30.06.2014, downloaded from: http://obcindia.co.in/obcnew/site/Basel-III_Disclosures_June_2014.pdf

Punjab National Bank Ltd. (2014), Pillar III Disclosure under Basel-III Framework for the Quarter ended 30th June, 2014, downloaded from: http://pnbindia.in/new/Upload/English/Financials/PDFs/Pillar3_Basel3_for_30062014.2014.pdf

Punjab & Sind Bank Ltd. (2014), Basel III Disclosure for the Quarter ended 30th June, 2014, downloaded from: https://www.psbindia.com/Basel_III_Disclosures_30.06.2014_English.pdf

Reserve Bank of India, 'Indian Banking at Crossroads – Challenge of Risk Management from Globalisation to Financial Inclusion', 2014. Available at: http://www.rbi.org, last accessed on 8 May 2014.

South Indian Bank Ltd. (2014), Disclosure under Basel III norms as on 30th June 2014, downloaded from: http://www.southindianbank.com/UserFiles/file/Basel-III%20.pdf

State Bank of India Ltd. (2014), Pillar 3 Disclosures (Consolidated) as at 30.06.2014, downloaded from: http://www.sbi.co.in/portal/documents/41076/905431/DF-2+TO+4.pdf/f97fc5a4-6bc8-4c43-9da6-481eef1a47c0

Syndicate Bank Ltd. (2014), Basel III, Pillar 3 Disclosures for the quarter ended 30.06.2014, downloaded from: //syndicatebank.in/downloads/BaselIII disclosures-30062014.pdf

Tamil Nad Mercantile Bank Ltd. (2014), BASEL III - Pillar 3 Disclosures as on 30th June 2014, downloaded from: http://www.tmb.in/doc/b3p3_20140630.pdf

UCO Bank Ltd. (2014), Basel III Pillar 3 Disclosure as on 30.06.2014 downloaded from: https://www.ucobank.com/investors/pdf/base-III-disclosures-30-06-14.pdf

United Bank of India Ltd. (2014), Pillar-3 Disclosure under Basel-III Norms (As on 30.06.2014), downloaded from: http://www.unionbankofindia.co.in/pdf/Basel-III_Pillar3_Jun14.pdf

Vaidyanathan K. Credit Risk Management for Indian Banks (2013), Sage Publications, New Delhi.

Vighneswara Swamy, Basel III – Implications for Indian Banking, Indian Institute of Banking & Finance (2012), ICFAI, IUP Publication Hyderabad.

Yes Bank Ltd. (2014), Disclosures under The Basel III Capital Regulations June 30, 2014, downloaded from: http://www.yesbank.in/images/all_pdf/Basel_III_Disclosure_June_30_2014.pdf

ANNEXURE

List of Banks taken as Sample

Private Banks
Axis Bank
Catholic Syrian Bank
City Union Bank
Development Credit Bank
Dhanalakshmi Bank
Federal Bank
ICICI Bank
IndusInd Bank
ING Vysya Bank
Karnataka Bank
Karur Vysya Bank
Kotak Mahindra Bank
Tamil Nad Merchnatile Bank
South Indian Bank
Yes Bank

Public Sector/Nationalized Banks
Allahabad Bank
Andhra Bank
Bank of Baroda
Bank Of India
Bank of Maharashtra
Canara Bank
Central Bank of India
Corporation Bank
Dena Bank
IDBI Bank
Oriental Bank of Commerce
Punjab National Bank
Punjab & Sind Bank
State Bank of India
Syndicate Bank
UCO Bank
United Bank of India

SECTION II

INTERNATIONAL FINANCIAL MARKETS

To Be or Not to Be
A Financial Perspective to Brand Equity

FREDA SWAMINATHAN
FORE School of Management, New Delhi
e-mail: freda@fsm.ac.in

ABSTRACT

Brand equity is the added intangible value that a brand brings to a market place. The price paid for a brand in earlier mergers and acquisitions was earlier seven to eight times its earnings. With brands being recognized as an asset in an organization's financial reports, the value has gone up considerably, between 20-25 times. This study looks at the annual reports of some brands listed in Interbrand's Top 100 Global brands, and raises the marketing and financial issues of brand equity. Brand equity valuation takes into consideration aspects of the brand that is disregarded in Accounting Standards. The intangible values in the annual report will be understood, from a Marketing and Finance perspective, and recommendations will be made on how the subject of brand equity should be looked at as an integration of Marketing and Finance orientation of an organization.

Keywords: Brand Equity, Accounting Standards, Good-will, Intangibles, Valuation

INTRODUCTION

Brand equity as a concept gained acceptance by industry during the 1980's. This was especially recognized as important when evaluating the asset value of an organization. Rather than look at an acquisition as that of only the product and the manufacturing assets, this started being looked as the acquisition of a brand. The former meant acquiring production capacity, whereas the latter signified acquiring a place in the consumer's mind. Traditionally, assets included manufacturing assets, land, buildings and financial assets like receivables and investments. Performance of an organization even today is measured through concepts like return on investment, and tangible assets or equity. Accounting book values do not take into account the value of intangibles. The International Financial Reporting Standard (2005) lays out the internationally agreed way of accounting for goodwill in acquisitions. Goodwill is the difference between the purchase price of a company and the book value of its assets. Nestle had bought Rowntree for five times its book value and Philip Morris had bought Kraft General Foods at a six times its book value.

Brand equity is the added intangible value that is endowed on products and services, because of the brand, and is reflected in the way consumers think, feel and act with respect to the brand. The measure of brand equity has been defined in terms of behavior that will create current and future cash flow. Keller, 2003 defined brand equity as the marketing effects or outcomes that accrue to a product with its brand name compared with those that would accrue is the same product did not have the brand name. The concept is not only used to assign a financial value to balance sheets and financial transactions. The measurement of brand equity guides marketing strategy and helps in tactical marketing decisions. Brand equity tracks the health of the brand, especially vis-à-vis competition and assesses the potential for brand extensions. Overall, brand equity helps marketers to evaluate the effectiveness of marketing decisions. The mood of the nation often gets reflected in financial markets, through share prices. This is also present in the way consumers think, feel and act towards a brand. Capturing the intangible value becomes often a point of conflict between Accountants and Marketing professionals. Mergers and acquisitions happen very often with a paradox. The Company being acquired is making a loss, but because of the future earning potential of the brands, owned by the Company, the equity value is high. The paper's theme – 'To be or not to be' looks into the intangibles being valued by annual reports of leading organizations, and raises the gaps in brand equity valuation.

The higher the brand equity, as per the valuations undertaken by leading research organizations like Interbrands, Milward Brown and Young & Rubicam, the better is the brand salience, perceptions of product performance and imagery. Consumer feelings towards a brand improves, and this brings about positive judgment, finally resulting in greater brand loyalty. The brand is able to charge a premium, enjoy larger margins, and becomes less vulnerable to competition. In terms of pricing strategies, the brand becomes more inelastic to price increases and more elastic to price decreases. Licensing opportunities and brand extension potential improves for the brand, and there is greater trade support and better integrated marketing communications effectiveness. The brand becomes less vulnerable to crisis situations.

Financial reporting in annual reports is a reporting of past performance of the organization. Equity valuation represents the future potential of the brands. Accounting standards ensure that the intangible values are within the rules set. However, because of the qualitative aspect of intangible valuation, the issue of 'To be or not to be' will tend to rise.

RESEARCH OBJECTIVES

The purpose of this paper is to study the following:

1. The role that the intangible value of brands play in the financial reporting of annual reports of leading brands, especially in the context of Mergers and Acquisitions.
2. To assess the challenges in the reporting of brand equity valuation.
3. To arrive at recommendations on how organizations should give a realistic picture of their brand's equity in the annual reports.

RESEARCH METHODOLOGY

The study is exploratory in nature. Secondary research was reviewed to assess the concepts of brand equity that get reflected in financial data. The annual reports of select organizations having leading brands, as per listed in Interbrand's Top 100 Global Brands, 2013 were studied. The Interbrand listing was selected because this is the leading brand valuation organization who was the pioneer and leader in brand equity valueation. An attempt was made to study the intangible values listed in the annual report and the valuation of 'good will'. The data has been collected from the figures given in the annual reports. The concepts of brand equity are then assessed to see whether full justification is being done in financial terms to the valuation of brand equity.

LITERATURE REVIEW

Intangible assets form an element in the Accounting Standards issued by the Institute of Chartered Accountants of India. An intangible asset is defined as "is an identifiable non-monetary asset, without physical substance, held for use in the production or supply of goods or services, for rental to others, or for administrative purposes". The AS26 also lists out methods for amortization or the systematic allocation of the depreciable amount of an intangible asset over its useful like. While intangible assets also include development word in R&D, this review will focus on intangible values of brands. During amalgamations, a purchaser may make a payment in anticipation of future economic benefits because of the brand being strong. This gets defined as 'goodwill'. It may be noted that internally generated intangible assets is not recognized as an asset because it is not easily identifiable in terms of being measured at cost. This includes internally generated brands, mastheads, publishing titles, customer lists and similar items.

Keller et al. (2011) has emphasized that the essentials of strategic brand management is the management of brand equity. Brand equity is created by planning and implementing brand marketing programs whether it is the selection of brand elements, designing of marketing programs including integrated marketing communication programs and the leveraging of secondary brand associations. The measurement and interpretation of brand performance becomes important in terms of developing measurement and management systems, capturing customer mind-set or the measuring of the outcomes of brand equity. Growing and sustaining brand equity is inherent in the implementation of branding strategies, new launches, revitalization of brands or the managing of brands across geographic boundaries and market segments.

Haxthausen and Kumar, 2013 identified a Brand Driver Framework which reduced the measures of brand equity to two : brand salience (or awareness) and brand impact on customers choice to purchase and consume one brand vis-à-vis competitors brands. The framework not only measures brand equity but can be used for brand and media planning and the measurement of the effectiveness of marketing programs.

Ailawadi et al. (2003) suggests that the "revenue premium as an outcome" becomes a measure of brand equity. They refer to Keller and Lehmann (2001) categorizing of brand equity measure to three categories: customer mindset, product market and financial market. The first measure is based on consumer research and therefore is not easy to compute to reflect in financial asset valuation. Product market outcome measure the performance of the brand in the market place. While this measure is more objective, it also is based on customer judgements and therefore could result in inaccurate valuation. Financial market measures are based on the price of a brand when it is bought or sold and the discounted cash flow valuation of licensing fees and royalties. Interbrand uses both product market and financial market measures. The Revenue Premium measure is recommended as it becomes a single, objective number based on available data and economic theory, where benchmark brands are identified and private labels are categorized as surrogate, to measure a revenue premium due to the brand.

Egan et al. (1994) raises the conflicts that arise between the valuation of brand equity and accounting practices. Brand equity is equated with acquisition value rather than customer value. He raises the issue that marketing expenses give value for a period beyond the accounting year. An estimate of brand valuation is better than no valuation at all. This should include value creators (advertising, product development and trade support), marketing assets (trademarks, brands, entry barriers, IT) and value manifestation (image, reputation, premium price and market share) and the cumulative competitive advantage that gives cumulative strategic value.

El-Tawy et al. (2008) set asset recognition criteria to assess the separable and inseparable valuation of the brand. The accounting profession needs to create 'boundaries' that make the method as objective and reliable as possible. The need of the day is that accountants recognize a brand valuation method with a 'multi-measurement' basis for the valuation. Separable measurement of an asset should be additive, based on an observation and measurement of bundles of assets should be avoided.

Bahadir, S.C. et al. (2008) considered the perceptual nature of valuation of brands in the case of mergers and acquisitions. After researching 133 M&Z transactions, the findings supported the hypothesis that both the acquirer and the target characteristics are of importance in valuating the firm's brands. The study indicated that the acquirer firm's marketing capabilities and brand portfolio diversity have positive effects on the financial value of the target firm's brand portfolio value. Therefore, both acquirer and target characteristics are important in determining the value attributed to the target firm's brands. The study also indicated that the positive impact of the acquirer's brand portfolio diversity and target marketing capability is lower when the M&A is synergistic than when it is non-synergistic. When an acquirer has strong marketing capabilities and a high brand portfolio diversity, the price of the brand acquisition can be higher.

Roslender, R. et al. (2003) begin by humorously writing about the contradictions between 'profligate marketers' and 'penny-pinching accountants', to reinforce the importance of customer profitability analysis (CFA) in both these functions. There is no provision for accounting standards to take into consideration 'home-grown brand' or the costs of developing databases of customers. CFA must take into account 'customers as sources of income streams'. The accountancy profession needs to take into consideration these values when preparing a financial statement.

Wiesel, T et al. (2008), proposes a method to report customer equity to allow investors to monitor a firm's performance with regard their customer assets. Investors should receive useful information about customer metrics (viz., retention and customer cash flow), the value of the customer base, life-time customer equity, its changes over time and its impact on customer metrics. A reporting technique was developed to consider the value of the customer base in the financial report as a separate section.

Mitchell, A. (2002) advocates that measuring profit should be about fact and not fiction. A company profits increase when employees are enriched. The wealth generated by the bottlers of Coke are not accounted in Coke's books of accounts. Reported profits reflect very little about the assets the organization is creating, or on the flip side, through environmental disasters, the wealth that is being destroyed. At the same time when intangibles account for a major proportion of a nation's economy, the 'real economy' is not reflected.

Bick, G.N.C. (2009) raises the issue that through 'myopic management' where there is no investment by organizations, brand equity and shareholder value was affected. The study distinguishes between brand equity and customer equity. While the former consists of the intangible assets and liabilities of a brand and focuses on product and brand investment decisions, the latter is the sum of the lifetime value of customers to a firm, and focuses on customer management decisions. Through rating research organizations like Interbrands, brand equity has become a concept that accounting principles are working to improve, customer equity also needs to be taken into consideration.

Knowles, J. (2008) has put the different perspectives on brand equity and has noted that the valuation of brand equity for different brands is very different, if one looks at those undertaken by Interbrands, Milward Brown and Brand Finance in 2007 of leading brands. The dilemma created by the concept of brand equity deals with the probability of future benefits - like the incremental cash flows generated by committed business versus those that may emerge because of the preference for a brand. Brand equity measures can be seen based on behavior and preference. Behavior-based measures of brand equity include purchase frequency, price premium, re-order rate, share of wallet and cross-sell ration. Preference-based measures of brand equity include relevant differentiation, willingness to recommend, worth paying a premium for and affinity. It is recommended that valuation models follow discipline and transparency. Examples of a systematic process is the 'relief from royalty method' where licensing revenues through licensing a trademark is assessed, or the net present value of the future stream of incremental cash flow derived from a Company owning a brand.

ANALYSIS

Though most research organization conceptually agree on the elements of brand equity, their different valuation models give rise to different values. Knowles (2008) had seen this difference in the figures given by the valuation organizations in 2007, and this may be seen again in the 2013 figures.

Table 1: Brand Valuation of Key brands by Different Valuators (figures in $ million)

Top 100 Brands	*Milward Brown*	*Interbrand*	*Brand Finance*
Apple	1,85,071 (Rank 1)	98,316 (Rank 1)	1,04,660 (Rank 1)
Google	1,13,669 (Rank 2)	93,291 (Rank 2)	68,620 (Rank 3)
IBM	1,12,536 (Rank 3)	78,808 (Rank 4)	41,513 (Rank 10)
McDonald's	90,256 (Rank 4)	41,992 (Rank 7)	26,047 (Rank 25)
Coke	78,415 (Rank 5)	79,213 (Rank 3)	33,722 (Rank 12)

Annual Reports from the following top brands were studied in order to look at how the issue of brand equity is dealt in financial reporting. 12 Annual reports were studied of top global brands, as per Interbrand. These were : Nestle, Pepsico, Samsung, Johnson & Johnson, Coke, Facebook, LVMH, McDonald's, 3M, BMW, Disney and Apple. The annual reports were studied to assess the following:

1. To study how the intangible element of brand is handled in annual reports.
2. To qualitatively assess how brands are dealt with in annual reports.
3. To look at the brand values of acquisitions made by organizations.
4. To analyze the above and arrive at recommendations.

Organizations are increasingly conscious of incorporating intangible values in the annual reports. This is of great significance in dealing whether to include or discontinue a brand that has been acquired or invest in it. For example when an annual report records good will in an acquisition, if the brand gets discontinued, it will reflect in the figures given as the asset value. All top brands seem to follow the latest accounting standards, usually, US GAAP or the European IFRS. Samsung follows K-IFRS, and thus it has recently changed, how goodwill should be reported.

Some of the stipulations of these accounting standards are that goodwill and intangible assets need to either be amortized as per the life of the asset or go through impairment test.

Goodwill is a term used in accountancy and law. It is an intangible asset of a business, and can include trademarks and patents, employees and their skill sets, the brand name and logo recognition, customer lists and relationships. When a company is purchased by another company, the difference between the purchase price and the book value of the purchased company is called goodwill. Goodwill is considered an intangible asset, meaning that is has no physical attributes. Being an asset, goodwill is recorded on the balance sheet of a company's financial statements. If the value is the same or higher than the initial valuation, the asset value on the balance sheet remains the same. If the impairment value is lower, the asset needs to be written down to the lower value.

Intangibles form a significant portion of total assets shown in annual reports. This is as low as 1.6% for Samsung, or as high as 57% for McDonald's or 54% for LVMH. Soft drink beverage brands like Coke and Pepsi have a share of 31% and 42.1% respectively. The value of the intangible reflects the Company's value on paper and its value in the stock exchange. The other way is the premium paid during an acquisition. A study by Interbrand concluded that on average brands account for more than one-third of shareholder value. The study reveals that brands create significant value either as consumer or corporate brands or as a combination of both.

Brands essentially form part of the intangible assets of the company. Brands are considered indefinite life intangible assets since there is no foreseeable limit to their useful economic life as they arise from contractual or other legal rights that can be renewed without significant cost and are the subject of continuous marketing support. They are tested for impairment annually or more frequently if an impairment indicator is triggered. The assessment of the classification of intangible assets as indefinite is reviewed annually.

It is interesting to note that a brand like Coca Cola that has been top of the list in the top global brands (Interbrand) for many years creates annual reports that communicate the image of the brand in a big way. The Coca-Cola Company classifies intangible assets into three categories: (1) intangible assets with definite lives subject to amortization, (2) intangible assets with indefinite lives not subject to amortization, and (3) goodwill. The intangibles include trademarks, bottlers franchise rights and customer relationships. With a key challenge of cola beverages being considered as unhealthy, the recent acquisition of Coca Cola is ZICOTM Pure Premium Coconut Water. In most acquisitions, the value of the brand plays a significant share (36 to up to 95%) of the value of the acquisition.

A conglomerate like LVMH, having luxury brands like Louis Vuitton has 54% of its total assets as intangibles. This includes, tradenames, licenses rights, leasehold rights, software, website and goodwill or reputation. Brands and intellectual rights account for 93% of the intangible asset values, and 87% of the goodwill. Essentially, acquisitions happen because of the high brand value of the luxury brands.

Changes in foreign exchange rates also affect the values of intangibles, impairment values and amortization. In all the annual reports studied, this was taken into consideration. This specially affects an organization like McDonald's whose goodwill primarily results from purchases of McDonald's outlets from franchisees and ownership increases in subsidiaries or affiliates all over the world.

Brand name rights are also an important aspect of intangibles. A good example is that of BMW. Intangible Assets of the company includes capitalized development costs on vehicle and engine projects as well as subsidies for tool costs, licenses, purchased development projects, software and purchased customer bases. It also include a brand-name right amounting to €43 million, goodwill of €369 million, and acquisition of licences amounting to €379 million. BMW in fact in 2003, it Rolls Royce from the VW Group leveraging the fact that it had already bought the RR Logo and the brand name Rolls Royce from the previous owner of Rolls Royce. VW Group, despite having bought Rolls Royce motors could not get it hands on the brand Rolls Royce which was already sold to BMW. This incident easily corroborates the importance and value of the brand name. Some of the Intangible assets acquired at the time of Rolls Royce acquisition were: Brand Name right: Rolls Royce, Brand Logo: RR, Mascot: Spirit of ecstasy and rights to the shape of the radiator grille.

Disney also has over 40% of its intangible assets as a percentage of its total assets. The business model of Disney is in fact dependent on high brand valuation. 43% of the revenues of the company are from royalties like Disney branded hotels, Japan amusement park and other stores around the world. Company licenses trade names, characters and visual and literary properties to various retailers, show promoters and publishers throughout the world. Brand Disney is reflected in terms of revenue (financial figure) in the annual report. The company acquires pictures and live action movies from other and sell and distribute under brand name Disney. The company derives royalties

(Disney character merchandise) from the sales of the licensed goods and services by third parties and the management of businesses operated under brands licensed from the Company. There are many games developed on different platform which use the Disney names and characters.

RECOMMENDATION

How does one create a win-win situation between marketers and accountants to the treatment of intangibles? Some principles that emerge are:

1. *Integration.* The asset value that is created by marketers in building brand equity needs to be assessed through a process that integrates marketing and accounting functions. The essence of a brand is the brand promise that it delivers. To fully comprehend this, brand managers and advertising experts need to work with consultancies to assess the real brand value – in terms of the brand's salience, performance, image, experience, responses and loyalty. Marketing needs to get more involved in this measure. This is also required to set impairment values and that on amortization.
2. *Market Orientation.* The success of a brand is relative to competition. Competitive analysis needs to be undertaken to get a 'real' value of intangibles. While this gets reflected in the valuation of goodwill, a more realistic valuation is required for home-grown brands.
3. *Brand Valuation.* The problem on the valuation of intangibles tends to be a lack of transparency. Brand details need to be specified while detailing intangible and goodwill values. This will indicate the contribution of each brand to the brand equity. Each brand will need to incorporate intangible values like brand imagery and associations, customer relationships, distribution network, CSR and other intangible aspects of a brand.

It may be noticed that organizations that build great brands are working towards building brand equity. Brand and trade names use methods of forecasting discounted cash flows or what LVMH refers to as 'comparable transactions' where they use the revenue and net profit coefficients employed for recent transactions involving similar brands, or of stock market multipliers. Other methods can be the royalty method, valuating the present value of royalties to be paid for a brand, or the brand reconstitution method involving the estimation of the amount of advertising and promotion expenses required to create a similar brand.

Today's industry has intangible assets listed in annual reports that tend to be conservative. One can appreciate accounting standards that support this because after all, an asset should also have a resale value or a potential to earn money. Intangibles are essentially not easy to trade and often involve a lengthy process of legal rights and valuation of the value that has been created beyond the intangibles.

CONCLUSION

The value of intangibles contributes greatly to the total current assets of an organization. The importance of its measurement therefore cannot be left to varying opinions of accountants, consultants or research agencies or the concept remaining abstract in nature. As the world economies are developing, research organizations like Interbrands are recognizing the importance of calculating brand values for country-specific brands. This tends to create even more points of discussion on the measurement techniques because of the cultural dimensions of each country. The importance of developing standardized brand valuation measurement techniques becomes that much more important because of the world becoming a global economy, where brands emerging from different parts of the world, be it Samsung or Whirlpool or Haier all compete for consumer imagery and preference.

The question is 'to be or not to be'. Professional organizations and accounting procedures need to ensure that the total assets of an organization in today's industry is much more that tangibles and goodwill, but includes all the nuances of a brand that adds to the brand equity or asset value.

REFERENCES

Ailawadi, K.L., Lehmann, D.R. & Neslin, S.A. (2003). Revenue Premium as an Outcome Measure of Brand Equity. Journal of Marketing. Vol.67, October, 2003, pp. 1–17.

Bahadir, S.C., Bharadwaj, S.G., Srivastava, R.K. (2008). Financial Value of Brands in Mergers and Acquisitions: Is Value in the Eye of the Beholder? *Journal of Marketing*, Vol. 72, November, 2008, pp. 49–64, @2008, American Marketing Association, ISSN: 0022-2429 (print), 1547-7185 (electronic).

Bick, G.N.C. (2009). Increasing Shareholder Value through building Customer and Brand Equity. *Journal of Marketing Management*, 2009, Vol. 25, No. 1-2, pp. 117–41. ISSN 0267-257X print/ISSN1472-1376 online © Westburn Publishers Ltd.

Egan, C. & Guilding, C. (1994). Dimensions of Brand Performance: Challenges for Marketing Management and Managerial Accountancy. 0267-257X/94/060449+241994 The Dryden Press.

El-Tawy, N. & Tollington, T. (2008). The recognition and measurement of brand assets: An exploration of the accounting/marketing interface. *Journal of Marketing Management*, 2008. Vol. 24, No. 7-8, pp. 711–31.

Haxthausen, Ove and Kumar, Pankaj (2013). Measure to Manage, An Actionable Model for Breaking free from the brand-equity paradox. *Marketing Insights*, Fall, 2013, pp. 26–31.

http://ec.europa.eu/finance/accounting/docs/arc/2005-11-30-annex-ifrs7 en.pdf. The International Financial Reporting Standard (2005).

Keller (2003). Brand Synthesis: The Multidimensionality of Brand Knowledge. *Journal of Consumer Research*, Vol. 29, March 2003.

Keller, K.L. & DR Lehmann (2001). How do Brands Create Value? *Marketing Management* 12(3), pp. 26–31.

Keller, K.L., Parameswaran, M.G., Jacob, I. (2011). Strategic Brand Management, 3rd Edition, Pearson Prentice Hall. ISBN 978-81-317-5689-8.

Knowles, J. (2008). Varying Perspectives on Brand Equity. *Marketing Management*, July/August, 2008, pp. 20–26.

Mitchell, A. (2002). Measuring Profit should be about Fact and not Fiction. *Marketing Week*, July 25, 2002, EBSCO Publishing.

Roslender, R. & Watt, Watt (2008). The Marketing/Accounting Synergy: A final word but certainly not the last word. *Journal of Marketing Management*, 2008, Vol. 24, No. 7-8, pp. 865–76. ISSN0267-257X print/ISSN1472-1376 online © Westburn Publishers Ltd.

Wiesel, T., Skiera, Bernd & Villanueva, J. Customer Equity: An Integral Part of Financial Reporting. *Journal of Marketing*, Vol. 72 (March 2008), pp. 1–14.

www.mca.gov.in/Ministry/notification/pdf/AS_26.pdf. Accessed on October 23, 2014 at 11.10 am.

Macroeconomic Determinants Impacting Exchange Rate in India

A Study

Pooja Misra and Tanvi Babbar

Birla Institute of Management Technology, Greater Noida, Uttar Pradesh
e-mail: pooja.misra@bimtech.ac.in; tanvi.babbar16@bimtech.ac.in

ABSTRACT

The exchange rate plays a key role in determining trade levels, that is, exports and imports of goods and services, foreign investment inflows and outflows, and balance of trade position of any country. One of the primary goals of any economy, whether developed or developing, is maintaining a stable exchange rate. Volatile exchange rates negatively impact international trade and these exchange rate risks discourage foreign financial investors from investing into India.

The volatility of the exchange rate of the Indian Rupee has been the topic of debate and worry not only for the financial markets, but also policy making circles. Currency rates are managed based on the economical evaluation of the currency of the particular economy. Currency exchange gives the rate of the currency in a pair of currency of two countries, that is, rate of Indian Rupee against the Dollar or against Pound Sterling, etc.

The Indian Rupee depreciated at a rapid pace, especially in the months of July and August 2013. The Rupee reached a lifetime low of 68.85 on 28 August 2013. It was recorded as the most affected Asian currency and depreciated 3.7 per cent in a single day. There could be varying macroeconomic determinants such as high inflation, interest rates, current account deficit, Gross Domestic Product (GDP) growth rate, etc., responsible for the sharp depreciation of the Indian Rupee.

The research paper seeks to understand and analyse the macroeconomic determinants that impact the exchange rate of the country's currency as against dominating currencies in the international market. It also seeks to determine the correlation between the strength of the relationship established of these macroeconomic determinants with specific reference to the exchange rate of the Indian Rupee as against US dollars.

Keywords: Exchange Rate, Inflation, Interest Rate, GDP Growth, Current Account

INTRODUCTION

One of the all-time concerning analysis during the past few years for India and particularly since January 2013 has been the cause for depreciation of the Indian Rupee as against the Dollar. The falling Indian Rupee has been the dominating debate in the financial markets and policy making circles. The Indian Rupee depreciated at a rapid pace, especially in the months of July and August 2013. The Rupee reached the life time low of 68.85 on 28 August 2013. It was recorded as the most affected Asian currency and depreciated 3.7 per cent in a single day. It was the worst fall that the Indian currency had seen in two decades. The currency had depreciated up to 20 per cent since the beginning of the calendar year 2013. The fall was steep enough that jokes on the currency started appreciating faster. 'The dollar is on an escalator and the rupee is on a ventilator' goes one witticism. Except for the Bangladeshi Taka and the Chinese Yuan, all the Asian and emerging markets had experienced a sharp depreciation in their respective currencies.

Volatile exchange rates create a negative impact on international trade and financial investment decisions. Volatility is a sign of the extent to which and how fast a variable changes over a period of time. In case of currencies which are highly volatile and unpredictable, high exchange rate risks can result in investors preferring to invest in domestic markets where profits are relatively lower in comparison to trading in foreign markets giving higher returns. Trading of currency in specific country's currencies is done based on future scope of profitability. Currency rates are managed based on the economical evaluation of the currency of the particular economy. Currency exchange gives the rate of the currency in a pair of currency of two countries, that is, the rate of Indian Rupee against the Dollar or against Pound Sterling, etc.

As a part of the liberalization and privatization process in 1991, India's exchange rate has evolved from being a pegged or fixed exchange rate to a floating exchange rate. Along with the opening up of the external sector of the Indian economy developments in the exchange rate policy took place. The exchange rate policy of India has progressed from a par value system to a basket peg and subsequently to a managed float exchange rate system. It was in the late 1980s and early 1990s that the Government realized that macroeconomic policies and other structural factors had largely contributed to a balance of payment difficulty for the country. Foreign currency assets had depleted to less than a billion dollars by July 1991, that is, less than two weeks' worth of imports into the country. It was in this light that the Government embarked on a series of structural and macroeconomic reforms with the objective of achieving higher growth rates. A framework was sought to be put in place by the High Level Committee on Balance of Payments for a realistic macroeconomic, structural, and stabilization programme encompassing industry outlook, trade circles, foreign portfolio investments, exchange rate, and, most importantly, foreign exchange reserves. For a stable and consistent exchange rate, it was foreseen that a thought needed to be given to a realistic exchange rate, maintaining a substantial level of foreign exchange to take care of short term fluctuations and volatility, working on the policy of free convertibility of the rupee and ensuring that there is an adequate level of focus and control on capital account transactions. It was seen that a stable and realistic exchange rate can be maintained by controlling inflation numbers through macroeconomic policy action. Also, a two-step downward exchange rate adjustment by 9 per cent and 11 per cent between 1 and 3 July 1991 was undertaken with a view to counter the massive drawdown in the foreign exchange reserves, and to establish confidence in the minds of the investors and improve domestic competitiveness in the international markets. In March 1993, the unified exchange rate system was put in place.

On an average, since 1993, the Rupee was seen to have generally depreciated against the dollar, with the exception of 2003–05 and 2007–08 when the Rupee had appreciated due to the weakening of the Dollar and inflow of large capital into India. It was also seen that the volatility of the exchange rate of the Rupee has been managed by the intervention of the Reserve Bank of India (RBI) in the foreign exchange market. The RBI has, on an average, reacted swiftly to the developments of the foreign exchange market by means of monetary and regulatory measures and through direct and indirect interventions whenever required.

Some of the macroeconomic determinants known to affect currency movement are inflation, lending rates, Gross Domestic Product (GDP) growth, and current account position. The purpose of the research study is to understand and analyse the important macroeconomic determinants affecting the valuation and exchange rate of the Indian Rupee.

FACTORS IMPACTING EXCHANGE RATE

Exchange rate is known to be influenced by numerous factors such as inflation levels in the country, lending rate differentials, Gross domestic product current account position of the country.

Movement of Exchange Rate

Exchange rate plays a key role in determining the volume of exports and imports of a country and its movement relative to other countries currency is keenly watched and analysed.

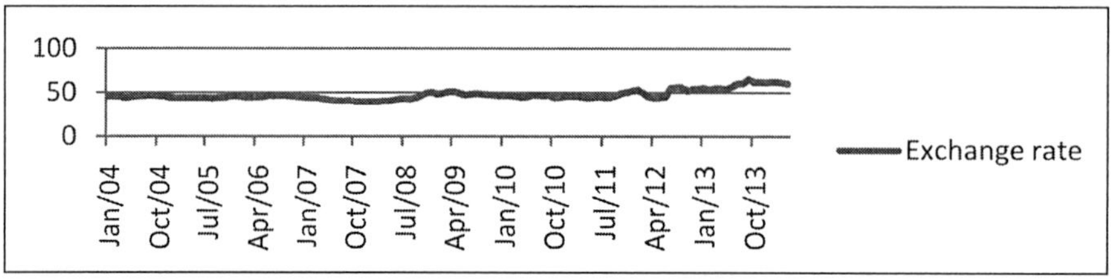

Figure 1: Exchange Rate of Indian Rupee as against USD

Inflation is defined as the sustained increase in general price level of goods and services in the country. If the rate of inflation in India is higher to other countries, it will lead to an increased price level of goods and services being produced in India, thereby making exports relatively more expensive in comparison to goods being produced in the rest of the world. On the other hand, it would make imports cheaper and, thus, demand for imports being made into the country would increase. Therefore, demand for foreign exchange to facilitate payments for imports will increase, whilst that of the Indian Rupee would decline, thereby leading to depreciation of the Indian currency.

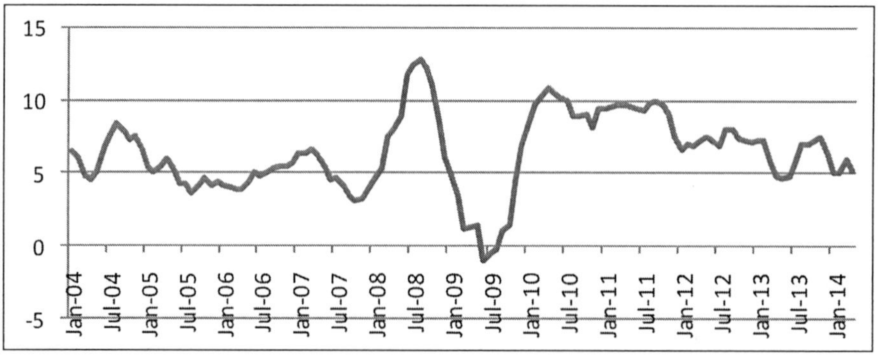

Figure 2: Rate of Inflation based on WPI in India; Base 2004-05 = 100 (%)

If the rate of interest in India or the lending rate in India is higher, relative to other countries, then foreign currency inflow into the country will increase as higher rates offer a higher return to lenders in the economy. Thus, higher lending rates attract inflow of capital into the country, causing the exchange rate to appreciate.

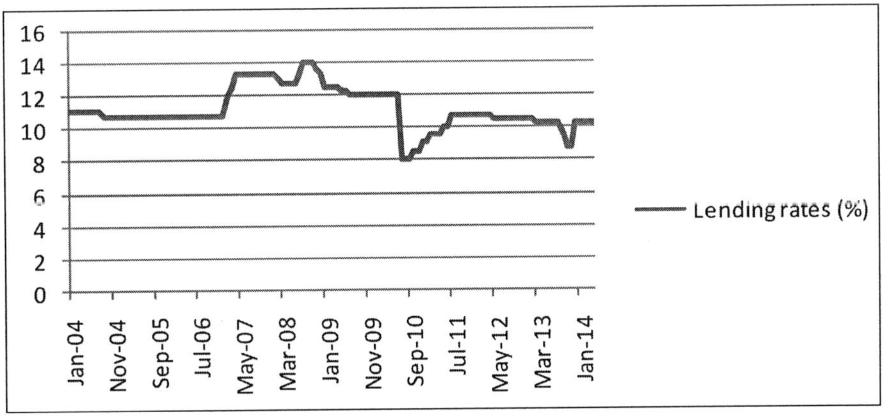

Figure 3: Lending Rate

The current account is a statement of the exports, imports, and net invisibles (comprising non-factor services, income, and transfers) of any country with the rest of the world. It is the balance of trade position of a country with its trading partners comprising goods, services, interests, and dividend payments. A deficit on the current account shows that the country is paying more in terms of foreign trade than it is earning, that is, the country is in need of foreign currency to pay for its imports in comparison to the money that the country earns by way of exports. A current account surplus

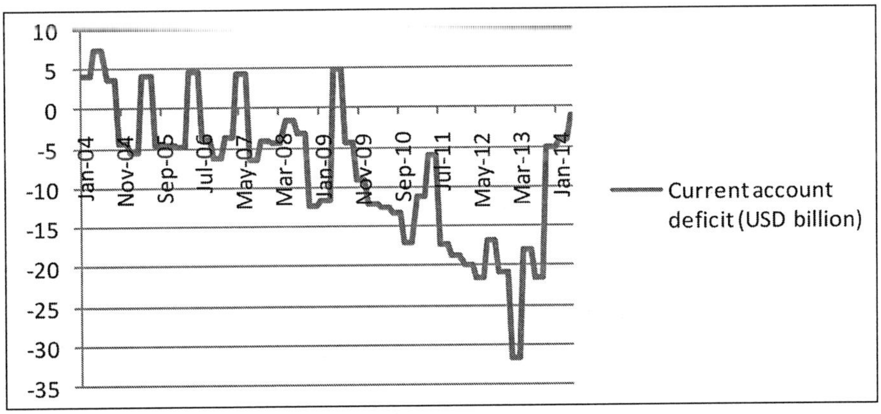

Figure 4: Current Account Deficit

is the vice versa situation, wherein the exports and net invisibles are higher than imports. Thus, a current account deficit results in a higher demand for foreign exchange in comparison to the home country's currency, thereby leading to a depreciation of the exchange rate. Hence, the current account deficit has a positive relationship with the exchange rate or an increase in current account surplus leads to an appreciation of the currency. Term of trade or balance of trade is exports minus imports.

Gross Domestic Product is the total money value of all final goods and services produced within the domestic boundaries of a country in a given time period. A higher GDP growth is reflective of strong fundamentals of the economy and vice versa.

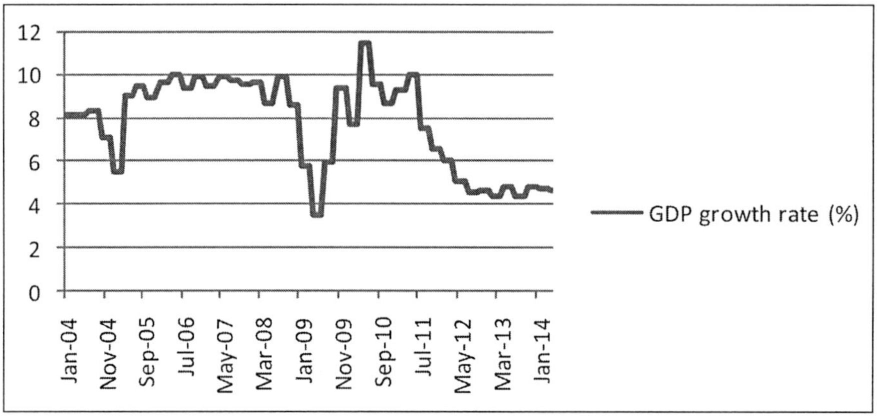

Figure 5: GDP Growth Rate

SCOPE OF THE RESEARCH

There could be varying macroeconomic determinants such as high inflation, interest rates or lending rates, current account deficit, GDP growth rate, etc., responsible for the fluctuation and the sharp appreciation or depreciation of the Indian Rupee.

1. The research has been undertaken to determine the macroeconomic factors which have impacted the volatility of foreign exchange rate with specific reference to the Indian Rupee as against US Dollars.
2. The study also seeks to analyse the strength of the relationship established amongst the exchange rate and identified macro-economic determinants with specific reference to the Indian Rupee.

The research is based on secondary monthly data available for 10, years taken on a monthly basis from January 2004–April 2014.

LITERATURE REVIEW

Hau (2002) in his study examined the relationship between trade openness and the real exchange rate, and stated that there is an inverse relationship between the two. Drine and Christophe (2005) concluded that the openness of the economy strongly influences the exchange rate of the currency. Xiaopu (2002) found that the terms of trade and capital flows were the main determinants of exchange rate.

Simon (1997) in his study stated that there exists a direct positive relationship between exchange rate and inflation and exchange rate and current account, and both these are influencing factors as far as exchange rates of a country are concerned. Bernhardsen and Roisland (2000) in their study on factors that impact the Krone exchange rate found that price differential and interest rate differential between countries impacted the Krone exchange rate. Akram (2000), in relation to Norway, found that if there is higher inflation in one country in comparison to its trading partners there is a tendency for that country's currency to depreciate. Edwards (2001 had analysed the relationship between exchange rates and capital flows in emerging markets and concludes that with apt policy measures in place floating exchange rates are effective and efficient. Taylor (2001) had concluded that money supply in the economy and credit given to firms have a direct association with international reserves, and thus, if there is an increase in capital inflows, the money supply and credit to firms increase resulting in a rise in domestic prices. On the other hand, Harberger (2004 found that there was no direct link between economic growth and real exchange rate of an economy. Garcia and Restrepo (2001) in their study found that exchange rate pass through and economic activity have a positive relationship between them, that is, the negative output gap offsets the inflationary impact of exchange rate depreciation for Chile. Husain et al. (2004) in their study established that there is no strong relationship between exchange rate and economic performance in developing countries. However, in the case of developed countries they found that these economies with a flexible exchange rate may experience a level of growth without a higher inflation rate. Due and Sen (2006) in their study for the period 1993 to 2004 found that real exchange rate, capital inflows, fiscal and monetary policy indicators, and the current account surplus are cointegrated. Aguire and Calderon (2007) found that real exchange rate correlates negatively with GDP per capita growth. Similarly, Prasad et al. (2007) found that capital inflows are positively related to real exchange rate. Gala (2008) found a negative relationship between GDP per capita growth and PPP based index of real exchange rate. Khattak (2012) in their research have analysed the macroeconomic factors that affect the nominal exchange rate of the Pakistan Rupee against the US Dollar and have established that factors such as trade balance, foreign exchange reserves, inflation, and interest rate have a long-run relationship with the Pakistan Rupee.

Mirchandani (2013) analysed various macroeconomic variables leading to variations in the exchange rate of the currency. She found that exchange rate has a either a direct, or inverse correlation with inflation, interest rate, and GDP growth rate, that is, there exists a moderate inverse relationship between exchange rate and inflation and between exchange rate and interest rate. While on the other hand, there exists a mild direct correlation between exchange rate and GDP growth rate. Patel et al. (2014) studied the factors influencing currency rates and found that inflation, rate of interest, capital account balance, speculators, debt of the country, GDP political stability, economic performance, employment data, and macroeconomic and geopolitical events have a bearing on the exchange rate of the currency.

HYPOTHESES

H1 Rupee exchange rate has no correlation with macroeconomic factors such as inflation, interest rate, GDP growth rate, current account, and foreign direct investment.

H2 Inflation has no relationship or influence on the exchange rate of the Indian Rupee in comparison to other international currencies.

H3 Interest rates or lending rate in statistical terms has a negative correlation with the Indian Rupee, that is, a higher interest rate will lead to an appreciation of the home currency.

H4 Current account in statistical terms has a negative correlation with the Indian Rupee as against international currencies, that is, a current account surplus will lead to an appreciation of the Indian currency.

H5 Gross Domestic Product growth rate in statistical terms has a negative correlation with the Indian Rupee, that is, a higher growth rate will lead to an appreciation of the Indian currency.

RESEARCH METHODOLOGY

The design of the study involved the use of secondary data from January 2004 to April 2014, collected from statistical handbooks, books, reports, journals, internet information for exchange rate, and macroeconomic determinants such as inflation, interest rates or lending rate, GDP growth rate, and current account position of India. Data was on a monthly basis and was collected to take care of any unwarranted fluctuations due to key influencing macroeconomic variables and other factors such as political stability, political risks and controls, speculation and liquidity, official monetary reserves, etc. The data was analysed with the help of the SPSS tool and Correlation and Regression analysis of the variables was done to understand the impact of the various independent variables, that is, inflation, current account, GDP growth, and interest rate or lending rate on the exchange rate of the Indian Rupee against the US Dollar (Table 1).

Table 1: Descriptive Statistics

	Mean	*Std. Deviation*	*N*
Exchange Rate	47.1813	5.60510	123
Inflation	6.4380	2.68869	123
Lending Rate	11.1443	1.32520	123
GDP Growth Rate	7.7073	2.11428	123
Current Account	−8.1539	8.86684	123

ANALYSIS AND DISCUSSION

Table 2: Correlations

Exchange Rate	Pearson Correlation	1	–0.25	–.418**	–.727**	–.416**
	Sig. (e-tailed)		.785	.000	.000	.000
	N	123	123	123	123	123
Inflation	Pearson Correlation	–.025	1	–.167	.215*	–.320**
	Sig. (e-tailed)	.785		.065	.017	.000
	N	123	123	123	123	123
Lending Rate	Pearson Correlation	–418**	–.167	1	.242**	.310**
	Sig. (e-tailed)	.000	.065		.007	.000
	N	123	123	123	123	123
GDP Growth Rate	Pearson Correlation	–.727**	.215*	.242**	1	.424**
	Sig. (e-tailed)	.000				.000
	N	123	123	123	123	123
Current Account	Pearson Correlation	–.416**	–.320**	.310**	.424**	1
	Sig. (e-tailed)	.000	.000	.000	.000	
	N	123	123	123	123	123

** Correlation is significant at the 0.01 level (2-tailed).

* Correlation is significant at the 0.05 level (2-tailed).

Table 2 shows that in statistical terms there is a moderate inverse correlation between lending rate and exchange rate, that is, – 0.418; and also between current account position and exchange rate of the Indian rupee, that is, −0.416. It also establishes that in statistical terms there is an inverse strong correlation between GDP growth rate and exchange rate of the Indian Rupee, that is, 0.727. This, thus, signifies that an increase in interest rates and lending rates in the Indian economy would result in an increase in capital inflows from other countries due to higher returns in India. Investment decisions by investors are primarily based on 'level of risk' and 'level of return'. On an increased expectation of higher returns in a country, foreign investors are attracted to invest and partake higher returns, resulting in an increased capital inflow. Therefore, there would be an increase in the inflow or supply of Dollars relative to the demand for Dollars or other international currency into the country, resulting in an increase in the demand for Indian Rupee, thereby leading to an appreciation of the exchange rate.

The inverse correlation established in statistical terms between current account position and exchange rate signifies that in case of increasing current account surplus the demand for Indian exports is higher than the demand for imports into India. This would result in increase of payment to exporters, that is, an increased inflow of Dollars or increase in supply of Dollars into the country, that is, India, leading to an increase in demand for the Indian Rupee, thereby appreciating the value of the Indian Rupee. The strong correlation between GDP growth rate and exchange rate of the Indian Rupee portrays the fact that an increase in GDP growth rate signifies strong fundamentals of the economy leading to foreign investors wanting and keen to invest in the country and be a part of the Indian growth story. This would consequently result in an increase in supply of Dollar, leading to an increase in demand for the Indian Rupee, thus, resulting in an appreciation on the exchange rate in terms of Indian Rupee.

Regression Analysis

Table 3: Model Summary*

Model	*R*	*R Square*	*Adjusted R Square*	*Std. Error of the Estimate*
1	0.774**	0.598	0.585	3.61180

* Dependent Variable: Exchange Rate.

** Predictors: (Constant), Current account, Lending rate, Inflation, GDP growth rate.

Regression analysis helps us understand how the typical value of the dependent variable changes when any one of the independent variables is varied, while the other independent variables are held fixed. Taking the following independent variables as fixed, that is, current account, lending rate, inflation, and GDP growth rate, the impact of these variables on the dependent variable, that is, exchange rate was analysed. The value of R^2 in the regression analysis was 0.598 which shows that 59.8 per cent of the variation can be explained by changes in the current account, lending rate, inflation and GDP growth rate.

Table 4: Coefficients[a]

Model		*Unstandardized Coefficients*		*Standardized Coefficients*	*t*	*Sig.*	*95% Confidence Interval for B*		*Correlations*		
		B	*Std. Error*	*Beta*			*Lower Bound*	*Upper Bound*	*Zero-order*	*Partial*	*Part*
1	(Constant)	70.727	3.256		21.722	.000	64.281	77.176			
	Inflation	.140	.142	.067	.985	.327	–.141	.421	–.025	.090	.057
	Lending Rate	–.986	.264	–.233	–3.731	.000	–1.510	–.463	–.418	–.325	–.218
	GDP Growth Rate	–1.772	.190	–.668	–9.328	.000	–2.148	–1.396	–.727	–.651	–.544
	Current Account	–.025	.046	–.039	–.535	.594	–.117	.067	–.416	–.049	–.031

[a] Dependent Variable: Exchange Rate.

The equation derived from regression analysis is: Exchange Rate = 70.728 – 0.986; Lending Rate – 1.772; GDP Growth Rate.

This shows that on a change of 1 per cent in the lending rate the exchange rate gets impacted to an extent of 0.986 and on a change of 1 per cent in the GDP growth rate, the exchange rate gets impacted to an extent of 1.772, that is, an increase of 1 per cent in the lending rate leads to an appreciation of the Indian Rupee to an extent of 0.986, and an increase of 1 per cent in the GDP growth rate leads to an appreciation of the Rupee exchange rate to an extent of 1.772. The minus sign portrays the existence of an inverse relationship in statistical terms between exchange rate and inflation, exchange rate and lending rates.

Thus, based on monthly secondary data from January 2004 to April 2014 it was seen that Hypothesis 1 has been largely reflected and a correlation between GDP growth rate, current account position and lending rate with the exchange rate has been established, whilst no correlation of the exchange rate has been established with inflation. In terms of the data taken, Hypothesis 2 has been accepted. Hypothesis 3 has been accepted and it was seen that interest rates or lending rate in statistical terms has a negative correlation with the Indian Rupee, that is, a higher interest rate will lead to an appreciation of the home currency. Hypothesis 4 is accepted. Current account, in statistical terms, has a negative correlation with the Indian Rupee as against international currencies, that is, a current account surplus will lead to an appreciation of the Indian currency. Hypothesis 5 has been accepted. The GDP growth rate in statistical terms has a negative correlation with the Indian Rupee, that is, a higher growth rate will lead to an appreciation of the Indian currency. It was also seen that in terms of regression, GDP growth rate has the highest impact on the exchange rate followed by the lending rate or interest rates in the economy, whilst the current account position does not impact the exchange rate to such a large extent. This could be due to the fact that the Government of any country tries to neutralize the current account position by the Capital account.

CONCLUSION

Based on our analysis of the monthly data from January 2004 to April 2014, it can be concluded that macroeconomic variables, such as GDP growth rate, current account position and lending rate or interest rate have proved to be an influencing factor as far as the Rupee exchange rate is concerned. The could be various reasons, such as with the fundamentals of the Indian economy becoming stronger post liberalization due to opening up of the economy, increased investment in infrastructure industry, rising disposable income, increasing working age population, increase in exports of goods and services, etc., that led to an increased inflow of Dollars into the country, and resulting in an appreciation of the Indian Rupee especially between 2004–07. It was only post 2008, when the financial crisis hit the rest of the world and also resulted in an economic slowdown for India, that there was an outflow of Dollars, especially the money earlier brought in by foreign institutional investors, negative impact on Indian exports, that is gems and jewellery industry, apparels, etc., which led to a depreciation of the Indian Rupee. With the domestic outlook becoming negative, the Indian Rupee depreciated. Also, the policy paralysis in the country in the past couple of years negatively influenced and discouraged investors, further exaggerating the depreciation pressures on the exchange rate. In the present scenario, with the developed economies expecting to recover and thereby increase interest rates leading to higher return, the Rupee is expected to remain highly volatile.

REFERENCES

A. Harberger, 'Economic Adjustment and the Real Exchange Rate', in S. Edwards and L. Ahamed, eds., *Economic Adjustment Exchange Rates in Developing Countries*, University of Chicago Press, vol.10, 2004, pp. 308–21.

A.M. Husain, A. Mody, and K.S. Rogoff, 'Exchange Rate Regime Durability and Performance in Developing Versus Advanced Economies', *Journal of Monetary Economics*, vol. 52, no. 1, 2004, pp. 35–64.

Anita Mirchandani, 'Analysis of Macroeconomic Determinants of Exchange Rate Volatility In India', *International Journal of Economics and Financial Issues*, vol. 3, no. 1, 2013, pp. 172–79.

C.J. Carcia and J.E. Restrepo, 'Price Inflation and Exchange Rate Pass-Through in Chile', Working Paper 128, November 2001.

Eswar S. Prasad, Raghuram G. Rajan, and Arvind Subramanian, 'Foreign capital and Foreign Capital and Economic Growth, IZA Discussion Paper No. 3186, November 2007.

H. Hau, 'Real Exchange Rate Volatility and Economic Openness: Theory and Evidence', *Journal of Money, Credit and Banking*, vol. 34, no. 3, 2002, pp. 611–30.

http://www.indiastat.com/economy/8/indices/132/inflation/32561/stats.aspx

http://www.rbi.org.in/scripts/PublicationsView.aspx?id=12252#EXC, July 2014

http://www.rbi.org.in/scripts/referenceratearchive.aspx

http://www.tradingeconomics.com/india/bank-lending-rate

http://www.tradingeconomics.com/india/currency

http://www.tradingeconomics.com/india/current-account

http://www.tradingeconomics.com/india/foreign-direct-investment

http://www.tradingeconomics.com/india/gdp-growth

I. Drine and R. Christopher, 'Learning About the Long-run Determinants of Real Exchange Rates for Developing Countries: A Panel Data Investigation', Volume 274, Panel Data Econometrics Theoretical Contributions and Empirical Applications, Emerald Publishing.

L. Taylor, 'Argentina: A Poster Child for Failure of Liberalised Policies?', Challenge, November–December, vol. 44, no. 6, 2001, pp. 28–44.

N.R. Khattak, M. Tariq, and J. Khan, 'Factors Affecting the Nominal Exchange Rate of Pakistan: An Econometric Investigation (1982–2008)', *Asian Economic and Financial Review*, vol. 2, no. 2, 2012, pp. 421–28.

P. Due and P. Sen, 'Capital Flow Volatility and Exchange Rates: The Case of India', Working Paper no. 144, Central for Development Economics, Department of Economics, Delhi School of Economics, 2006.

P.J. Patel, N.J. Patel, and A.R. Patel, 'Factors Affecting Currency Exchange Rate, Economical Formulas and Prediction Models', *International Journal of*

Application or Innovation in Engineering and Management, www.ijaiem.org, vol. 3, Issue 3, 2014.

Paulo Gala, 'Real Exchange Rate Levels and Economic Development: Theoretical Analysis and Econometric Evidence', *Cambridge Journal of Economics*, vol. 32, no. 2, 2008, p. 273.

Qaisar Farooq Akram, 'PPP Despite Real Shocks: An Empirical Analysis of the Norwegian Exchange Rate', Working Paper 2000/7, Norges Bank, 2000.

Roberto Hausmann, Lant Pritchett, and Dani Rodrik, 'Growth Accelerations', *Journal of Economic Growth*, vol. 10, no. 4, 2005, pp. 303–29.

S. Edwards, 'Exchange Rate Regimes, Capital Inflows and Crisis Prevention', Working Paper, NBER and University of California, 2001. 8529.

T. Bernhardsen and O. Roisland, Norges Bank, *Economic Bulletin*, 71, 4, 2000, p. 143.

W.L.S. Simon, 'Is There Life Outside the ERM? An Evaluation of the Effects of Sterling's Devaluation on the UK Economy', *International Journal of Finance and Economics*, vol. 2, 1997, pp.199–216.

Z. Xiaopu, 'Equilibrium and Misalignment: An Assessment of the RMB Exchange Rate from 1978 to 1999', Center for Research on Economic Development and Policy Reform Working Paper, no. 127, 2002.

Impact of Global Capital Flows on Indian Real Estate and Stock Market

Taral Pathak

Post Graduate Institute of Management, Ahmedabad University, Gujarat
e-mail: taralspathak@yahoo.com, taral.pathak@ahduni.edu.in

ABSTRACT

The last two decades have witnessed unprecedented amount of international capital flows into emerging economies with an altering trend from official capital flows to private flows, leading to a shift in the nature of the capital flows from long-term to short-term. Concomitant with these trends is the increasing incidence of financial crisis and its contagion effect.

The present paper examines the impact of Foreign Institutional Investment (FII) on the variations in the BSE Index, its volume, return, and market capitalization. It also looks into the variations caused in the housing prices [as measured by Consumer Price Index (CPI) of the housing sector and bank credit due to Foreign Direct Investment (FDI) flows].

Monthly data from January 2004 to December 2013 is subjected to a Granger-causality approach to investigate the causality between Foreign Institutional Investment (FII) flow, FDI flow and other macroeconomic variables like Foreign exchange reserves, Money supply, and Foreign exchange rates. The Augmented Dickey Fuller (ADF) test has been used to test the stationary nature of data and Johansen's Co-integration Test is used for validating the association of various macroeconomic variables.

The results indicate that housing price index granger causes FDI flow in India, while the reverse is not true, though FDI and FII when combined do have a lagged impact on the housing sector.

Conversely the FII flows do not granger cause the BSE returns. Neither does the BSE return cause FII flows to India. There is no causality observed between FII flows and the BSE market capitalization, although FDI and FII taken together granger cause the foreign exchange rate and a unidirectional causality from Foreign exchange reserves to FDI and FII flows is noted. It is also observed that money supply, as measured by M3, granger causes FDI and FII flows to India, while the reverse causality is not seen, that is, FDI and FII flows do not granger cause money supply.

Keywords: Foreign Direct Investment (FDI), Foreign Institutional Investments (FII's), Indian Stock Market, Indian Real Estate Market, Granger Causality

INTRODUCTION

India opened its door to the rest of the world in 1991. It had a closed capital account before 1991 and during this era it witnessed restrictions on capital mobility. Foreign Direct Investment (FDI) was the first to be liberalized, followed by portfolio flows. The process of liberalization, which started in 1991, actually involved removal of distortions in the economy caused by government intervention, tax reforms, setting up of disinvestment ministry, de-licensing of various industries, and relaxing the Monopolies and Restrictive Trade Practices (MRTP) Act. These reforms gave greater operational flexibility to the industry and were ably accompanied by reforms in the financial sector and capital markets. Researchers have since a long time spent considerable time and energy in researching about the impact of the reforms in the financial sector and capital markets on the performance of the industry and the economy as a whole. Allowing international capital flows into the Indian economy is perceived as a turning point in the Indian economy landscape.

History has also shown that the global factors affecting foreign investment tend to have an important cyclical component, which has given rise to repeated booms and busts in capital inflows. The surge in portfolio flows to the Asian and Latin American countries was accompanied by sharp increases in stock and real estate prices (Guillermo et al., 1996)

It's been two decades since India has witnessed international capital flows. Initially, the domestic growth rates, sound economic policies, and perception towards India's economy were touted as the reasons behind attracting international capital flows. As Tewari and Pathak (2013) say 'the mass media coverage about India in the foreign media has positively impacted the Foreign Institutional Investments (FIIs) about India as a destination. The positive coverage about India in foreign media and a lagged rise in FII investment is a clear indication of the *information effect.'*

However, it was soon clear that excess liquidity around the world was also a major reason for the influx of foreign capital and not just the domestic factors. It is therefore thought important to study the desirability of the inflow of international capital flows.

THEORETICAL FOUNDATION AND REVIEW OF LITERATURE

Literature indicates ample instances which illustrate the negative, as well as positive impact of Global capital flows to emerging countries. An influx of capital increases the liquidity and thereby increases consumption, leading to increase in domestic growth rates. Foreign Direct Investment has also resulted into technology transfer resulting into more efficient operations for the domestic sector. On the other hand, inflows have resulted into widening of the current account deficit, volatility in exchange rates, and increase in inflation of financial, as well as non-financial assets. Some of the key relationships that literature outlines have been discussed below and these are conditional to the manner in which the cash flows are modelled by the Central Bank of a country.

Foreign Exchange Reserves

According to Kohli (2000 a,b), 'the Reserve Bank of India has typically absorbed fifty percent of the net capital inflows as foreign exchange reserves. The rate of growth of foreign exchange reserves in India averaged 25.2 percent during 1991 and 2000 as against a negative average of 7.06 percent for 1985-90'. A similar pattern was observed during 1990 to 1994 when the portion of the flows going to reserves was 59 per cent in Asia and 35 per cent in Latin America (Guillermo et al., 1996). This goes to show that most Central Banks have initially taken an approach to safeguard their economies by allowing the building up of foreign exchange reserves.

Current Account Deficit

An increase in foreign exchange reserves balance is accompanied by a decline in the current account deficit. The pace of reserve accumulation has definitely slowed down during the more recent periods. The widening of the current account deficit basically involved the reduction in national savings and an increase in private consumption. The difference between the two is nothing else but current account deficit. Kohli (2003) observed the reduction in India's current account deficit in the late 1990s and early 2000.

National Savings and Private Consumption

Most economies have witnessed a consumption boom with a fall in the national savings. Depending upon the policies adopted by the Central Bank of each country and the resultant foreign exchange rate, the consumption could be accompanied by rising imports and/or complemented by an increase in domestic growth rates. Most emerging economies have had an impressive rate of growth to showcase.

Money Supply

Kamin and Wood (1998) examined that countries experienced growth in money supply, both in real and nominal terms. The growth in money supply may have a possible inflationary impact on various assets through the transmission mechanism, stocks and real estate in particular. There have been several instances where the Reserve Bank of India (RBI) has overshot its target of money supply. However, during such times policy action in the form of reserve requirements has often worked. It is evident that increased reserve requirements have managed to control the flow of credit into specific sectors and in totality. Calvo et al. (1994) argues that allowing the real exchange rate to appreciate would allow no expansion in the monetary base. Alternatively, banks can carry out 'sterilized intervention.' This involves purchasing foreign exchange by the Central Bank, accompanied by issue of Government bonds to suck out excess liquidity from the market. However, the only issue with this policy in the long-term is that it results in accumulation of debt by the Government which involves an interest burden in the immediate future and unsustainable levels of debt in the long-term.

Real Exchange Rate

Under a fixed exchange rate system money market equilibrium is achieved by an increase in the accumulated reserve balance as accompanied by an increase in money supply. However, under a flexible exchange rate regime the Central Bank has the leverage to allow the exchange rate to appreciate and thus take away the possible inflationary impact. Typically, Central Banks across the world have the incongruous dual objectives of controlling inflation and ensuring foreign exchange rate stability.

Output and Growth

As per Singh and Weisse (1998) the World Institute for Development Economics Research (WIDER) had argued for developing countries to change their internal financial market regulations to attract foreign equity flows so that it could boost the output and growth in the developing economies. India opened up its economy post the Balance of Payment (BOP) crisis in 1991 with a similar objective. Sethi and Patnaik (2007) examined the impact of Global capital flows on India's growth using monthly data from April 1995 to July 2005. They conclude that FDI positively affects the economic growth, while FII negatively affects economic growth in India.

Stock and Real Estate Prices

A lot of literature is available which considers the impact of FII flows on the stock market prices, returns, volatility, and its performance. Bekaert and Harvey (1998) and Errunza (2001) have found evidences that FII flows do not have a significant effect in increasing the volatility of stock returns. However, Jo (2002) suggested that stock market volatility did increase in the presence of FII flows.

Equity market returns were found to have a significant impact on FII investments, and a significant positive correlation was also reported by Singh et al. (2014), Chandra (2012), Bohn and Tesar (1996), and Brennan and Cao (1997)

Some authors have reported that lagged stock market returns have a greater impact on the FII investment flows. Many researchers did not find causation from FII to stock market returns (Rai and Bhanumurthy, 2003), but in some cases researchers have found bi-directional causality between FII and the stock market (Chandra, 2012; Goudarzi and Ramanarayanan, 2010).

Therefore, there is considerable contradiction in the findings related to the impact of FII on the Indian stock market and it definitely requires to be researched upon.

Comparatively the available research on the Indian housing sector is not as abundant. Mallick and Mahalik (2010) used cointegration tests and the Vector Error Correction Model to study the causal relationship between house price and its five determinants—real income, short-run real interest rates, real stock price index, real effective exchange rate, and real non-food bank credit. They observed that 'with faster rise in growth of income, the emerging economies are witnessing structural changes with regard to their pattern of consumption and investments. There is an increasing demand for housing as an asset for future returns and an asset to live. This is backed up by increasing speculations by the foreign investors in the housing market of emerging economies depending on the degree of their entry restrictions in different markets.' The study of the housing market would differ from one economy to another because of the complexities involved in operations of the industry and the financing patterns used by the housing sector and the consumer involved. The empirical research on housing market in India is scarce due to the paucity of information. However, international literature is quick to point out housing loan rate (Apergis and Rzitis, 2004) and real income (Abelson et al., 2005) as the most important and significant factors that explain the changes in housing prices. India's case is different since country-wide rent figures that can be measured easily are not available. Usually an increase in housing price is accompanied by an increase in rent levels as well. Therefore, the ratio of housing price to rentals remains constant even after an increase in housing prices. However, this is true for an economy where majority of the demand for housing is fuelled by genuine customers willing to occupy premises. In India, the market for owner occupied housing and investor category housing cannot be easily segregated. As a result it is difficult to study whether increase in housing prices are backed by an increase in income levels (fuelled by domestic savings, a phenomenon usually seen in owner occupied housing) or it is simply because of foreign savings that flow into the country (a phenomenon usually seen in the investor category housing). Jud and Winkler (2002) observed that 'stock market appreciation imparts a strong current and lagged wealth effect on growth of housing prices.' There is, therefore, a strong case to study the impact of FDI inflows on the housing sector. Since the stock markets exhibit a transmission through the wealth channel, it makes sense to look into the impact of FII flows, as well on to the housing sector. The combined impact of FDI and FII flows could have a stronger relationship with the housing prices in India.

The Government of India took the bold step of liberalizing the housing sector in 2005. The Government decided to allow FDI upto 100 per cent under the automatic route in townships, housing, built up infrastructure, and construction development projects, which include commercial premises, hotels, hospitals, recreational facilities, and regional level infrastructures.

Given the above relationships, the present paper studies the housing price behaviour in India within a partial macroeconomic framework.

RESEARCH METHODOLOGY

To examine the impact of international capital flows on various macroeconomic variables, as well as stock market and the housing market pair-wise, the Granger causality test (1969) is used. However, the non-stationary nature of most time-series data and the need to avoid spurious regressions necessitates the use of a unit root test. A unit root test for each of the variables in the model is conducted. Augmented Dickey Fuller (ADF, 1979) is the most popular test for stationary.

Secondly, a Cointegration test using the Johansen Method is taken up. This detects the presence of the long-run equilibrium relationship between two or more variables in a single equation system. This multiple Cointegration test can be very sensitive to the lag length used in the test; so, the Akaike Information Criteria (AIC) is used, as Ivanov and Kilian (2001) suggest that with monthly data, AIC tends to be more accurate, especially in the context of Vector autoregression (VAR) models.

RESEARCH OBJECTIVE AND DATA SOURCE

The research objectives for the study were as follows:

1. To study the impact of international capital flows on the stock market.
2. To study the impact of international capital flows on the housing market.
3. To study the impact of international capital flows on select macro-economic variables.

Monthly data from January 2004 up to December 2013 was collected from the *Handbook of Statistics on Indian Economy*, RBI, and the Indiastat website. The data on 11 variables was collected – total bank credit (BKCR), FII flows (FII), FDI flows (FDI), combined FDI and FII flows (FDINFII), housing price index out of the Consumer Price Index (CPI) (HCPI), foreign exchange reserves balance (FXRES), monthly average foreign exchange rates (FXRATE), money supply (M3), BSE monthly return (BSERET), BSE monthly turnover (BSETOVER), and BSE monthly market capitalisation (BSEMKTCAP).

Since the data on housing price index underwent a change in its base year, therefore the series was re-cast using the adjustment factor recommended by RBI. All the data was converted in natural logarithms with the exception of FII inflows, FDI inflows, and BSE monthly return.

EMPIRICAL RESULTS AND ANALYSIS

Unit Root test is run for each variable at level, as well as at first difference of non-stationary variables. The results of the test are outlined in Table 1 which clearly shows that all the variables – BSE return, FDI, FII and combined FDI and FII inflows are stationary at their level. However, the other non-stationary variables were found to be stationary at their first differences and therefore are integrated as order one.

Table 1: Unit Root Test-Augmented Dickey Fuller Test Results

Variable	*ADF Test Statistic*	*Critical Value at 5%*	*Probability*	*Order of Integration*
FDI	−5.504990	−3.486064	0.0000	I (0)
FII	−7.284138	−3.486064	0.0000	I (0)
FDI & FII	−11.19859	−3.486064	0.0000	I (0)
BSERET	−9.884033	−2.885863	0.0000	I (0)
LBKCR	−12.06152	−2.886074	0.0000	I (1)
LBSEMKTCAP	−9.613900	−2.886074	0.0000	I (1)
LBSETOVER	−12.55021	−2.886074	0.0000	I (1)
LFXRES	−7.203692	−2.886074	0.0000	I (1)
LFXRATE	−7.632283	−2.886074	0.0000	I (1)
LHCPI	−11.10413	−2.886074	0.0000	I (1)
Lm3	−11.22446	−2.886074	0.0000	I (1)

Since the above variables are found to be integrated of the first order, a linear combination between them is checked to ensure that they are stationary. A possibility of co-integration amongst these variables is checked and the test for co-integration is applied to check for long-run equilibrium relationship between any pair of variables. The Johansen's Cointegration test is applied on the above 11 variables which are stationary and the results are

Table 2: Unrestricted Cointegration Rank Test (Trace)

Hypothesized No. of CE(s)	*Trace Statistic*	*5% Critical Value*	*Probability***
None*	440.9413	285.1425	0.0000
At most 1*	334.7107	239.2354	0.0000
At most 2*	263.2164	197.3709	0.0000
At most 3*	205.0738	159.5297	0.0000
At most 4*	163.0941	125.6154	0.0000
At most 5*	124.4003	95.75366	0.0001
At most 6*	88.83296	69.81889	0.0007
At most 7*	58.86574	47.85613	0.0033
At most 8*	36.79715	29.79707	0.0066
At most 9*	20.26253	15.49471	0.0088
At most 10*	7.580211	3.841466	0.0059

Trace test indicates 11 cointegrating eqn(s) at the 0.05 level.
* denotes rejection of the hypothesis at the 0.05 level; **MacKinnon-Haug-Michelis (1999) p-values.

summarized in Table 2 and Table 3. It can be seen that the trace statistic value is greater than the critical value and the probability value is less than 5 per cent in most cases. The results indicate that there are 11 cointegrating equations.

Table 3: Unrestricted Cointegration Rank Test (Maximum Eigenvalue)

Hypothesized No. of CE(s)	*Max-Eigen Statistic*	*5% Critical Value*	*Probability***
None*	106.2306	70.53513	0.0000
At most 1*	71.49426	64.50472	0.0094
At most 2*	58.14261	58.43354	0.0534
At most 3*	41.97967	52.36261	0.3789
At most 4*	38.69389	46.23142	0.2546
At most 5*	35.56730	40.07757	0.1478
At most 6*	29.96721	33.87687	0.1366
At most 7*	22.06859	27.58434	0.2169
At most 8*	16.53462	21.13162	0.1951
At most 9*	12.68232	14.26460	0.0876
At most 10*	7.580211	3.841466	0.0059

Max-eigenvalue test indicates 2 cointegrating eqn(s) at the 0.05 level.

Pair-wise Granger Causality Tests

As per the literature in econometrics, one variable is said to Granger cause another if it helps to make a more accurate prediction of another than had only the lagged variable of the latter was used as the predictor. Granger causality shows that one variable can help predict the other variable better and not necessarily an actual causal relationship. Given two time series X_t and Y_t, X_t is said to have granger caused Y_t if Y_t can be better predicted using the histories of both X_t and Y_t than it can be done by history of Y_t alone. This relationship can be formulated in an equation form as under:

$$Y_t = \sum_{i=t}^{n} \alpha_i X_{t-i} + \sum_{j=i}^{n} \beta_j X_{t-j} + u_{1t} \qquad ...(1)$$

$$X_t = \sum_{i=t}^{n} \lambda_i X_{t-i} + \sum_{j=i}^{n} \delta_j Y_{t-j} + u_{2t} \qquad ...(2)$$

In the above equations are parameters. The absence of Granger causality is tested by estimating the above VAR model.

Testing H_0: $\alpha_1 = \alpha_2 = ... \alpha_i = 0$

against

$H_1 = \text{Not } H_0$

is a test that X_t does not Granger cause Y_t. In each case rejection of the null hypothesis implies that there is Granger causality between variables. In testing for Granger causality it is possible to arrive at any one of the following four results:

1. Unidirectional Granger causality from variable X_t to Y_t;
2. Unidirectional Granger causality from variable Y_t to X_t;
3. Bi-directional causality; or
4. No causality.

The analysis of the results is segregated into three sections, that is, assessing the impact on the stock markets, housing markets, and other macro-economic indicators.

Assessing the Impact on the Stock Markets

The following variables were considered:

(a) Foreign Institutional Investment flows – FII flows
(b) BSE return – BSERET
(c) BSE market capitalization – BSEMKTCAP
(d) BSE turnover – BSETOVER

The results are summarized in Table 4.

Table 4: Results of Pairwise Granger Causality Tests – Stock Markets

Null Hypothesis: No Causality	*Observations*	*Lags*	*F-statistic*	*Probability*	*Decision*	*Type of Causality*
FII – BSERET	118	2	0.16291	0.84987	Accept Null	None
BSERET- FII			0.16932	0.84445	Accept Null	None
LBSEMKTCAP-FII	118	2	0.36065	0.69802	Accept Null	None
FII-LBSEMKTCAP			0.08124	0.92203	Accept Null	None
LBSETOVER-FII	118	2	0.82747	0.43978	Accept Null	None
FII-LBSETOVER			4.62525	0.01173	Reject Null	Unidirectional

The above table indicates that FII flows do not granger cause the BSE returns. Neither does the BSE return cause FII flows to India. There is no causality observed between FII flows and the BSE market capitalization. However, the null hypothesis is accepted in case of the FII-BSE turnover relationship. FII flows do granger cause the BSE turnover. This is consistent, considering the huge quantum of cash flows that the FII's trade in. However, higher volumes of trade have not resulted into return generation for the BSE sensex.

Assessing the Impact on the Housing Markets

The following variables were considered:

(a) Housing Index, which is a part of the CPI for Industrial workers (HCPI), is considered as a proxy for measuring the housing prices all over India. Data for the same is collected from the RBI web site. According to the Labour Bureau, Ministry of Labour, GOI, the weightage of housing price in the overall basket of CPI for industrial workers is 22.53 per cent. Housing thus plays a critical role in determining the CPI number.

(b) Total bank credit (BKCR) is taken as a variable which measures the liquidity in the banking sector.

(c) Foreign Direct Investment flow is used as the exogenous variable. The combined impact of FDI and FII (FDINFII) is also considered to measure the impact on the housing sector.

(d) The return on the BSE sensex (BSERET) is considered as an important variable which affects the housing prices since there are investors who consider the stock market and housing market as complimentary products for investment.

The results of the test are summarized in Table 5.

Table 5: Results of Pairwise Granger Causality Tests – Housing Market

Null Hypothesis: No Causality	*Observations*	*Lags*	*F-statistic*	*Probability*	*Decision*	*Type of Causality*
LHCPI- LFDI	116	4	2.69818	0.03453	Reject Null	Unidirectional
LFDI-LHCPI			0.75471	0.55705	Accept Null	None
LBKCR-LFDI	118	2	4.06207	0.01979	Reject Null	Unidirectional
LFDI- LBKCR			0.16388	0.84904	Accept Null	None
LHCPI- LFDINFII	26	8	0.83444	0.59540	Accept Null	None
LFDINFII-LHCPI			4.28393	0.02189	Reject Null	Unidirectional
LBKCR- LFDINFII	87	1	8.55653	0.00443	Reject Null	Unidirectional
LFDINFII-LBKCR			0.52384	0.47122	Accept Null	None
LHCPI-LBSERET	17	3	0.48568	0.69975	Accept Null	None
LBSERET-LHCPI			5.45231	0.01759	Reject Null	Unidirectional

The above table indicates that the housing price index granger causes FDI flows to India. However, the reverse is not true, that is, FDI flows do not granger cause the housing price index. It is interesting to note that when the combined flows, that is, FDI and FII are considered, then there is causality towards housing price index. This does go on to imply that there could be an inflationary effect in the housing sector because of FDI and FII inflows taken together. However, there is a lagged effect and not an immediate one. These are results which are supported by literature. Guillermo et al. (1996) clearly underline a similar effect on housing/real estate sector. There is unidirectional movement from Bank credit to housing price Index, which clearly underlines the liquidity impact. Economic literature confirms that the availability of ample capital will push up asset prices, which is true for housing prices as reflected by the housing index. Bank credit granger causes FDI flows and it also granger causes FDI and FII flows when considered together. Interestingly, the BSERET granger causes the housing index. This shows that when the stock markets are doing good and delivering impressive returns, then it reflects in higher housing prices or at least there is a causal relationship. There is a bit of a lag involved in this causality which is understandable, since shifting between asset classes is not an easy decision.

Assessing the Impact on Other Macroeconomic Variables

The following variables were considered:

(a) Foreign exchange reserves (FXRES)

(b) Foreign exchange rate (FXRATE) used is the average foreign exchange rate for the month. Average FXRATE for the month is calculated by considering the daily foreign exchange closing rates as reported by RBI.

(c) Money supply (M3) includes time deposits and narrow money.

The results of the test are summarized in Table 6.

Table 6: Results of Pairwise Granger Causality Tests – Select Macro-economic Variables

Null Hypothesis: No Causality	*Observations*	*Lags*	*F-statistic*	*Probability*	*Decision*	*Type of Causality*
LFDINFII- LFXRATE	60	3	2.81886	0.04772	Reject Null	Unidirectional
LFXRATE-LFDINFII			0.90178	0.44652	Accept Null	None
LFXRES-LFDINFII	73	2	4.99438	0.00947	Reject Null	Unidirecional
LFDINFII- LFXRES			0.28652	0.75178	Accept Null	None
LM3-LFDINFII	73	2	4.42285	0.01564	Reject Null	Unidirectional
LFDINFII-LM3			0.17214	0.84222	Accept Null	None

The results as per the above table indicate that FDI and FII, taken together, granger cause the foreign exchange rate. As per literature, this is possible in case of a flexible exchange rate regime if the Central Bank of the country choses to do so. In case of India, it should be noted that the exchange rate had recently depreciated considerably because of the slowing down of foreign capital flows during the post-2008 subprime crisis phase. It was also the case during the pre-election period in 2014, when the inability of the Government to push certain key reforms had resulted into reversal of foreign capital flows. The second pair-wise test indicates unidirectional causality from foreign exchange reserves to FDI and FII flows. This clearly indicates a country's ability to attract foreign capital based on a robust reserve base. A higher reserve balance provides foreign investors with the confidence and the comfort that the Government will be able to meet import bills while maintaining the exchange rate favourably during times of reversal of international cash flows. Money supply as measured by M3 granger causes FDI and FII flows to India. The reverse causality is not seen, that is, FDI and FII flows do not granger cause money supply. This means that the Government has been particularly careful in not allowing the foreign capital flows to affect the domestic liquidity. It has instead allowed the exchange rate to appreciate which is visible in the earlier result. This may also indicate that the RBI has resorted to sterilized intervention in the market. However, one needs to look into the public debt amount carefully before confirming this.

PRACTICAL SIGNIFICANCE

The overall aim of the paper is to investigate the impact of foreign capital flows on the Indian stock market, housing market, and select macro-economic variables. The results derived for the stock markets are useful for investors who consider that the returns of the market are closely associated with the FII investment activity. The results prove that this is not the case.

The housing market findings are important for policy makers since the impact of FII and FDI flows on the housing index is clearly visible. Further research is possible in this area to check if this causes excess variability in the housing market. A variance decomposition approach can be taken up to understand the factors responsible for the variations in the housing index. Capital flows may turn out to be an important factor in that case too.

The impact on select macro-economic variables is useful from the point of an academician since the findings fall in line with the standard open economy models that suggest that a surge in capital inflows is likely to be accompanied by a rise in consumption and investment, an increase in money balances and foreign exchange reserves, appreciation in exchange rate, and widening of the current account deficit. The findings from the current study can be used to establish the usefulness of economic models.

CONCLUSION

The results indicate that housing price index granger causes FDI flow in India, while the reverse is not true, though FDI and FII, when combined, do have a lagged impact the housing sector. Conversely, the FII flows do not granger cause the BSE returns. Neither does the BSE return cause FII flows to India. There is no causality observed between FII flows and the BSE market capitalization, although FDI and FII taken together granger cause the foreign exchange rate and a unidirectional causality from foreign exchange reserves to FDI and FII flows is noted. Added, Money supply, as measured by M3, granger causes FDI and FII flows to India, while the reverse causality is not seen, that is, FDI and FII flows do not granger cause money supply.

REFERENCES

A. Chandra, 'Cause and Effect between FII Trading Behavior and Stock Market returns,' *Journal of Indian Business Research,* vol. 4, no. 4, 2012, pp. 286-300.

A. Guillermo, L. Leiderman and C. Reinhart, 'Inflows of Capital to Developing Countries in the 1990s', *The Journal of Economic Perspectives*, vol. 10, no. 2, Spring, 1996, pp. 123–39.

A. Singh and B. Weisse, 'Emergiing Stock Markets, Portfolio Capital Flows and Long-term Economic Growth: Micro and Macroeconomic Perspectives', *World Development,* vol. 26, no. 4, 1998, pp. 607-22.

C. Granger, 'Investigating Causal Relationships by Econometrics Models and Cross Spectral Methods', *Econometrica*, vol. 37, 1969, pp. 425–35.

D. Dickey and W. Fuller, 'Distribution of estimators for autoregressive time series with a unit root', *Journal of American Statistical Association*, 74, 1979, pp. 427–31.

D. Jud and D. Winkler, 'The Dynamics of Metropolitan Housing Prices', *Journal of Real Estate Research,* vol. 23, no. 2, 2002.

G. Calvo, L. Leiderman and C.M. Reinhart, 'Capital Inflows to Latin America: The 1970s and 1990s', in Edmar L. Bacha (ed.), *Economics in a Changing World,* London: Macmillan, 1994, pp. 123–48.

Gab-Je Jo, 'Foreign Equity Investment in Korea', For presentation at the Association of Korean Economic Studies, Seoul, 2002.

H. Bohn and L. Tesar, 'US Equity Investment in Foreign Markets: Portfolio

Rebalancing or Return Chasing?' *American Economic Review*, vol. 86, May 1996, pp. 77–81.

H. Goudarzi and C. Ramanarayanam, 'Empirical Analysis of the Impact of Foreign Institutional Investment on the Indian Stock Market Volatility during World Financial Crisis 2008-09', *International Journal of Economics and Finance*, vol. 3, no. 3, 2010.

H. Mallick, and M. Mahalik, 'Constructing the Economy: The Role of Construction Sector In India's Growth', *Journal of Real Estate Finance and Economics*, vol. 40, no. 3, 2010, pp. 368.

J. MacKinnon, 'Critical Values for Cointegration Tests', in R.F. Engle and C.W.J. Granger, eds., *Long-Run Economic Relationships: Readings in Cointegration*, Oxford, Oxford University Press, 1991.

K. Rai and N. Bhanumurthy, 'Determinants of Foreign Institutional Investments in India: The Role of Return, Risk and Inflation', *The Developing Economies*, vol. XLII-4, 2003, pp. 479–93.

M. Brennan and H. Cao, 'International Portfolio Investment Flows', *Journal of Finance*, vol. LII, no. 5, December 1997, pp. 1851–80.

N. Apergis and A. Rezitis, 'Housing Price and Macro Economic Factors in Greece: Prospects Within the EMU', *Applied Economic Letters*, vol. 10, no. 12, 2004, pp. 561–65.

N. Sethi and U. Patnaik, 'International Capital Flows on India's Economic Growth – In View of Changing Financial Market', *The Indian Journal of Economics*, vol. 45, no. 348, 2007.

P. Abelson, R. Joyeux, G. Milunovich and D. Chung, 'House Prices in Australia: 1970 to 2003: Facts and Explanations', 2005, http://www.econ.mq.edu.au/research/2005/HousePrices.pdf). Accessed on 8th May, 2015.

R. Kohli, 'Aspects of Exchange Rate Behaviour and Management in India 1993-98', *Economic and Political Weekly*, vol. 35, no. 5, 29 January–4 February 2000.

R. Kohli, 'Capital Flows and Domestic Financial Sector in India', *Economic and Political Weekly*, February 2003.

R. Tewari and T. Pathak, 'Framing India – Pre-post Globalization', *Journal of Media Studies*, vol. 28, no. 1, December, 2013.

S. Kamin and P. Wood, 'Capital Inflows, Financial Intermediation, and Aggregate Demand: Empirical Evidence from Mexico and Other Pacific Basin Countries', in R. Glick, ed., *Managing Capital Flows and Exchange Rates: Perspectives from the Pacific Basin*, Cambridge University Press, Cambridge, 1998.

S. Singh, L. Tripathi and A. Pardesi, 'FII Flow and Indian Stock Market: A Causal Study', *Asian Journal of Research in Business Economics and Management*, vol. 4, no. 1, 2014, pp. 202-09.

T. Bekaert and R. Harvey, 'Capital Flows and the Behavior of Emerging Market Equity Returns', in Sebastian Edwards, ed., *Capital Flows and the Emerging*

Economies: Theory, Evidence, and Controversies, University of Chicago Press, Chicago, 1998, pp. 159–97.

V. Errunza, 'Foreign Portfolio Equity Investments, Financial Liberalization, and Economic Development', *Review of International Economics,* vol. 9, no. 4, 2001, pp. 703-26.

V. Ivanov and L. Kilian, 'A Practitioners Guide to Lag-order Selection for Vector Autoregressions', CEPR Discussion paper no. 2685, London, Centre for Economic Policy, 2001.

Stock Price Reactions to Cash Dividend Announcements

Evidence from Bombay Stock Exchange

Pawan Kumar Jha

School of Management, Kathmandu University, Pinchhe Tole, Sasatancha, Lalitpur, Nepal

e-mail: pawan@kusom.edu.np; pawan_jha2011@yahoo.com

ABSTRACT

This paper is an attempt to examine stock price reactions around cash dividend announcements during the sample period of 1 January 2009 to 29 June 2013. For this purpose, Event study methodology has been used to examine the significance of mean abnormal return on and around the announcement date. A sample of 44 companies from Banking, IT, Trading, Automobile, and Pharmaceutical Sectors listed at Bombay Stock Exchange (BSE) have been selected based on market capitalization, which in all had made 200 final cash dividend announcements during the sample period. The results show that most of the t-statistics of Average Abnormal Returns (AARs) and Cumulative Average Abnormal Returns (CAARs) during event window period are not close to zero, which indicates that stock price of sample companies mostly react to cash dividend announcements during the event window period. Likewise, it has been observed the similar results for selected sectors. In general, the findings strongly support the dividend signaling hypothesis in explaining the stock price reactions to an announcement of cash dividend.

Keywords: Signaling Hypothesis, Event Study, Cash Dividend Announcement, Stock Price Reaction, Cumulative Average Abnormal Return

INTRODUCTION

Dividend policy decision is an integral part of a company's financial policy since it is explicitly related to the other two major decisions-investment and financing decision. It involves the portion of a firm's net earnings which are paid out to the shareholders and remaining is ploughed back in the company for its growth. It can also be defined as the practice that corporate management follows in making dividend payout decisions (Lease, et al., 2000). The decisions regarding the amount and regularity of dividends are exclusively at the prudence of the company's board. Shareholders like mostly cash dividend since it is predictable than future gain in the form of capital gains (Brealey and Stewart, 1998). In addition to cash dividend, a company may also issue bonus shares to its existing shareholders by means of capitalization of its free reserves. Dividends convey the management's expectation of future profitability and prosperity to the shareholders (Archer and George,1985).

The issue of corporate dividends has a long history and the development of dividend payments to shareholders has been tied up with the development of the corporate firm itself (Frankfurter and Wood,1997). Since the dividend policy determines whether to distribute the earnings to shareholders or self-finance through retained earnings, so it is an important issue that receives more attention these days from financial analysts, academics, and practitioners. The crux of debate on the dividend policy is the division of net earnings between dividend and retained earnings. In a perfect capital market, dividend policy is irrelevant and is not deterministic of the market value. Therefore, investors are indifferent between dividends and capital gains (Miller and Modigliani, 1961). However, real financial markets don't seem to be perfect due to presence of market imperfections, such as taxes, asymmetric information, agency costs, and transaction costs. According to the signaling theory of dividend, dividends changes trigger stock returns as they convey new information about the firm's future profitability.

REVIEW OF LITERATURE

There is an extensive 'event study' literature that investigates the informational content of market announcements such as firm's cash dividend announcements. The theoretical literature on dividend effects has been well developed. Researchers have largely accepted that dividend per-se has no impact on the shareholder's value in a perfect economy. However, in a real financial world, the dividend announcement is important to the shareholders because of its tax effect and information content.

Pettit (1972) found that dividend announcements do convey valuable information. Unexpected changes in dividend policy are associated with stock price reactions in the same direction (1980, Aharony). A widely accepted explanation for this well-established empirical finding, which was first suggested by Miller and Modigliani (1961), emphasizes the role of information asymmetry.

Grinblatt et al. (1984) examined the announcement period effect of stock dividends and splits of more than 10 per cent at the New York Stock Exchange (NYSE) and AMEX-listed securities between 1967 and 1976. They concluded that stock dividends and splits convey information about future cash flows even in the absence of cash dividends.

Merton and Rock (1985) concluded that the earnings surprise and the net dividend surprise can convey the same information and that an unexpected increase in dividends will increase the value of the enterprise.

Healy and Palepu (1988) indicated that the information conveyed by dividend initiations and omissions are related to earnings changes following the announcement of dividend policy changes. Investors therefore, interpret dividend initiations and omissions as changes in the management's earnings forecast.

McNichols and Dravid (1990) provided evidence to support the signaling hypothesis. They reported positively significant abnormal returns on the day of stock dividend announcement.

Lonie et al. (1996) found that investors respond to the increase or decrease in dividends. However, their findings also revealed that, even for companies with no change in dividends, the average abnormal returns one day prior to the announcements were significantly different from zero as indicated by the t-statistic.

Anderson et al. (2001) reported that there is significant abnormal return around announcement period. Their sample of non contaminated announcements show significant two day returns. However, this is not significantly different when compared with the remaining contaminated announcements.

Adelegan (2003) conducted a study to analyze the reaction of stock prices to dividend announcements and capital market efficiency in Nigeria. The standard Event study methodology had been used to test the semi-strong form of market efficiency and found that the Nigerian stock market was inefficient in its semi-strong form.

Uddin and Chowhury (2005) investigated dividend announcements on the Dhaka Stock Exchange (DSE) and found that there were no statistically significant abnormal returns and that dividends had no information content for stock returns and prices in the DSE.

Akbar and Baig (2010) suggested negligible abnormal returns for cash dividend announcements. However, the average abnormal and cumulative average abnormal returns for stock and simultaneous cash and stock dividend announcements are mostly positive and statistically significant.

Mahmood et al. (2001) found that there are positive returns in the pre-event window which show the signs of insider trading, while positive returns in post-event windows are evidences of a weak form of market efficiency and also arbitrage profit opportunities. Hence, the results confirm the positive value relevance of dividend announcements.

DATA AND METHODOLOGY

This paper is an attempt to analyse the stock price reaction around cash dividend announcements using Event study methodology. For the study purpose, the event window of 41 days has been considered (= –20 days to the date of announcement, 0 to 20 days after the cash dividend announcement, +20). A total of 44 companies from the Banking, IT, Trading, Automobile, and Pharmaceutical sectors listed at the Bombay Stock Exchange (BSE) have been selected, which, in all, had made 200 final cash dividend announcements during the sample period (1 January 2009 to 29 June 2013). The secondary data of stock and index prices were collected from the official website of BSE and the sample companies. We have used the price of each stock, that is, stock returns and the BSE-500 index values, that is market returns for 120 days, 20 days prior to the announcement day (AD 120 days to AD = –20 days) to estimate the market model.

The daily Abnormal Returns (ARs) are estimated for each event window period as follows:

$$AR_{it} = e_{it} = [R_{it} - E(R_{it})] = R_{it} - (\alpha_i + \beta_i R_{mt}) \quad ...(1)$$

where, R_{it} is the actual return for company's stock i at time t; $E(R_{it})$ is the expected return on company's i stock at time t; α_i is constant term; β_i is beta coefficient, and R_{mt} is the market return.

The value of alpha, beta coefficient, and expected return are estimated on the daily data for an estimated period (clean period) of 120 trading days prior to the window period of 20 trading days prior to announcement date.

The daily Average Abnormal Returns (AARs) for cash dividend announcement in 41 days windows are estimated by taking the average of the ARs of the sample companies:

$$AAR_{it} = \frac{1}{n}\sum_{i}^{n} AR_{it} \quad ...(2)$$

where, t is – 20 to + 20 and n is the number of cash dividend announcements made by the sample companies.

Further, the Cumulative Average Abnormal Returns (CAARs) of cash dividend announcement in 41 days window are estimated by summing the AARs in the respective window.

$$CAAR = \sum_{-20}^{+20}\left(\frac{1}{n}\sum_{i}^{n} AAR_{it}\right) = AAR_{it} + CAAR_{it-1} \quad ...(3)$$

If the markets are efficient, the AARs and CAARs should be close to zero. To test whether the AAR_{it} and $CAAR_{it}$, are statistically different from zero, the Independent t-test was applied. The t-statistics for AAR_{it} and $CAAR_{it}$ for each day during the event window are calculated as:

$$t = \frac{AAR_t}{SE_{AAR_t}} \quad ...(4)$$

$$t = \frac{CAAR_t}{SE_{CAAR_t}} \quad ...(5)$$

where, SE_{AAR} and SE_{CAAR} represent the standard error of average abnormal return ($\sigma_{AAR}/\sqrt{n}$) and standard error of cumulative average abnormal return ($\sigma_{CAAR}/\sqrt{n}$).

RESULTS AND DISCUSSION

The stock price reactions around the announcements of cash dividends for the overall sample followed by sectoral analysis during events window were analysed:

Total Sample Results

Table 1 presents the results of stock price ARs and their t-statistics at the examination window (day = –20 to day +20) for the total sample with 200 cash dividend announcements. It is observed that most of the t-statistics of AARs and CAARs during the event window periods are not close to zero and statistically significant, which indicates that the stock prices of sample companies react to cash dividend announcement. However, t-statistics of AARs and CAARs on day = –6 is found insignificant (*AR = –6 = –0.01660, t = –6 = –1.35978; CAAR = –6 = –0.02496, t = –6 = –1.02955*). It indicates that there is no effect of cash dividend announcement on stock price on Day 6 before cash event day (0). Similarly, t-statistics of CAARs on days +2 and +10 are also found statistically insignificant. It shows that there is no effect of cash dividend announcement on stock price cumulatively on Day 2 and 10 after the event day (0).

Table 1: AARs, CAARs, and t-test Results for Cash Dividend Announcements (Total Sample, N = 200)

Days	*AAR (%)*	*t-value*	*CAAR (%)*	*t-value*
= –20	= –0.06885	= –5.63973*	= –0.06885	= –2.83951*
= –19	0.15998	13.10379*	0.09112	3.75802*
= –18	0.21717	17.78817*	0.30829	12.71407*
= –17	= –0.16388	= –13.42389*	0.14440	5.95537*
= –16	0.04222	3.45838*	0.18663	7.69661*
= –15	0.09525	7.80215*	0.28188	11.62486*
= –14	= –0.02991	= –2.44997**	0.25197	10.39134*
= –13	0.20007	16.38757*	0.45204	18.64221*
= –12	= –0.07716	= –6.32060*	0.37487	15.45989*
= –11	= –0.06313	= –5.17156*	0.31174	12.85609*
= –10	0.20425	16.73019*	0.51599	21.27947*
= –9	= –0.20010	= –16.39146*	0.31587	13.02664*
= –8	= –0.05423	= –4.44255*	0.26163	10.78989*
= –7	= –0.22007	= –18.02584*	0.04156	1.714179***
= –6	= –0.01660	= –1.35978	0.02496	1.02955
= –5	0.14922	12.22243*	0.17418	7.18334*
= –4	= –0.12681	= –10.38687*	0.04737	1.95372***
= –3	0.06052	4.957579*	0.10790	4.449782*
= –2	0.17287	14.15960*	0.28077	11.57890*
= –1	0.01551	1.27105	0.29628	12.21886*
0	= –0.06838	= –5.60166*	0.22789	9.39851*
1	= –0.08734	= –7.15431*	0.14055	5.79643*
2	= –0.10092	= –8.26672*	0.03962	1.63428
3	= –0.08193	= –6.71083*	= –0.04230	= –1.74451***
4	0.25804	21.1365*	0.21574	8.89738*
5	0.27467	22.4985*	0.49042	20.22503*
6	0.12256	10.03883*	0.61298	25.27942*
7	= –0.34939	= –28.6188*	0.26358	10.87029*
8	0.03171	2.59764*	0.29530	12.17816*
9	= –0.20139	= –16.49580*	0.09390	3.87280*
10	= –0.10628	= –8.70554*	= –0.01237	= –0.51029
11	= –0.24085	= –19.72820*	= –0.25322	= –10.44311*
12	0.06220	5.09509*	= –0.19102	= –7.87781*
13	0.07755	6.35251*	= –0.11346	= –4.679428*
14	= –0.12760	= –10.45227*	= –0.24107	= –9.941973*
15	0.05411	4.43229*	= –0.18696	= –7.710386*
16	0.13798	11.30194*	= –0.04898	= –2.02004**
17	= –0.02076	= –1.70111***	= –0.06975	= –2.876528*
18	= –0.04672	= –3.82724*	= –0.11647	= –4.803483*
19	= –0.39880	= –32.66600*	= –0.51528	= –21.25026*
20	= –0.30223	= –24.75553*	= –0.81752	= –33.71426*

*Significant at 0.01 level; ** significant at 0.05 level; and *** significant at 0.10 level

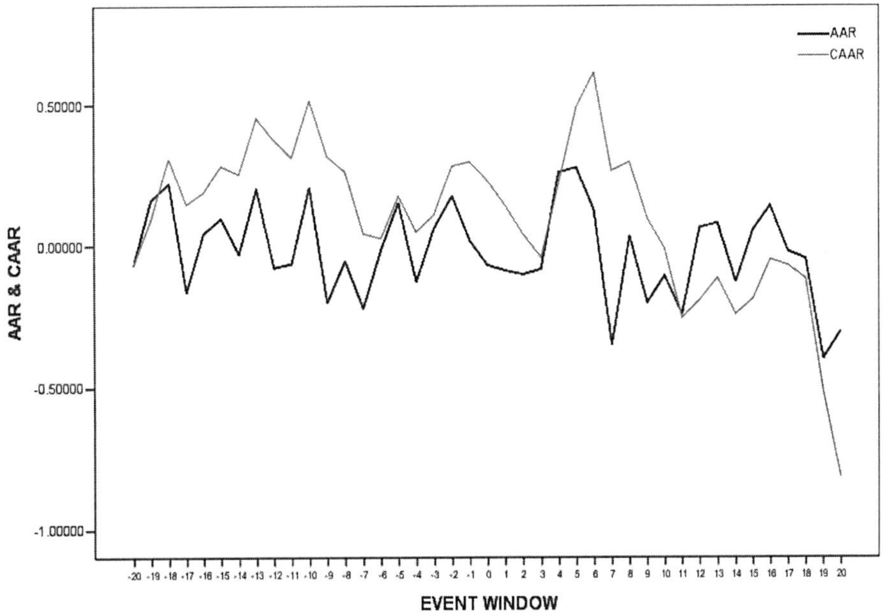

Figure 1: AAR and CAAR Graph for Cash Dividend Announcements (total sample)

Sectoral Results

Table 2 depicts the results of stock price ARs and their t-statistics at the examination window (day = –20 to day +20) for the Banking sector with 50 cash dividend announcements. It has been observed that most of the t-statistics of AARs and CAARs during the event window periods are not close to zero and statistically significant, which indicates that the cash dividend announcement affects the stock price in the Banking Sector. However, t-statistics of AARs on day = –15, = –13, = –12, 11, 13 and 17 are found insignificant. Similarly, t-statistics of CAAR on day = –19, = –18, 7, 9, 10, and 11 are also found statistically insignificant.

In Table 3 the results of stock price ARs and their t-statistic at the examination window (day = –20 to day +20) for the IT Sector with 35 cash dividend announcements has been provided. It may be observed that most of the t-statistics of AARs and CAARs during the event window periods are not close to zero and statistically significant, which indicates that there a frequent effect of cash dividend announcement on stock price in this sector. However, t-statistic of AARs on day = –17, = –15, = –5, = –3, = –1, 2, 4, 7, 10, and 17 are found insignificant. Similarly, t-statistic of CAAR on day = –19 to = –9 except = –12 day are also found statistically insignificant.

Table 2: AARs, CAARs, and t-test Results for Cash Dividend Announcements (Banking Sector, N = 50)

Days	*AAR (%)*	*t-value*	*CAAR (%)*	*t-value*
= –20	= –0.39512	= –9.55746*	= –0.39512	= –2.07167**
= –19	0.44343	10.72582*	0.04830	0.25325
= –18	0.19610	4.74343*	0.24440	1.28144
= –17	0.09936	2.40336**	0.34376	1.80239***
= –16	0.07440	1.79963***	0.41817	2.19248**
= –15	0.01341	0.32455	0.43158	2.26283**
= –14	= –0.10553	= –2.55265**	0.32605	1.70951***
= –13	0.04583	1.10867	0.37189	1.94983***
= –12	0.00643	0.15559	0.37832	1.98356**
= –11	0.05182	1.25345	0.43014	2.25526**
= –10	= –0.07762	= –1.87750***	0.35252	1.84829***
= –9	0.13273	3.21050*	0.48525	2.54420**
= –8	0.25904	6.26591*	0.74430	3.90239*
= –7	0.01122	0.27151	0.75552	3.96125*
= –6	0.05556	1.34408	0.81109	4.25259*
= –5	0.10989	2.65816*	0.92098	4.82877*
= –4	= –0.28239	= –6.83063*	0.63859	3.34816*
= –3	0.05499	1.33012	0.69358	3.63648*
= –2	= –0.16974	= –4.10577*	0.52384	2.74652*
= –1	0.37004	8.95080*	0.89388	4.68669*
0	0.31712	7.67077*	1.21101	6.34940*
1	= –0.39654	= –9.59180*	0.81446	4.27029*
2	= –0.42827	= –10.35911*	0.386199	2.02485**
3	= –0.24232	= –5.86144*	0.14387	0.75432
4	0.53492	12.93882*	0.67879	3.55894*
5	0.30500	7.37751*	0.98379	5.15809*
6	= –0.10763	= –2.60357**	0.87616	4.59374*
7	= –0.68212	= –16.49939*	0.19403	1.01733
8	0.16042	3.88042*	0.35446	1.85846***
9	= –0.39572	= –9.57189*	= –0.04126	= –0.21633
10	0.14541	3.51730*	0.10415	0.54607
11	= –0.03573	= –0.86446	0.06841	0.35868
12	0.49556	11.98695*	0.56398	2.95697*
13	0.06025	1.45735	0.62423	3.27287*
14	0.28092	6.79519*	0.90516	4.74579*
15	0.27970	6.76557*	1.18486	6.21229*
16	0.30873	7.46775*	1.49360	7.83100*
17	0.00589	0.14264	1.49949	7.86192*
18	0.47626	11.52003*	1.97576	10.35900*
19	= –0.22220	= –5.37480*	1.75355	9.19396*
20	= –0.88381	= –21.37786*	0.86974	4.56010*

*Significant at 0.01 level; ** significant at 0.05 level; and *** significant at 0.10 level

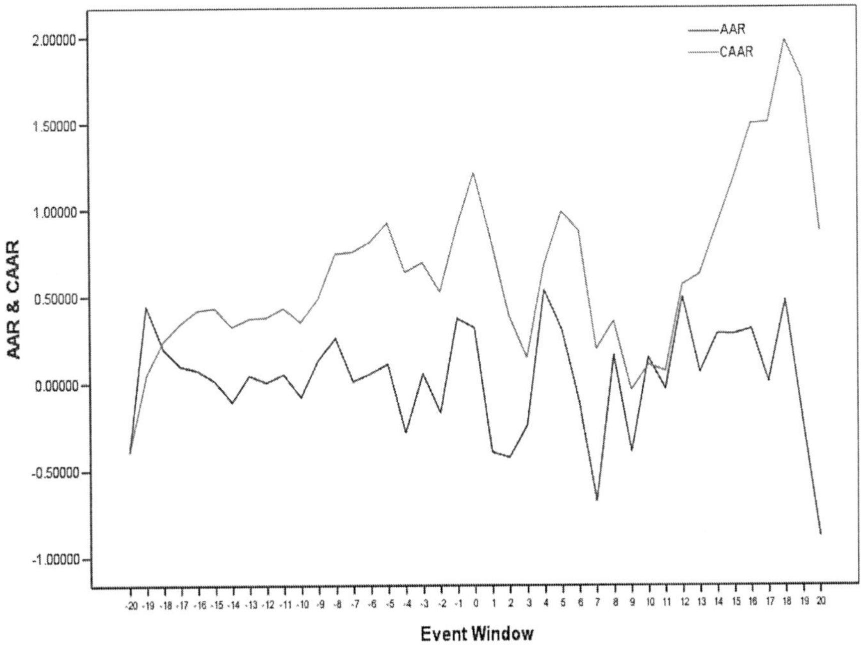

Figure 2: AAR and CAAR Graph for Cash Dividend Announcements (banking sector)

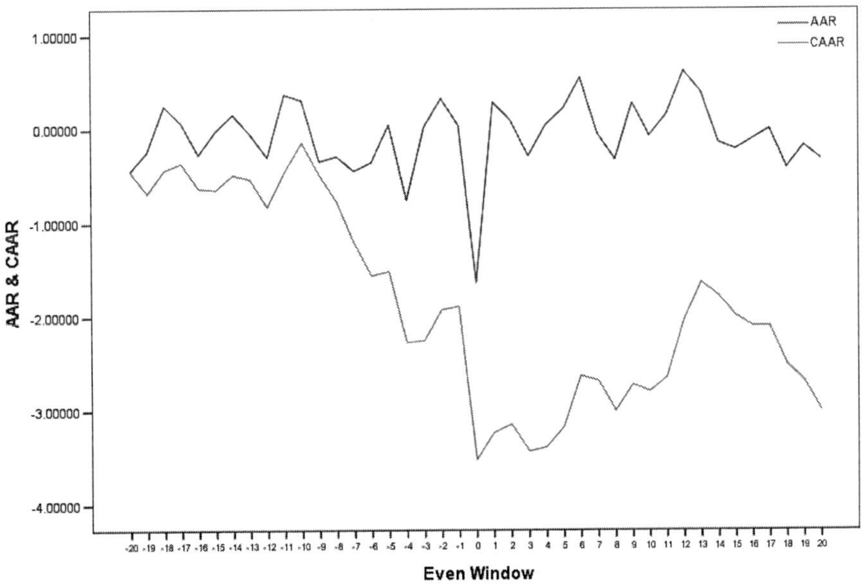

Figure 3: AAR and CAAR Graph for Cash Dividend Announcements (IT sector)

Table 3: AARs, CAARs, and t-test results for Cash Dividend Announcement (IT Sector, N = 35)

Days	*AAR (%)*	*t-value*	*CAAR (%)*	*t-value*
= –20	= –0.44241	= –8.05115*	= –0.44241	= –1.09789
= –19	= –0.23525	= –4.28118*	= –0.67766	= –1.68169
= –18	0.249582	4.541984*	= –0.42808	= –1.06232
= –17	0.070818	1.288771	= –0.35726	= –0.88658
= –16	= –0.26631	= –4.84646*	= –0.62357	= –1.54746
= –15	= –0.01584	= –0.2883	= –0.63942	= –1.58678
= –14	0.157878	2.873117*	= –0.48154	= –1.19499
= –13	= –0.04599	= –0.83698	= –0.52753	= –1.30912
= –12	= –0.29566	= –5.38046*	= –0.82319	= –2.04282*
= –11	0.372541	6.779637*	= –0.45065	= –1.11832
= –10	0.310885	5.657611*	= –0.13976	= –0.34683
= –9	= –0.33954	= –6.17911*	= –0.4793	= –1.18944
= –8	= –0.28791	= –5.23958*	= –0.76722	= –1.90393***
= –7	= –0.4417	= –8.03814*	= –1.20891	= –3.00004*
= –6	= –0.35182	= –6.40255*	= –1.56073	= –3.87312*
= –5	0.048462	0.881937	= –1.51227	= –3.75286*
= –4	= –0.75623	= –13.7621*	= –2.2685	= –5.62952*
= –3	0.017251	0.313941	= –2.25125	= –5.58671*
= –2	0.328218	5.97303*	= –1.92303	= –4.7722*
= –1	0.035697	0.649633	= –1.88733	= –4.68362*
0	= –1.63587	= –29.7702*	= –3.52321	= –8.74321*
1	0.287203	5.226629*	= –3.236	= –8.03048*
2	0.090335	1.643947	= –3.14567	= –7.80631*
3	= –0.28741	= –5.23046*	= –3.43308	= –8.51955*
4	0.043063	0.78368	= –3.39002	= –8.41269*
5	0.216735	3.944228*	= –3.17328	= –7.87484*
6	0.545278	9.923184*	= –2.628	= –6.52167*
7	= –0.05280	= –0.96092	= –2.68081	= –6.65270*
8	= –0.32291	= –5.87647*	= –3.00372	= –7.45404*
9	0.279911	5.093918*	= –2.72381	= –6.75942*
10	= –0.07289	= –1.32648	= –2.7967	= –6.94030*
11	0.152805	2.780795*	= –2.64389	= –6.56110*
12	0.615115	11.1941*	= –2.02878	= –5.03463*
13	0.394952	7.187482*	= –1.63383	= –4.05451*
14	= –0.14378	= –2.61658*	= –1.77761	= –4.41132*
15	= –0.21368	= –3.88868*	= –1.99129	= –4.94160*
16	= –0.10697	= –1.94676***	= –2.09826	= –5.20706*
17	0.00027	0.004984	= –2.09799	= –5.20638*
18	= –0.40882	= –7.43986*	= –2.50681	= –6.22091*
19	= –0.17645	= –3.21118*	= –2.68326	= –6.65880*
20	= –0.32016	= –5.82635*	= –3.00342	= –7.45331*

*Significant at 0.01 level; ** significant at 0.05 level; and *** significant at 0.10 level

Table 4 gives the results of stock price ARs and their t-statistics at the examination window (day = –20 to day +20) for the Trading sector with 31 cash dividend announcements. It has been observed that most of the t-statistics of AARs and CAARs during the event window periods are not close to zero and statistically significant, which indicates that there is frequent effect of cash dividend announcement on stock price in the Trading sector. However, the t–statistic of AARs on day = –17, = –16, = –14, = –8, = –6, 4, 6, 7, 13, 14, and 19 are found to be insignificant, while t-statistic of CAAR on day = –20, = –19, = –3, 5, 6, 7, and 9 are also found to be statistically insignificant.

Table 5 shows the results of stock price ARs and their t-statistics at the examination window (day = –20 to day +20) for the Automobile sector with 44 cash dividend announcements. It has been observed that most of the t-statistics of AARs and CAARs during the event window periods are not close to zero and statistically significant, which indicates that there is a frequent effect of cash dividend announcement on stock price in the Automobile sector. However, the t-statistic of AARs on day = –19, = –14, = –6, 1, and 8 are found insignificant.

Table 6 presents the results of stock price ARs and their t-statistic at the examination window (day = –20 to day +20) for the Pharmaceutical sector with 40 cash dividend announcements. It has been observed that

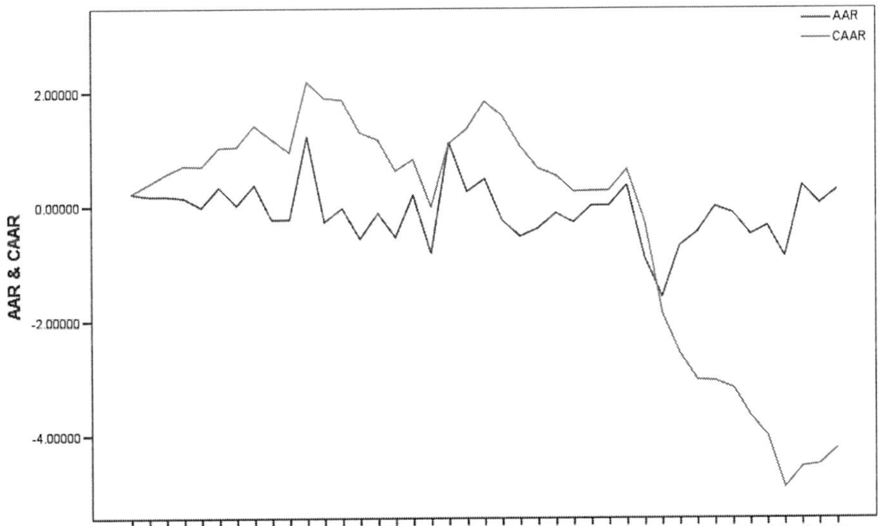

Figure 4: AAR and CAAR Graph for Cash Dividend Announcements (trading sector)

Table 4: AARs, CAARs, and t-test Results for Cash Dividend Announcement (Trading Sector, N = 31)

Days	*AAR (%)*	*t-value*	*CAAR (%)*	*t-value*
=–20	0.219583	2.388414**	0.219583	0.890556
=–19	0.174671	1.899907***	0.394254	1.598964
=–18	0.174058	1.893233***	0.568312	2.304884**
=–17	0.145555	1.583209	0.713867	2.895207*
=–16	-0.01930	=–0.20994	0.694565	2.816927*
=–15	0.332831	3.620217*	1.027396	4.166779*
=–14	0.014199	0.154448	1.041595	4.224367*
=–13	0.371914	4.045322*	1.413509	5.732726*
=–12	=–0.23477	=–2.55360**	1.178739	4.780577*
=–11	=–0.23062	=–2.50851**	0.948115	3.845243*
=–10	1.22904	13.36833*	2.177155	8.829822*
=–9	=–0.27768	=–3.02034*	1.899475	7.703644*
=–8	=–0.03488	=–0.37942	1.864593	7.562172*
=–7	=–0.57252	=–6.22734*	1.292072	5.240217*
=–6	=–0.12291	=–1.33693	1.169159	4.741721*
=–5	=–0.54621	=–5.94115*	0.622949	2.526476**
=–4	0.1976	2.149304**	0.820549	3.327876*
=–3	=–0.83392	=–9.07056*	=–0.01337	=–0.05422
=–2	1.114142	12.11857*	1.100774	4.464375*
=–1	0.25794	2.805626*	1.358714	5.510495*
0	0.479831	5.219141*	1.838544	7.456529*
1	=–0.25219	=–2.74311*	1.586352	6.433718*
2	=–0.53032	=–5.76833*	1.05603	4.28291*
3	=–0.39041	=–4.24654*	0.665617	2.699523*
4	=–0.12407	=–1.34951	0.541547	2.196337**
5	=–0.28333	=–3.08183*	0.258214	1.047232
6	0.00721	0.078424	0.265424	1.076473
7	0.009107	0.099059	0.274531	1.113409
8	0.367342	3.995598*	0.641874	2.603227*
9	=–0.92161	=–10.0244*	=–0.27973	=–1.13451
10	=–1.59492	=–17.348*	=–1.87466	=–7.60299*
11	=–0.69619	=–7.57254*	=–2.57085	=–10.4265*
12	=–0.45952	=–4.99818*	=–3.03037	=–12.2902*
13	=–0.01154	=–0.12549	=–3.0419	=–12.337*
14	=–0.12692	=–1.38053	=–3.16882	=–12.8517*
15	=–0.50034	=–5.44227*	=–3.66917	=–14.8809*
16	=–0.35071	=–3.81473*	=–4.01988	=–16.3033*
17	=–0.89514	=–9.73647*	=–4.91502	=–19.9337*
18	0.361203	3.928828*	=–4.55382	=–18.4688*
19	0.041562	0.452074	=–4.51226	=–18.3002*
20	0.286611	3.117486*	=–4.22564	=–17.1378*

*Significant at 0.01 level; ** significant at 0.05 level; and *** significant at 0.10 level

Table 5: AARs, CAARs, and t-test Results for Cash Dividend Announcement (Automobile Sector, N = 44)

Days	*AAR (%)*	*t-value*	*CAAR (%)*	*t-value*
= –20	0.408739	7.236089*	0.408739	3.077066*
= –19	= –0.02053	= –0.3635	0.388206	2.922493*
= –18	= –0.0934	= –1.65351***	0.294806	2.219357**
= –17	= –0.56505	= –10.0034*	= –0.27025	= –2.03446**
= –16	0.316899	5.610199*	0.046654	0.351217
= –15	0.202393	3.583049*	0.249046	1.874869***
= –14	= –0.02752	= –0.48725	0.221524	1.667672***
= –13	0.262696	4.650621*	0.484219	3.645297
= –12	= –0.17609	= –3.1174*	0.30813	2.319659**
= –11	= –0.14285	= –2.5289**	0.165282	1.244271
= –10	= –0.2195	= –3.88586*	= –0.05422	= –0.40815
= –9	= –0.39836	= –7.05239*	= –0.45258	= –3.4071*
= –8	= –0.40501	= –7.17008*	= –0.85759	= –6.45609*
= –7	= –0.16699	= –2.95634*	= –1.02458	= –7.71324*
= –6	0.031742	0.561945	= –0.99284	= –7.47428*
= –5	0.23886	4.228658*	= –0.75398	= –5.6761*
= –4	= –0.49665	= –8.7924*	= –1.25063	= –9.414978*
= –3	= –0.20624	= –3.65111*	= –1.45686	= –10.9676*
= –2	0.136503	2.416576**	= –1.32036	= –9.93994*
= –1	0.224992	3.983128*	= –1.09537	= –8.24616*
0	0.322875	5.716007*	= –0.77249	= –5.81549*
1	0.089037	1.576266	= –0.68346	= –5.1452*
2	0.271348	4.803788*	= –0.41211	= –3.10244*
3	= –0.11243	= –1.99032**	= –0.52454	= –3.94881*
4	= –0.21365	= –3.78234*	= –0.73819	= –5.5572*
5	0.353195	6.252766*	= –0.38499	= –2.89828*
6	= –0.19411	= –3.43636*	= –0.5791	= –4.35956*
7	= –0.54534	= –9.65436*	= –1.12444	= –8.46497*
8	0.009954	0.176225	= –1.11448	= –8.39003*
9	0.109545	1.939318***	= –1.00494	= –7.56536*
10	0.496033	8.781492*	= –0.5089	= –3.83113*
11	= –0.48061	= –8.5085*	= –0.98952	= –7.44927*
12	= –0.16271	= –2.88046*	= –1.15222	= –8.67416*
13	= –0.21296	= –3.77021*	= –1.36519	= –10.2774*
14	= –0.375	= –6.63877*	= –1.74019	= –13.1005*
15	0.529379	9.371836*	= –1.21081	= –9.11519*
16	= –0.23783	= –4.21048*	= –1.44864	= –10.9056*
17	0.139152	2.463478**	= –1.30949	= –9.85808*
18	= –0.52323	= –9.26289*	= –1.83271	= –13.797*
19	= –0.72608	= –12.8541*	= –2.55879	= –19.2631*
20	= –0.14576	= –2.58053*	= –2.70455	= –20.3604*

*Significant at 0.01 level; ** significant at 0.05 level; and *** significant at 0.10 level

Table 6: AARs, CAARs, and t-test Results for Cash Dividend Announcement (Pharmaceutical Sector, N = 40)

Days	*AAR (%)*	*t-value*	*CAAR (%)*	*t-value*
=–20	=–0.236980	=–4.05006*	=–0.23698	=–1.00654
=–19	0.03304	0.56466	=–0.20394	=–0.86621
=–18	0.54767	9.35998*	0.34373	1.45998
=–17	=–0.75701	=–12.93750*	=–0.41327	=–1.75530***
=–16	0.22083	3.77418*	=–0.19243	=–0.81732
=–15	=–0.18598	=–3.17845*	=–0.37841	=–1.60725
=–14	=–0.49170	=–8.40331*	=–0.87011	=–3.69567*
=–13	0.32352	5.52921*	=–0.54658	=–2.32153**
=–12	0.16696	2.85348*	=–0.37962	=–1.61237
=–11	=–0.30218	=–5.16432*	=–0.68179	=–2.89583*
=–10	0.53247	9.10020*	=–0.14932	=–0.63420
=–9	=–0.01968	=–0.33632	=–0.16900	=–0.71779
=–8	0.06658	1.13800	=–0.10241	=–0.43496
=–7	=–0.34254	=–5.85416*	=–0.44495	=–1.88987***
=–6	=–0.00628	=–0.10737	=–0.45123	=–1.91655***
=–5	0.48845	8.34782*	0.03722	0.15809
=–4	0.48706	8.32401*	0.52428	2.22681**
=–3	0.22043	3.76729*	0.74471	3.16307*
=–2	=–0.21087	=–3.60386*	0.53384	2.26743**
=–1	=–0.42848	=–7.32291*	0.10536	0.44750
0	0.12747	2.17862**	0.23283	0.98895
1	=–0.27934	=–4.77403*	=–0.04650	=–0.19751
2	=–0.12157	=–2.07774**	=–0.16808	=–0.71388
3	0.53163	9.08587*	0.36356	1.54418
4	0.64645	11.04807*	1.01001	4.28989*
5	0.35406	6.05110*	1.36407	5.79374*
6	0.49467	8.45408*	1.85875	7.89479*
7	=–0.11576	=–1.97840**	1.74298	7.40311*
8	=–0.04965	=–0.84858	1.69333	7.19221*
9	=–0.26872	=–4.59260*	1.42461	6.05084*
10	=–0.23333	=–3.98771*	1.19128	5.05980*
11	=–0.33975	=–5.80645*	0.85152	3.61675*
12	=–0.23438	=–4.00562*	0.61715	2.62126*
13	0.13552	2.31609**	0.75267	3.19686*
14	=–0.11987	=–2.04856**	0.63280	2.68775*
15	0.25007	4.27391*	0.88288	3.74992*
16	0.62958	10.75988*	1.51247	6.42401*
17	0.14477	2.47417*	1.65724	7.03891*
18	=–0.25677	=–4.38821*	1.40047	5.94833*
19	=–0.54193	=–9.26182*	0.85854	3.64654*
20	=–0.29444	=–5.03209*	0.56410	2.39594**

*Significant at 0.01 level; ** significant at 0.05 level; and *** significant at 0.10 level

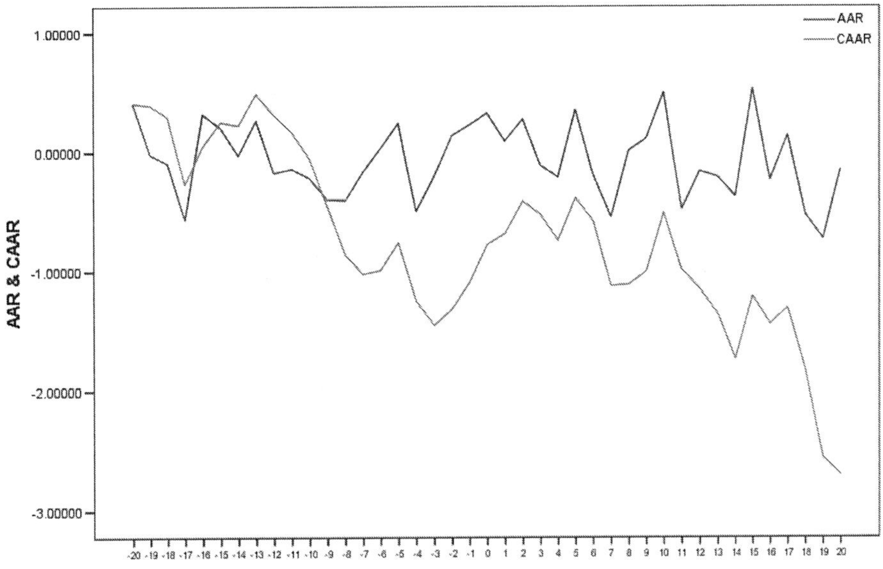

Figure 5: AAR and CAAR Graph for Cash Dividend Announcements (automobile sector)

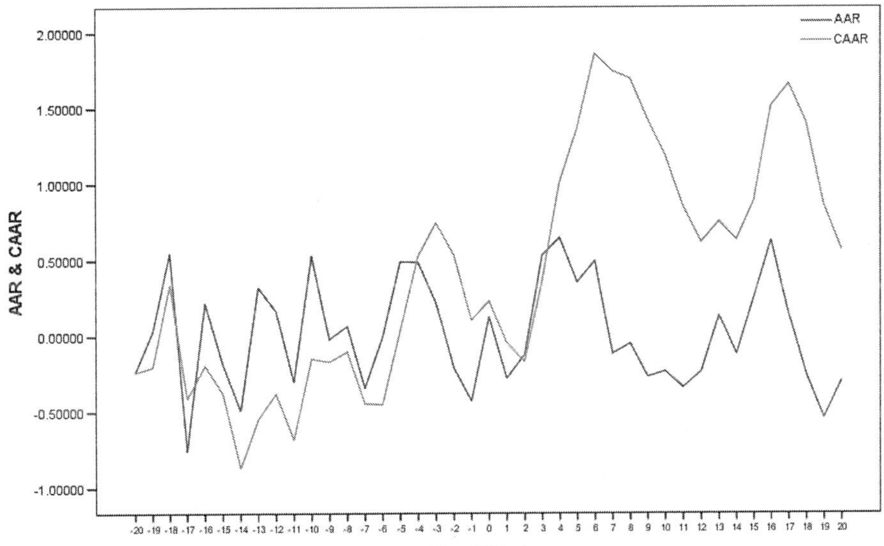

Figure 6: AAR and CAAR Graph for Cash Dividend Announcements (pharmaceutical sector)

most of the t-statistics of AARs and CAARs during the event window periods are not close to zero and statistically significant, which indicates that there is a frequent effect of cash dividend announcement on stock price in this sector. However, the t-statistics of AARs on day = –19, = –9, = –8, = –6, and 8 are found to be insignificant. The t-statistic of CAAR on day = –16, = –11, and = –10 are also found to be statistically insignificant.

CONCLUSION

The present paper analyses the stock price reaction around cash dividend announcements using the Event study methodology. A total of 44 companies from Banking, IT, Trading, Automobile, and Pharmaceutical sectors listed at BSE-500 have been selected, which, in all, had made 200 final cash dividend announcements during the sample period, that is 1 January 2009 to 29 June 2013. If the markets are efficient, the AARs and CAARs should be close to zero. So, the overall conclusions would be based on the results of t-values on AAR_{it} and $CAAR_{it}$ for the 41 days event window. The findings show that most of the t-statistics of AARs and CAARs during the event window period are not close to zero, which indicates that the stock price of sample companies mostly react to cash dividend announcements during the event window period. Likewise, similar results have been observed for the selected sectors. In general, the findings strongly support the dividend signaling hypothesis in explaining the stock price reactions to an announcement of cash dividend.

REFERENCES

A.A. et al., 'The Stock Market Reaction to Dividend Announcements: A UK Study of Complex Market Signals', *Journal of Financial Studies*, vol. 23, 1996, pp. 32–52.

G.M. Frankfurter, and B. Wood, 'The Evolution of Corporate Dividend Policy', *Journal of Financial Education*, vol. 23, 1997, pp. 16–33.

H. Anderson, S. Cahan, and L. Rose, 'Stock Dividend Announcement Effects in an Imputation Tax Environment', *Journal of Finance and Accounting*, vol. 28, no. (5/6), 2001, pp. 653–69.

H.M. Merton and K. Rock, 'Dividend Policy under Asymmetric Information', *The Journal of Finance*, vol. 40, 1985, pp. 1031–51.

J.S. Aharony, 'Quarterly Dividend and Earning Announcements and Stockholders' Return: An Empirical Analysis', *Journal of Finance*, vol. 35, no. (1), 1980, pp. 1–12.

M. Akbar, M., and H. Baig, 'Reaction of Stock Prices to Dividend Announcements and Market Efficiency in Pakistan', *The Lahore Journal of Economics*, vol. 15, no. (1), 2010, pp. 103–25.

M. Grinblatt, R. Masulis, and S. Titman, 'The Valuation Effects of Stock Splits and Stock Dividends', *Journal of Financial Economics*, 1984, pp. 461–90.

M. McNichols and A. Dravid, 'Stock Dividends, Stock Splits, and Signalling', *Journal of Finance*, vol. 45, no. (3), 1990, pp. 857-879.

M. Miller and F. Modigliani, 'Dividend Policy, Growth, and the Valuation of Shares', *Journal of Buiness*, vol. 34, no. (4), 1961, pp. 411-433.

M.H. Uddin and G.M. Chowdhury, 'Effect of Dividend Announcement and Shareholders' Value: Evidence from Dhaka Stock Exchange', *Journal of Business Research*, vol. 7, 2005, pp. 61-72.

O.J. Adelegan, 'Capital Market Efficiency and the Effects of Dividend Announcements on Share Prices in Nigeria', *African Development Review*, vol. 15, 2003, pp. 218-236.

P.M. Healy and K. Palepu, 'Earnings Information Conveyed by Dividend Initiations and Omissions', *Journal of Financial Economics*, 1988, pp. 149-175.

R. Pettit, 'Dividend Announcements, Security Performance, and Capital Market Efficiency', *Journal of Finance*, vol. 27, no. (5), 1972, pp. 993-1007.

R.A. Brealey and M.C. Stewart, Principles of Corporate Finance. New Delhi: Tata McGraw-Hill Publishing Company Limited, 1998.

R.C. Lease et al., Dividend Policy:Its Impact on Firm's Value, Boston, Massachusttes: Harvard Business School Press, 2000.

S.H. Archer, G., M.C., and George, R., Financial Management. New York: John Wiley and Sons, 1985.

S. Mahmood, M.F. Sheikh and A.Q. Ghaffari, 'Dividend Announcements and Stock Returns: An Event Study on Karachi Stock Exchange', *Interdisciplinary Journal of Contemporary Research in Business*, vol. 3, no. (8), 2011, pp. 972-981.

APPENDIX

List of Sample Companies Listed at BSE
(The Market Capitalization as on 29 April 2013 was used as sorting criteria)

Company Name		*(INR Crore)*
S. No.	*Banking Sector*	*Market Capitalization*
Public Sector Banks		
1.	State Bank of India (SBI)	1,56,520.65
2.	Bank of Baroda	29,696.83
3.	PNB	27, 889.05
4.	Bank of India	19, 623.06
5.	Canara Bank	18, 809.78
Private Sector Banks		
6.	HDFC	1,65, 384.54
7.	ICICI Bank	1,33, 237.97
8.	Axix Bank	69, 277.36
9.	Kotak Mahindra	52, 904.72
10.	Induslnd Bank	25,126.02

	Company Name	*(INR Crore)*
S. No.	*Banking Sector*	*Market Capitalization*
Information Technology (IT) Sector		
11.	Tata Consultancy Services (TCS)	2,68, 149.06
12.	Infosys	1,27, 991.50
13.	Wipro	84, 232.37
14.	HCL Tech	48, 766.55
15.	Tech Mehindra	12, 128.75
16.	Mphasis	7,860.02
17.	Financial Tech	3,875.20
18.	MindTree	3,371.83
Trading Sector		
19.	Adani Enterprise	23, 915.37
20.	MMTC Ltd.	21, 600.00
21.	PTC India	1,776.05
22.	Ushdev Int	1144.11
23.	Swan Energy	1122.43
24.	STC India	1023.60
25.	Ind Motor Parts	351.13
Automobile Sector		
26.	Tata Motors	95, 017.60
27.	Mahindra and Mahindra Ltd	55, 331.95
28.	Bajaj Auto Ltd.	55, 130.20
29.	Maruti Suzuki	50, 898.98
30.	Hero Motorcorp	33, 195.05
31.	Eicher Motors Ltd.	7, 911.29
32.	Ashok Leyland Ltd.	5, 999.83
33.	Force Motors	503.33
34.	Maharashtra Scooters	945.09
Pharmaceuticals Sector		
35.	Sun Phrama	98, 483.84
36.	Dr Reddys Lbs	34, 134.58
37.	Cipla	32, 626.71
38.	Lupin	30, 665.38
39.	Wockhardt	20, 557.85
40.	GlaxoSmithKline	19, 187.77
41.	Rambaxy Labs	18, 859.73
42.	Cadila Health	15, 922.27
43.	Divis Labs	14, 215.84
44.	Glenmark	13, 116.81

SECTION III

CORPORATE GOVERNANCE ISSUES AND BEHAVIORAL FINANCE

Corporate Governance
Enacting Financial Discipline and Reporting

Ambrish Gupta
FORE School of Management, New Delhi
e-mail: ambrish@fsm.ac.in

ABSTRACT

The genesis of corporate governance is traced back to the Cadbury Committee Report of 1992 in Britain which was necessitated by the changing economic order of the public sector to privatization, manifesting among others in accounting scandals (BCCI and Maxwell, for example). In this background, the title of the committee's report was 'The Financial Aspects of Corporate Governance' showing its focus area. The committee stated 'Corporate governance is the system by which companies are directed and controlled. Boards of directors are responsible for the governance of their companies. Within that overall framework, specifically the financial aspects of corporate governance (the Committee's remit) are the way in which boards set financial policy ... and the process whereby they report on the activities and progress of the company to the shareholders'.

The subject gained the real impetus with the unfolding of accounting scandals of WorldCom (Y2000) and Enron (Y2001) in the USA. This led to the enactment of The Accounting Industry Reforms Act, 2002, popularly known as Sarbanes-Oxley Act. The focus of the act inter alia was on strengthening and restoring confidence in the accounting profession and to improve disclosure and financial reporting.

India also followed the suit and enacted corporate governance norms through Clause 49 of the listing agreement in Y2000. The clause includes mandatory as well as eight voluntary norms. There are four specific voluntary norms, namely, Independent directors' tenure (limitation of 9 years), Whistle Blower policy, Audit Qualifications: move towards unqualified report, and Shareholders' right to receive half yearly financial reports, which revolve around board independence, control on financial scandals, financial policies, and reporting to the shareholders. This paper examines the extent of compliance of these norms by the listed companies to ascertain the corporate sector's response towards voluntary compliance. It is found that overall, while the companies seem to be conscious of enacting financial discipline, they seem to be lacking in stakeholder reporting which creates information asymmetry and puts retail investors at greater risk.

Keywords: Clause 49, Corporate Governance, Non-mandatory Requirements, BSE Sensex

INTRODUCTION

The genesis of the concept of corporate governance is traced back to the Cadbury Committee Report of 1992 in Britain which was necessitated by the changing economic order of the public sector to privatization, manifesting, among others, in accounting scandals (BCCI and Maxwell for example). In this background the title of the committee's report was 'The Financial Aspects of Corporate Governance' showing its focus area. The committee stated:

> Corporate governance is the system by which companies are directed and controlled. Boards of directors are responsible for the governance of their companies. The shareholders' role in governance is to appoint the directors and the auditors and to satisfy themselves that an appropriate governance structure is in place. The responsibilities of the board include setting the company's strategic aims, providing the leadership to put them into effect, supervising the management of the business and reporting to shareholders on their stewardship. The board's actions are subject to laws, regulations and the shareholders in general meeting. Within that overall framework, specifically the **financial aspects** of corporate governance (the Committee's remit) are the way in which:
>
> - Boards set financial policy and oversee its implementation, including the use of financial controls, and
> - The process whereby they report on the activities and progress of the company to the shareholders.

The subject, however, gained the real impetus with the unfolding of accounting scandals of WorldCom (Y2000) and Enron (Y2001) in the USA. Both these companies used to resort to inflate their profits artificially. The bubble had to bust and it did, sooner than later. This led to the enactment of The Accounting Industry Reforms Act, 2002, popularly known as Sarbanes-Oxley Act, named after its propounders. The Sarbanes-Oxley Act has become a benchmark the world over and has its imprint on all global efforts towards strengthening the corporate governance of the public corporations (Gupta, 2012). The focus of the act inter alia was on:

1. Strengthening and restoring confidence in the accounting profession;
2. Improving disclosures in the periodic financial statements; and
3. Reporting thereof, that is, keeping the shareholders well informed through financial reporting.

THE INDIAN SCENE

India also followed the suit and enacted corporate governance norms through Clause 49 of the listing agreement in Y2000, amended from time to time. The code is divided into mandatory and eight non- mandatory requirements. It is applicable to entities seeking listing for the first time and for existing listed entities having a paid up share capital of INR 3 crore and above or net worth of INR 25 crore or more at any time in the history of the company. Clause 49 requires listed companies to annex a separate section on corporate governance in the annual report of the company, with a detailed compliance report thereon. Non-compliance of any mandatory requirement of this clause with reasons, and the extent to which the non-mandatory requirements have been complied with/not complied with needs to be specifically highlighted. Further, the companies are also required to submit a quarterly compliance report to the stock exchanges within 15 days from the closure of the quarter in the prescribed format (BSE, n.d.1). The following paragraphs carry a discussion on those requirements of Clause 49 which are 'financial discipline and reporting' centric (BSE).

REQUIREMENTS EMPHASIZING FINANCIAL DISCIPLINE AND REPORTING

Of the mandatory norms, requirements of:

1. Independent directors on the board,
2. Constitution of audit committee, and
3. Disclosures related to the basis of related party transactions, accounting treatment, risk management and utilization of proceeds from public/rights/preferential issues, etc.,

are specifically directed towards ensuring board independence, financial discipline and reporting.

Of the non-mandatory norms, the following four norms specifically revolve around board independence, control on financial scandals, financial policies and reporting to the shareholders:

1. Independent directors' tenure to be limited to 9 years (board independence);
2. Whistle Blower policy (financial scandals);
4. Audit qualifications: Move towards unqualified report (financial scandals, financial policies and quality of financial statements); and
5. Shareholders' right to receive half yearly financial reports (reporting to the shareholders)

Board independence is supposed to be the enabler of financial discipline, control, and reporting.

NON-MANDATORY (VOLUNTARY) REQUIREMENTS

Non-mandatory (Voluntary) Requirements Revolving Around Board Independence, Control on Financial Scandals, Financial Policies and Reporting to the Shareholders. For the mandatory requirements it will be reasonable to presume that the companies will comply with them as they are bound to do so. However, for non-mandatory requirements Clause 49 provides that they may be implemented as per the discretion of the company. The clause further requires that disclosures of the adoption/non-adoption of the non-mandatory requirements need to be made in the section on corporate governance in the annual report. Apart from the four requirements mentioned above, Clause 49 additionally proposes the following four: office for non-executive chairman, constitution of remuneration committee, training of board members, and mechanism to be put in place for evaluating non-executive board members' performance.

Following is a full listing of the four requirements which specifically revolve around board independence, control on financial scandals, financial policies, and reporting to the shareholders, thus enabling financial discipline and reporting as given in annexure 1D of Clause 49 (BSE):

1. *Independent Directors' Tenure:* 'Independent directors may have a tenure not exceeding, in the aggregate, a period of nine years, on the board of a company. The company may ensure that the person who is being appointed as an independent director has the requisite qualifications and experience which would be of use to the company and which, in the opinion of the company, would enable him to contribute effectively to the company in his capacity as an independent director'.
2. *Whistle Blower Policy:* 'The Company may establish a mechanism for employees to report to the management concerns about unethical

behaviour, actual or suspected fraud or violation of the company's code of conduct or ethics policy. This mechanism could also provide for adequate safeguards against victimization of employees who avail of the mechanism and also provide for direct access to the chairman of the audit committee in exceptional cases. Once established, the existence of the mechanism may be appropriately communicated within the organization'.

3. *Audit Qualifications:* Move towards unqualified report: 'Company may move towards a regime of unqualified financial statements'.
4. *Shareholders' Right to Receive Half Yearly Financial Reports:* 'A half-yearly declaration of financial performance including summary of the significant events in the last six-months, may be sent to each household of shareholders'.

REVIEW OF LITERATURE

Literature is replete with research on various aspects of Indian corporate governance. A study by Srinivasan and Srinivasan (2011) even assesses the status of corporate governance research 'on' India. A few studies which address the issue of compliance with the corporate governance requirements of Clause 49, both mandatory and non-mandatory, are briefed here under.

Pahuja and Bhatia (2010) conducted a study on 'Determinants of Corporate Governance Disclosures: Evidence from Companies in Northern India'. The study examined the annual corporate governance reports of 50 listed companies. They found that 'there was a substantial scope for improvement in the corporate governance disclosure practices and that the size of the corporation was a significant determinant of the disclosures'.

Bhasin (2010) conducted a case study of Reliance Industries Ltd. for the year 2008–09 and observed that the company had complied with some of the important non-mandatory requirements stipulated under Clause 49 and that the company had a whistle-blower policy and enforcement mechanism in place.

Sareen and Chander (2009) carried out an empirical investigation on 'Firms' Attributes and Corporate Governance Disclosure Practices' in India. Their study was based on secondary data taken from 100 selected BSE listed companies. They found a 'positive relationship between selected company attributes and 'extent of corporate governance disclosures'.

Gupta (2006) carried out a comparative study of corporate governance practices in selected companies in the automobile industry in Haryana. The data was collected from the corporate governance reports of the related companies for the year 2004–05. The study did not find any significant deviations in actual practices, vis-a-vis the norms stipulated in Clause 49.

Literature is replete with research on various aspects of corporate governance. Coming specifically to compliance with voluntary norms, a few studies related to the Indian context are available. Gupta, Nair, and Gogula (2003) carried out an analysis of corporate governance practices, on the basis of corporate governance reports for the years 2001–02 and 2002–03, of 30 selected Indian companies listed in the Bombay Stock Exchange (BSE). They found 'variations in the reporting practices of the companies, and in certain cases, even omission of mandatory requirements of clause 49'.

It is clear that research studies on 'compliance of corporate governance requirements' on India either focus on only the mandatory requirements or both altogether. Further, most of the studies are limited to just one company, one industry, and one geographical area. It is therefore felt that an exclusive study on compliance with non-mandatory requirements covering a larger sample of companies and industry sectors with an all India impact be carried out. The studies cited above are general in nature. They do not specifically address the issues of enacting financial discipline and reporting, the basic purpose of corporate governance mechanism. Hence, this study has been attempted.

OBJECTIVES OF THE STUDY

In this backdrop the objective of this research is to assess whether India Inc. follows the four specific voluntary norms, namely, Independent Directors' tenure (limitation of 9 years), Whistle Blower policy, Audit Qualifications: move towards unqualified report, and Shareholders' right to receive half yearly financial reports, which revolve around board independence, control on financial scandals, financial policies, and reporting to the shareholders. This paper examines the extent of compliance of these norms by the listed companies to ascertain the corporate sector's response towards ensuring financial discipline and reporting.

HYPOTHESIS

Towards the objectives of this study following hypotheses have been formed:

H1: Indian corporate sector is not in full compliance with the four specified corporate governance norms aimed at enacting financial discipline, control, and shareholder reporting thereof.

H2: Indian corporate sector is in full compliance with the four specified corporate governance norms aimed at enacting financial discipline, control, and shareholder reporting thereof.

DATA COLLECTION AND METHODOLOGY

This paper is based on secondary, nonetheless original, data and proceeds with the following research methodology:

1. Constituent companies of Bombay Stock Exchange Sensitivity Index (BSE Sensex), numbering 30, have been considered as representing the Indian corporate sector since the Sensex stocks represent large, well-established, and financially sound companies across key sectors and the Sensex itself is considered as the barometer of Indian capital market (BSE). These companies enjoy leadership positions in their respective industries, and corporate reporting practices followed by them are keenly watched by, and influence, the reporting practices of the entire corporate sector. Their market capitalization (as on 3 October 2014) at INR 44,48,066 crore (BSE, 2014a) represents 48 per cent of the total market capitalization of all BSE listed companies amounting to INR 93,60,220 crore (BSE, 2014 b). Annexure 1 provides a listing of these companies (BSE, 2014 c) together with their segmentation based on industry sector (sub sector), business house, and ownership.
2. The corporate governance reports of all these companies as contained in their respective annual reports for the latest financial year 2013–14 were scanned to find out the details about adoption/non-adoption of non-mandatory requirements of Clause 49. These details were tabulated and aggregated company-wise and requirement-wise. Annexure 2 provides the details.
3. In a few cases information on adoption/non adoption of non-mandatory requirements was not provided under a separate head. Therefore, information was culled out in bits and pieces from the entire corporate governance report/auditors' report/directors' report. Though every effort has been made to ensure accuracy in those cases, inadvertent omissions might be remotely possible.

COMPLIANCE/NON-COMPLIANCE OF THE FOUR VOLUNTARY NORMS: ANALYSIS, DISCUSSION AND FINDINGS

Detailed objectives and methodology of this research study have been stated earlier. This section seeks to ascertain whether India Inc. follows the corporate governance requirements meant to enact financial discipline and stakeholder reporting thereof, and to what extent. The section is divided into two parts:

1. Requirement-wise Compliance/Non-compliance
2. Company-wise Compliance/Non-compliance

Requirement-wise Compliance/Non-compliance

Table 1 provides details of requirement-wise compliance / non-compliance.

Table 1: Requirement-wise Compliance / Non-compliance of Four Specified Non-Mandatory Requirements

Req. No.	*Requirements*	*Compliance*		*Non-compliance (%)*
		%	*Rank*	
1	Independent Directors' tenure (limitation of 9 years)	27	3	73
2	Whistle Blower Policy	87	1	13
3	Audit Qualifications: Move towards Unqualified Report	77	2	23
4	Shareholders' Right to receive half yearly financial reports	23	4	77
	Total	53		47

Data source: Author's research based on Annexure 2.

Findings

1. No requirement being complied with 100 per cent.
2. Compliance of different requirements in descending order:
   (a) Highest compliance – 87 per cent – Whistle Blower Policy – Rank 1.
   (b) Second highest – 77 per cent – Audit Qualifications: Move towards unqualified report – Rank 2.
   (c) Next – 27 per cent – Independent Directors' tenure (limitation of 9 years) – Rank 3.
   (d) Lowest compliance – 23 per cent – Shareholders' right to receive half yearly financial reports – Rank 4.

Analysis

1. Compliance with whistle blower policy by 87 per cent companies is quite significant because this policy is perceived as being instrumental in maintaining financial discipline by bringing scandals to the fore.
2. It is also commendable that the requirement 'Audit qualifications: Move

towards unqualified report' is complied with by a high 77 per cent of the companies. In the backdrop of financial scandals that led to the genesis of corporate governance, high compliance levels of these two requirements assume great significance. The corporate sector, however, further needs to strive to achieve 100 per cent compliance on both these counts.

3. However, the tendency to prefer the same directors for reappointment as independent directors is quite disturbing. This tendency is bound to create conflict of interest and jeopardise the very independence of the directors.
4. Companies also need to be investor friendly and keep them regularly informed of the financial performance.
5. Hence, while the companies seem to be conscious of enacting financial discipline, they seem to be lacking in stakeholder reporting which creates information asymmetry and puts retail investors at greater risk.

Company-wise Compliance/Non-compliance

Table 2 provides the details of company-wise compliance/non-compliance.

Table 2: Company-wise Compliance/Non-compliance of Four Specified Non-Mandatory Requirements

Sl. No.	*Company*	*Compliance*		*Non-compliance (%)*
		%	*Rank*	
1	Axis Bank	50	3	50
2	Bajaj Auto	100	1	0
3	Bharti Airtel	50	3	50
4	BHEL (PSU)	50	3	50
5	Cipla	0	5	100
6	Coal India (PSU)	75	2	25
7	Dr Reddy's Lab	50	3	50
8	Gail India (PSU)	100	1	0
9	HDFC Bank	75	2	25
10	HDFC	50	3	50
11	Hero MotoCorp	0	5	100
12	Hindalco	50	3	50
13	Hindustan Unilever	25	4	75
14	ICICI Bank	50	3	50
15	Infosys	25	4	75
16	ITC	75	2	25
17	L & T	25	4	75

Sl. No.	Company	Compliance		Non-compliance (%)
		%	Rank	
18	Mahindra & Mahindra	50	3	50
19	Maruti Suzuki	25	4	75
20	NTPC (PSU)	75	2	25
21	ONGC (PSU)	50	3	50
22	Reliance	75	2	25
23	SBI (PSU)	75	2	25
24	SSLT (Sesa Sterlite)	25	4	75
25	Sun Pharma	25	4	75
26	TATA Motors	75	2	25
27	TATA Power	75	2	25
28	TATA Steel	75	2	25
29	TCS	75	2	25
30	Wipro	50	3	50
	Aggregate	53		47

Findings

1. There is wide diversity among Sensex companies in complying with the four specified non-mandatory requirements of Sensex companies.
2. Put together, they have complied with the four specified non-mandatory requirements to the extent of only 53 per cent. A very high non-compliance of 47 per cent is indicated.

Further Rank-wise Grouping of Corporate Compliance

To facilitate better comprehension, the data of Table 2 has been regrouped in order of ranks in Table 3.

Findings of Rank-wise Grouping of Corporate Compliance

1. Only two companies, that is, Bajaj Auto, a private sector undertaking, and GAIL (India), a Public Sector Undertaking (PSU) have scored the first rank, that is, 100 per cent compliance.
2. Only 40 per cent (12) companies fall in the first two ranks. Out of them four are PSUs—GAIL (India) in the first rank, and remaining three, that is, Coal India, NTPC, and SBI in the second.
3. The largest private enterprise, Reliance and all the four Sensex TATA companies have scored second rank, having complied with three requirements.

Table 3: Rank-wise Grouping of Companies' Compliance of Four Specified Non-Mandatory Requirements

Sl. No.	*Compliance (%)*	*Rank*	*Number of Companies*	*% to Total*	*Company/ies*
1	100	1	2	7	Bajaj Auto, GAIL (PSU)
2	75	2	10	33	Coal India (PSU), HDFC Bank, ITC, NTPC (PSU), Reliance, SBI (PSU), TATA Motors, TATA Power, TATA Steel, TCS
3	50	3	9	30	Axis Bank, Bharti Airtel, BHEL (PSU), Dr Reddy's Lab, HDFC, Hindalco, ICICI Bank, Mahindra & Mahindra, ONGC (PSU)
4	25	4	7	23	Hindustan Unilever, Infosys, L&T, Maruti Suzuki, SSLT (Sesa Sterlite), Sun Pharma, Wipro
5	0	5	2	7	Cipla, Hero MotoCorp
Total			30	100	

4. A high 60 per cent (18) fall in the next three ranks, out of which two, that is, BHEL and ONGC are PSUs.
5. Infosys is a big disappointment at the fourth rank.
6. Cipla and Hero MotoCorp have surprisingly not complied with any requirement, falling in the lowest rank of 5.

Analysis

Sensex companies are all blue chip companies and their market capitalization, as noted earlier, is 48 per cent of the total Indian market's capitalization. These companies thus represent almost half of the market on this parameter. However, their performance in enacting financial discipline and reporting through corporate governance is totally unsatisfactory. Non-compliance of even a single norm by companies like Cipla and Hero MotoCorp is highly disappointing. Even the two Maharatna PSUs, BHEL and ONGC have complied with only two requirements. Overall, the total average compliance of the Sensex companies at 53 per cent is far from satisfactory. Corporates need to introspect.

CONCLUSION

This research proves that the Indian corporate sector has to go a long way in complying with the four non-mandatory voluntary requirements of corporate governance meant to enact financial discipline, control, and shareholder reporting.

More specifically, the track record of financial discipline (Whistle Blower policy compliance of 87 per cent and 'Audit Qualifications: Move towards unqualified report' compliance of 77 per cent) is suggestive of high quality financial statements with a very low risk of fraudulent occurrences. Companies, however, do not seem to be serious about sharing the financial information in print with the shareholders (just 23 per cent compliance). E-mailing, etc., is fine, but that is no substitute to hard documents. Moreover, not all individual shareholders have either access to the net or are tech savvy. Keeping them away from the reports leads to information asymmetry and inefficiency in the market and exposes the individual investors to avoidable market risks.

Again, the tendency to appoint and reappoint the independent directors for tenures exceeding the threshold limit of 9 years is very disturbing. Corporate performance in complying with this key norm of independent directors' tenure to be limited to 9 years at 27 per cent is grossly unsatisfactory. In fact, they should be appointed for not more than one term. This could also act as a catalyst in improving and bringing the compliance of the other three requirements to the level of 100 per cent.

Thus, our hypothesis, 'H1: Indian corporate sector is not in full compliance with the 4 specified corporate governance norms aimed at enacting financial discipline, control and shareholder reporting thereof' is proved. Overall, the study finds that while the companies seem to be conscious of enacting financial discipline they seem to be lacking in stakeholder reporting which creates information asymmetry and puts retail investors at greater risk.

REFERENCES

A. Gupta, A.P. Nair and R. Gogula, 'Corporate Governance Reporting by Indian Companies: A Content Analysis Study', *The ICFAI Journal of Corporate Governance*, vol. 2, no. 4, 3003, pp. 7–18.

A. Pahuja and B.S. Bhatia, 'Determinants of CG Disclosures: Evidence from companies in Northern India', *The IUP Journal of Corporate Governance*, vol. 9, no. 3, 2010, pp. 69–88.

Ambrish Gupta, *Financial Accounting for Management: An Analytical Perspective,* 4th edn, Delhi: Pearson Education, 2012, pp. 493–96.

BSE (n.d.1), 'Clause 49 of the Listing Agreement', Retrieved from http://www.bseindia.com/Static/about/Listing_Agreement.aspx?expandable=2

BSE (n.d.), 'S&P BSE SENSEX – The Barometer of Indian Capital Markets', Retrieved from http://www.bseindia.com/indices/DispIndex.aspx?iname=BSE30&index_Code=16&page=B16FEF6B-3A5C-45B8-89F9-C79E884CC716

BSE (2014a), 'Market Capitalization of BSE Sensex Companies', 3 October 2014, Retrieved from http://www.bseindia.com/sensexview/indexview_new.aspx?index_Code=16&iname=BSE30#

BSE (2014b), 'Market Capitalization of BSE Listed Companies', 3 October 2014, Retrieved from http://www.bseindia.com/markets/equity/EQReports/TopMarketCapitalization.aspx?expandable=3

BSE (2014c), 'S&P BSE SENSEX Index Constituents', Retrieved from http://www.bseindia.com/sensexview/IndicesWatch_weight.aspx?iname=BSE30&index_Code=16

Committee on the Financial Aspects of Corporate Governance (1992), Cadbury Committee Report on Financial Aspects of Corporate Governance, December 1992, Retrieved from http://business.gov.in/outerwin.php?id =http://www.ecgi.org/codes/documents/cadbury.pdf

K.C. Gupta, 'A Comparative Study of Corporate Governance Practices in Selected Companies of Automobile Industry in Haryana (An Indian State)', *Punjab Journal of Business Studies*, vol. 1, no. 2, 2006, pp. 58–71.

Madan Lal Bhasin, 'Corporate Governance Disclosure Practices: The Portrait of a Developing Country', *International Journal of Business and Management*, vol. 5, no. 4, 2010, pp. 150–67.

P. Srinivasan and V. Srinivasan, 'Status of Corporate Governance Research on India: An Exploratory Study', Working Paper No. 334, Indian Institute of Management, Bangalore, 2011.

V.K. Sareen and S. Chander, 'Firm's Attributes and Corporate Governance Disclosure Practices: An Empirical Investigation', *Indian Journal of Corporate Governance*, vol. 2, no. 1, 2009, pp. 117–37.

ANNEXURES

Annexure 1

Constituent Companies of S&P BSE Sensex (as on 29 October 2013)

Sl. No.	*Company*	*Scrip Code*	*Industry sector (sub sector)*	*Business house*	*Ownership*
1	Axis Bank	532215	Finance (Banks)	UUUTI/LIC	Private
2	Bajaj Auto	532977	TE (2/3 wheelers)	Bajaj	Private
3	Bharti Airtel	532454	Telecom (Telecom services)	Bharti	Private
4	BHEL	500103	CG (Heavy Electrical Equipment)	*Govt. of India*	**Public**
5	Cipla	500087	Healthcare (Pharmaceuticals)	Y. K. Hamied	Private
6	Coal India	533278	MMPM (Coal)	*Govt. of India*	**Public**
7	Dr Reddy's Lab	500124	Healthcare (Pharmaceuticals)	Dr Reddy's	Private
8	Gail India	532155	Oil & Gas (Utilities: Non-Elec.)	*Govt. of India*	**Public**
9	HDFC Bank	500180	Finance (Banks)	HDFC group	Private
10	HDFC	500010	Finance (Housing Finance)	HDFC group	Private
11	Hero MotoCorp	500182	TE (2/3 wheelers)	Munjal (Hero)	Private
12	Hindalco	500440	MMPM (Aluminium)	Aditya Birla	Private
13	Hindustan Unilever	500696	FMCG (Personal Products)	MNC Associate-Unilever	Private
14	ICICI Bank	532174	Finance (Banks)	ICICI group	Private
15	Infosys	500209	IT (IT Consulting & Software)	N.R. Narayanmurthy	Private
16	ITC	500875	FMCG (Cigarettes, Tobacco Products)	MNC Associate-ITC	Private
17	L & T	500510	CG (Construction & Engineering)	L & T group	Private
18	Mahindra & Mahindra	500520	TE (Cars & Utility Vehicles)	Mahindra	Private

Sl. No.	*Company*	*Scrip Code*	*Industry sector (sub sector)*	*Business house*	*Ownership*
19	Maruti Suzuki	532500	TE (Cars & Utility Vehicles)	MNC Associate-Suzuki	Private
20	NTPC	532555	Power (Electric Utilities)	*Govt. of India*	**Public**
21	ONGC	500312	Oil & Gas (Exploration & Production)	*Govt. of India*	**Public**
22	Reliance	500325	Oil & Gas (Integrated Oil & Gas)	Mukesh Ambani	Private
23	SBI	500112	Finance (Banks)	Govt. of India	Public
24	SSLT (Sesa Sterlite)	500295	MMPM (Iron & Steel/Intermediate Products)	Vedanta	Private
25	Sun Pharma	524715	Healthcare (Pharmaceuticals)	Dilip Singhvi	Private
26	TATA Motors	500570	TE (Commercial Vehicles)	TATA	Private
27	TATA Power	500400	Power (Electric Utilities)	TATA	Private
28	TATA Steel	500470	MMPM (Iron & Steel/Intermediate Products)	TATA	Private
29	TCS	532540	IT (IT Consulting & Software)	TATA	Private
30	Wipro	507685	IT (IT Consulting & Software)	Azim Premji	Private

Notes:

1. Sesa Sterlite was earlier known as Sterlite Industries.
2. Industry sectors/sub sectors have been identified as per the information available at www.bseindia.com.
3. Business houses have been identified as per the information available at www.bseindia.com and Capitaline Neo database.

Annexure 2

Break-up of Requirement-wise Compliance/Non-compliance of Four Specified Non-mandatory Requirements of Clause 49

Sl. No.	*Company*	*Requirement No.*				*Aggregates*		*Compliance (%)*	*Non-compliance (%)*
		1	*2*	*3*	*4*	*Y*	*N*		
1	Axis Bank	N	Y	Y	N	2	2	50	50
2	Bajaj Auto	Y	Y	Y	Y	4	0	100	0
3	Bharti Airtel	N	Y	Y	N	2	2	50	50
4	BHEL	Y	N	Y	N	2	2	50	50
5	Cipla	N	N	N	N	0	4	0	100
6	Coal India	Y	Y	Y	N	3	1	75	25
7	Dr Reddy's Lab	N	Y	Y	N	2	2	50	50
8	Gail India	Y	Y	Y	Y	4	0	100	0
9	HDFC Bank	Y	Y	Y	N	3	1	75	25
10	HDFC	N	Y	Y	N	2	2	50	50
11	Hero MotoCorp	N	N	N	N	0	4	0	100
12	Hindalco	N	Y	Y	N	2	2	50	50
13	Hindustan Unilever	N	Y	N	N	1	3	25	75
14	ICICI Bank	N	Y	Y	N	2	2	50	50
15	Infosys	N	Y	N	N	1	3	25	75
16	ITC	Y	Y	Y	N	3	1	75	25
17	L & T	N	Y	N	N	1	3	25	75
18	Mahindra & Mahindra	N	Y	Y	N	2	2	50	50
19	Maruti Suzuki	N	Y	N	N	1	3	25	75
20	NTPC	Y	Y	Y	N	3	1	75	25
21	ONGC	N	Y	Y	N	2	2	50	50

Sl. No.	Company	Requirement No.				Aggregates		Compliance (%)	Non-compliance (%)
		1	2	3	4	Y	N		
22	Reliance	N	Y	Y	Y	3	1	75	25
23	SBI	Y	Y	Y	N	3	1	75	25
24	SSLT (Sesa Sterlite)	N	Y	N	N	1	3	25	75
25	Sun Pharma	N	N	Y	N	1	3	25	75
26	TATA Motors	N	Y	Y	Y	3	1	75	25
27	TATA Power	N	Y	Y	Y	3	1	75	25
28	TATA Steel	N	Y	Y	Y	3	1	75	25
29	TCS	N	Y	Y	Y	3	1	75	25
30	Wipro	N	Y	Y	N	2	2	50	50
	Aggregates:	...	...	...	...	64	56	53	47
	Y	8	26	23	7	64			
	N	22	4	7	23	56			
	Total	30	30	30	30	120			
	Compliance (%)	27	87	77	23	53			
	Non-compliance (%)	73	13	23	77	47			

Legend: Req. 1: Independent directors' tenure (limited to 9 years); Req. 2: Whistle Blower policy; Req. 3: Audit qualifications: Move towards unqualified report; Req. 4: Shareholders' right to receive half yearly financial reports.

Notes:

1. Y: Compliance
2. N: Non-compliance.
3. In a few cases information on adoption/non adoption with non-mandatory requirements was not provided under a separate head. Therefore, information was culled out in bits and pieces from the entire corporate governance report/auditors' report/directors' report. Every effort has been made to ensure accuracy in those cases. However, inadvertent mistake could be possible.

Interlinkages of Ownership Structure, Corporate Governance and Firm Performance

An Empirical Sectoral Validation

Namita Rajput, Bharti[1] and Shelly Oberoi

Sri Aurobindo College, University of Delhi, Delhi

[1] USMS, GGS Indraprastha University, New Delhi

e-mail: namitarajput27@gmail.com; bharti.1119@gmail.com; shellyoberoi83@gmail.com

ABSTRACT

The subject of corporate governance has received major consideration on account of its influence on the economic and financial health of the corporation especially after plenitude of recent company shake downs and frauds. Fair, principled and high ethical values of the companies can help in reducing costs and benefitting the organizations in a long way. The issue of improvement of corporate governance is of prime importance in India to sustain future developments. The Indian government has realized that good corporate governance is necessary to improve corporate competitiveness and to attract foreign investors. With better corporate governance, listed firms can reduce agency costs, become more competitive in global markets, improve their financial performance and thus lead to wealth maximization of the shareholders. Current literature does not provide any conclusive evidence in proving the relationship between shareholder types and firm performance. Our study is a modest attempt in this direction to add knowledge and address the noticeable gap in Indian literature. The regular types of shareholders among listed companies in India are institutions, government, managers, foreigners and diverse shareholders. Using panel regression , the relationships between shareholder types and financial performance as measured by Tobin's Q, ROA, ROE were tested taking a sample of BSE100 companies excluding banking and insurance companies. The variables were tested on four different sectors of the economy namely- Fast Moving Consumer

Goods (FMCG), Information Technology (IT), Automobile and Pharmaceuticals. The overall results for all sectors are quite similar. However, variables like advertising spent in FMCG and IT sectors have a significant positive impact on firm performance. The analysis of the result also shows foreign institutional investors and family shareholder types have a significant positive influence on ROE whereas government and retail shareholder affect ROE negatively. Also, the corporate governance index has a significantly negative impact on ROE. However, the relationship of CGI with ROA and Tobin's Q was not found to be significant.

Keywords: Corporate Governance, Agency Cost, Wealth Maximization, Shareholder Types, Firm Performance, Corporate Governance Index

INTRODUCTION

Corporate Governance may be defined as a set of systems, processes and principles which ensure that a company is governed in the best interest of all stakeholders. The concept is about promoting corporate fairness, transparency and accountability to do 'good business'. Corporations around the world are increasingly recognizing that sustained growth of their organization requires cooperation of all stakeholders, which requires adherence to the best corporate governance practices. In this regard, the management needs to act as trustees of the shareholders at large and prevent asymmetry of benefits between various sections of shareholders. It is about commitment to values and about ethical business conduct. Ethical dilemmas arise from conflicting interests of the parties involved. In this regard, managers make decisions based on a set of principles influenced by the values, context and culture of the organization. Ethical leadership is good for business as the organization is seen to conduct its business in line with the expectations of all stakeholders.

The aim of 'Good Corporate Governance' is to ensure commitment of the board in managing the company in a transparent manner for maximizing long-term value of the company for its shareholders and all other parties. It integrates all the participants involved in a process, which is economic, and at the same time social.

Today adoption of good Corporate Governance practices has emerged as an integral element for doing business. It is not only a pre-requisite for facing intense competition for sustainable growth in the emerging global market scenario but is also an embodiment of the parameters of fairness, accountability, disclosures and transparency to maximize value for the stakeholders. The topic has received major consideration on account of its influence on the economic and financial health of the corporation especially after plenitude of recent company shake downs and frauds. In the changing global scenario, it has become necessary to bring in effective governance practices in the corporate sector. Accordingly, several codes, guidelines and principles have been made and implemented covering varied aspects of corporate governance.

Confederation of Indian Industries lead the Indian corporate sector to formulate a voluntary code of Corporate Governance (CG) post liberalization followed by clause 49 of listing agreement that necessitated the appointment of independent directors. *Naresh Chandra Committee* laid major emphasis on independent oversight of board and audit, and improvements in disclosures (financial as well as non-financial). In the years that followed, committees constituted under the leadership of Mr Narayan Murthy and Mr J.J. Irani, emphasised explicitly for bringing in best practices from around the world to create a well regulated environment that promotes entrepreneurship. The Satyam debacle in 2009 shocked the industry overall but brought the importance of indispensable governance necessary for growth and development. Since then The Ministry of Corporate Affairs (MCA) came out with guidelines in 2009 in the form of Clause 49 called 'Corporate Governance', that contains eight sections dealing with the Board of Directors, Audit Committee, Remuneration of Directors, Board Procedure, Management, Shareholders, Report on Corporate Governance, and Compliance. Firms that do not comply with Clause 49 can be de-listed and face financial penalties. Now, the Companies Act, 2013 which has been enacted recently, has further strengthened the CG norms.

Hence, in the years to come, corporate governance will become more relevant and a more acceptable practice worldwide. This is easily evident from the various activities undertaken by many companies in framing and enforcing codes of conduct and honest business practices; following more stringent norms for financial and non-financial disclosures, as mandated by law; accepting higher and appropriate accounting standards; enforcing tax reforms coupled with deregulation and competition; etc. Evidence in the present study underlines the relationship between types of shareholders and financial performance of the companies in four different sectors of the economy namely – Fast Moving Consumer Goods (FMCG), Information Technology (IT), Automobile and Pharmaceuticals. Financial performance can be measured using indicators like profitability, efficiency, leverage and liquidity. The present research uses three measures of performance indicators for the purpose of analysis, namely ROA, ROE and Tobin's Q. The independent variables taken are seven in number – Retail Shareholding, Institutional Shareholders, Government Ownership, Family Shareholding, FII Shareholding, Corporate Shareholding and Corporate Governance Index. The control variables such as firm's size, proxy by total assets, firm's age since its inception and leverage proxy by debt equity ratio are considered as exogenous variables. Advertising expenses and board size of the sample firms have also been included.

To achieve the objective, the paper is divided into following sections, i.e. the present section gives the insights of corporate governance and its various parameters, followed by next section which gives a brief review of literature. Third section presents research objectives and hypothesis followed by fourth section which deals with data and methodology. Fifth section entails the analysis and interpretation of empirical results which are divided into two parts, first, gives the aggregate of all sectors, the relationship between shareholder types and ROE and second that analyses the relationship between ownership structure and ROA for all four types of sectors namely, Auto, FMCG, IT and Pharmaceuticals. It is followed by the summary, conclusion and implications of the research contained in sixth section and nomenclature in seventh section. References form the part of last section.

REVIEW OF LITERATURE

Present section gives a snapshot of the existing literature done in India and across the globe on the topic. The inter linkage between ownership pattern and firm performance has been a subject of debate in the corporate finance theory and it dates back to the Berle and Means (1932) thesis. The thesis concluded a negative relationship between the diffuseness of shareholdings and firm performance. Demsetz (1983) challenged this view and argued that the ownership structure of a corporation should be thought of as an endogenous outcome of decisions that reflect the influence of shareholders and of trading on the market for shares. Rapidly increasing empirical research shows that the pattern of share holding can be an important source of incentive for managers, boards of directors and outside shareholders (Milgrom and Roberts, 1992). Developing economies face heavily concentrated firm ownership structures (Blasi and Shleifer, 1996; Claessens et al., 1996; Claessens, 1997; Xu and Wang, 1997; La Porta et al., 1998; Yee, 1998; Wiwattanakantang, 1999; Yeh, et al., 2001; and Joh, 2003).

McConnell and Servaes (1990) research gives evidence on the relationship between the distribution of equity ownership and corporate value. The author studies the cross sectional relation between Tobin's Q and equity ownership from the sample and the firm value is taken as a function of distribution of equity ownership amongst corporate insiders, individual shareholders, block shareholders and institutional investors. The author concludes that insider ownership and Q have a curvilinear relationship, i.e value of Q initially rises first to a maximum and then declines on further rise in insider equity ownership. Institutional investors have a significant positive influence on the firm value while block shareholders have no significant relationship with the value of the firm. Shleifer and Vishny (1997) focus on the theme of corporate governance from the perspective of agency problem, sometimes referred to as the separation of ownership and control and emphasize on the question as to how investors get the managers to give them back their invested money. The authors take into account ownership by small investors and concentrated ownership; i.e. by large shareholders which reduces agency costs and thereby improves corporate governance and firm performance and also discuss the negative impact of state ownership on company performance. Thomsen Pedersen (1998) study the sample of the largest companies from 12 European nations to find the link between ownership structure and company economic performance. Ownership structure is measured by the identity and share of the largest owner and performance is measured by ROA, market to book values and sales growth controlling for industry. Thcy conclude presence of a bell-shaped (first increasing and then decreasing) effect of ownership share on ROA and market-to-book values of equity. Companies whose largest owner is a financial institution have higher market-to book values than companies in which the largest owner is a family, another company or the government. The effects on asset returns are qualitatively identical, but weaker and insignificant except for a negative effect of government ownership. In contrast, companies whose largest owner is a family or another company have significantly higher sales growth. Xu Xiaonian, Wang Yan (1997) study the publicly-listed companies in China on and SZSE for the years 1993, 1994 and 1995 to investigate whether ownership pattern has significant effects on the performance. The authors use three accounting ratios to measure the firm's performance, the market-to-book value ratio (MBR), ROE, and ROA and it is concluded that the firm's performance is positively correlated with legal persons(institutional shareholders). In contrast, the fraction of equity owned by individual shareholders, has a significant negative effect on the market-to-book ratios. Also the authors conclude a negative relationship between the shares owned by the state and firm performance.

Repei (2000) researched on the sample of 318 companies for 1997–1998 years from all regions of Ukraine covering 15 sectors including fast moving service and finance to test if corporate performance varies according to the shareholder structure and concludes that private ownership lead to higher performance than state one as the latter demonstrates failure in enterprise restructuring because of economically harmful political objectives, and outside owners provide much better governance of assets, while private individuals are very ineffective owners due to "free-riding" problem. Bertrand et al., 2002 concludes that Asian countries particularly India face more family control in businesses probably due to the ineffectiveness of the legal system in protecting property rights.

Kumar (2004), from a sample of the Indian corporate firms over 1994-2000 empirically observed the relationship between the ownership structure and firm performance using a panel method and found that foreign shareholding pattern did not influence the firm performance significantly. Dwivedi and Jain (2005) studied 340 large listed Indian firms from 1997-2001 across 24 industry groups using regression model and measured firm performance by Tobin's Q. The results provided a positive correlation between foreign shareholding and market value while insignificant relationship between Indian institutional shareholders with firm performance. A weak positive association is present between board size and firm value while public shareholding has a linear negative relation. Christoph and Moldenhauer (2005) examine a data set of 245 German firms to answer the question whether there is any empirical relationship between corporate performance and insider ownership. They find evidence for a positive and significant relationship between corporate performance, as measured by stock price performance as well as by Tobin's Q, and insider ownership. Imam and Malik (2007) analyzed the listed non financial firms on Dhaka Stock Exchange and provide evidence that institutional and foreign holding is positively and significantly related to the firm performance as measured by firm's holding period returns and Tobin's Q, and the relationship is a monotonic one. Basically, foreign holdings are increasing in those firms that have good governance and through these good governance practice firm will improve by doing better for all of its stakeholders. Also, sponsor ownership is negatively related and in case of the other dimensions it is positively related, but the result except foreign holding turns out to be insignificant.

Ongore O. Vincent, K'Obonyo O. Peter, Ogutu Martin (2011), analyzed forty-two firms in Kenya using Pearson's Product Moment Correlation and Logistic Regression. The results of ownership identity were analyzed based on five elements: government; foreign; institution; diverse; and manager (insider). The study concluded that foreign ownership, institutions, insiders and diverse shareholders have a significant positive relationship on firm performance whereas government affects the firm performance significantly negatively.

The existing corporate finance literature points conclusively that foreign ownership effect is significant and positive on the firm performance while the government as a stakeholder affects the firm negatively. Also the impact of private individuals and retail owners is mostly ineffective in increasing the financial performance. There is a lack of studies revealing the impact of shareholder types, corporate governance on financial performance. Our study is a modest attempt in this direction.

RESEARCH OBJECTIVES AND HYPOTHESIS

Shareholding pattern varies across the firms and therefore would contribute differently to the firm performance. In the research, we have attempted to examine the relationship between firm performance and ownership structure in 76 companies (from BSE 100, excluding banking and financial sector companies) for four major sectors namely, Automobile, IT, Pharmaceuticals and FMCG. Following are the objectives of the research:

1. To study effects of ownership structure (shareholding pattern) on performance of firms of all the four sectors in India.
2. To study the effect of corporate governance measured by Corporate Governance Index on financial performance of a firm of all four sectors.

DATA AND METHODOLOGY

Daily data from BSE 100 Index was taken from 01st April 2007 to 31st March 2014. The data sources were the annual reports of the companies, corporate database (PROWESS) maintained by the CMIE, the Center for Monitoring the Indian Economy, and the reports filed by companies with the BSE as part of the listing requirements. The sample size studied is of 76 companies from BSE100 excluding banking and financial services companies since they are governed by the Banking Regulation Act and not by the Companies Act.

Key Variables

For research following variables were used:

Measurement of Corporate Performance

Two measures of performance, as supported in the finance and accounting literature were chosen for the purpose of analysis.

- *Tobin's Q:* Tobin and Brainard (1968) and Tobin (1969) designed a measurement of corporate performance, which is equal to the ratio of market value of equity and debt divided by the replacement costs of total assets. Companies displaying Tobin's Q greater than unity are considered to be using scarce resources effectively, while those with Tobin's Q less than unity as using resources poorly.

  Tobin's Q has been computed as [MV of common stock + BV of preference stock + BV of borrowings + BV of CL] / [BV of total assets as denoted by FA + INV + CA] with all values computed at the year end.
- *Return on Assets (ROA):* The accounting variable chosen was calculated as the ratio of net profit to assets. Total assets include value of fixed assets, investments, and current assets.
- *Return on Equity (ROE):* The ratio of net profit to equity capital. Equity Capital is the total outstanding paid up equity capital of the firm as at the end of the accounting period. Shares issued but not paid-up or pending allotments do not form part of equity capital. This includes bonus equity shares issued, if any, by the firm in the past. ROE = Net Profit/Equity Capital

Ownership and Governance Variables

The ownership structure and corporate governance mechanisms can influence company performance. The ownership and governance measures were analyzed as independent variables.

- *Ownership structure*: The shareholding has been classified according to a standard taxonomy of investors' categories and definitions as provided under Clause 35 (Appendix III) and 40A of the Listing Agreement (Appendix IV). For the cross-sectional and pooled panel regression analysis the study considers only six major groups of ownership, viz., Retail shareholders, family ownership, foreign institutional investors, domestic institutional investors, government, corporate.

H1: There is a significant relationship between retail shareholding and return on equity.

H2: There is a significant relationship between Institutional shareholding and return on equity.

H3: There is a significant relationship between Government shareholding and return on equity.

H4: There is a significant relationship between family shareholding and return on equity.

H5: There is a significant relationship between FII shareholding and return on equity.

H6: There is a significant relationship between corporate shareholding and return on equity.

- *Board size:* There is a view that larger boards are better for corporate performance because they have a range of expertise to help make better decisions and are harder for a powerful CEO to dominate. However, recent thinking has leaned towards smaller boards. Board size has been measured as the total number of directors on the board.

  H5: There is a significant relationship between board size and return on equity.

Control Variables

In order to control for the other possible determinants of performance not captured by the ownership variables, some observed company characteristics have been included as control variables. The control variables used in the study have been selected with reference to those employed in earlier studies.

- *Age:* It is argued that effects of learning curve and survivor bias old companies are more efficient and therefore promise better performance. However, older companies are prone to inertia, and rigidities in adaptability, which may lead to lower performance. Age has been measured as the number of years for which the company has been in existence since incorporation to the date of observation.
- *Size:* A vast amount of literature has investigated the relation between size and performance of firms. Pervan and Josipa (2012) concluded that firm size has significant positive impact on profitability. Lang and Stulz (1994) reported significant negative correlation between size and Tobin's Q. Gilson (1997) measured the natural log of total assets as a proxy of firm size. In the study, size has been measured by the natural logarithm of total assets of firms.

- *Debt-Equity:* Theories on the role of debt provide us with a complementary corporate governance mechanism that monitors the management (Jensen, 1989; and Thomsen and Pedersen, 2000).

  Following regression equation for our research has been formulated:

  FIRM PERFORMANCE, ROE (RSH, IISH, GSH, FSH, FIISH, CSH, S, CGI, ADVT, BS, AGE, DEBT)

  We have used pooled panel regression model. The data are usually collected over time and over the same individuals and then a regression is run over these two dimensions. The regression has been applied on the entire sample in total.

ANALYSIS AND INTERPREATIONS OF EMPIRICAL RESULTS

Relationship Between Shareholder Types and ROE

Table 1: Aggregate Results of Pooled Panel Regression

Independent Variables	*Dependent Variables*	
	Coefficients	*ROE (p-value)*
Intercept	90.7234	0.0790
Retail Shareholding	–0.230325	0.3542
Institutional Investors Shareholding	0.068730	0.4167
Government	–0.103891	0.0200
Family Shareholding	0.818756	0.0053
FII Shareholding	0.390567	0.0008
Corporate Shareholding	–0.042546	0.356
Size	–16.56712	0.019
Log Advertising	2.089602	0.0125
CGI	–15.81236	0.001
Board Size	1.356901	0.0829
Age	0.153892	0.2178
Debt-Equity	–1.9876	0.4256
R Squared	0.21659	

The table is a snapshot of the regression results on an aggregate basis for all the firms in the sample. The retail shareholders have a negative relationship with financial performance as measured by ROE, though not significant. As per Repei (2000), the problem of 'free riding' make the ownership by individual shareholders ineffective. Therefore we reject the null hypothesis that retail shareholders have significant impact on ROE. Institutional investors have a positive correlation with firm performance although insignificant as they help in reducing the information asymmetry associated with ownership and control and have better access to information that helps in decision making (Shleifer and Vishny, 1986). Hence the null hypothesis that impact of institutional shareholders on ROE is significant is also rejected. The impact of government ownership on firm performance is significantly negative at 5% level as governments are likely to pay special attention to political goals, many of which may be negatively correlated with the ROE (Pedersen and Thomsen, 1998). In fact the rationale for government ownership in welfare economics is non- profit making (Arrow, 1969; Shephard, 1989). Thus, the null hypothesis is accepted. The ownership control by family has a positive and significant impact on the financial performance of the company and can be explained using the incentive alignment argument when family members also act as managers. The long term orientation of the family owner and reduction in principal-agent conflicts are some reasons (Reeb, 2003; Górriz & Fumás, 2005). This is also supported by the argument that instead of focusing on short term profit maximization, family owners have a long term commitment to the firm and are willing to invest in the capacities that will create competitive advantages which require large investment in the beginning. Null hypothesis is thus accepted. FII also have a positive and significant impact at 5% level on ROE. Aydin, Sayim and Yalama, 2007 have concluded that on an average multinational corporations have performed better than the domestically owned firms mainly due to the better ability of foreign owners to monitor managers and provide performance based incentives and avoid behaviors that undermine the wealth creation motivation of the firm owners. Moreover, due to transfer of new and better technology and globally tested management practices, the operating expenses decrease which enhances efficiency and generate savings (Ongore, K'Obonyo and Ogutu, 2011). Null hypothesis is therefore accepted. The presence of corporate ownership has a negative impact on ROE, though insignificant. As is widely expected, the large amount of assets, or size of the firm should have been positively correlated with ROE as more assets provide the company with cushion to raise capital easily. However the firm performance is significantly negatively correlated with asset size. It is argued that as the size increases, efficiency reduces as control by top managers over strategic and operational activities decreases. On the other hand, advertising expenses of the firm yield positive and significant relationship with ROE at 5% and can be explained on account of increased visibility of the firm in the market. Joshi and Hanssens, 2010 posit that advertising spending has a positive effect on the market capitalization of the firm and a negative impact on the valuation of the competitor of comparable size. The Corporate Governance Index, CGI, is significantly negatively correlated with the firm performance mainly because of negative and significant impact of CEO Duality, audit committee size, board meetings and presence of non-executive directors who may not have total commitment to the cause of the company because of other commitments which limits their contribution. According to Baysinger and Heskisson, 1990, non-executive directors are limited in scope and understanding when it comes to complexities involving decision making because of their temporal position. According to Wu Ming-Cheng et al. (2005), board size and CEO Duality have a significant negative impact on firm performance. The analysis also shows that board size has a significant and positive effect in increasing the ROE at 10% significance level. As concluded by Coles et al., 2008 and Linck et al., 2008, greater knowledge of various board members can improve firm performance. The age of the firm as explained by experience shows a positive relationship although insignificant in improving performance. Due to economies of scale, older firms enjoy better performance (Kumar, 2004). ROE is negatively related with debt at 5% significance level as high debt in a company leads to increased cost of capital along with risk of financial distress.

R-squared value is 21.65% for ROE.

Regression Results: Sectoral Index Basis

In this section, regression on performance as measured by ROE of all the four sectors has been applied.

The table gives a snapshot of the regression results on sectoral basis for the sample. It is evident that institutional shareholders have a positive impact on the firm performance, although the effect is significant only in case of auto sector. Retail shareholders have a negative relationship with financial performance as measured by ROE, though not significant. The impact of government ownership on the firm performance for all four sectors is significantly negative at 5% level. Family shareholding has a positive relation with ROE, though it is significant only for Auto sector at 5% level. Foreign institutional investors have a positive impact on firm performance as measured by ROE and significant for all sectors except FMCG. Corporate ownership has a negative insignificant impact on ROE. Size of the firm, measured by asset base is negatively related with ROE while it is significant only for Auto and FMCG sector. Log of advertising is significant and positive for FMCG

Table 2: Snapshot of the Regression Results on Sectoral Basis for the Sample

Independent Variables	*Auto Sector*		*FMCG Sector*		*Pharma Sector*		*IT Sector*	
	Coefficients	*p- value*	*Coefficients*	*p- value*	*Coefficients*	*p- value*	*Coefficients*	*p- value*
Intercept	16.2654	0.6945	285.3401	0.2381	131.0836	0.1523	–4.28912	0.6531
Retail Shareholding	–0.236712	0.3451	–0.76589	0.4382	–0.41926	0.5627	–0.573105	0.3014
Institutional Investors Shareholding	0.238451	0.0296	0.205631	0.7561	0.003561	0.8931	0.106539	0.2162
Government	–0.120973	0.0231	–0.341905	0.0315	–0.328101	0.0157	–0.23418	0.0326
Family Shareholding	0.21345	0.0234	0.014372	0.5611	0.016713	0.439	0.105621	0.3142
FII Shareholding	0.4871	0.0003	0.50319	0.6529	0.671209	0.00265	0.453191	0.03481
Corporate Shareholding	–0.03289	0.3471	–0.34801	0.5719	–0.519021	0.6712	–0.43812	0.763
Size	–23.43	0.0001	–49.7123	0.0641	4.23012	0.7531	–2.51902	0.5181
Log Advertising	–1.89452	0.6589	36.56289	0.02513	–16.90132	0.4431	0.963163	0.0021
CGI	–0.987612	0.4576	–12.6732	0.6913	–1.6529	0.4591	–1.452901	0.2418
Board Size	1.025476	0.2567	–1.05478	0.6455	1.945121	0.0731	1.12819	0.0261
Age	–0.30981	0.0845	0.29871	0.0067	0.02412	0.7929	0.051591	0.7821
Debt-Equity	7.45391	0.169	–0.92375	0.523	–19.34198	0.2153	10.5419	0.0002
R Squared	0.356719		0.572139		0.341392		0.421891	

sector as advertising is a very crucial means of promotion of products for the industry, as shown by a very high coefficient. Also it is significant and positive for IT sector. Corporate Governance Index (CGI) has a negative impact on ROE, although insignificant for all sectors. Board size impacts pharma and IT sector positively at 10% and 5% significance level respectively. Board matters to the investors as they provide business focus and vision along with commitment to achieve long term goals (The Economic Times dated 10/10/2014). The age of the firm has a significant and negative relationship with ROE for of auto sector at 10% significance level, whereas its positively and significantly related for FMCG sector at 1% level. The degree of leverage has a positive impact on IT sector at 1% level, whereas for FMCG and pharma sector the relationship is negative, although insignificant.

The intercept coefficients are insignificant for all sectors and these results are consistent with the ones obtained on an aggregate basis. Further R-Squared values are 35.67%, 57.21%, 34.13% and 42.18% for auto, FMCG, pharma and IT sector respectively.

SUMMARY, CONCLUSIONS AND IMPLICATIONS

This paper analyses the impact of shareholder types on firm performance from Indian companies taking data from BSE. To conclude, the research questions are answered with evidence from non-financial companies. The ownership structure and its effect on firm performance was analyzed for listed Indian companies using pooled panel regression. It is found that retail shareholders have no significant impact on firm performance as measured by ROE, while government ownership affects the performance of a company negatively and significantly for all sectors. Foreign shareholders too affect the firm performance significantly whereas institutional investors and family shareholding affects the performance significantly only in case of auto sector. The various arguments in support of the relationship between ownership structure and firm performance can be explained in terms of incentive alignment argument and long-term orientation argument for family ownership; institutional myopia argument and cost-efficiency of monitoring argument for institution ownership; information asymmetry of bureaucracy argument and dual-role argument for government ownership. The impact of type of shareholder on performance of the firm varies among varied types of ownership patterns because the different owner has its own preference on firm strategic goals and varies in incentive and capability to deal with agency problems. Some of the control variables had a significant effect on the corporate performance. Board size plays a significantly conducive role in increasing the performance of IT sector firms. The age of the firm affects auto sector negatively whereas it is insignificant for other sector types. ROE of IT sector is positively correlated with level of debt in capital structure. Large asset base significantly reduces the firm performance for auto and FMCG sector. Advertising has a significant positive impact on ROE of FMCG and IT sectors as brand visibility and business development activities lead to more projects and contracts. Corporate governance index had a negative impact on ROE, though not significant. The reason could be that the components of CGI are negatively related to the firm performance . Also, although the relationship between CGI and ROE, ROA and Tobin's Q is observed to be negative, but the impact of CGI is significant only in case of ROE.

IMPLICATIONS OF THE STUDY

- The findings imply that individual and retail investors are insignificant whereas family ownership is dominant followed by institutional investors. Since maximum powers of the board are derived from dominant shareholders, disciplining them is the key but is not feasible leading to ineffectiveness of the board. There thus exists a dual challenge of resolving not just principal-agent conflict, but also dominant-minority shareholders conflict. Shleifer and Vishny (1986) argue that large shareholders have a strong incentive to monitor managers because of their significant economic stakes.
- Foreign investors need sound corporate governance mechanisms to invest in the country. Thus, implementation of these policies is crucial so as to tap tremendous opportunities for investment and growth which the Indian economy provides.
- Government due to excessive bureaucracy, nepotism, political expediency impacts the firm negatively. The current study reinforces the result. Thus, more private players, increased privately managed companies and provision for divestiture program to attract more private individuals and institutions to co-own the public sector undertakings should be undertaken.
- In line with the above, the private players should have a stake in the projects launched by the government and more PPP projects should be undertaken.
- The positive and significant relationship between foreign ownership and firm performance should be utilized by having more access to efficient management systems and massive resource base.

- The board composition especially size and independence is imperative to improve effectiveness of corporate governance practices. Further the powers of independent directors should increase so as to monitor managers. A major problem, however, is the limited availability of trained independent directors who are well versed with the procedures, tasks and responsibilities expected of them. One solution to this challenge is business leadership training of existing and potential independent directors in India. Hillman et al.(2000) posit to have board members with varied skills such as being insiders in the firm, business experts, support specialists for better performance.
- The study recommends larger board size, although the relationship is not significant. However, the logic is to bring in a large board with the required expertise and knowledge to efficiently run the company.

NOMENCLATURE

Table 3: Symbols Used

Variables Used	*Definition*	*Symbol Used*
Return on Equity	Net profit as a percentage of shareholder's equity	ROE
Return on Assets	Net profit as a percentage of total assets	ROA
Tobin's Q	Market value of equity plus book value of debt and preference share capital divided by total assets	Tobin's Q
Retail Shareholding	Percentage of shares held by individuals	RSH
Institutional Shareholding	Percentage of shares held by institutions	IISH
Government Shareholding	Percentage of shares held by Government	GSH
Family Shareholding	Percentage of shares held by family	FSH
FII Shareholding	Percentage of shares held by foreign institutional investors	FIISH
Corporate Shareholding	Percentage of shares held by corporate bodies, excluding those already covered	CSH
Size	Firm size in terms of total assets owned	S
Advertising Expenses	Includes sum of advertising, marketing and distribution expenses	ADVT
Corporate Governance Index	Includes the corporate governance parameters like Duality, number of directors, proportion of Non-executive directors, proportion of independent directors, number	CGI

Variables Used	*Definition*	*Symbol Used*
	of board meetings held, average attendance of audit committee meetings, average attendance of board meeting, number of audit committee meetings, number of remuneration meetings, number of nomination committee meetings, proportion of independent directors in nomination committee, profile of directors, minutes of different meetings, whistle blowing policy, related party disclosure	
Board Size	Number of directors on board	BS
Age	Number of years between observation year and year of incorporation	AGE
Debt Equity Ratio(Leverage)	Ratio of long term debt to equity	DEBT

REFERENCES

Agrawal, A. and C. Knoeber (1996), 'Firm Performance and Mechanisms to Control Agency Problems Between Managers and Shareholders', *Journal of Financial Quantitative Analysis*, 31, 3: 377-397.

Anderson, R.C. and D.M. Reeb (2008), 'Founding-Family Ownership and Firm Performance: Evidence from the S&P 500', *The Journal of Finance*, LVIII (3), June, 1301-1328.

Aydin, N., Sayim, M. and Yalama A. (2007), 'Foreign Ownership and Firm Performance: Evidence from Turkey', *International Research Journal of Financial Economics*, Issue 11.

Band, R. (1981), 'The Relationship between Return and Market Value of Common Stocks', *Journal of Financial Economics*, 9, 3–18.

Baysinger, B. and Heskisson, R.E. (1990), 'The Composition of Boards of Directors and Strategic Control: Effects on Corporate Strategy', *Academy of Management Review*, Vol. 15, No. 1, 72-87.

Berle, A., and G. Means (1932), The Modern Corporation and Private Property. The Macmillan Company, New York.

Bertrand, M., P. Mehta, and S. Mullainathan (2002), 'Ferreting out Tunnelling: An Application to Indian Business Groups', *Quarterly Journal of Economics*, 117(1), 121–148.

Bhattacharya, S. and Graham, M. (2007), 'Institutional Ownership and Firm Performance: Evidence from Finland'.

Blasi, J. and A. Shleifer (1996), Corporate Governance in Russia: An Initial Look, in Frydman, Roman, Cheryl W Gray and Andrzej Rapaczynshil, eds. *Corporate*

Governance in Central Europe and Russia, Volume 2, Insiders and the State, Budapest, Hungary: CEU Press.

Chemin, M. (2007), 'The Impact of the Judiciary on Economic Activity: Evidence from India', Working Paper 07-24.

Christoph, K., and Moldenhauer, B. (2005), 'Insider Ownership and Corporate Performance – Evidence from Germany', Working Paper, Center for Entrepreneurial and Financial Studies (CEFS), and Department for Financial Management and Capital Markets.

Claessens, S. (1997), 'Corporate Governance and Equity Prices: Evidence from the Czech and Slovak Republics', *Journal of Finance*, 52(4), 1641-1658.

Claessens, S., Djankov, S., Fan P.H.J and Lang H.P.L. (1999), 'Expropriation of Minority shareholders: Evidence from East Asia'.

Claessens, S., Djankov, S. and Pohl, G. (1996), 'Ownership and Corporate Governance: Evidence from the Czech Republic'.

Coles, J.L., Daniel, N.D. and Naveen, L. (2008), 'Boards: Does one size fit all?', *Journal of Financial Economics*, 87, 329-356.

Cubbin, J. and D. Leech (1983), 'Ownership Structure and Economic Performance in the Largest European Companies', *Strategic Management Journal*, 21, 6: 689-705.

Demsetz, H. (1983), 'The Structure of Ownership and the Theory of the Firm', *Journal of Law Economics*, 7: 26375-390.

Demsetz, H. and K. Lehn (1985), 'The Structure of Corporate Ownership: Causes and Consequences', *Journal of Political Economy*, 93: 1155-77.

Demsetz, H., and Villalonga, B. (2001), 'Ownership Structure and Corporate Performance', *Journal of Corporate Finance*, Vol. 7, pp. 209-233. Available at SSRN: http://ssrn.com/abstract=304181.

Dwivedi, N. and Jain, A.K. (2005), 'Corporate Governance and Performance of Indian Firms: The Effect of Board Size and Ownership', *Employees Responsibilities and Rights Journal*, Volume 17(3), pp. 161-172.

Gilson, S. (1997), 'Transaction Costs and Capital Structure Choice: Evidence from Financial Distressed Firms', *Journal of Finance*, 52, 161–195.

Górriz, C.G. and Fumás, V.S. (2005), 'Family Ownership and Performance: The Net Effect of Productive Efficiency and Growth Constraints', SSRN eLibrary.

Imam, M.O. and Malik, M. (2007), 'Firm Performance and Corporate Governance Through Ownership Structure: Evidence from Bangladesh Stock Market', *International Review of Business Research Papers*, Vol. 3, No. 4, pp. 88-110. Available at SSRN: http://ssrn.com/abstract=2256480

Jensen, M. and Meckling, W. (1976), 'Theory of the Firm: Managerial Behavior, Agency Costs and Ownership Structure', *Journal of Financial Economics*, 3: 305–360.

Jensen, M.C. (1989), 'Eclipse of the Public Corporation', *Harvard Business Review*,

Sept.-Oct. Available at SSRN: http://ssrn.com/abstract=146149 or DOI: 10.2139/ssrn.10.2139/ssrn.146149.

Joh, S.W. (2003), 'Corporate Governance and Firm Profitability: Evidence from Korea before the Economic Crisis', *Journal of Financial Economics*, 68(2), 287-322.

Joshi, A. and Hanssens, D.M. (2010), 'The Direct and Indirect Effects of Advertising Spending on Firm Value', *Journal of Marketing*, Vol. 74, 20–33.

Kaur, P. and Gill, S. (2007), 'The Effects of Ownership Structure on Corporate Governance and Performance: An Empirical Assessment in India', Research Project, NFCG.

Kumar, J. (2004), Does Ownership Structure Influence Firm Value? Evidence from India, December, Available at http://www.stmarys.ca/academic/commerce/economic/IAFEP/papers/kumar.pdf.

La Porta R., Lopez-de-Silanes F., Shleifer A. and Vishny R. (1999), 'Corporate Ownership Around the World', *Journal of Finance* 54: 471– 517.

La Porta, R., F. Lopez-de-Silanes and A. Shleifer (1998), 'Corporate Ownership Around the World', *Journal of Finance*, 54, 842–893.

La Porta, R., F. Lopez-de-Silanes and A. Shleifer (1998), 'Law and Finance', *Journal of Political Economy*, 106, 1113-5.

La Porta, R., F. Lopez-de-Silanes, A. Shleifer, R. Vishny (2000), 'Investor Protection and Corporate Governance', *Journal of Financial Economics*, 58, 3-27.

La Porta, R., F. Lopez-de-Silanes, A. Shleifer, R. Vishny (2002), 'Investor Protection and Corporate Valuation', *Journal of Finance*, 57, 1147-70.

La Porta, R., F. Lopez-de-Silanes, and A. Shleifer (2006), 'What Works in Securities Laws', *Journal of Finance*, Vol. 61, 1-32.

Lang, L.H.P. and R.M. Stulz (1994), 'Tobin's q, Corporate Diversification and Firm Performance', *Journal of Political Economy*, 102, 1248-1281.

Linck, J., Netter, J. and Yang, T. (2008), 'The Determinants of Board Structure', *Journal of Financial Economics*, 87, 308-328.

McConnell, J.J. and Servaes, H. (1990), 'Additional Evidence on Equity Ownership and Corporate Value', *Journal of Financial Economics.*

Milgrom, P. and J. Roberts (1992), Economics, Management and Organization, Englewood Cliffs, NJ: Prentice Hall.

Ongore, O.V., K'Obonyo O.P., Ogutu, M. (2011), 'Implications of Firm Ownership Identity and Managerial Discretion on Financial Performance: Empirical Evidence from Nairobi Stock Exchange'.

Pervan, M. and Višić, J. (2012), 'Influence of Firm Size on Its Business Success', *Croatian Operational Research Review*, Vol. 3, No. 1, pp. 213-223.

Reinganum, M. (1981), 'Misspecification of Capital Asset Pricing: Empirical Anomalies based on Earnings' Yields and Market Values', *Journal of Financial Economics*, 9, 19–46.

Repei, V. (2000), 'Ownership Structure, Corporate Governance, and Corporate Performance: Evidence from Ukraine'.

Sarkar, Jayati, and Sarkar, S. (2000), 'Large Shareholder Activism in Corporate Governance in Developing Countries: Evidence From India', *International Review of Finance* 1, no. 3, 161–194.

Shleifer, Andrei, and Robert W. Vishny (1986), 'Large Shareholders and Corporate Control', *Journal of Political Economics* 94, no. 3, 461–488.

Shleifer, A. Vishny W.R. (1997), 'A Survey of Corporate Governance', *The Journal of Finance*, Vol. 52, No. 2, pp. 737-783.

Thomsen, S. and Pedersen, T. (2000), 'Ownership Structure and Economic Performance in the Largest European Companies', *Strategic Management Journal*, 21, 689-705.

Thomsen, S., Pedersen, T. (1998), 'Ownership Structure and Economic Performance in the Largest European Companies'.

Tobin, J. (1969), 'A General Equilibrium Approach to Monetary Theory', *Journal of Money, Credit, and Banking*, 1, 15–29.

Tobin, J. and W. Brainard (1968), 'Pitfalls in Financial Model Building', *American Economic Review*, 59, 99–102.

Wiwattanakantang, Y. (1999), 'An Empirical Study on the Determinants of the Capital Structure of Thai Firms', *Pacific-Basin Finance Journal*, 7, 371-403.

Xu Xiaonian and Wang Yan (1997), 'Ownership Structure, Corporate Governance, And Corporate Performance: The Case of Chinese Stock Companies'.

Yee, H.S. (1998), 'A Study on Relationship between Ownership and Return in Malaysia', MBA thesis, University of Malaya, Kuala Lumpur.

Yeh, Y.H., T.S. Lee, and T. Woidtke (2001), 'Family Control and Corporate Governance: Evidence from Taiwan', *International Review of Finance*, 2, 21-48.

Websites

http://www.bseindia.com

http://www.competition-commission-india.nic.in

http://www.economictimes.indiatimes.com

http://www.finmin.nic.in

http://www.icai.org

http://www.irdaindia.org

http://www.mca.gov.in

http://www.rbi.org.in

http://www.sebi.gov.in

http://www.sec.gov

http://business.gov.in

An Analytical Study of Behavioural Biases
From Investors Perspective

T.V. Raman and Neha Agarwal

Department of Accounting and Finance, Amity Business School, Noida, Uttar Pradesh

e-mail: drtvraman@gmail.com; tvraman@amity.edu; neha.agarwal.2@gmail.com

ABSTRACT

Today, many types of investment options are available with the investors, whether to invest in real assets or financial assets. Investors are loaded with information to choose an appropriate portfolio. The securities industry is a gigantic machine for extracting money from ordinary investors, and does so in a way that makes it all seems perfectly reasonable. One cannot take chance while investing as the economic well being in the long run depends on the investors' investing decision. Investors cannot behave rational all times. Human nature usually serves us well in coping with day-to-day life. But it can also get in the way of achieving success in long term activities such as saving and investing. There is no – 'cure' – for human nature but greater awareness of biases can help the investors and avoid major pitfalls. Several unconscious drivers affect the way investors make decisions about money, these are called behavioural biases. There are different types of behavioural biases, which intend to kick away any illusions an investor may have about himself or herself and his or her investing abilities and trample them into the dust. These biases can be caused due to time cost and capacity constraints, insufficient information, information overloaded and distractions and resistance to change. Behavioural Finance is a part of finance that deals with behavioural biases and argues that emotions and sentiments play a crucial role in determining the behaviour of investors in the market place and very often they act irrationally due to the influence of psychological factor. In this paper we study how portfolio choice depends on two well -known behavioural phenomena: -herding and overconfidence and optimism. Correlation and Regression model and other suitable techniques were used to investigate whether investment decision is affected by these biases.

Keywords: Behavioural Finance, Behavioural Biases, Correlation, Herding, Overconfidence and Optimism, Regression

INTRODUCTION

Albert Einstein said, 'Everything should be as simple as it is but not Simpler.' This phrase perfectly fits with the term Investment. The word Investment looks simple but it is not as simple as one thinks. Even for a small investment a person has to consider many factors. Investing is simple but the industry has made it complicated. Investing is not just analysing numbers and making decisions to buy and sell asset securities, it is much wider than this. In fact a larger part of investing involves individual behaviour. Investors have to be aware about this behaviour because ignoring this behaviour can influence portfolio performance. The securities industry serves as a gigantic machine for extracting money from ordinary investors and does so in a way that it looks perfectly reasonable. But one cannot take a chance while investing as the economic well being in the long run depends on our investing decision. Investors cannot behave rational at all times, sometimes they behave irrational. Investing is all about having the patience to hold on to one's conviction.

Earlier there was a concept of traditional finance, which was based on four assumptions: (1) Investors have well defined stable preferences, even if those preference are never explained or challenged, (2) Investors base their preference between choices on expected outcomes, (3) Investors maximise their own well-being; and (4) Investors discount their future payoff by geometrically increasing the amounts to obtain their present value. But now modern theory comes in a market. It suggests that investors cannot behave rationally at all times while making an investment decisions. They deal with several psychological and cognitive errors, even the ones which they are not aware of.

According to classical economist, investors make decisions based on only the available information. But the real world assumes that investors are both equally well informed and use that information in predictable ways. They are not always risk averse but often risk seekers while they make an investment decisions.

Human nature usually serves us well in coping with day-to-day life. But it can also get in the way of achieving success in long term activities such as saving and investing. There is no 'cure' for human nature, but greater awareness of biases can help the investors and avoid major pitfalls. Several unconscious drivers affect the way investors make decisions about money, these are called behavioural biases. There are different types of behavioural biases like overconfidence, disposition effect, loss aversion, gambling, herding and many more, which intend to kick away any illusions the investors have about himself or herself and his or her investing abilities and trample them into the dust. These biases can be caused due to time cost and capacity constraints, insufficient information, information overloaded and distractions and resistance to change. Figure 1 clearly explains the psychology of the investors, at the time of investment.

Behavioural Finance is a part of finance that deals with behavioural biases and argues that emotions and sentiments play a crucial role in determining the behaviour of investors in the market place and very often they act irrationally due to the influence of psychological factors. Behavioural Finance aims to find out the reason why people forget fundamentals and make investment decisions which are influenced by their emotions.

The whole concept of Behavioural Finance was introduced by Daniel Kahneman and Amol Tversky in late 1960s. They are called as the father of Behavioural Finance. Their observation began to kick off a whole range

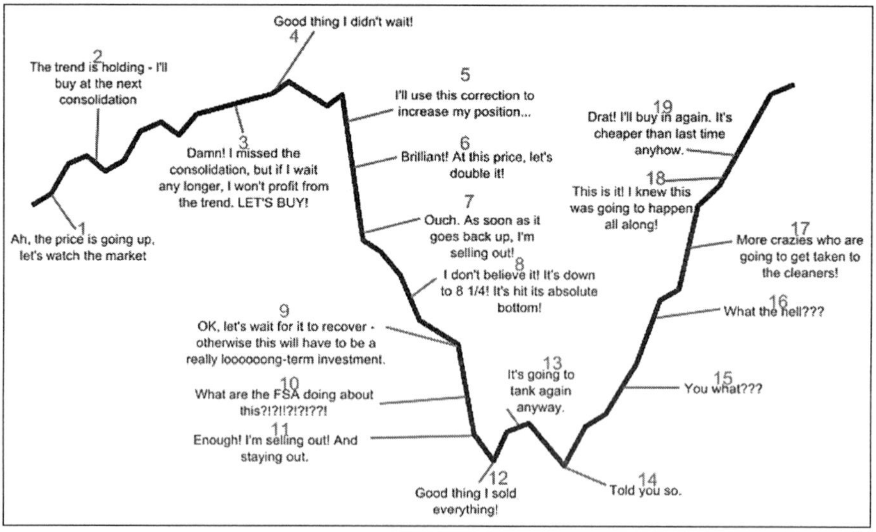

Figure 1: The Psychology of Investing

Source: http://www.tudorinvest.com.au/newsletter/psychology-of-investing

of discoveries, with ramifications that investors cannot afford to ignore. Later, Tversky and Kahneman began to uncover previously searched series of behavioural bias that causes investors to act irrationally. In 2002, Daniel Kahneman received the Noble Memorial Prize for his contribution to the study of rationality in economics. Understanding Behavioural Finance and how it affects the markets is the key to a successful investment strategy.

First sentence of the book on behavioural asset pricing by Hersh Shefrin states 'Behavioural Finance is the study of how psychological phenomena impact financial behaviour.' To understand the developments in Behavioural Finance one needs to understand how financial decisions are made under uncertainty. This problem is addressed by two different branches of Economics: the economics of uncertainty and the economics of information. Economics of uncertainty says that the investors understand and accept the limitation of their knowledge and try to make the best possible decision they can; while the economics of information says that investors try to seek the maximum possible information before taking the financial decision.

OVERCONFIDENCE AND OPTIMISM

Overconfidence is a bias in which investors have too much faith in the precision of their estimates, causing them to underestimate the range of possibilities that actually exist. One should not be confused with the two biases here. One is optimism, believing that he or she will earn 20 per cent return on his or her portfolio, but in reality he or she will be lucky if he or she earn 10 per cent. The other is overconfidence which is about his or her ability to invest well and choose a portfolio that will produce a 20 per cent return and when if something goes wrong he or she should be grateful for 15 per cent. More or less, there is not a clear difference between overconfidence and optimism. Therefore we can call this bias as overconfidence optimist bias.

Shum in 2006 conclude that there are two types of overconfidence, namely 'better-than-average' effect (I am better than average driver) and illusion of control (I won't have car accident). The illusion of control bias describes the tendency of human being to believe that they can control or at least influence outcome, when, in fact, they cannot.

Due to their overconfidence behaviour, investors trade too much or take too much risk because they are certain about their opinions. They believe they can predict the winner. Figure 2 helps us to understand the behaviour of overconfident investors.

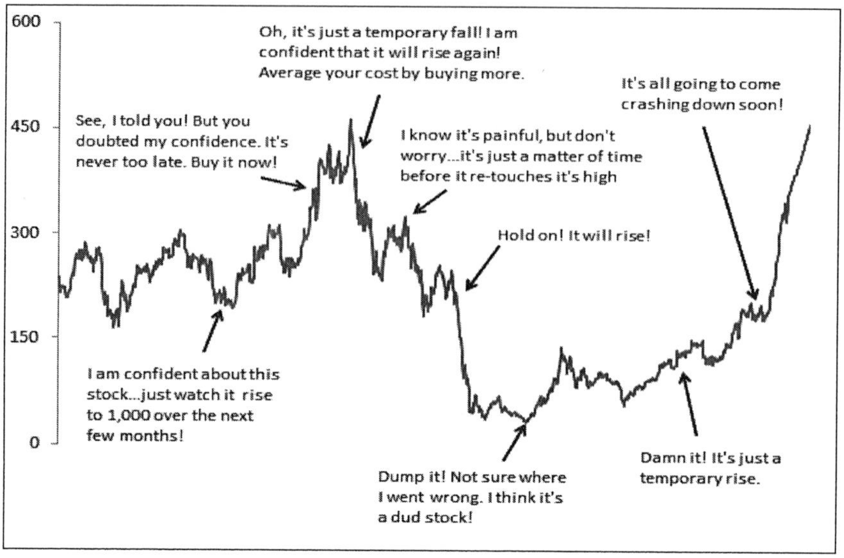

Figure 2: Are You an Overconfident Investor?

Source: http://www.safalniveshak.com/are-you-overconfident-investor/

According to Shefrin (2008) there are two implications of Investors Overconfidence. The first is that investors take bad bets because they fail to realize that they are at an informational disadvantage. The second is that they trade more actively than prudent, which leads to excessive trade volume.

HERDING

Herd behaviour is the tendency of people to follow the action of a larger group irrespective of their decision whether it's rational or irrational. Herding is a very common investor behavioural trait, where people copy each other. When we don't know what to do, we tend to copy each other. Similarly, when investors are exposed to conditions of uncertainty, they adjust their investment based on what other people are doing and invest where others are investing, rather than trying to search for information and doing fundamental analysis of their own. The problem is that they think that the other person is very confident and knows everything, so they blindly follow him or her. But if no one knows what to do and investors just outsourcing their judgement to other people who actually don't have any clue of what's really going on and have no better idea than them.

Herding can be classified as rational herding and irrational herding. In rational herding investors or participants behave to the information about the behaviour of other investors or participants rather than the behaviour of the market. Participants follow others, believing that others are better informed than themselves. Irrational herding is something that is caused by the investor's own belief, sentiments and positive feedback. A substantial herding behaviour can affects both individual and professional investor's attitude.

However it's not true that herding is always bad for investors, sometimes it proves to be good also but following other people without thinking is not good at all.

REVIEW OF LITERATURE

Kahneman, (1974) said that heuristic biases are quite useful but sometimes they lead to systematic and severe errors. He talks about three heuristic biases: (1) Representativeness, which is usually employed when people are asked to judge the probability that an object or event A belongs to class or process B; (2) Availability, which is often employed when people are asked to assess the frequency of a class; and (3) Adjustment from an anchor, which is usually employed in numerical predictions when a relevant value is available. He concluded that better understanding of these biases helps to reduce the errors in decision making.

Brad M. Barber, (1999) describes how investors overestimate the precision of their information and show biases in their interpretation of that information. Overconfident Investors believe more strongly in the valuation of stock rather than grapevine communication.

Ritter (2003), suggests that Behavioural Finance is based in Psychology. Behavioural Finance recommends that human decision processes are subject to several cognitive illusions. The illusions are classified into two groups: illusions caused by heuristic decision process, and illusions rooted from the adoption of mental frames grouped in the prospect theory.

Curtis (2004), concluded that we need both Modern Portfolio Theory (MPT) and Behavioural Finance for helping us in designing and managing successful investment portfolios, as individually both are incomplete. The MPT represents the best learning we investors have about how capital markets actually operate, while Behavioural Finance offers the best insights into how investors actually behave.

R. Agnew (2006), suggests that behavioural biases vary across individuals. He takes a deeper look of three behavioural biases: two allocation biases (naive diversification bias and company stock evidence) and one participation bias. His finding suggests that higher salaried employees tend to make significantly better investment choices in all three cases. Women also appear to make a better choice in two of the three cases. Lack of participation can stand out as the most obvious investment mistake an individual can make.

Seppala (2009), conducted a research on whether behavioural biases like hindsight, overconfidence and self-attribution possessed by investment advisors have any impact on clients' decision making, who take the advices of these advisors, because decision process is more or less influenced by these behavioural biases. Hindsight bias creates a hurdle of learning from past and makes the people not to learn from the past that again leads them to provide wrong advices regarding investing. Also overconfidence and self-attribution leads to this type of behaviour. The result indicates that advisors possess these three biases but hindsight is less than two other biases.

Bashir (2013), investigated the relationship of demographics and the Big Five personality traits with investment biases and risk taking behaviour by constructing the two structure equation models. He concluded that personality traits influence the two investment biases (overconfidence and herding) and risk taking behaviour while demographics do not have a significant relationship with investment biases and risk taking behaviour.

T. Bashir (2013), conducted a research on the influence of behavioural biases on cognitive abilities. He used the Cognitive Reflection Test (CRT) to investigate whether behavioural biases play a major role in financial decision making. The CRT experiment showed that individuals are susceptible of many behavioural biases. Low CRT individuals reflected low patience level and demand returns immediately as compared to high CRT individuals. The experiment proved that people with low cognitive abilities are more affected by the biases.

Ivanova (2013), identifies Behavioural Finance theories, their needs and possibility for use in the financial decision-making process of a household. He finds that a majority of respondents (60 per cent) are non-conscious risk takers and 27 per cent are conscious risk takers. He concluded that behaviour features of literate households confirm the necessity to consider the behavioural factor in managing the financial decisions of an individual.

Statman (2014), identifies that Behavioural Finance substitute normal people for the rational people in standard finance. Behavioural Finance also substitutes the Behavioural Portfolio Theory for the Mean-variance Theory and behavioural asset pricing models for the CAPM and other models where expected returns are determined only by risk. Behavioural Finance explores the saving and spending behaviour, beyond portfolio formation, and it also explores the financial choices affected by culture, fairness, social responsibility, and other expressive and emotional wants.

RESEARCH OBJECTIVE

It is very important to understand how overconfidence and herding affects the investment performance. The main objective of the paper is to test whether the overconfidence and herding variables affect the decision making process of investors.

METHODOLOGY

The study includes only primary data, which was collected through a questionnaire. The target population was 500 individual investors located at Noida. Stratified sampling was used to send the questionnaire to the respondent. The questionnaire was sent only to the investors. The questionnaire is divided into two parts: Investor's profile and behavioural analysis of investors. Data collected for this study was analysed by using SPSS. Statistical techniques which were used for analysis include descriptive statistics and multiple regressions analysis.

RESEARCH ANALYSIS

Demographic

The demographic summary of investors is given in Table 1. The total sample size is of 500 investors, which consisted of (290) male and (210) female investors. The age group is categorized as below 30 years, between 30-40 years, between 40-50 years, and above 50 years. The age group of 30-40 years is highly represented in the sample as compared to other age group. The occupations of the investors were categorized as salaried, businessman and housewife. Majority of the respondent was businessmen. The average monthly income of the investors was categorized as below INR 50,000, between INR 50000–1,00,000, between INR 1,00,000–1,50,000 and above INR 1,50,000. The highest number of investors earned above INR 1.5 lac. In terms of marital status, 465 were married and only 35 were unmarried. Investors mostly invested 20 per cent to 40 per cent of their income and the 3 rest of the income was kept for personal use. Majority of the investors preferred to invest in shares followed by bonds, insurance and others investment options.

Table 1: Demographic Summary of Investors

Title	*Category*	*Number*
Gender	Male	290
	Female	210
Age Group	Below 30	45
	Between 30-40	265
	Between 40-50	125
	Above 50	65
Occupation	Salaried	150
	Businessman	270
	Housewife	80
Income Group (Monthly) (INR)	Below 50000	20
	Between 50000 to 100000	105
	Between 100000 to 150000	160
	Above 150000	215
Marital status	Married	465
	Unmarried	35
Percentage of income investors invest	0–20	115
	20–40	250
	40–60	85
	Above 60	50
Types of Investment	Bank Deposit	45
	Post Office Scheme	50
	Shares	175
	Mutual Funds	20
	Real Estate	45
	Insurance	55
	Bonds	60
	Forex Market	50

Behavioural Analysis

Influence of Overconfidence Variables on Individual Investors Decision Making

Table 2: Influence of Overconfidence Variables

Overconfidence Variables	*Mean*	*Standard Deviations*
Compared with the investors you are acquainted with, you believe your investment performance is...	1.52	0.609
Overconfidence in investment performance related with the market as a whole When considering the next three months, do you have confidence in beating the market as a whole?	1.66	0.621

Overconfidence Variables	*Mean*	*Standard Deviations*
For your next investment, do you take decision based to your previous investment?	1.38	0.486
Suppose you are related to a group of people who have a similar background and social status as you. Generally, when compared with them, you will most probably feel that you are...	1.85	0.767

$R^2 = .118$, $F = 16.594$

The result show that the previous investment decision variable (Mean = 1.38) has a very low impact while taking decision for future investment as compared to other variables. Overconfidence in investment performance variable (Mean = 1.66) has a higher impact on individual investors' decision. All other variables have moderate an impact on investors.

Influence of Overconfidence Factors on Individual Investment Performance

H0 There is positive effect of overconfidence factors on individual performance.

H1 There is negative effect of overconfidence factors on individual performance.

Table 3: Multiple Regression Analysis with Gender as Dependent Variable

Model	*Unstandardized Coefficient*		*Standardized Coefficients*	*t*	*Sig.*
	B	*Std. Error*	*Beta*		
(Constant)	2.049	0.109		18.218	0.000
Suppose you are related to a group of people who have a similar background and social status as you. Generally, when compared with them, you will most probably feel that you are...	–0.049	0.028	–0.076	–1.764	0.078
Compared with the investors you are acquainted with, you believe your investment performance is...	0.003	0.035	0.004	0.097	0.923
Overconfidence in investment performance related with the market as a whole When considering the next three months, do you have confidence in beating the market as a whole?	–0.038	0.034	–0.048	–1.123	0.262
For your next investment, do you take decision based to your previous investment?	–0.348	0.043	–0.342	–8.046	0.000

The result of the analysis shows that only one overconfidence factor; 'compared with the investors you are acquainted with, you believe your investment performance is...' has a positive effect on individual investors' performance. The other three factors have a negative effect on individual performance. R^2 denotes that overall there is 11.8 per cent variation in individual investors' performance. However, the remaining 88.2 per cent variability is not explained. Overall the result of overconfidence variables suggests that overconfidence factors do not have a positive impact on individual investors' performance. Therefore, H1 hypothesis is not accepted as the overconfidence variables have negative impact on individual investors' performance and we accept hypothesis H2.

Influence of Herding Variables on Individual Investors Decision Making

Table 4: Influence of Herding Variables

Herding Variables	*Mean*	*Standard Deviation*
Suppose Company X is an immensely interesting investment but you do not have enough information to be sure of this investment. Suddenly a large number of your colleagues decide to go through with the investment of Company X. How does this sudden movement from your colleague's affect you in your decision?	1.84	0.957
Now imagine that you have bought stocks of Company X. Immediately a large number of your companions decide to sell the stocks and do so accordingly. How does this affect your attitude towards the same stock?	2.54	0.670
Do you generally behave to the changes of other investor's decision and sometimes blindly chase their reaction?	1.46	0.499

The result shown in Table 4 explain that the attitude towards the same stock variable (Mean = 2.54) has a high impact on individual investors' decision making. Changes of other investor's decision variable (Mean = 1.46) has a low impact on investor's decision, while the other variable has a moderate impact.

Influence of Herding Factors on Individual Investment Performance

H3 There is positive effect of herding factors on individual performance.

H4 There is negative effect of herding factors on individual performance.

Table 5: Multiple Regression Analysis with Gender as Dependent Variable

Model	*Unstandardized Coefficient*		*Standardized Coefficients*	*t*	*Sig.*
	B	*Std. Error*	*Beta*		
(Constant)	1.021	0.129		7.935	0.000
Suppose Company X is an immensely interesting investment but you do not have enough information to be sure of this investment. Suddenly a large number of your colleagues decide to go through with the investment of Company X. How does this sudden movement from your colleague's affect you in your decision?	0.035	0.023	0.067	1.501	0.134
Now imagine that you have bought stocks of Company X. Immediately a large number of your companions decide to sell the stocks and do so accordingly. How does this affect your attitude towards the same stock?	0.143	0.033	0.194	4.358	0.000
Do you generally behave to the changes of other investor's decision and sometimes blindly chase their reaction?	–0.019	0.045	–0.019	–0.425	0.671

$R^2 = 0.042$, $F = 7.236$

The result of the analysis shows that only one herding factor; 'Do you generally behave to the changes of other investors' decision and sometimes blindly chase their reaction' has a negative effect on individual investors' performance. The other two factors have a positive effect on individual performance but statistically not very significantly. R^2 denotes that overall there is 4.2 per cent variation in individual investors' performance on the basis of herding. However, the remaining 95.8 per cent variability is not explained. Result of Analysis of Variance (ANOVA) suggests that $F = 7.236$, $p < 0.01$, that is the model is significant. As there is very low variation between gender and herding variables, that is, 4.2 per cent, the result of herding variables suggests that herding factors do not have a positive impact on individual investors' performance. Therefore hypothesis H3 is rejected.

CONCLUSION

The study concluded that investors more or less are affected by behavioural biases. Here we have talked about two biases, overconfidence and herding. We concluded that overall both herding and overconfidence biases have a negative effect on investors' performance, although some variables of herding and overconfidence have a positive impact. Therefore, we can say that the investors' future investment decision is not much influenced by herding and overconfidence.

REFERENCES

A. Alam, *Behavioural Biases,* 3 June 2011. Retrieved from www.scribd.com, http://www.scribd.com/doc/57032684/Behavioural-Biases, 25-10-2014.

A. Seppala, 'Behavioural Biases of Investment Advisors: The Effect of Overconfidence and Hindsight Bias', *Helsinki School of Economics*, Thesis No. 12150, 2009.

A.T. Kahneman, 'Judgement Under Uncertainty:Heuristics and Biases', *Jstor*, vol. 185, no. 4157, 1974.

D.J. Ivanova, *Behavioural Finance: Theory and Survey*, 2013.

D.T. Bashir, 'Are Behavioural Biases Influenced by Demongrafuc Characteristics and Personality Traits? Evidence From Pakistan', *European Scientific Journal*, vol. 9, no. 29, 2013.

F.K. Taqadus Bashir, 'Influence of Behavioural Biases on Cognitive Abilities', *IOSR Journal of Business and Management*, vol. 12, no. 2, 2013, pp. 68–73.

G. Curtis, 'Modern Portfolio Theory and Behavioural Finance', *The Journal of Wealth Management*, vol. 7, 2004.

H.B. Ricciardi, *How Biases Affect Investor Behaviour*, 27 July 2014. Retrieved from www.valuewalk.com, http://www.valuewalk.com/2014/07/how-biases-affect-investor-behaviour/

H. Shefrin, *A Behavioural Approach to Asset Pricing,* New York: Academic Press, 2008.

J.R. Ritter, 'Behavioural Finance', *Pacific-Basin Finance Journal*, vol. 11, no. 4, 2003.

J.R. Agnew, 'Do Behavioural Biases vary across Individuals? Evidence from Individual Level 401(k) Data', *Journal of Financial and Quantitaive Analysis*, vol. 41, no. 4, 2006.

M. Brad and T.O. Barber, 'The Courage of Misguided Convinction', *Financial Analysts Journal*, 1999.

M. Statman, 'Behavioural Finance: Finance with Normal People', *Borsa Istanbul Review*, 2014.

P. Parikh, *Value Inveting and Behavioural Finance,* Tata McGraw-Hill Education, 2009.

T. Richards, *Investing Psychology,* Hoboken, New Jersy: John Wiley & Sons, 2014.

W. Forbes, *Behavioural Finance,* John Wiley and Sons, Inc., New Delhi, 2012.

Financial Exclusion in India

Causes and Remedies

MUKTA MANI AND ANUPAM NARULA[1]

Department of Humanities and Social Sciences, Jaypee Institute of Information Technology, Noida, Uttar Pradesh

[1] FORE School of Management, New Delhi

e-mail: mukta.mani@gmail.com; anupam@fsm.ac.in

ABSTRACT

Financial Inclusion means access of financial products and services to each member of the society. In India around 51 per cent of the population is still excluded from the financial system. Even in urban areas the coverage of loan accounts is only 14 per cent, against 9.5 per cent in rural areas. These figures from the National Sample Survey Organization provide a glimpse of the problem of Financial Exclusion in India. A large number of studies are available on the problem of Financial Exclusion; however, there are few studies that strive to find out the reasons behind low level of Financial Inclusion in India. The objective of this study is to investigate the causes of financial exclusion and suggest some solutions. An exploratory research has been conducted to find out the causes of Financial Exclusion. Further, an in-depth review of literature has been carried out and secondary data has been collected to analyse the causes. On the basis of data analysis, some remedial actions have been suggested. The data has been collected from various government bodies and banks. The data analysis reveals that there are a large number of factors responsible for the high level of Financial Exclusion in India. The main causes have been divided as – market factors, societal factors, and behavioural factors. The market factors include demand side factors, supply side factors, and government policies, etc. The societal factors include illiteracy, low income levels, lack of awareness, cultural factors, etc. The behavioural factors include self exclusion, saving habits, trust and confidence, etc.

Keywords: Financial Inclusion, Financial Exclusion, Banking, Financial Markets

INTRODUCTION

Financial Inclusion is the process of bringing all sections of the society under the umbrella of formal financial system. The formal financial system, that is, organized and regulated financial services and products are still unavailable to the weaker sections of society and low income people. Such sections are called financially excluded. The financial excluded sections are forced to resort to private money lenders, pawn brokers, etc., for their financial needs. The private money lenders provide the credit at their own terms and conditions and very high interest rates. It leads to exploitation of the poor borrowers and ultimately forces them to take extreme steps like suicide. Financial Inclusion is an initiative to provide access to appropriate financial products and services needed by all sections of the society at an affordable cost and in a fair and transparent manner by mainstream institutional players (Ravikumar, 2014; Aduda and Kalunda, 2012).

According to the International Monetary Fund's financial access survey (2011), the performance of India on measures of Financial Inclusion is quite poor. India has less than 11 bank branches per 1,00,000 adults, compared with nearly 24 in China. After 68 years of independence of India, 68 per cent of the Indian population is without a formal bank account. The data in Table 1 shows the actual amount of deposits and loans per person in rural versus urban areas. The amounts reflect a wide gap in rural and urban areas (Ravikumar, 2014).

Table 1: Population-wise Deposits and Loans per Person

Population as per Census 2011		*Rupee Deposits per Person*	*Rupee Loans per Person*	*Rupee Deposits per Person*	*Rupee Loans per Person*
Number in Millions		*March 2012*		*March 2013*	
Rural	833	6,941	4,557	8,101	5,476
Urban	377	1,48,433	1,16,795	1,69,138	1,33,960

Source: Author's calculation on the basis of data from RBI website.

Figure 1 shows the growth of commercial bank branches population-wise areas from the year 2006 to 2013. It indicates major growth in Metropolitan, Urban and Semi-urban areas, and a very marginal growth in rural areas.

To deal with the problem of Financial Exclusion, the Indian government has taken many initiatives from time to time. The most prominent strategy is the priority sector lending, which requires commercial banks to lend 40 per cent of their lending to agricultural purposes. The governments Self Help Group-Bank linkage programme (SBLP), *Kisan* Credit Card (KCC) scheme

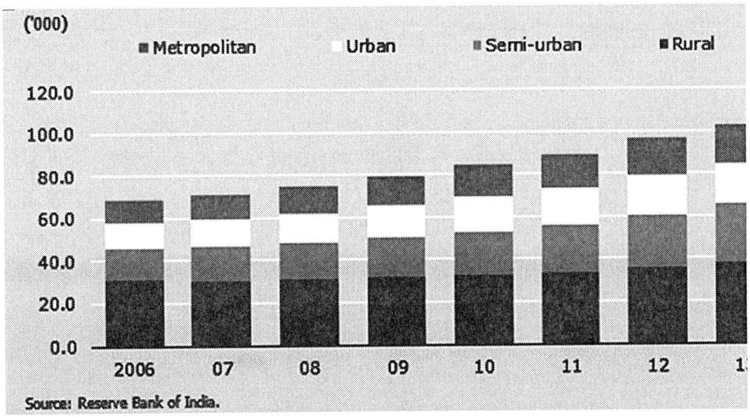

Figure 1: Commercial Bank Branches Area-wise

for farmers, *Rashtriya Swashtya Bima Yojana* (RSBY), Direct Benefit Transfer (DBT) are other such initiatives. The most recent *Pradhan Mantri Jan Dhan Yojna* (PMJDY), started in August 2014, is aimed to provide 'universal access to banking facilities' starting with Basic Banking Accounts with overdraft facility of INR 5,000 after six months and RuPay Debit card with inbuilt accident insurance cover of INR 1 lakh and RuPay Kisan Card.

REVIEW OF LITERATURE

A thorough review of literature reveals that, not only in India, Financial Exclusion is a major problem in most of the developing countries. A large section of the population in developing countries is deprived of formal financial products and services (Peachy and Roe, 2004; Chaia et al., 2009). To deal with the situation, the governments have made policy changes like microfinance and technology innovations. In India, the economy has recorded a good growth in the past few decades; however, the economic growth has not been inclusive. The icons of development like increased usage of mobile phones, e-mail, e-commerce, ATMs, etc., are available only to a small section of the population (Sing and Khurana, 2003). A report on the policy level response to Financial Exclusion in developing countries suggests that the major causes of Financial Exclusion are refusal by banks, identity requirements, terms and conditions for opening accounts, bank charges, physical access problems caused by bank branch closures, and psychological and cultural barriers.

The policymakers in India are aware of the fact and have been taking actions time to time. The Reserve Bank of India (RBI) has emphasized the importance of Financial Inclusion in its announcements and initiatives. The RBI has issued guidelines to banks like opening of 'No frills' accounts, relaxation in Know Your Customer (KYC) norms, General purpose Credit Cards (GCC), settlement of small loans, and services of Non-Government Organizations (NGOs) and Self Help Groups (SHGs) to achieve more Financial Inclusion (Shafi and Medabesh, 2012). In 2014, the RBI accepted one of the major recommendations by the Nachiket Mor Committee on Financial Inclusion. The committee recommended that a new class of banks – to be called Payment Banks – be created. These banks, meant to reach hitherto unbanked customers, can accept deposits and handle remittances. However, they cannot have their own treasury operations. They have to invest their deposits in government securities. To drive Financial Inclusion, RBI also gave new banking licenses – one to IDFC and the other to Bandhan, a Kolkata headquartered Micro Finanace Institution (Rajshekhar, 2014).

Despite serious efforts by policymakers and the government, the Financial Inclusion has not yet picked up in India. The factors behind the failure have been discussed by many researchers. A fair share of the failure can be attributed to poor governance of Financial Inclusion framework. It is clearly due to lack of accountability and a problem of attitude. Many of the banks have not developed an appropriate, cost-effective delivery model for Financial Inclusion and therefore, they are still not thoroughly convinced about Financial Inclusion being a profitable business opportunity. Resultantly, they still perceive this to be a social/regulatory obligation and consequently their efforts are half-hearted (Chakrabarty, 2014). The other factors are refusal by banks due to no credit history, identity requirements, terms and conditions, bank charges, and physical access problems caused by bank branch closures (Kempson et al., 2004). It is observed in general that access to formal financial services requires documents of proof regarding a person's identity, income, etc. Generally, the poor people do not have these documents and thus are excluded from these services. Also, these people may subscribe to the services initially, but may not use them subsequently as actively as others because of factors such as long distance between the bank and their residence, poor infrastructure, etc. (Vighneswara Swamy, 2011). Non-availability of competing financial services, no or limited consumer protection requirements, prohibitive market factors, geographical barriers, infrastructure, and connectivity barriers also contribute to the failure of Financial Inclusion drives (Atkinson and Messy, 2013).

On the other hand, there are behavioural factors like the psychological and cultural barriers (Kempson et al., 2004). Research in behavioural economics has revealed that many people are not contented with using formal financial services. The reasons of course are the difficulty in understanding the language, and various documents and conditions that accompany the financial services (Vighneswara Swamy, 2011). Moreover, in the Indian context the problem of financial illiteracy is more acute, with awareness levels of the rural population regarding the benefits of linking with mainstream financial institutions being extremely poor (Chakrabarty, 2014; Bihari, 2011). It has also been observed that the poor living in urban areas do not utilize the financial services as they find that the financial services are costly and thus are unaffordable. In view of this, even if financial services are available, the high costs deter the poor from accessing them (Vighneswara Swamy, 2011). Thus, the demand side factors are financial vulnerability caused by personal circumstances, low level of financial literacy, reduced social and technological inclusion, and cultural or psychological barriers (Atkinson and Messy, 2013).

The objective of this study is to investigate the causes of Financial Exclusion and suggest some solutions for better Financial Inclusion.

CAUSES OF FINANCIAL EXCLUSION

The study reveals that there are a large number factors responsible for the high level of Financial Exclusion in India. The main causes have been divided as – market factors, societal factors, and behavioural factors.

Market Factors

There are many market factors that influence the Financial Exclusion.

Demand-side Factors

The market demand of financial products and services depends on the various voluntary exclusion factors and involuntary exclusion factors that affect the needs of customers. The voluntary exclusion factors include taking credit from informal sources of finance like family, friends, etc., and not opening a bank account because one family member already has an account. In such cases the customer voluntarily chooses not to open a bank account.

The involuntary exclusion factors are as follows:

1. *Poor Infrastructure:* Unavailability of bank branches in the area or the bank branch is too far to approach easily.
2. *Affordability:* The financial services are too costly and thus unaffordable.

3. *Documentary Proofs:* Proofs such as identity and address proofs are required to open a bank account. Low income group people may not have such documents to provide (Fungacova and Weill, 2014).
4. *Language Problem:* Difficulty in understanding the language and financial documents.

Supply-Side Factors

The financial service providers deny financial services to people with low income, as they consider them to be highly risky. Banks use sophisticated techniques to classify customers into profitable and risky. This can lead to denial of credit to small customers who can't provide guarantees and securities. Even after policy initiatives from the government it has been observed that banks are reluctant to provide banking facilities to rural areas and low income group people. The basic reason is that the banks don't consider the rural areas and low income group as a profitable business opportunity. Secondly, the financial products available in the market are not suitable for the low income group customers. Banks need to provide a new range of products keeping in mind the need of such kind of customers.

Societal Factors

The societal factors include illiteracy, low income levels, lack of awareness, cultural factors, etc.

Cultural Factors

Due to cultural beliefs, there are many misleading presumptions about financial services. For example, Islam prohibits interest, so followers of Islam might be reluctant to have a formal account in a bank. Islamic banks are there to comply with the principles of Sharia to serve the Muslim community. However, in the absence of Islamic banks, a large section of the Muslim community may remain unbanked.

Illiteracy

The literacy rate is very poor in rural areas in India. Due to illiteracy, people are not aware of the benefits of accessing formal financial services. They consider it too complicated to understand and thus remain away from it. Even if one has a bank account, due to his or her inability to read and write, he or she becomes dependent on someone to operate the bank account. Under this situation he or she becomes vulnerable to the risk of cheating and frauds.

Low Levels of Income

Individuals with very low income levels may not be able to afford financial services. There are many services that demand some investment of money or payment of fee. For example, processing fee of loans is to be paid by the borrowers, and an annual fee is to be paid for having a locker. The saving bank accounts require a minimum balance to be kept in the account. Debit card and credit cards carry annual fee. Some banks impose a fee on branch banking.

Behavioural Factors

The behavioural factors include self exclusion, saving habits, lack of consumer trust and confidence, etc.

Self Exclusion

Some sections of the society are excluded due to circumstances such as migrant status. They lack knowledge and familiarity with technologies and ability to communicate in the local language. Thus, they keep themselves excluded from the formal financial system and remain aloof of the mainstream society.

Saving Habits

In rural areas, people prefer to invest their savings in physical assets like gold and land rather than financial products like fixed deposits. Even today the housewives in rural, as well as urban areas collect their small savings to buy gold ornaments which serve a dual purpose for them. Firstly, the ornaments can be used for wearing and then the gold ornaments provide them wealth which they consider to be their own. While keeping money in bank accounts makes it visible to the male members of the family, the female has a fear that they lose control over the money. Moreover, keeping money in bank accounts make them dependant on male members of the family to operate the account.

Lack of Consumer Trust and Confidence

Even if the people are literate, they lack awareness about various financial services and benefits of getting involved in the financial services. People lack trust and confidence in the financial markets. Many stock market scams, banking frauds, government's indifferent attitude, and lethargic legal system leads to a mindset that the financial system is very complicated, it is highly risky, and therefore one should avoid it (Fungacova and Weill, 2014).

DATA ANALYSIS

In Table 2, State-wise data has been collected on two Financial Inclusion parameters namely, Per Capita Deposits and Per Capita Credit. The State-wise data has also been collected on some demographic factors such as literacy rate, per capita income, and population per bank office. The demographic factors' data has been collected from the government database of Census 2011. The Financial Inclusion parameter data has been taken from the RBI database (Kumar, 2013).

A State-wise comparison in Table 2 reveals that the highest deposits per capita are found to be in National Capital Territory (NCT) of Delhi, while lowest per capita deposits are in Bihar. The highest credit per capita is in Chandigarh, while lowest is in Bihar. The NCT of Delhi also records the highest per capita income, while lowest is recorded again for Bihar. The literacy rate is highest for Kerala and lowest for Bihar. Population per bank office is a negative indicator, which shows the number of bank offices in comparison to the population of the State. A high value shows the poor condition of availability of banking services, while a low figure indicates good condition. The highest value is recorded for Manipur and the lowest value is shown for Goa.

Table 2: State-wise Financial Inclusion Indicators and Demographic Factors

S. No.	*Region/State/UT*	*Per Capita Deposits (in INR)*	*Per Capita Credit (in INR)*	*Per Capita Income (in INR)*	*Literacy Rate (in %)*	*Population Per Bank Office*
		2012	*2012*	*2011–12*	*2011*	*2012*
1	Andaman & Nicobar Islands	53,314	20,252	82,272	87	8,498
2	Andhra Pradesh	40,507	44,549	71,540	67	10,773
3	Arunachal Pradesh	43,222	9,718	62,213	65	15,558
4	Assam	21,304	7,950	33,633	72	20,116
5	Bihar	13,310	3,876	24,681	62	23,577
6	Chandigarh	3,73,290	4,24,171	N.A	86	3,620
7	Chhattisgarh	26,435	14,139	46,573	70	17,129
8	Dadra & Nagar Haveli	44,401	15,291	N.A	76	8,958
9	Daman & Diu	82,007	14,100	N.A	87	7,924
10	Goa	2,49,532	72,148	1,92,652	89	3,049

S. No.	*Region/State/UT*	*Per Capita Deposits (in INR)*	*Per Capita Credit (in INR)*	*Per Capita Income (in INR)*	*Literacy Rate (in %)*	*Population Per Bank Office*
		2012	*2012*	*2011–12*	*2011*	*2012*
11	Gujarat	49,806	34,729	N.A	78	11,643
12	Haryana	56,806	44,888	1,09,227	76	8,961
13	Himachal Pradesh	55,380	20,582	73,608	83	6,104
14	Jammu & Kashmir	38,647	13,241	41,833	67	11,911
15	Jharkhand	26,431	8,887	31,982	66	15,884
16	Karnataka	66,364	46,873	69,493	75	9,110
17	Kerala	59,789	45,169	83,725	94	7,014
18	Lakshadweep	87,318	8,462	N.A	92	5,402
19	Madhya Pradesh	22,848	12,841	N.A	69	16,075
20	Maharashtra	1,39,715	121,663	N.A	82	12,600
21	Manipur	15,360	4,620	32,284	79	31,696
22	Meghalaya	36,962	9,345	56,643	74	13,157
23	Mizoram	30,787	11,730	N.A	91	10,705
24	Nagaland	29,491	7,895	56,116	80	19,998
25	NCT of Delhi	4,01,757	3,82,983	1,75,812	86	6,410
26	Odisha	29,503	13,842	46,150	73	13,301
27	Puducherry	60,158	43,090	95,759	86	7,921
28	Punjab	62,140	50,711	78,171	76	6,794
29	Rajasthan	21,721	19,579	N.A	66	14,771
30	Sikkim	67,444	21,603	N.A	81	6,987
31	Tamil Nadu	54,786	63,624	84,058	80	10,096
32	Tripura	28,099	8,785	50,750	87	14,486
33	Uttar Pradesh	21,385	9,369	29,417	68	17,575
34	Uttarakhand	55,098	19,623	75,604	79	7,339
35	West Bengal	40,855	25,646	55,864	76	15,967

Source: RBI website and Census 2011 data.

In order to verify the opinions presented under the causes of Financial Inclusion, a correlation analysis has been conducted among the Financial Inclusion factors and demographic factors as shown in Table 3. The analysis shows that there is a positive correlation between the Financial Inclusion factors and the literacy rate and per capita income. It establishes that the States with a high level of literacy demonstrate better Financial Inclusion and vice versa. The correlation between the Financial Inclusion factors and per capita income is highly positive. Thus, we can propose that the Financial Inclusion is high in the States where per capita income is high and vice versa. Low level of income is highly related to low level of Financial Inclusion.

Population per bank office is an indicator of availability of banking facilities to the population. A negative correlation between Financial Inclusion factors and the population per bank office clearly suggests that the Financial inclusion is low where lesser number of bank branches are available.

Table 3: Correlation between Financial Inclusion Factors and Demographic Factors

Financial Inclusion Factors	*Demographic Factors*	*Literacy Rate*	*Per Capita Income*	*Population per Bank Office*
		2011	*2012*	*2012*
Per Capita Deposits	2012	0.43	0.87	–0.51
Per Capita Credit	2012	0.30	0.70	–0.39

Source: Authors' calculations.

Table 4: State-wise Level of Financial Inclusion

Low	*Medium*	*High*
Bihar	Chhattisgarh	Haryana
Manipur	Rajasthan	Puducherry
Assam	Mizoram	Kerala
Uttar Pradesh	Odisha	Punjab
Jharkhand	Meghalaya	Karnataka
Madhya Pradesh	Jammu & Kashmir	Tamil Nadu
Tripura	Arunachal Pradesh	Maharashtra
Nagaland	Dadra & Nagar Haveli	Goa
	West Bengal	NCT of Delhi
	Andaman & Nicobar Islands	Chandigarh
	Uttarakhand	
	Himachal Pradesh	
	Gujarat	
	Andhra Pradesh	
	Sikkim	
	Lakshadweep	
	Daman & Diu	

Source: Authors' calculations.

Table 4 shows the level of Financial Inclusion in different States and Union territories of India. All the States and UTs have been divided into three categories on the basis of Financial Inclusion factors taken in Table 2. The States that show very high performance on these two factors have been kept in High category and the States that show poor values have been placed in the Low category.

SUGGESTIONS FOR FINANCIAL INCLUSION

On the basis of the above analysis it could be understood that there are many factors related to the problem of Financial Exclusion. The policymakers need to address all the issues together to reach to the desired level of Financial Inclusion.

Banking System

On one side there are market factors like lack of suitable financial products, reluctance of banks in opening accounts for low income group customers, documentary requirements, etc. To address the market factors the government needs to frame strict policies to make it mandatory for the commercial banks to open new bank branches in rural areas and open accounts for the weaker sections of the society, and design new financial products which are suitable to both the buyer and the issuer. Unavailability of bank branches and the poor infrastructure in the bank branches is one of the major issues for Financial Exclusion. Moreover, banks need to consider the lower sections of the society as a business opportunity. Serving to the hitherto unbanked areas may help banks expand their deposits base. The government may relax the documentary requirements for opening plain saving bank accounts (Ranganath and Rao, 2013).

Education System

The demand side factors like language problems and lack of awareness may be addressed by increasing the literacy level in the country. The financial literacy may be promoted among the lower sections of the society. Even the illiterate people may be made aware of the benefits of connecting to the formal financial system. Financial management has always been a part of India's history and culture. Indian history has witnessed many great economists like Kautilya and Amartya Sen. Our education system may strive to relate better financial practices to our culture and tradition. There is a need to inculcate the financial wisdom from the very early stages of education. We may teach our children about financial wisdom through short stories, comics, etc.

Media and Technology

The responsibility of achieving greater Financial Inclusion also lies with electronic media. Television and mobile phones have reached in the remotest areas. We may create better awareness by spreading messages through mass media. Information Technology can also be of great help, as mobile banking can be made available to the customers where it is not possible to open bank branches in vicinity (Srinivas, 2014).

CONCLUSION

Financial Inclusion means access of financial products and services to each member of the society. In India around 51 per cent of the population is still excluded from the financial system. Even in urban areas the coverage of loan accounts is only 14 per cent, against 9.5 per cent in rural areas. These figures from the National Sample Survey Organization provide a glimpse of the problem of Financial Exclusion in India. The analysis of State-wise data reveals that there are many States in India where the reach of formal financial system is very limited. The study highlights the major causes of Financial Exclusion. The major causes are classified into market factors, societal factors and behavioural factors. The most important factors are found to be – lack of awareness, lack of availability of bank branches, and some cultural and religious factors. To achieve greater Financial Inclusion the policymakers, bankers, education system, media, and technology need to work together. The government needs to provide a better policy framework. The banking industry needs to consider Financial Inclusion as a potential business opportunity. The education systems needs to widespread the benefits of formal financial system and promote financial literacy. Media and technology are required to be used more effectively to promote the Financial Inclusion. There is a scope of further research in this study. The researcher might investigate the causes of Financial Exclusion by conducting a cause-effect analysis among the variables.

REFERENCES

A. Atkinson and F. Messy, 'Promoting Financial Inclusion through Financial education: OECD/INFE Evidence, Policies and Practice', *OECD Working Papers on Finance, Insurance and Private Pensions*, no. 34, OECD Publishing, 2013.

A. Chaia et al., 'Half the World is Unbanked', *Financial Access Initiative, Framing Note*, October 2009, State of financial inclusion policy in developing countries AFI, 2009.

E. Kempson, A. Atkinson, and O. Pilley, 'Policy Level Response to Financial Exclusion in Developed Economies: Lessons for Developing Countries', The Personal Finance Research Centre, University of Bristol, September 2004.

G. Srinivas, 'Innovation, Financial Inclusion and Oversight', Report Information from ProQuest, ProQuest.

J. Aduda and E. Kalunda, 'Financial Inclusion and Financial Sector Stability With Reference To Kenya: A Review of Literature', *Journal of Applied Finance & Banking*, vol. 2, no. 6, 2012, 95–120; ISSN: 1792-6580 (print version), 1792-6599 (online) Scienpress.

K.C. Chakrabarty, 'Inclusion, Growth and Governance – Issues and Way Forward', *RBI Monthly Bulletin*, Reserve Bank of India, May 2014.

M. Rajshekhar, 'Financial Inclusion Takes a New Form', *The Economic Times*, 28 August 2014, p. 13.

M. Shafi and A.H. Medabesh, 'Financial Inclusion in Developing Countries: Evidences from an Indian State', *International Business Research*, Canadian Center of Science and Education, vol. 5, no. 8, 2012; ISSN 1913-9004, E-ISSN 1913-9012.

N. Kumar, 'Financial Inclusion and its Determinants: Evidence from India', *Journal of Financial Economic Policy*, vol. 5, no. 1, 2013, pp. 4–19.

N.S. Ranganath and G.T. Rao, 'Banking and Financial Inclusion in India – A need for Innovation', *Srusti Management Review*, vol. VI, Issue 1, January, 2013, pp. 37–42.

P. Sing and M.R. Khurana, *Economic Reforms in India: From First to Second Generation and Beyond*, New Delhi: Deep and Deep Publications Pvt. Ltd, 2003.

P.M. Vighneswara Swamy, 'Financial Inclusion in India: An Evaluation of the Coverage, Progress and Trends', *The IUP Journal of Financial Economics*, vol. IX, no. 2, 2011.

S. Peachy and A. Roe, *Access to Finance – What does it Mean and how do Savings banks Foster Access?* Brussels: World Saving Bank Institute, 2004.

S.C. Bihari, 'Growth through Financial Inclusion in India', *Journal of International Business Ethics*, vol.4, no.1, 2011, pp. 28–41.

T. Ravikumar, 'Role of Banks in Financial Inclusion Process in India', Report Information from ProQuest, ProQuest, 2014.

Z. Fungacova and L. Weill, 'A View on Financial Inclusion in Asian Countries', BOFIT Policy Brief, 8/2014, Institute for Economies in Transition, Bank of Finland, 2014, pp. 3–13.

SECTION IV

CORPORATE FINANCE

Correlation Structure, Portfolio Size and Diversification Benefits

Mean-Variance Optimization vs Market Model

Himanshu Joshi
FORE School of Management, New Delhi
e-mail: himanshu@fsm.ac.in

ABSTRACT

Portfolio diversification benefit and optimum portfolio size depends upon the internal correlation structure of the market, as well as its correlation with other economies. A higher correlation amongst the stocks in a market requires lesser number of securities for constructing diversified portfolio, but results in reduced diversification benefit. In the present paper the correlation for stocks in the Indian and US market are calculated to know the optimal size of portfolios in these countries. Returns on NIFTY 50 and NASDAQ 100 are considered for calculating average correlations for Indian and US stock indices for 3 years. Results shows higher correlations for the NASDAQ 100 in comparison to NIFTY 50, which indicate that the Indian equity market provides better opportunity for international diversification for the American investors. Lower correlations for NIFTY 50 require a larger number of shares to be included in the portfolio to diversify the systematic risk.

The present paper then calculates the diversification benefits using the traditional approach of mean-variance analysis. However, implementation of mean-variance analysis produces wildly unrealistic portfolios with huge short positions and correspondingly imaginary long positions. In many cases short sales are caused by bad historical returns that are not necessarily indicative of future anticipated returns. To overcome these limitations, a single factor model, that is, the Market Model is then used. This Market Model assumes that asset returns are related to each other through their correlations with one single variable or factor, which is market returns in this case. Results show that the Market Model indicates lesser diversification benefit using the same set of assets in comparison to the mean-

variance approach. However, results of the market model are more realistic and reliable, as it does not indicate unrealistic short positions.

Keywords: Portfolio Diversification, Correlation Structure, Mean-variance Optimization, Market Model

INTRODUCTION

There can be firm-specific risk, as well market-wide risk in equity investments. When all risk is firm-specific, diversification can reduce risk to arbitrarily low levels. The reason is that with all the risk sources independent, the exposure to any particular source of risk is reduced to negligible level. However, when common sources of risk affect all firms, even extensive diversification cannot eliminate risk. In this case the portfolio standard deviation falls as the number of securities increases, but it cannot be reduced to zero. The risk that remains even after extensive diversification is called systematic risk, or non-diversifiable risk. In contrast, the risk that can be eliminated by diversification is called nonsystematic risk or diversifiable risk.

Average standard deviation of any randomly selected portfolio does fall with diversification, but the power of diversification to reduce risk is limited by systematic or common source of risk. Portfolio diversification benefit and optimum portfolio size depends upon the internal correlation structure of the market, as well as its correlation with other economies. A higher correlation amongst the stocks in a market requires lesser number of securities for constructing diversified portfolio, but results into reduced diversification benefit. In the present paper the correlation for stocks in the Indian and US market are calculated to know the optimal size of portfolios in these countries. Returns on NIFTY 50 and NASDAQ 100 are considered for calculating average correlations for Indian and US stock indices for the last 3 years. Results shows higher correlations for the NASDAQ 100 in comparison to Nifty 50, which indicate that the Indian equity market provides better opportunity for international diversification for U.S. investors. Lower correlations for NIFTY 50 require a larger number of shares to be included in the portfolio to diversify the systematic risk.

The present paper then calculates diversification benefits using the traditional approach of mean-variance analysis. However, implementation of mean-variance analysis produces wildly unrealistic portfolios with huge short positions and correspondingly imaginary long positions. In many cases short sales are caused by bad historical returns that are not necessarily indicative of future anticipated returns. To overcome these limitations, a single factor model, that is, the Market Model is then used. This market model assumes that asset returns are related to each other through their correlations with one single variable or factor, which is market returns in this case. The Market Model describes a regression relationship between the returns on an asset and the returns on the market portfolio. Results show that the Market Model indicates lesser diversification benefit using the same set of assets in comparison to the mean- variance approach. However, results of the Market Model are more realistic and reliable, as it does not indicate unrealistic short positions.

LITERATURE REVIEW

The discussion of the theoretical model of portfolio selection started more than 50 years ago. The theoretical models of portfolio selection developed by H. M. Markowitz (1952) and J. Tobin (1952) provide a positive explanation and normative rules for the diversification of risky assets. However, the history of research about the international diversification is about 40 years old. Most of the research on international diversification analyses the benefits from an American standpoint. In the early period of the research about international diversification, only the benefits are certified.. Levy and Sarnat (1970), in their paper, recommend that the American investor should never restrict his or her portfolio to developing countries. The gaining of international diversification is related to the correlation between the US market and the target country market. A high correlation between the two markets may cause little gain when combing them in a portfolio of their own. For example, Belgium, France, Germany, and Italy's markets have very high correlation with the US market, so the American investors should not take the assets of these countries into the portfolio. Conversely, they should invest in countries which have low, even minus, correlation with the US market such as Austria, Denmark, Japan, and Mexico. Solnik (1974) shows the degree of risk reduction when diversified internationally. The primary motivation in holding a diversified portfolio of stocks is to reduce risk. The risk of a portfolio in terms of variability of returns will be less than the risk of its separate parts. The reason is that the greater the number of securities in a portfolio, the less the portfolio is likely to lose as the result of one company's misfortune. He compared the portfolio diversification in foreign securities with the domestic common stocks and reached a conclusion for from the American standpoint. However, the quantities analysis is not applied in the early research. The reason is that such models are difficult to use and tend to result in portfolios that are badly behaved.

Study of co-movements and stock market integration has been well documented in the literature with respect to developed markets. Nevertheless, emerging markets such as India have received less attention (Modi et al., 2010; Wong et al., 2004). The Indian stock market provides a unique perspective for analysing co-movements and stock market integration because of its burgeoning economy and its subsequent linkages to other economies. For example, Modi et al. (2010) examined the stock market indices of India, Hong Kong, China, Mexico, Brazil, the UK, and the US from 1 July 1997 to 30 June 2008. Using a multivariate analysis consisting of co-integration and principal component analysis, they found that low correlations exist between Indian stock markets and Mexico, the UK, and the US. Modi et al. also found that the lowest correlations exist between the India (SENSEX) and US (NASDAQ) stock exchanges. The implications are that investors can diversify their portfolios by investing in stocks listed on the SENSEX and NASDAQ simultaneously.

Wong et al. (2004) observed this relationship by evaluating the long-run and short-run relationship and linkages between the Indian Stock Exchange (BSE 200) and the US (S&P 500), Japan (Nikkei 225), and UK (FTSE 100) stock exchange from 1 January 1991 to 31 December 2003. They found that the Indian stock market is integrated with developed markets and is sensitive to the dynamics of these markets in the long run. The researchers also found that short-run stock returns in the US and Japan Granger affect the Indian stock markets, but not the opposite. Granger causality is a technique that examines the relationship between two or more time series by examining whether times series are co-integrated over both the short and long run. This information is important for international investors in aiding in decision making with respect to diversification and investing in the Indian stock market. The implications are that the Indian stock market is integrated with other world markets in the long run and this is important when attempting to diversify portfolios.

Although the study of co-movements has been well documented in the literature with respect to developed markets, the Indian stock markets have received less attention. Also, correlation structures between the international markets and amongst the securities of the local market is time varying; thus this study fills the gap by calculating the correlations using returns on NIFTY 50 and NASDAQ 100 for the Indian and US stock indices, respectively, for the period of 3 years that is 2010–13. This study also captures the post- global financial crisis behaviour of cross-country returns for the Indian and US markets.

RESEARCH METHODOLOGY

For calculating correlations between the returns on securities in the Indian and US market, daily weighted share indices were collected from Yahoo Finance and NSE websites and analysed for the period of April 2010 through March 2013. All indices of NASDAQ 100 were denominated in Dollars and NIFTY 50 was denominated in INR. The daily returns were calculated on basis of this data. For calculating variance of the portfolio a general formula was used:

$$\sigma p^2 = \sum_{i=1}^{n} \sum_{j=1}^{n} wi\ wj\ Cov\ (ri, rj) \qquad ...(1)$$

A correlation matrix among these share indices, making up the sample population, was computed. To examine the potential benefits that are available from diversification, correlation analysis was done. The results were then used to determine the benefits of diversification to an Indian investor wishing to invest over a long-term period.

To establish the relationship between systematic risk and security correlations, the present study considered the naïve diversification strategy in which an equally weighted portfolio is constructed, meaning that $wi = 1/n$ for each security. In this case Equation (1) can be rewritten as follows:

$$\sigma p^2 = \frac{1}{n} \sum_{i=1}^{n} \frac{1}{n} \sigma i^2 + \sum_{\substack{j=1 \\ J \neq 1}}^{n} \sum_{i=1}^{n} \frac{1}{n^2} Cov(ri, rj) \qquad ...(2)$$

There are n variance terms and $n(n-1)$ covariance terms in Equation (2). If average variance and average co-variances of the securities in the market are defined as:

$$\sigma^2 = \frac{1}{n} \sum_{i=1}^{n} \sigma i^2$$

$$Cov = \frac{1}{n(n-1)} \sum_{\substack{i=1 \\ J \neq 1}}^{n} \sum_{i=1}^{n} Cov(ri, rj)$$

Then portfolio variance can be expressed as:

$$\sigma p^2 = \frac{1}{n} \sigma^2 + \frac{n-1}{n} Cov \qquad ...(3)$$

Equation (3) establishes a very important link between the portfolio variance σp^2 and the number of securities considered in the portfolio n, when there is no diversification, that is, where all the investment goes into only one security, variance of the portfolio will be equal to the average variance of the securities, and as n increases, the dependence of portfolio variance on the average variance of securities decreases and it is explained more by the average covariance among securities.

To further see the fundamental relationship between systematic risk and security correlations, it is assumed that all securities have a common standard deviation, σ, and all securities' pairs have a common correlation coefficient, ρ. Then the covariance between all pairs of securities is $\rho\sigma^2$, and Equation (3) can be rewritten as:

$$\sigma p^2 = \frac{1}{n}\sigma^2 + \frac{n-1}{n}\rho\sigma^2 \qquad ...(4)$$

Equation (4) explains the effect of correlation on portfolio variance explicitly. When $\rho = 0$, insurance principle is obtained, where portfolio variance approaches zero as n becomes greater. For $\rho > 0$, however, portfolio variance remains positive. In fact, for $\rho = 1$, portfolio variance equals σ^2, regardless of n, demonstrating that diversification is of no benefit; in the case of perfect correlation, all risk is systematic. More generally, as n becomes greater, Equation (4) shows that systematic risk becomes $\rho\sigma^2$. In the current paper, average correlation for stocks in the Indian and US market are calculated to know the optimal size of portfolios in these countries.

The paper then calculates diversification benefits using the traditional approach of mean-variance analysis for five randomly selected stocks from the Indian market. This approach involves calculating means, variances, and correlations directly from historical data. A variance-covariance matrix is constructed for calculating the portfolio variance. The historical method requires estimating a very large number of parameters when we are optimizing for even a moderately large number of assets. The number of parameters needed to determine the minimum-variance frontier depends on the number of potential stocks in the portfolio. If a portfolio has n stocks, then it requires:

1. n parameters for the expected returns to the stocks;
2. n parameters for the variances of the stock returns; and
3. $n(n-1)/2$ for the covariances of all the stock returns with each other.
4. Total parameters $n^2/2 + 3n/2$.

Thus, for the present study of five stocks in the portfolio, 20 parameters are computed. Implementation of mean-variance analysis, however, produces wildly unrealistic portfolios with huge short positions and correspondingly imaginary long positions. In many cases short sales are caused by bad historical returns that are not necessarily indicative of future anticipated returns. To overcome these limitations, a single factor model, that is, the

Market Model is then used. This Market Model assumes that asset returns are related to each other through their correlations with one single variable or factor, which is market returns in this case. The Market Model describes a regression relationship between the returns on an asset and the returns on the market portfolio. For asset i, the return to the asset can be modeled as:

$$Ri = \alpha i + \beta i\, Rm + \varepsilon i \qquad \text{...(5)}$$

where Ri = the return on asset i;

Rm = the return on the market portfolio;

αi = average return on asset i unrelated to the market return;

βi = the sensitivity of the return on asset i to the return on the market portfolio; and

εi = an error term.

The Market Model makes the following predictions about the expected returns, as well as the variances and covariances of asset returns. First, the expected return for asset i depends on the expected return to the market, $E(Rm)$, the sensitivity of the return on asset i to the return on the market, βi, and the part of the returns on asset i that are independent of market returns, αi.

$$E(Ri) = \alpha i + \beta i\, E(Rm) \qquad \text{...(6)}$$

Second, the variance of the return to asset i depends on the variance of the return to the market, σm^2, the variance of the error for the return of asset i in the Market Model, $\sigma_{\varepsilon i}^{\ 2}$, and the sensitivity, βi.

$$Var(Ri) = \beta i^2\, \sigma m^2 + \sigma \varepsilon i^2 \qquad \text{...(7)}$$

Third, the covariance of the return to asset i and the return to asset j depends on the variance of the return to the market, σm^2, and on the sensitivities βi and βj.

$$Cov\,(Ri, Rj) = \beta i\, \beta j\, \sigma^2 m \qquad \text{...(8)}$$

The Market Model is used to estimate αi and βi by using a separate linear regression for each asset, using historical data on asset returns and market returns. The Market Model reduces the computational task of providing the inputs to a mean-variance optimization.

FINDINGS AND ANALYSIS

Table 1 and Table 2 show the average correlation of stock returns for the Indian and US market, respectively, using all the stocks in NIFTY 50 for India and NASDAQ 100 for the US, for 3 years, that is, the period 2010–13. This time period happens to be a very important phase of the markets for the study because it represents the period immediately after the two major global

Table 1: Correlation of Returns for Indian Market using NIFTY-50 Stocks

Year	2010–11	2011–12	2012–13
Average Correlation	0.254	0.312	0.194

Table 2: Average Correlation of Returns for US Market using NASDAQ 100 Stocks

Year	2010–11	2011–12	2012–13
Average Correlation	0.403	0.482	0.296

financial crises, that is, the 2008 US subprime mortgage crisis, and the more recent 2009–10 European debt crisis. The average correlation for the Indian market is relatively low in comparison to the US market for all the years under study. A less correlated market signifies more scope of diversification in comparison to a highly correlated market.

Both the markets show a very similar pattern in terms of the correlation structure over the 3 years. Correlations are increasing from 0.254 to 0.312 for India and 0.403 to 0.482 for the US from the year 2010–11 to 2011–12, and then decreasing for the years 2011–12 to 2012–13 for India from 0.312 to 0.194 and for US from 0.482 to 0.296. Increasing correlation among the securities shows that the market is influenced more by some common factors (systematic risk) and decreasing correlation signifies dominance of unsystematic risk. Unsystematic risk is diversifiable, so it is beneficial for the portfolio investors.

Table 3 and Table 4 provide the optimal portfolio size computed, based on the average correlation of the market, and minimum possible portfolio variance for India and US, respectively.

It is evident from Table 3 and Table 4 that the minimum possible portfolio variance for a diversified portfolio is lower for the Indian market than the US market for all the years under study. However, in India, the portfolio manager needs to hold more stocks to diversify the unsystematic risk completely.

Table 3: Average Number of Securities Needed to Hold a Completely Diversified Portfolio Based on Average Correlation for India

Financial Year	*NIFTY 50 Securities Correlation*	*No. of Securities Needed to Hold a Completely Diversified Portfolio*	*Min. Possible Portfolio Variance for Diversified Portfolio*
2010–11	0.254943	30	0.279778
2011–12	0.312106	25	0.339622
2012–13	0.193748	50	0.209873

Table 4: Average Number of Needed to Hold a Completely Diversified Portfolio Based on Average Correlation for US

Financial Year	*NYSE Securities Correlation*	*No. of Securities Needed to Hold a Completely Diversified Portfolio*	*Min. Possible Portfolio Variance for Diversified Portfolio*
2010–11	0.403424	23	0.429362
2011–12	0.48258	19	0.509813
2012–13	0.296507	30	0.319957

Lower correlation for stock return for the Indian market in comparison to the US indicates that average portfolio size in India is supposed to be larger than the US

Table 5 shows the correlation between NIFTY 50 and NASDAQ 100 for 3 years, that is, 2010–13. The lowest correlation is recorded in the year 2011–12, and the highest is recorded in the year 2012–13. A very low correlation of 0.061 in the year 2011–12 is beneficial for foreign investors originating from the US for investing in Indian market as it provides very good diversification opportunity. In fact, for all the years under study the average correlation for stock returns between India and US are quite low, which provides diversification benefit to the foreign investors originating in U.S.

In the second part of the paper the diversification benefits are calculated using the traditional approach of mean-variance analysis for five randomly selected stocks from the Indian market. This approach involves calculating means, variances, and correlations directly from historical data. A variance-

Table 5: Correlation between NIFTY 50 and NASDAQ 100 Indices for Years 2011–13

Year	*Correlation between NIFTY 50 and NASDAQ 100*
2010–11	0.146
2011–12	0.061
2012–13	0.257

Table 6: Correlation Data for Five Randomly Selected Stocks

Company	*HDFC*	*GAIL*	*BHEL*	*Zee Ent.*	*BAG Films*
HDFC	1				
GAIL	–0.168	1			
BHEL	–0.775	0.634	1		
Zee Ent.	0.895	–0.183	–0.723	1	
BAG Films	0.0316	0.166	0.278	0.188	1

covariance matrix is constructed for calculating portfolio variance. Table 6 shows the correlation data for the five randomly selected securities.

There are many firm pairs in Table 6, which show either negative or very low correlations. For example, the BHEL and HDFC pair shows a highly negative correlation of –0.775, the highest correlation being 0.85 between HDFC and Zee Entertainment. Negative and low correlations contribute towards significant reduction in portfolio risk. For calculating portfolio variance a variance-covariance matrix has been prepared. Table 7 shows the variance-covariance matrix.

First, the standard deviation and variance for the portfolio is calculated using equal weights for all the securities. Then the portfolio is optimized for weights to obtained minimum standard deviation using MS Excel Solver. Table 8 summarizes the results obtained for the optimized portfolio.

It is clearly evident from Table 8 that both, naïve strategy using equally weighted portfolio, and quantitatively optimized portfolio using solver produce significant diversification benefit, as the diversification ratio is quite good at 69 per cent and 31 per cent, respectively. Diversification ratio is significantly low for quantitatively optimized portfolio in comparison to the equally weighted portfolio. However, it comes with severe limitations. Implementation of quantitative optimization produces wildly unrealistic portfolios with huge short positions and correspondingly imaginary long positions. In many cases short sales are caused by bad historical returns that are not necessarily indicative of future anticipated returns. It is also

Table 7: Variance-Covariance Matrix for Randomly Selected Stocks

Company	*HDFC*	*GAIL*	*BHEL*	*ZEE*	*BAG*
HDFC	46.21	–7.76	–52.80	44.49	2.42
GAIL	–7.76	45.97	43.06	–9.07	12.73
BHEL	–52.80	43.06	100.28	–52.94	31.51
ZEE	44.49	–9.06	–52.94	53.44	15.54
BAG	2.42	12.73	31.52	15.54	127.44

Table 8: Portfolio Standard Deviation and Diversification Ratios using Equal Weights, Varying Weights, and Market Model

S.D for Random selection of Securities	*Equally Weighted Portfolio*		*Optimized Portfolio*		*Market Model based Portfolio*	
	S.D	*Diversification Ratio*	*S.D*	*Diversification Ratio*	*S.D*	*Diversification Ratio*
8.43	5.86	0.69	2.62	0.31	5.32	0.63

evident from Table 6 that many security pairs show a negative correlation, which results in negative weights being assigned to some securities in the optimization process. To overcome these limitations, a single factor model, that is, the Market Model is then used. Standard deviation according to the Market Model is 5.32 per cent with 63 per cent of the diversification ratio. The Market Model produces a lesser diversification benefit using the same set of assets, in comparison to the mean-variance approach. However, the results of the Market Model are more realistic and reliable, as it does not indicate unrealistic short positions.

CONCLUDING REMARKS

The average correlation for stock returns for the Indian market is relatively low in comparison to the US market for all the years under study. A less correlated market signifies more scope of diversification in comparison to a highly correlated market; however, it requires a larger portfolio size for diversification of the unsystematic risk. Both the markets show very similar pattern in terms of correlation structure over the three years. Correlations increase from year 2010–11 to 2011–12, and then decrease from 2011–12 to 2012–13 for both India and the US. Increasing correlation among the securities shows that the market is influenced more by some common factors (systematic risk) and decreasing correlation signify dominance of unsystematic risk. A low correlation between Indian and US stock indexes provides a good opportunity for international diversification for the foreign investors. For portfolio optimization, the Market Model indicates lesser diversification benefit in comparison to quantitative optimization using mean -variance approach; however results of the Market Model are more realistic and reliable, as it does not indicate unrealistic short positions. The reason for producing short positions for many assets in quantitative optimization using traditional mean-variance approach is that the correlations between asset returns are in some cases large. Large correlations for a particular stock can lead the investors to prefer other stocks with smaller returns, but more moderate correlations. In the present selection of stocks there are many asset pairs showing a large negative correlation.

REFERENCES

C. Bengtsson and J. Holst, 'On Portfolio Selection: Improved Covariance Matrix Estimation for Swedish Asset Returns', Working Paper, Lund University and Lund Institute of Technology, 2002.

E. Fama, and K. French, 'Industry Costs of Equity', *Journal of Financial Economics*, vol. 43, 1997.

E.J. Elton, M.J. Gruber, and T. Ulrich, 'Are Betas Best?', *Journal of Finance*, vol. 23, 1978.

F. Black, 'Capital Market Equilibrium with Restricted Borrowing'', *Journal of Business*, vol. 45, 1972.

________, 'Equilibrium Exchange Rate Hedging', NBER Working Paper Series: Working Paper No. 2947, April 1989a.

________ and R. Litterman, 'Global Asset Allocation with Equities, Bonds, and Currencies', *Fixed Income Research*, Goldman, Sachs and Company, October 1991.

________, 'Global Portfolio Optimization', *Financial Analyst Journal*, September/ October, 1992, pp. 28–43.

H.M. Markowitz, 'Portfolio Selection', *The Journal of Finance*, March 1952, pp. 77–91.

L. Chan, J. Karceski, and J. Lakonishok, ('On Portfolio Estimation: Forecasting Covariances and Choosing the Risk Model', Review *of Financial Studies*, vol, 12, 1999.

R. Litterman and K. Winkelmann, 'Estimating Covariance Matrices', *Risk Management Series*, Goldman Sachs & Company, January 1998.

R.C. Green, 'Positively Weighted Portfolios on the Minimum-Variance Frontier', Journal *of Finance*, vol. 41, 1986.

W.F. Sharpe, 'Capital Asset Prices: A Theory of Market Equilibrium', *Journal of Finance*, September 1964, pp. 138–50.

________, 'Imputing Expected Security Returns from Portfolio Composition', *Journal of Financial and Quantitative Analysis*, June 1974, pp. 463–72.

W. Lee, *Advanced Theory and Methodology of Tactical Asset Allocation*. New York: John Wiley and Sons, 2000.

Z. Bodie et al., *Investments*, 8th ed., Tata McGraw-Hill, New Delhi, 2009.

Determinants of Corporate Credit Ratings in India

Rachan Sareen and Madhu Vij[1]

Department of Commerce, S.G.T.B. Khalsa College, University of Delhi, Delhi

[1] Faculty of Management Studies (FMS), University of Delhi, Delhi

e-mail: rachansareen@gmail.com; madhufms@gmail.com

ABSTRACT

Credit rating agencies (CRAs) play a key role in financial markets. They help to reduce the information asymmetry about the creditworthiness of companies between investors and issuers. The CRAs claim that they use financial and non-financial information to assign credit ratings. Nevertheless, it is difficult to understand the ratings assigned by the rating agencies as there is an element of subjective judgement involved. The present paper attempts to empirically analyse the relationship of corporate governance, financial and non-financial characteristics with the credit ratings using the multinomial logistic regression model. The results depict a significant relationship between the credit ratings and the selected variables. The independent variables that have been found to be significant determiners of credit ratings are Interest Coverage Ratio, Leverage Ratio, Profitability Ratio, and Size and Disclosure policies. The model is able to classify ratings with reasonable accuracy.

Keywords: Corporate Governance, Credit Ratings, Governance Indices, Multinomial Logistic Regression

INTRODUCTION

The inability of the credit rating agencies to predict the 1997–98 Asian crises, 2007–09 subprime crises, and the bankruptcies of Enron, WorldCom and Parmalat have earned them severe criticism. This has also prompted legislators to regulate rating agencies. Nevertheless, their role as guards to the capital markets remains firmly in place. The rating agencies' role has expanded with financial globalization. It has received an additional boost from Basel II that incorporates the ratings of CRAs into the rules for setting weights for credit risk.

Internationally, there are three credit rating agencies which hold a reputed position: Moody's Investors Service, Fitch Ratings and Standard and Poor's. In India, the ratings industry has been built up to its present position over a period of 25 years. The ratings have been operating in India since 1988. There are five credit rating agencies recognized by Securities and Exchange Board of India (SEBI). Credit Rating and Information Services of India Limited (CRISIL), Investment Information and Credit Rating Agency of India Limited (ICRA) and Fitch India have collaborative arrangements with S&P, Moody's and Fitch respectively. Credit Analysis & Research Ltd. (CARE) is promoted by IDBI & Canara Bank. Brickworks, the latest entrant, was established in 2008. The Indian credit rating industry is next to USA in terms of number of ratings issued.

It is crucial that the credit rating agencies maintain their reputation as reliable and objective source of information. In the aftermath of default scandals like Enron, WorldCom and Parmalat, there has been a lot of discussion about the reliability and relevance of the information provided by credit ratings. Closer to home, big corporate giants like Satyam and non-banking finance companies floated by C.R. Bansali (CRB scam) with favourable credit ratings and audit reports collapsed causing losses to many small investors. The accuracy and timeliness of ratings have been debatable. The present research work examines some of the determinants of credit ratings. The objective of the paper is (1) to examine the relationship of corporate governance measures, financial and non-financial characteristics with credit ratings, and (2) to develop a credit rating classification model and determine its accuracy.

LITERATURE REVIEW

There are many studies that have examined the relationship of financial determinants and credit ratings. The econometric methods for analysing categorical dependent variables have evolved over a period of time. These techniques include Multiple Regression Analysis (Horrigan, 1966; Pogue and Soldofsky, 1969; West, 1970), Multiple Discriminant Analysis (Pinches and Mingo, 1973), Ordered Linear Probit Model (OLPM) (Kaplan and Urwitz, 1979; Blume et al., 1998; Poon, 2003; Amato and Furfine, 2004;

Roje, 2005; Gray and Raghunathan, 2006; Hwang et al., 2009; Purda, 2008; Tanthanongsakkun and Treepongkaruna, 2008). There are few which have used machine learning techniques, for example, Artificial Neural Networks (Kumar and Haynes, 2003).

The main drawback of the earlier studies was that the dependent variable (credit ratings) was considered as a continuous variable. In the later studies, the Ordered Probit Model was used. This has the theoretical advantage of treating credit ratings as ordinal discrete variables.

All studies pointed out that credit rating agencies use both quantitative and qualitative information to arrive at credit ratings. Earlier studies have been able to develop models that could classify 60 per cent to 75 per cent of the actual bond ratings. A higher percentage of correct classifications has not been possible because of the subjectivity involved in the rating process.

Although corporate governance is a well-researched topic, there are very few studies which investigate the relationship between corporate governance and credit ratings. Bhojraj and Sengupta (2003), Ashbaugh-Skaife et al. (2006) and Alali et al. (2012) provide empirical evidence that corporate governance affects the credit ratings. In the earlier studies, corporate governance has been studied with relation to the cost of equity, firm's performance, capital structure, and cost of debt. Some empirical studies (Ashbaugh-Skaife et al., 2006; Drobetz et al., 2004; Chen et al., 2003) agree that high corporate governance standards have a positive impact on the access and cost of equity capital. There is empirical evidence (Kumar, 2005; Jiraporn and Gleason, 2007; Alba et al., 1998) linking high leverage with weak governance. Corporate governance also influences the cost of debt (Beekes and Brown, 2006). There is an extensive literature (Klapper and Love, 2004; Gompers et al., 2003; Drobetz et al., 2004) that associate corporate governance with financial performance. Although there is little research dedicated to its association with credit ratings, a firm's performance and cost of capital are in a way reflected in credit ratings. A credit rating is meant to impart a message of a company's efficiency (strong corporate governance), dynamism (performance), and credit worthiness (access and cost of finance).

Most of these studies have been conducted in the US market, Australia, China and the Nordic countries. With reference to India, most of the studies evaluate the performance of rating agencies in terms of their usefulness to individual and institutional investors in India. A report on Comprehensive Regulation for Credit rating agencies (2010) by Reserve Bank of India, and Ohta (2010) focus on how regulatory framework can be made more comprehensive for a more effective and efficient operation of Credit rating agencies in India.

METHODOLOGY

The present paper attempts to empirically analyse the relationship of financial characteristics, non-financial characteristics, and corporate governance measures with the credit ratings in 219 companies in three industries in the manufacturing sector of India – Textile, Steel, and Paper. This section describes the dependent and the independent variables. This is followed by the description of the sample design and the statistical and econometric model used in the study.

Dependent Variable

The dependent variable (*Y*) is the long-term rating of a company assigned by credit rating agencies in India as on 1 July 2012. The long-term ratings for the selected companies were obtained from the Centre for Monitoring Indian Economy (CMIE) database. The long-term credit ratings are issued in alphabetic form and are categorized in six investment grades and four non-investment grades. They further classify companies into subcategories by attaching a suffix '–' or '+' to indicate the relative position of the issuer within the same category. The ratings have been converted to a numerical score for the purpose of statistical analysis. The present study focuses on broad categories. Therefore, positive or negative signs suffixed to ratings are ignored while assigning numerical values. As there were a few observations in the highest categories (A, AA, AAA) and the lowest categories (D, C, CC and CCC), they were merged with the nearest category. Therefore, the present study considers five categories of credit ratings ranging from 1 to 5, where 1 denotes the lowest rating and 5 denotes the highest rating. The lowest value is assigned to the lowest rating (highest credit risk). The categorization of the credit ratings into numeric classes, in ascending order, is presented as follows:

$$Y_i = \begin{cases} 1 \text{ if rating} = \text{D, C, CC, CCC} \\ 2 \text{ if rating} = \text{B} \\ 3 \text{ if rating} = \text{BB} \\ 4 \text{ if rating} = \text{BBB} \\ 5 \text{ if rating} = \text{A, AA, AAA} \end{cases}$$

The dependent variable (Y_i) includes the ratings assigned to all bonds, non-convertible debentures, and other debt instruments (excluding public deposits) with original maturity exceeding one year.

Independent Variables

In the present study, corporate governance, financial and non-financial characteristics are the independent variables. These are as follows:

Corporate Governance

A set of 47 questions was formulated on the basis of previous literature, mandatory and non-mandatory requirements given in Clause 49 of the listing agreement. The questions focus on the board composition, qualifications, meetings, various committees, and their composition, disclosure practices and policies followed by an enterprise. The responses to these questions have been manually recorded using the corporate governance reports and the respective websites of the companies. It has been found that the SEBI last amended Clause 49 of the listing agreement pertaining to corporate governance norms in December, 2003.[1] It has been observed after examining various corporate governance reports that compliance of the companies did not change much in the period 2009–12. Therefore, it has been decided to consider corporate governance compliance of financial year 2011–12 for the present study. The various aspects of corporate governance have been grouped under four subheadings.

1. Board of Directors
2. Disclosure practices
3. Audit committee
4. Other Committees

The favourable aspects of corporate governance have been reflected by using a binary scale in most cases – a higher value of one is assigned if the company either follows the mandatory or non-mandatory requirements in the listing agreement, or complies with certain mechanisms that have been empirically proven relevant in the earlier studies. There are other attributes which are assigned scores by developing thresholds for identifying better governance practices. For example, Clause 49 does not make any recommendation about the size of the board, but there is empirical evidence (Yermack, 1996) that neither too large nor too small a board is beneficial for companies. Therefore, the companies have been divided into quartiles

[1] A consultative paper on review of norms of corporate governance in India suggesting further amendments in Clause 49 was published in January, 2012.

based on the range of the size of the board in the given sample. A higher score of '2' is assigned to the companies in the second and third quartile and lower score of '1' to companies in the first and fourth quartiles. The sum of the values assigned to individual attributes under the four subheadings gave four sub- indices. The four sub-indices have been further transformed into two categories on the basis of their respective median values. A category with value '1' implies strong corporate governance and a category with value '0' implies weak corporate governance. If the computed sub index is found to be above its median value, it is assigned category '1' and if the sub index is found to be below the median value, it is assigned the category '0'.

Financial Variables

The present study includes only those financial indicators that have been used either in explaining credit ratings in the extant literature, or they are considered relevant by the rating agencies. The majority of these indicators are in the form of ratios. The use of financial ratios facilitates the comparison of financial indicators of companies of different size. The financial ratios that have been used are as follows:

1. Interest Coverage Ratio (Fund flow from operations/interest)
2. Leverage Ratio (Debt /Equity)
3. Profitability Ratios (PBITDA/Sales, PBIT/Average total assets, Standard deviation of earnings/Total assets)
4. Liquidity Ratio (Cash Ratio)

Non-financial Variables

1. Size (Average total assets)
2. Industry (Steel, Paper And Textile)

The financial information for four year period (2008–09 to 2011–12) has been used to compute the explanatory variables and it has been extracted from CMIE database. The variables are transformed since they are highly skewed, possessed a high range and variance using data transformation techniques. The data is also checked for outliers and influential cases.

Multinomial Logit Regression

This technique has been used to investigate the impact of the explanatory variables on the credit ratings. The credit ratings, Y, of a company i, (Y_i) have been studied as a function of the explanatory variables in the following model:

Credit Ratings (Y_i) = f (corporate governance, financial characteristics, size and industry)

Logistic regression models the probability of one of the two outcomes using the independent variables. The logistic regression equation is as follows:

Log (Prob ($Y_i^\star$) / Prob ($Y_k^\star$) = $\alpha_i + \beta_j X_j$,

where Log (Prob ($Y_i^\star$)/Prob ($Y_k^\star$) is the log of odds of i outcomes with respect to a referent outcome k (i varies from 1 to k–1). This can be presented as follows:

$$\log\frac{\Pr\left(Y_i^* = 1\right)}{\Pr\left(Y_i^* = k\right)} = \alpha_i + X_j\beta_{1j}$$

$$\log\frac{\Pr\left(Y_i^* = 2\right)}{\Pr\left(Y_i^* = k\right)} = \alpha_2 + X_j\beta_{2j}$$

....

$$\log\frac{\Pr\left(Y_i^* = k-1\right)}{\Pr\left(Y_i^* = k\right)} = \alpha_{k-1} + X_j\beta_{k-1j}$$

The probabilities of each category can be found by exponentiating the log of odds (Exp ($\alpha_i + \beta_j X_j$)) as shown below:

$$\Pr[Y_i^* = 1] = \frac{\exp^{\alpha i + Xj\beta 1j}}{1 + \sum_{i=1}^{k-1} \exp^{\alpha i + Xj\beta ij}}$$

$$\Pr[Y_i^* = 2] = \frac{\exp^{\alpha i + Xj\beta 2j}}{1 + \sum_{i=1}^{k-1} \exp^{\alpha i + Xj\beta ij}}$$

....

$$\Pr[Y_i^* = k-1] = \frac{\exp^{\alpha i + Xj\beta(k-1)j}}{1 + \sum_{i=1}^{k-1} \exp^{\alpha i + Xj\beta ij}}$$

Multinomial logistic regression[2] is an extension of the binary logistic regression. It generalizes logistic regression by allowing more than two outcomes of dependent variables which may be non-metric – nominal or ordinal. The independent variable may be metric or non-metric. It describes polytomous responses by a sequence of binary models. If the ordinal

[2] P.L. Flom (n.d.), 'Multinomial and Ordinal Logistic Regression Using PROC LOGISTIC', National Development and Research Institutes, Inc. Retrieved on 7 May 2013 from http://www.nesug.org/proceedings/nesug05/an/an2.pdf

dependent variable is divided into *k* categories, it compares the probability of being in each of the ($k-1$) categories compared to a reference category *k*.

ANALYSIS AND INTERPRETATION OF RESULTS

The preliminary investigations included correlation statistics, descriptive statistics, and frequency distribution of assigned ratings. They confirmed that the transformed data did not suffer from multicollinearity or heteroskedacity (Table 1).

Table 1: Frequency Distribution of Ratings Assigned in the Given Sample

Rating Code	*Ratings*	*Frequency*	*Percent*
1	D, C, CC, CCC	34	15.5
2	B	17	7.8
3	BB	54	24.7
4	BBB	66	30.1
5	A, AA, AAA	48	21.9
		219	100

Of the companies that were included in the sample, 52 per cent had investment grade and 48 per cent had speculative grade. The multinomial logistic regression has been used to examine the relationship of the predictors and credit ratings. The results of the regression technique have been discussed in Table 2.

Table 2: Parameter Estimates

Explanatory Variables	*−2 log Likelihood*	*p-value*
EBITDA/Interest	419.49	0.010
Debt/Equity	429.31	0.000
PBITDA/Sales	407.97	0.795
PBIT/Average Total Assets	427.28	0.000
Std deviation of earnings/Total assets	412.28	0.200
Cash ratio	407.70	0.842
Average Total Assets	473.00	0.000
Board of Directors	411.42	0.274
Disclosures practices	423.57	0.002
Audit Committee	410.77	0.345
Other Committee	407.07	0.942
Industry	416.12	0.277
Overall model fit		0.000
Pseudo R-square		0.73

On the basis of the likelihood ratio test, the model with the 12 selected explanatory variables depicts a significant relationship between the credit ratings and the selected predictors. The Nagelkerke R^2 is 73 per cent which implies that the selected variables explain approximately 73 per cent of the variation in the outcome variable, that is, credit ratings. There are five independent variables found to be significant determinants of credit ratings – Interest Coverage Ratio, Leverage Ratio, Profitability Ratio, Size, and Disclosure policies.

If an independent variable has an overall significant relationship with the dependent variable, it is not necessary that it will be statistically significant in differentiating between pairs of categories defined by the dependent variable. The interpretation for an independent variable focuses on its ability to distinguish between pairs of credit ratings' categories and the contribution

Table 3: Interpretation of Significant Independent Variables and Credit Ratings (with reference category BBB)

BBB	*CCC, CC, C, D*	*B*	*BB*	*A, AA, AAA*
	β-coefficient *Standard error*			
EBITDA/ Interest	–0.006	0.001	−0.005	0.000
	0.003	0.001	0.002	0.001
	5.071	0.758	4.651	0.041
	0.024	0.384	0.031	0.840
Debt/Equity	0.003	0.003	0.003	−0.014
	0.002	0.003	0.002	0.004
	1.397	1.522	2.712	11.055
	0.237	0.217	0.100	0.001
PBIT/Average	−0.264	−0.239	−0.004	0.183
	0.100	0.102	0.079	0.084
Total Assets Average	6.933	5.470	0.002	4.812
	0.008	0.019	0.964	0.028
	−1.240	−0.898	−2.343	3.574
Total Assets	0.694	0.782	0.607	0.779
	3.196	1.319	14.890	21.051
	0.074	0.251	0.000	0.000
Disclosure practices	1.947	2.533	0.954	−0.697
	0.682	0.795	0.549	0.685
	8.145	10.322	3.016	1.035
	0.004	0.001	0.082	0.309

that it makes to change the odds of being in one credit rating group rather than the other.[3] In Table 3, interpretation of only those independent variables has been given that have been proved significant in the overall relationship with the credit ratings.

As there are five possible outcomes considered in the sample, the multinomial logistic regression estimates four models for a given reference category. In the following tables, the fourth category (BBB) has been treated as referent category and models have been estimated relative to that category. Therefore, for a unit change in the explanatory variable, the logit of outcome, *m*, relative to the referent category is expected to change by its respective parameter estimate (which is in log-odds units) given the other variables in the model are held constant. For instance, if EBITDA to Interest Ratio was to increase by one unit, multinomial log-odds of being in category CCC, CC, C and D relative to BBB would be expected to decrease by 0.006 units while holding all other variables in the model constant.

The odds ratio for relevant variables in the different categories have been found by exponentiation of beta coefficients (Table 4).

Table 4: Odds Ratios [Exp (β)]

Independent Variable	*Comparison Categories*	*Odds Ratio Exp (β)*
EBITDA/Interest Debt/Equity	CCC, CC, C, D & BBB	0.994
	BB & BBB	0.995
	A, AA, AAA & BBB	0.986
PBIT/Average Total Assets	CCC, CC, C, D & BBB	0.768
	B & BBB	0.787
	A, AA, AAA & BBB	1.201
Average Total Assets	BB & BBB	0.096
	A, AA, AAA & BBB	35.642
Disclosure Practices	CCC, CC, C, D & BBB	7.005
	B & BBB	12.842

Table 4 summarizes the effect of each predictor found significant in the overall model in differentiating between different categories of credit ratings:

Interest Coverage Ratio as a predictor is able to differentiate between CCC, CC, C, D as one category, BB and BBB. Since the odds ratio is less than 1, an increase in Interest Coverage Ratio of a company makes it more probable for the company to get a higher credit rating (BBB in this

[3] 'Multinomial Logistic Regression', Retrieved on 5 May 2013, from www.utexas.edu/.../MultinomialLogisticRegression_BasicRelationships.ppt

case). The odds ratio for CCC, CC, C, D as one category, and BB is 0.998 (= 0.994/0.995). However, it is not able to differentiate between higher categories.

Leverage Ratio as a predictor is able to differentiate between A, AA, AAA as one category and BBB. The odds ratio is less than 1. This indicates that as the debt portion increases in the capital structure, the probability of being rated in the lower categories increases.

Profitability Ratio as a predictor is able to distinguish between all categories except BB. The odds ratio is less than 1 when category BBB is compared with lower categories (B and CCC, CC, C, D) and more than 1 when it is compared with higher categories (A, AA, AAA as one category), indicating that as the profitability increases, the probability of being rated in the higher categories also increases.

Size as a predictor is able to differentiate between A, AA, AAA as one category, BB and BBB. The odds ratio is less than 1 when category BBB is compared with a lower category (BB), and more than 1 when it is compared with higher categories (A, AA, AAA). This implies that larger companies are rated higher than the smaller companies.

Disclosure practices as a predictor is able to differentiate between CCC, CC, C, D (as one category), B and BBB. The odds ratio is more than 1 indicating that a company following efficient disclosure practices is likely to be assigned higher ratings.

CLASSIFICATION RESULTS

The accuracy of the multinomial logit regression model in classifying the credit ratings can be found by cross tabulation of observed credit ratings and predicted credit ratings. The classification results have been shown in Table 5.

Table 5: Classification Table

Observed	*Predicted Ratings*					
	C, CC, CCC, D	*B*	*BB*	*BBB*	*A, AA, AAA*	*% Correct*
C,CC,CCC,D	22	0	6	6	0	64.7
B	6	0	6	4	1	0.0
BB	4	2	38	9	1	70.4
BBB	2	0	8	49	7	74.2
A, AA,AAA	0	0	2	9	37	77.1
Overall %	15.5	0.9	27.4	35.2	21.0	66.7

The proportional by-chance accuracy rate is computed by calculating the proportion of cases for each category in the given sample, and then squaring and summing the proportion of cases in each category ($0.155^2 + 0.078^2 + 0.247^2 + 0.301^2 + 0.219^2 = 0.227$) (from Table 1). The proportional by-chance accuracy criteria (Schwab, 2007) is 28 per cent ($1.25 \times 22.7\% = 26\%$). The given model is considered useful as it makes correct predictions to the extent of 66.7 per cent with maximum correct predictions (77.1 per cent) made in the fifth category (A, AA, AAA) followed by the fourth (74.2 per cent in BB) and third category (70.4 per cent in B). It is also observed that 21 per cent of predictions missed the perfect prediction by only one category. Hence, the given model is able to classify with reasonable accuracy.

CONCLUSION

The relationship of corporate governance, financial and non-financial variables with credit ratings is assessed using the multinomial logit regression model on a sample of 218 companies. On the basis of the likelihood ratio test, the model, with the 12 selected explanatory variables, depicts a significant relationship between the credit ratings and the selected predictors. There are four independent variables found to be significant determiners of credit ratings – Interest Coverage Ratio, Leverage Ratio, Profitability Ratio, Size and Disclosure policies.

The given model is considered useful as it makes correct classifications to the extent of 66.7 per cent with maximum correct classifications (74.2 per cent) made in the second category (BBB) followed by the first (77.1 per cent in AAA, AA and A) and third category (69.4 per cent in BB). It is also observed that 22 per cent of the ratings missed the perfect classifications by only one category. Therefore, the model is able to make classifications with reasonable accuracy.

The accreditations assigned by the rating agencies certify the financial instrument of the issuer. This ensures that the issuer is able to raise funds at a reasonable cost. The present study may provide guidance for the firms in the quest for rating solicitation. It may also help the investors to interpret ratings and make the correct investment decision. The empirical evidence also confirms the positive role of corporate governance for companies relying on debt. The time, effort, and cost invested by a company in implementing corporate governance practices may translate into good credit ratings and, thus, lower the cost of debt.

REFERENCES

D. Yermack, 'Higher Market Valuation of Companies with a Small Board of Directors', *Journal of Financial Economics*, vol. 40, no. 2, 1996, pp. 185–211.

F.A. Alali, A. Anandrajan, and W. Jiang, 'The Effect of Corporate Governance on Firm's Credit Ratings: Further Evidence Using Governance Score in the United States', *Journal of Accounting & Finance*, vol. 52, no. 2, 2012, pp. 291–312.

G. Roje, 'The role of accounting determinants in predicting long term credit ratings', *Proceedings of the European Accounting Association Congress*, 2005.

G.E. Pinches and K.A. Mingo, 'A Multivariate Analysis of Industrial Bond Ratings', *Journal of Finance*, vol. 28, 1973, pp. 1–18.

H. Ashbaugh-Skaife, D.W. Collins, and R. LaFond, 'The Effects of Corporate Governance on Firms' Credit Ratings', *Journal of Accounting and Economics*, vol. 42, no. 1, 2006, pp. 203–43.

H. Ohta, 'The Finance in the Capital Market and Credit Rating in India'.2010, Retrieved on 23 June,2011 from www.eco.nihon-u.ac.jp/center/ccas/pdf/wp011.pdf

J. Kumar, 'Corporate Governance Mechanisms and Firm Financing in India', *In Proceedings of the International Conference on Emerging Securities Market: Challenges and Prospects*, The Securities Exchange Board of India (SEBI) and the ICFAI University, Mumbai, 2005.

J.A. Schwab, 'Multinomial Logistic Regression: Basic Relationships and Complete Problems', 2007. Retrieved on 7 May, 2012 from http://www.utexas.edu/courses/schwab/sw388r7/SolvingProblems.

J.D. Amato C.H. Furfine, 'Are Credit Ratings Procyclical?' *Journal of Banking and Finance*, vol. **28**, 2001, pp. 2641–77.

J.O. Horrigan, 'The Determination of Long-term Credit Standing with Financial Ratios', *Journal of Accounting Research*, vol. 4, 1966, pp. 44–62.

K. Kumar and J.D. Haynes, 'Forecasting Credit Ratings Using and Statistical Techniques', *International Journal of Business Studies*, vol. 11, 2003, pp. 91–8.

K.C.W. Chen, K.C.J. Wei, and Z. Chen, 'Disclosure, Corporate Governance and the Cost of Equity Capital from Asia's Emerging Markets', 2003. Retrieved on 31 May 2013 from http://ssrn.com/abstract=422000.

L. Purda, 'Risk Perception and Financial System', *Journal of International Business Studies*, vol. 39, no. 7, 2008, pp. 1178–96.

L.F. Klapper and I. Love, 'Corporate Governance, Investor Protection, and Performance in Emerging Markets', *Journal of Corporate Finance*, vol. 10, no. 5, 2004, pp. 703–28.

M.E. Blume, F. Lim, and A.C. MacKinlay, 'The Declining Credit Quality of U.S. Corporate Debt: Myth or Reality?' *Journal of Finance*, vol. 53, 1998, pp. 1389–414.

M. Gray and V. Ragunathan, 'The Determinants of Credit Ratings: Australian Evidence', *Australian Journal of Management*, vol. 31, 2006, pp. 333–54.

P. Alba, S. Claessens and S. Djankov, *Thailand›s Corporate Financing and Governance Structures,* No. 2003), World Bank Publications, 1998.

P. Gompers, J. Ishii, and A. Metrick, 'Corporate Governance and Equity Prices', *Quarterly Journal of Economics,* vol.16, no.1, 2003, pp. 107–31.

P. Jiraporn and K.C. Gleason, 'Capital Structure, Shareholder Rights, And Corporate Governance', 2007. Retrieved on 6 June 2013 from http://dx.doi.org/10.2139/ssrn.792604.

R.C. Hwang, H. Chung, and C.K. Chu, 'Predicting Issuer Credit Ratings using a Semiparametric Method', *Journal of Empirical Finance,* vol. 17, 2009, pp. 120–37.

R.R. West, 'An Alternative Approach to Predicting Corporate Bond Rating', *Journal of Accounting Research,* 1970, pp. 118–27.

R.S. Kaplan and G. Urwitz, 'Statistical Models of Bond Ratings: A Methodological Inquiry', *Journal of Business,* vol. 52, 1979, pp. 231–61.

Report of the Committee on Comprehensive Regulation for Credit Rating Agencies Reserve Bank of India (2010). Available at www.rbi.org.in

S. Bhojraj and P. Sengupta, 'Effect of Corporate Governance on Bond Ratings and Yields: The Role of Institutional Investors and Outside Directors', *Journal of Business,* vol. 76, no. 3, 2003, pp. 455–75.

S. Tanthanongsakkun and S. Treepongkaruna, 'Explaining Credit Ratings of Australian Companies-an application of Merton Model', *Australian Journal of Management,* vol. 33, no. 2, 2008, pp. 261–75.

T.F. Pogue and R.M. Soldofsky, 'What's in a Bond Rating?' *Journal of Financial and Quantitative Analysis,* vol. 4, 1969, pp. 201–28.

W. Beekes and P. Brown, 'Do Better-Governed Australian Firms Make More Informative Disclosures?' *Journal of Business Finance & Accounting,* vol. 33, nos. 3–4, 2006, pp. 422–50.

W. Drobetz, A. Schillhofer and H. Zimmermann, 'Corporate Governance and Expected Stock Returns: Evidence from Germany', *European Financial Management,* vol.10, no.2, 2004, pp. 267–93.

W.P.H. Poon, 'Are Unsolicited Credit Ratings Biased Downward?' *Journal of Banking and Finance,* vol. 27, 2003, pp. 593–614.

Financial Determinants of Firm's Value

Evidence from Indian Firms

Pushpendra Singh
G L Bajaj Institute of Management and Research, Grater Noida, Uttar Pradesh
e-mail: Pushpendra.ssb@gmail.com

ABSTRACT

Businesses or fractional interests in businesses may be valued for various purposes such as mergers and acquisitions, sale of securities, and taxable events. An accurate valuation of companies largely depends on the reliability of the firm's historic financial information, financial statements that are audited by Certified Chartered Accountants, and overseen by a government regulator. Alternatively, private firms do not have government oversight – unless operating in a regulated industry – and are usually not required having their financial statements audited. Moreover, managers of private firms often prepare their financial statements to minimize profits and, therefore, taxes. Alternatively, managers of public firms tend to want higher profits to increase their stock price. Therefore, a firm's historic financial information may not be accurate and can lead to over- and undervaluation. In an acquisition, a buyer often performs due diligence to verify the seller's information.

This paper investigates empirically the determinants of firm value creation. For this, 16 companies of four sectors, namely Metal, Fast Moving Consumer Goods (FMCG), Information Technology (IT) and Automobile industry listed on the Bombay Stock Exchange (BSE) from 2004 to 2013 were identified on the basis of market capitalization in their industry. Taking evidence from numerous literatures, various factors have been identified, that is, Net Sales, Profit, Fixed Assets, dividend pay-out ratio, and capital structure as the financial variables affecting a firm's value. Data from 2004 to 2013 were collected for all these companies from Money-Control, Business-Line, and company websites. Hence, data under consideration are all secondary data. Correlation tool was applied to identify multiple correlations among variables, if any. The Augmented Dickey Fuller (ADF) test was applied to check stationarity of data and thereafter Pooled Regression Model (PRM) was applied to identify the significant factors. The finding of the research goes along with the proposition of Modigliani and Miller, that is, capital structure doesn't influence the value of a firm. But at the same time, this research outcome suggests that the Weighted Average Cost of Capital (WACC) has a significant impact on the value of the firm. Other significant factors identified through the proposed model are fixed assets, net sales, and profit. The research will help managers and policy makers to take rational decisions while evaluating different financial parameters in-order to increase the value of the firm.

Keywords: Financial Leverage, Market Capitalization, Pooled Regression, Unit Root Test

INTRODUCTION

In analysing a company's financial health or taking its ownership, the most crucial aspect is the firm's value. Greater the value better is the position of the firm financially and better is the prospects for prospective investors. Market capitalization has been taken as a proxy for a firm's value in many literatures. Market Capitalization is determined by multiplying a number of outstanding shares and the current market price of one share. It is generally used to determine a company's size, as opposed to sales or total assets. Considering the number of outstanding shares to be constant (except in the case of buyout or split share), a firm's value is largely affected by the market price of the firm.

In order to enhance a firm's value, an important question is determining the factors that play a key role in affecting the market price of the firm. Taking evidence from numerous literatures, various factors can be identified, namely Net Sales, Profit, Fixed Assets, and most importantly capital structure. Capital structure refers to the way a firm's assets are financed out of long-term sources of finance. Long-term sources of finance include net-worth and long-term debt. Determining the proportionate relation of debt and equity is a key decision in corporate finance. Although, Modigliani and Miller in their path breaking paper showed that the value of a firm depends upon its investment decision and not on the way it finances its investment, that is, the value of a firm is independent of its capital structure. However, a number of researchers are of the view that capital structure has a significant impact on the value of the firm.

The effect of capital structure on firm's value is determined in terms of debt-equity ratio, as well as Weighted Average Cost of Capital (WACC).

Both debt-equity ratio and WACC have been taken as separate factors in this paper because it may be that debt-equity ratio is high, but the cost of debt is low, so the overall WACC is low, having a positive impact on a firm's value. Analysis may reveal that WACC is a more powerful factor in a firm's value as compared to debt-equity ratio. Apart from capital structure, various factors have been identified which may affect a firm's value. Net sales, as well as profit can be factors directly affecting the value of a firm. Greater turnover and greater profit is preferred because achieving the objective of profit maximization is essential before reaching for wealth maximization. Also, fixed assets possessed by the firm can also be an important factor as it improves the solvency position of the firm by giving an additional protection to creditors and shareholders. Other than these, dividend payout ratio can also be considered as one of the key factor affecting the value of a firm because regular dividend payment provides an investment-recovery mechanism for investors, and hence, is valued as a better company from the perspective of investors looking for liquidity in their investment objectives.

The basic model of equity valuation also suggests that the market value of equity depends on dividend payout ratio, as well as on discount rate and is given as:

$$MV = DPS/(Ke - g) = EPS\,(1 - b)/(Ke - g) \qquad \ldots (1)$$

where MV is market value of equity, DPS is dividend per share, Ke is cost of equity, and g is the expected growth rate.

REVIEW OF LITERATURE

The value of a firm is determined by the market price of the firm's common stock, which in turn is a reflection of the firm's investment, and financial and dividend decisions (Van Home, 1992). A firm's investment is reflected from the fixed asset possessed; financing decisions depends upon debt-equity and WACC, whereas, dividend payout ratio is the indicator of the firm's dividend decisions.

An empirical study investigating the shareholders' value creation (Asogwa, 2009) concluded that the dividend policy is more important for value creation than profitability and earnings growth, whereas, capital structure has no affect in this regard. A study concluded that earning per share and dividend per share explains the variance of equity share price.

Evidence from American firms (Gill, 2012; Biger 2012) indicates that profitability, turnover and market ratio have a significant impact on stock return (Khairurizka, Martani and Mulyono, 2009). This result is consistent with previous studies by Hobart (2006), and Utama and Santoso (1998). Hence, net sales and profit are also taken as the factors under consideration.

Short-term debt, long-term debt, and equity have an influence on the value of firms (Mikail, 2009; Arkan, 2004). Ross's model (1977) suggested that the value of firms will rise with the leverage. A study by Messbacher (2004) also concluded that the choice between debt and equity aims to find the right capital structure that will maximize shareholders wealth.

The WACC is used to define a firm's value by discounting the future cash flows. Minimizing the WACC of any firm will maximize value of firm (S.A, 1977). On the contrary, Rayan (2008) proposed that financial leverage has a negative correlation with a firm's value. From the management point of view, Leland and Poyle (1977) proposed that managers take the debt-equity ratio as a signal by the fact that high leverage implies higher bankruptcy risk and costs for firms which have weak financial conditions. Rasol and Waqas (2011) also supported that management can increase the performance and profit indicators just by changing the debt-equity structure. This study was, however, confined to Pakistan. The WACC has a direct impact on the value of a firm (Johannes and Dhamraj, 2007). Also, Chowdhury and Chowdhury (2010) concluded that by changing the capital structure composition, a firm can increase its value in the market, whereas, the cost of capital has a negative correlation in this decision. This study was confined to Bangladesh.

RESEARCH METHODOLOGY

To identify the determinants impacting the value of a firm, 16 companies from four different dominant sectors of India were identified. The companies selected were from the Metal, Fast Moving Consumer Goods (FMCG), Information Technology (IT), and Automobile industry. The basis of selection of these companies (as per market capitalization) was the top four companies of their sectors. Data from 2004 to 2013 were collected for all these companies from money-control, business line, and company websites. Hence, data under considerations are all secondary data.

A correlation tool was applied on the selected variables to identify whether there was any multiple correlations among them. The correlation matrix output is shown in Table 1.

Table 1: The Correlation Matrix Output Amongst Variables

	Market Capitalization	*Net Sales*	*Profit*	*Debt-Equity Ratio*	*Dividend Payout*	*Fixed Assets*	*WACC*
Market Capitalization	1	0.62	0.74	– 0.25	– 0.05	0.27	0.08
Net Sales		1	0.08	0.05	– 0.13	0.01	– 0.01
Profit			1	– 0.08	– 0.11	0.42	– 0.16
Debt-Equity Ratio				1	– 0.30	0.44	– 0.11
Dividend Payout					1	−0.30	– 0.02
Fixed Assets						1	– 0.04
WACC							1

The output suggests that there are no multiple correlation problems among variables, and hence, all variables under consideration can be taken as explanatory variables in the proposed model. As the data is a time-series data, hence, unit root was applied to check the stationarity of data. Unit root test was applied separately for each company to identify the stationarity of data within the group as well. To check the unit est Augmented Dickey Fuller (ADF) test was applied. The presence of non-stationarity makes the analysis erroneous. The ADF test is a well-accepted test for unit root testing of time series data.

The outcome of ADF test is given in Table 2.

Table 2: Outcome of ADF Test

Method	*Statistic*	*Prob.***
ADF – Fisher Chi-square	8.64338	0.00232
ADF – Choi Z-stat	4.22058	0.00159

The output suggests that data taken under consideration is stationary over the period, as the null hypothesis of ADF test is H_0: Unit root. At a probability value of less than 0.05, we reject the null hypothesis, that is, in this case data taken under consideration is having unit root, that is, data is stationary. To identify the factors affecting the value of a firm significantly, pooled regression was applied with the value of firm as dependent variable, and net sales, profit, debt-equity ratio, dividend payout ratio, fixed assets and WACC as independent variables.

$$\text{Market Cap} = C(1) + C(2)^{\star}\text{ Net sales} + C(3)^{\star}\text{ Profit} + C(4)^{\star}\text{ Debt equity Ratio} + C(5)^{\star}\text{ Dividend Payout Ratio} + C(6)^{\star}\text{ Fixed Assets} + C(7)^{\star}\text{ WACC} \quad \ldots (2)$$

The output of regression is as given in Table 3.

Table 3: Output of Regression

Dependent Variable: MARKET CAPITALIZATION
Method: Least Squares
Sample: 1160
Included observations: 160

	Coefficient	*Std. Error*	*t-Statistic*	*Prob.*
C(1)	5210.771	3869.681	1.346563	0.1801
C(2)	1.635516	0.287776	5.683305	0.0000
C(3)	12.43083	1.209578	10.27700	0.0000
C(4)	−3782.734	4589.706	−0.824178	0.4111
C(5)	−4115.354	4680.364	−0.879281	0.3806
C(6)	−4.081178	0.883968	−4.616887	0.0000
C(7)	15628.83	3986.785	3.920159	0.0001

R-squared	0.703321	Mean dependent var	26177.73
Adjusted R-squared	0.691686	S.D. dependent var	31005.65
S.E. of regression	17216.20	Akaike info criterion	22.38785
Sum squared resid	4.53E+10	Schwarz criterion	22.52239
Log likelihood	−1784.028	Durbin-Watson stat	2.03231

The output suggests that coefficient C(2), C (3), C(6), C(7) are having significant impacts on value of firm while C(1), C(4), C(5) are having no significant impact. R-square = 70.33% also suggests that the model is a best fit model and explains 70.33% variance of the dependent variable. The Durbin-Watson statistics of 2.03231 indicates that there is no auto-correlation problem with the variables, and hence, from all aspects the model explains the dependent variable and is a best fit model. Therefore, the model suggests that profit is the most significant factor affecting the value of a firm, sale is the second best explanatory variable, and then the WACC . This outcome suggests that if the objective of profit creation for the shareholders is fulfilled by a firm, it is reflected on its market capitalization, that is, increase in the value of the firm.

CONCLUSION

This study makes an approach to identify factors affecting the value of a firm. Data of last 10 years were collected for the analysis. Pooled regression was applied on this data to evaluate the determinants. The outcome suggests that profit, sales, fixed assets and the WACC affect the value of a firm significantly.

Out of these, profit impacts the value of a firm most, followed by sales, and then the WACC, as against the popular theory of the value of firm, which suggests that the WACC is the prime determinant.

This paper has taken only four sectors into consideration and a total of 16 companies' data over a 10 year period, which is a limitation of this paper. In future, there is a need to broaden the scope of the paper by identifying whether the result is biased towards a sector by including more sectors and companies for consideration.

REFERENCES

Amarjit Gill, ed., 'Determinants of Equity Share Prices: Evidence from American Firms', *International Research Journal of Finance and Economics*, Issue 9, 2012, pp. 176–92.

Anup Chowdhury and Suman Paul, 'Impact of Capital Structure on Firm's Value: Evidence from Bangladesh', *Business and Economic Horizones*, vol. 3, 2010, pp. 111–22.

B. Jovanovic, 'Selection and Evolution of Industry', *Econometrica*, vol. 50, no. 30, 1982, pp. 649–70.

Dwi Martani, Mulyono, and Rahfiani Khairurizka, 'The Effect of Financial Ratios, Firm Size, and Cash Flow from Operating Activities in the Interim Report to the Stock Return', *Chinese Business Review*, vol. 8, no. 6 (Serial No. 72), 2009.

H. Leland and H. Poyle, 'Informational Asymmetries, Financial Structure, and financial Intermediation', *Journal of Finance*, vol. 32, no. 2, 1977, pp. 371–87.

Kuben Rayan,'Financial Leverage and Firm Value', *Thesis, Gordon Institute of Business Science*, University of Pretoria, 2008.

M. Altan, ed., 'Relationship between Firm Value and Financial Structure: A Study on Firms in ISE Industrial Index', *Journal of Business and Economic Research*, vol. 9, no. 9, 2009, pp. 61–6.

Robert Asogwa, 'Measuring the Determinants of Value Creation for Publicly listed Banks in Nigeria: A Random Effects Probit Model Analysis', Paper presented at *14th Annual Conference on Econometric Modelling for Africa*, 2009.

S.A. Ross, 'The Determination of Financial Structure: The Incentive-Signalling Approach', *The Bill Journal of Economics*, vol. 8, no. 1, 1977, pp. 23–44.

U. Messbacher, 'Does Capital Structure Influence Firm Value?' University of Ulster, 2004.

SECTION V

BANKING AND FINANCE (Liquidity, Mergers and Other Issues)

Dividend Signalling Effect

An Emperical Study of Indian Mid-Cap Companies

Pervin A. Gandhi and Neha Taneja

B.K. Majumdar Institute of Business Administration, Ahmedabad University, Ahmedabad

e-mail: pervin.gandhi@bkmiba.edu.in; neha.taneja@bkmiba.edu.in

ABSTRACT

Dividend decision, in addition to being one of the most important strategic corporate financial decisions, can also play a significant role in influencing the investing pattern of the investors. The present paper attempts to investigate the Dividend Signalling Effect of selected 20 companies which are part of S&P Bombay Stock Exchange(BSE) Mid-Cap Index and announced considerable dividend from 1 January 2013 to 31 August, 2014. In order to analyse the impact, Abnormal Returns(AR), Average Abnormal Returns(AAR) and Cumulative Average Abnormal Returns (CAAR) are worked out for an event window of 20 days prior to and 20 days after the dividend announcement (event) date. The study observes the high increase in the frequency of dividend announcements and the amount of Dividend per share (DPS) in 2014 as compared to previous the period. There are significant wealth effects around dividend changes as proposed by the signalling models.

Keywords: Dividend, Dividend Signalling, Event Study, Shareholder's Wealth

INTRODUCTION

Dividend decision, in addition to being one of the most important strategic corporate financial decisions, has remained the most interesting puzzle for financial managers and researchers till date, as rightly mentioned by Black (1976) in his article 'The Dividend Puzzle'. In finance literature Signalling models have been widely used to understand the dividend policy of corporate firms as the decision of pay-out or ploughing back is critical to attain the corporate goal of maximising the shareholder's wealth. Though Modigliani and Miller (1958) proposed the Irrelevance Theory, they also suggested that dividends may convey information not otherwise known to the market. This argument is theoretically proposed in a number of signalling models. Taneem and Yuce (2011) also stated that dividend changes trigger stock returns as they reflects changes in management assessment of a firm's future profitability. As suggested by Ross Watt (1973) the 'Information content of dividend' phrase refers to the dividend hypothesis for conveying information about future earnings which eventually enables market participants to forecast future earnings more accurately.

This study aims to provide further evidence on the signalling mechanism by studying the information content of dividend through investigating the market reaction to considerable dividend announcements by Indian companies listed on Bombay Stock Exchange (BSE) Mid Cap. Launched on 11 April 2005, the S&P BSE Mid-Cap index is designed to measure the performance of Mid-Cap companies with relatively smaller market capitalizations, listed at BSE Ltd. (S&P Dow Jones Indices LLC and BSE Ltd.). The motivation for the research is to check dividends as a signalling mechanism in such an environment since the medium capitalized segment of the stock market is being increasingly perceived as an attractive investment segment with high growth potential [National Stock Exchange (NSE)].

LITERATURE REVIEW

Large number of 'event study' research has been carried out in the past to investigate the impact of the information content of various market announcements, including dividend announcements. Some of the important contributors to this study are Ball and Brown (1968), Fama et al. (1969), Brown and Warner (1985), Oppenheimer and Dielman (1988), Fama (1991), Kaleem and Salahuddin (2006), Mallikarjunappa and Manjunatha (2009), and Taneem and Yuce (2011). The current study is based on the available framework (models) of the event study literature and particularly studies the impact of considerable dividend announcement by Mid-Cap companies listed at the BSE Ltd.

Academic literature provides two contrary views for dividend theory, that is, the Irrelevance Theory proposed by Miller and Modigliani in 1961 and the Relevance Theory proposed by Walter and Gordon in 1956 and

1959, respectively. Miller and Modigliani (1961) proposed that a dividend policy is irrelevant under a perfect market situation as it will not affect the value of the firm. Walter (1956) argues that the choice of dividend policy almost always affects the value of a firm. According to him, there is a relation between a firm's rate of return and cost of capital in determining the dividend policy, which eventually will maximize the wealth of shareholders. Gordon (1959) seconds Walter's proposition and proposes that the market value of a firm is explicitly related to the dividend policy of the firm. Lintner (1956) also suggested that the current dividends depend on future, as well as past earnings. The Finance Theory also suggests three forms of capital market efficiency, that is, weak, semi-strong and strong form of efficiency. Fama et al. (1969) have conducted a study on the semi-strong form of market efficiency through event study to determine the effect of new information on stock prices.

The following literature reviews the Dividend Signalling effect in the recent Indian, as well as international scenario in chronological order.

Oppenheimer and Dielman (1988) measured the returns of the firms listed on either the New York Stock Exchange (NYSE) or American Stock Exchange (AMEX) at the time of dividend change for 200 days prior to announcement until 21 days prior to announcement. They concluded that the investors, for the most part, do not anticipate large changes in dividend rate, but dividend announcements produce large impacts. These impacts are much larger for negative than for positive dividend change announcements. They also found that the impact of dividend announcement is larger than that of earnings' announcements.

Kaleem and Salahuddin (2006) in their study on 24 companies listed on the Lahore Stock Exchange found that investors do not benefit from the dividend announcements by the companies. Infact, the investors were found to incur losses up to 2.5 per cent over the period starting 30 days prior to dividend to 7 days after the dividend date.

Chander et al. (2007) studied the impact of dividend announcement considering 188 events of dividends' announcement for Group A listed stocks of the BSE during the period January 2004 through December 2005. In the Capital Asset Pricing Model (CAPM) framework, a lesser (close to zero) positive incidence of average abnormal return was noticed around (4 weeks pre / post announcement) the dividend announcement date. The same were noticed to be gaining momentum and were magnified in the negative direction as the event horizon widened.

Dasilas et al. (2009) found that dividend initiation announcements are trustworthy mechanisms to convey information about the firm's future prospects and are associated with rises in shareholders' wealth through stock price increase. Specifically, the dividend initiation brings about a Cumulative Abnormal Returns (CAR) of more than 2.3 per cent in the event period. The magnitude of the price reaction to dividend initiation announcements differs across information environments. For the pre- and post-event windows CAR is higher for the portfolio of firms in the 'low' information environment than in the 'high one. The study was based on 38 Greek listed firms.

The positive abnormal returns persist several days after the dividend announcements by the companies. The number of days on which positive returns are earned is more than the number of days on which negative returns are recorded. The trend of positive returns is more pronounced after the event-day. The positive Cumulative Average Abnormal Returns (CAARs) can be earned by buying the stocks after the dividend announcements. The study was conducted on 149 companies which are part of the BSE200 Index that announced dividends for the financial year 2002 (Mallikarjunappa and Manjunatha, 2009)

Lukose and Sapar (2010) studied a large sample of firms listed on the BSE to examine the stock price reaction to dividend changes and the relevance of signalling models. The study finds significant wealth effects around dividend changes as proposed by the signalling models. There is a strong positive relationship between dividend changes and profitability during the year of dividend change, but little evidence exists about profitability in the future years. Dividend initiating (omitting) firms have large increase (decrease) in earnings in the year of change, compared to the moderate change in earnings in case of dividend increasing (decreasing) firms.

Ahmed et al. (2010), in their study on market reaction to dividend and earnings' announcement by 120 companies listed on Malaysian Stock Exchange, found on the announcement date or day 0, that the Average Abnormal Returns(AARs) for all companies how a positive figure of 0.15 per cent. The small gain on AARs implies that the market does not fully react to the information since significant abnormal returns are only realized on day +1 and day +6 post-announcement day. Throughout the 11-day event period, there is a significant change in stock prices due to increasing dividend announcements. In addition, about 70 per cent of the companies in the sample earned positive abnormal returns on this day, compared to only 47.5 per cent of companies earning positive abnormal returns both on day –1 and day 0. This result suggests that there is a delayed response from the market as stock prices adjust slowly to the new information.

Taneem and Yuce (2011) focussed on the information content of dividend policies through a 20 day window of share price reaction of 82 companies listed in the BSE. Average mean daily returns are positive on almost all days for good news sample, as well as bad news sample; but on the day of the event return for bad news sample is negative, while that for good news sample is positive. Companies that increased dividend amounts had higher abnormal, as well as cumulative abnormal return. They concluded that investors have the perception, that if the companies increase their dividend payment amount, this means that the company is in a better position.

SAMPLE, DATA AND METHODOLOGY

The study measures the signalling effect of considerable corporate dividend announcement on the ability of investors to earn abnormal returns. Event study methodology which examines the behaviour of firms' stock prices around corporate events is adopted for the purpose of this study.

Sample Level

The companies selected for this study are those which are a part of S&P BSE Mid-Cap Index and announced considerable dividend from 1 January 2013 to 31 August 2014. As the paper aims to find out the Dividend Signalling effect, the companies selected for the purpose of study are only those companies which declared dividend per share of INR 15 or more, irrespective of par value and market value of share (that is considered as 'Considerable' dividend for the purpose of study). As a result, out of 220 dividend announcements by BSE Mid-Cap companies during the period under study, 40 dividend announcements were initially selected, out of which a sample of 33 dividend announcements by 20 Mid-Cap companies was finally considered based on criteria of:

1. No other concurrently announced corporate events (such as announcements of Bonus Issue, Right Issue, stock splits, mergers and acquisitions, etc.), within a 20-day window surrounding the dividend announcement to be able to check the impact of dividend announcement only.
2. Dividend announcement includes final, as well as special dividends declared by the companies under study.

Sample represents good mix of different industries in the Mid-Cap Segment (Annexure I).

Data

For the purpose of the study the dividend declaration date has been considered as an Event date (Day 0). Data has been collected for an event window of 20 days prior to and 20 days after the dividend announcement (event) date. Dividend declaration data for all the Mid-Cap companies is procured from the PROWESS database maintained by the Centre for Monitoring Indian Economy (CMIE) under a licensing agreement. The event dates were cross verified from BSE and the Electronic database of *The Economic Times* maintained by *The Times of India* (*Economic Times*). Daily market prices' data with respect to each security, as well as for BSE Mid-Cap Index were collected from the BSE website for calculating Abnormal Returns.

Methodology

Event studies serve an important purpose in capital market research for testing the market efficiency (Brown and Warner, 1980; Fama, 1991). Systematically non-zero abnormal security returns that persist after a particular type of corporate event are inconsistent with market efficiency.

An event study typically tries to examine the return behaviour for a sample of firms experiencing a common type of event (e.g. a stock split, dividend, bonus, etc.). The event might take place at different points in calendar time or it might be clustered at a particular date. Two main changes in methodology have taken place over the years. First, the use of daily(and sometimes intraday) rather than monthly security return data has become more prevalent as it results in a more precise measurement of abnormal returns and gives better information about the impact of the announcements. Second, the methods used to estimate abnormal returns have become more sophisticated (Eckbo, 2007)

To examine the return behaviour for a sample of firms experiencing a common event of dividend declaration, Abnormal Returns (AR), AAR and CAA Rare calculated around the dividend announcement day (for the event window of 20 days).

The AR is a direct measure of the (unexpected) change in the security holder's wealth associated with the event (Eckbo, 2007). For each security in the sample the AR_{it} for a stock *i* in given period *t* is obtained by finding the difference between actual return and expected return.

$$AR_{it} = R_{it} - K_{it} \quad ...(1)$$

where, R_{it} = Daily return of security *i*,

K_{it} = Expected (Normal) return of security

Daily return (R_{it}) is calculated by finding the relative difference between the security prices for two consecutive days.

$$R_{it} = \frac{P_{it} - P_{i(t-1)}}{P_{i(t-1)}} * 100 \qquad ...(2)$$

where, P_{it} = Price of security i on day t

$P_{i(t-1)}$ = Price of security on day $t - 1$.

Expected Return (K_{it}) is calculated using the CAPM, one of the basic models to determine the expected return for stock. This model was developed and extensively used by Sharpe (1964), and Lintner (1965) to generate expected return.

$$K_{it} = Rf_t + \beta_i [Rm_t - Rf_t] \qquad ...(3)$$

where, Rf_t = Risk free rate of return in the given period t

Rm_t = Expected rate of return on market portfolio (BSE Mid-Cap Index) in the given period t

β_i = Non-diversifiable risk of security i (Pandey, 2010).

Risk free rate of return in the given period $t(Rf_t)$ is calculated using an average of 91 days t-bill rate of return for 2013–14 (RBI). The expected rate of return on market portfolio in the given period t (Rm_t) is calculated by finding the relative difference between the BSE Mid-Cap Index Value price for two consecutive days as per equation 4.

$$Rm_t = \frac{V_t - V_{t-1}}{V_{t-1}} * 100 \qquad ...(4)$$

where, V_t = BSE Mid-Cap Index value on day t

V_{t-1} = BSE Mid-Cap Index value on day $t - 1$

Non-diversifiable risk, that is, beta (β) is calculated as the ratio of change in daily return of security to change in daily market return for each day of the event window. βi of the security i is determined by taking the average of the value of β for security i for all the days of the event window.

The AAR is calculated with respect to each day in the event window. In order to find a day-wise AAR, the average of ARs of all the dividend announcements for each day surrounding the event-day (i.e. −20 to 20 days) are calculated using the following formula (Mallikarjunappa and Manjunatha, 2009).

$$AAR_t = \frac{\sum_{i=1}^{n} AR}{n} \qquad ...(5)$$

where, N = Total number of dividend announcements, that is, 33.

t = The day of the event window for which AAR is calculated. AAR is calculated for each day of the event window (i.e. from $t = -20$ ..., 0, ... + 20).

To know the cumulative effect of AARs on days surrounding the event, these are added to get the CAAR. The cumulative daily abnormal returns for the securities are aggregated throughout the particular portfolio within the event window, that is, day –20 to +20, day –15 to +15, day –10 to +10, day –5 to +5, day –2 to +2, and day –1 to +1, relative to the event-day is calculated using Equation (6).

$$CAAR_{t_1,t_2} = \sum_{t_1}^{t_2} AAR \quad ...(6)$$

where, CAAR denotes cumulative average abnormal returns for the period t_1 to t_2.

FINDINGS

There is considerable increase in the frequency and amount of dividend declared in the year 2014 (till August) as compared to previous years by companies listed on S&P BSE Mid-Cap Index (Table 1). As per Table 2, it has been observed that AR was maximum on days −4, 1 and 9 for nine announcements out of total announcements, and was found to be minimum on day 1,that is, post the event-day for five announcements.

The values of AAR (Annexure II) show that they are fluctuating, yielding both positive and negative returns around the event-day. It is negative on eight days (40 per cent) before and six days (30 per cent) days after the event-day. It is positive on 12 days (60 per cent) before and 14 days (70 per cent) days after the event-day.

Hence, AAR is found to be negative on 40 per cent of the days and positive on 60 per cent of the days during the event window. This indicates that these returns are positive for more days than they are negative, both before and

Table 1: Year-wise Break-up of Dividend Announcements

	Total Dividend Announcements	*Dividend Announcements with DPS ≥15*	*% of Considerable Dividend Announcements*	*Minimum DPS (INR)*	*Maximum DPS (INR)*	*Average DPS (INR)*
2014	169	18	10.65	15	75	30
2013	51	15	29.41	15	500	61.81
Total	220	33	15.00			

Table 2: Security-wise Break-up of Abnormal Return (AR) for Sample

Security	*AR*	*Highest*	*Day of Highest AR*	*Lowest*	*Day of Lowest AR*
1	0.408	9.6968	17	−3.4014	12
2	−1.0522	6.0266	−18	−8.2884	1
3	0.3358	7.6275	15	−2.3444	0
4	0.3302	7.6825	1	−3.2760	18
5	−0.1646	8.2457	6	−4.6412	0
6	0.6417	5.6692	−6	−4.8961	4
7	0.2393	4.3284	4	−5.1710	8
8	−0.1644	3.9063	−3	−6.0923	19
9	0.8432	9.4684	6	−5.7635	11
10	0.4984	5.7387	9	−6.1775	16
11	−0.8389	2.3931	−6	−4.6864	20
12	0.0297	4.3539	−8	−2.6474	−16
13	−0.3437	5.9895	10	−5.0045	1
14	0.6458	6.6171	−1	−4.5847	−7
15	0.7106	4.1003	−4	−8.3546	0
16	0.2320	6.2297	−8	−5.9159	12
17	0.3024	7.1934	−4	−18.1595	11
18	0.1006	2.7409	−11	−3.1365	−16
19	0.6729	6.7170	−4	−2.0898	3
20	−0.0510	2.9476	9	−2.8948	1
21	0.2140	14.2561	9	−5.4698	1
22	0.5069	4.5925	10	−2.4544	4
23	0.9348	-0.9348	18	−0.0029	19
24	0.0029	5.8883	1	−4.2602	−20
25	0.0183	3.5556	3	-3.7061	1
26	0.6992	2.8630	−1	−1.6074	−4
27	0.1410	6.5064	1	−3.3605	16
28	−0.1279	3.6847	−20	−5.5642	−14
29	1.4593	9.0654	12	−8.8769	−2
30	0.2486	5.6652	0	−4.5079	16
31	−0.9834	8.0470	17	−12.9562	−5
32	0.1011	2.5350	18	−3.2015	3
33	−2.0477	7.4394	16	−57.1971	6

after the event-day. Therefore, the trend indicates that it is possible to earn positive returns on majority of the days surrounding the event-day.

Maximum positive AAR before the announcement is found to be on Day −1 (i.e. 0.5447), and after the announcement day it is found to be on Day

18 (i.e. 0.8547). Maximum negative AAR before the announcement is found to be on Day −7 (i.e. −0.8247), and after the announcement day it is found to be on Day 7 (i.e. −1.6814). For 40 per cent of the companies maximum AAR is found to be before the announcement date and for 60 per cent of the companies maximum AAR is found to be after the announcement date, whereas, only 20 per cent of the companies have minimum AAR before the announcement date and 80 per cent of the companies have minimum AAR after the announcement date.

The value of AAR is found to be more than 0.5 on the days −18, −4, −1, 5, 6, 10, 17 and 18 with the highest positive AAR on day 18 and less than minus 0.5 on the days −11, −10, −7, 11, 7, 8, 11, 16 with the highest negative AAR on Day 7.

The CAAR is the cumulative deviations of the securities' returns from their expected market returns over the periods surrounding the event-day. This shows the cumulative effects of the residuals of all stocks on a given day. The values of CAARs are calculated in three series. In the first series, the values of AARs are cumulated from specified number of days before the event to the same number of days after the event. In the second series, AARs are cumulated for specified number of days before the event, whereas, in the third series AARs are cumulated for specified number of days after the event (Table 3).

Table 3: Cumulative Average Abnormal Return (CAAR)

	Days (t_1, t_2)	*CAAR*
Series 1	–20 to +20	2.4131
	–15 to +15	0.9277
	–10 to +10	0.4670
	–5 to +5	2.4657
	–2 to +2	1.4384
	–1 to +1	0.7241
Series 2	−6 to −1	1.6895
	−10 to −1	0.1918
	−10 to −2	−0.3529
	−20 to −1	0.1342
	−20 to −2	−0.4104
Series 3	1 to 6	1.6469
	1 to 9	−0.2678
	1 to 10	0.2983
	1 to 20	2.3020

In the first series, the CAARs are positive for all the time intervals taken into consideration, with a 20 day window and five day event window yielding maximum CAAR. In series 2 and 3, CAARs are significantly positive for six days before the event and six days after the event. Series 2 helps us understand that the AAR on Day −1 is high, which helps to get a positive CAAR for the pre-event period. If Day −1 is not considered, CAAR becomes negative in the pre-event period. CAAR of Series 3 indicates that after the event-day, the CAAR rises, with some corrections in the process around eighth and ninth day where it becomes negative, and then rises further as we move towards Day 20. The analysis of CAAR indicates that positive ARs exist both before and after the event-day, but more so in the post event-days.

CONCLUSION

The study observes that systematically non-zero average abnormal security returns that persist after a particular type of corporate event are inconsistent with market efficiency (Eckbo, 2007). Therefore, AARs can neither be positive nor negative consistently for a long time, either before or after the event-day. The analysis also shows that the number of days on which positive returns are earned is more than the number of days on which negative returns are recorded. The trend of positive returns is more prominent after the event-day, also found by Mallikarjunappa and Manjunatha (2009). The research shows that the positive CAARs can be earned by buying the stocks after the dividend announcements for Indian Mid-Cap companies.

REFERENCES

A. Ahmed, B.M. Hussin, and T.C. Ying, 'Semi-strong Form Efficiency: Market Reaction to Dividend and Earnings Announcements in Malaysian Stock Exchange', *IUP Journal of Applied Finance*, vol. 16, no. 5, 2010, pp. 36–60.

A. Dasilas, K. Lyroudi, and D. Ginoglou, 'The Impact of Dividend Initiations on Greek Listed Firms' Wealth and Volatility Across Information Environments', *Managerial Finance*, vol. 35, no. 6, 2009, pp. 531–43.

A. Kaleem and C. Salahuddin, 'Impact of Dividend Announcement on Common Stock Prices at Lahore Stock Exchange (Pakistan)', *South Asian Journal of Management*, vol. 13, no. 2, 2006, p. 86.

B.E. Eckbo, ed., *Handbook of Empirical Corporate Finance SET,* vol. 1, Elsevier, 2007.

Bombay Stock Exchange. Retrieved October 2014, from BSE Website: http://www.bseindia.com/sensexview/IndexArchiveData.aspx?expandable=3.

Economic Times, *Economic Times Website.* Retrieved October 2014, from http://economictimes.indiatimes.com/markets/stocks.

E.F. Fama, 'Efficient Capital Markets: II', *The Journal of Finance*, vol. 46, no. 5, 1991, pp. 1575–617.

E.F. Fama et al., 'The Adjustment of Stock Prices to New Information', *International Economic Review*, vol. 10, no. 1, 1969, pp. 1–21.

F. Black, 'The Dividend Puzzle', *The Journal of Portfolio Management*, vol. 2, no. 2, 1976, pp. 5–8.

F. Modigliani and M.H. Miller, 'The Cost of Capital, Corporation Finance and the Theory of Investment', *The American Economic Review*, vol. 48, no. 3, 1958, pp. 261-297.

F.W. Sharpe, 'Capital asset prices: A theory of market equilibrium under conditions of risk', *The Journal of Finance*, vol. 19, no. 3, 1964, pp. 425-442.

H.R. Oppenheimer and T.E. Dielman, 'Dividend and Earnings Announcements and Stockholders' Returns: Further Empirical Evidence', *Managerial Finance*, vol. 14, no. 1, 1988, pp. 34–42.

I.M. Pandey, *Financial Management,* New Delhi: Vikas Publishing House, 2010.

J. Lintner, 'Distribution of Incomes of Corporations among Dividends, Retained Earnings, and Taxes', *The American Economic Review*, vol. 46, no. 2, 1956, pp. 97–113.

J. Lintner, 'The Valuation of Risk Assets on the Selection of Risky Investments in Stock Portfolios and Capital Budgets', *Review of Economics and Statistics,* vol. 47, no. 1, 1965, pp. 13–37.

J.E. Walter, 'Dividend Policies and Common Stock Prices', *The Journal of Finance*, vol. 11, no. 1, 1956, pp. 29–41.

M.H. Miller and F. Modigliani, 'Dividend Policy, Growth, and the Valuation of Shares', *The Journal of Business*, vol. 34, no. 4, 1961, pp. 411–33.

M.J. Gordon, 'Dividends, Earnings, and Stock Prices', *The Review of Economics and Statistics*, vol. 41, no. 2, part 1, 1959, pp. 99–105.

NSE. Retrieved October 2014, from National Stock Exchange Website: http://www.nseindia.com/products/content/equities/indices/cnx_midcap_200.htm.

P.J. Lukose and N. Sapar, 'Dividend Changes and Profitability: An Empirical Study of Indian Manufacturing Firms', *The IUP Journal of Applied Finance*, vol. 16, no. 1, 2010, pp. 5–26.

R. Ball and P. Brown, 'An Empirical Evaluation of Accounting Income Numbers',*Journal of Accounting Research*, vol. 6, no. 2, 1968, pp. 159–78.

RBI. Retrieved October 2014, from Reserve Bank of India Website: http://dbie.rbi.org.in/DBIE/dbie.rbi?site=publications.

R. Chander, R. Sharma, and K. Mehta, 'Dividend Announcement and Informational Efficiency: An Empirical Study of Indian Stock Market', *The ICFAI Journal of Applied Finance*, vol. 13, 2007, pp. 29–42.

R. Watts, 'The Information Content of Dividends', *The Journal of Business*, vol. 46, no. 2, 1973, pp. 191–211.

S. Taneem and A. Yuce, 'Information Content of Dividend Announcements: An Investigation of the Indian Stock Market', *International Business & Economics Research Journal (IBER)*, vol. 10, no. 5, 2011, pp. 49–58.

S.J. Brown and J.B. Warner, 'Measuring Security Price Performance', *Journal of Financial Economics*, vol. 8, no. 3, 1980, pp. 205–58.

S.J. Brown, and J.B. Warner, 'Using daily stock returns', *Journal of Financial Economics*, vol. 14, no. 1, 1985, pp. 3–31.

S&P Dow Jones Indices LLC and BSE Ltd. Retrieved October 2014, from Asia Index Pvt. Ltd.: http://www.asiaindex.co.in/indices/equity/sp-bse-mid-cap.

T. Mallikarjunappa and T. Manjunatha, 'Stock Price Reactions to Dividend Announcements', *Journal of Management and Public Policy*, vol. 1, no. 1, 2009, pp. 43–56.

ANNEXURES

Annexure I: Sectorial Breakdown of the Considerable Dividend Announcements

Sr. No.	*Sector*	*% of Considerable Dividend Announcements*
1	Agro Chemicals – Pesticides	3
2	Banks – Private Sector	6
3	Consumer Durable – Domestic Appliance	6
4	Finance & Investment	18
5	FMCG – Cigarettes	25
	FMCG – Paint	
	FMCG – Personal Care	
6	Healthcare – Pharmaceuticals	12
7	IT – Computers Hardware	12
	IT – Computers Software	
8	Refineries – Oil & Gas	3
9	Service – Couriers	6
10	Textiles – Machinery	9
	Textiles – Readymade Apparels	
Total		100

Annexure II: Results of Average Abnormal Return during the 20 Day Event Window

Day	*AAR*	*Day*	*AAR*
−20	−0.0588	1	0.2025
−19	0.0184	2	0.4300
−18	0.5429	3	0.1931
−17	0.0762	4	−0.4400
−16	−0.6316	5	0.6931
−15	0.3699	6	0.5681
−14	−0.1429	7	−1.6814
−13	0.2635	8	−0.6020
−12	0.0574	9	0.3687
−11	−0.5526	10	0.5661
−10	-0.5287	11	−0.7619
−9	−0.2303	12	0.4072
−8	0.0861	13	−0.0258
−7	−0.8247	14	0.4917
−6	0.2794	15	0.3542
−5	−0.0462	16	0.2891
−4	0.5310	17	0.6981
−3	0.0963	18	0.8547
−2	0.2843	19	0.0022
−1	0.5447	20	−0.3058
0	−0.0231		

Effect of Merger on Financial Performance in Banking Industry

A Case Study of ICICI Bank and BoR

Megha Aggarwal

SBI School of Commerce and Banking, WISDOM, Banasthali Vidyapith, Rajasthan
e-mail: meghamba86@gmail.com

ABSTRACT

In the era of twenty first century, companies adopt various strategies to grow rapidly in their sector or new origin or field. One major aspect of such strategies is Merger and Acquisition, commonly known as M&A, widely used by the organizations. Where merger is a mutually agreed decision by the companies, acquisitions are the takeovers or unwilling deals between the organizations. Major benefit as considered by any organization is the benefit of synergy that is, creating value which is greater than the simple total of its parts. Experiencing for other benefits such as entering in new market, cost reduction, cross selling, risk diversification, increasing shareholder's value, M&A can be done within the industry or outside the industry. Reports on daily basis are provided by media for various updates of any of the industry either Bollywood for latest releases, sports for world cup matches, or stock market for ups and downs. The Banking Industry in India is also in the news for its various deals of M&A since long. Various mergers have taken place in the industry for example, the State Bank of India acquired the Bank of Bihar Ltd. and National Bank of Lahore in the year 1969 and 1970, respectively. ICICI Bank has done many mergers with different banks. It started to acquire banks with Bank of Madura Ltd. in 2001, ICICI Personal Finance Services Ltd. and ICICI Capital Services Ltd. in 2002, Sangli Bank Ltd. in 2007, and the Bank of Rajasthan (BoR) in 2010. This paper focuses on one of these mergers, that is, ICICI Bank (Acquirer) and The Bank of Rajasthan (Target). The main objective of this paper is to analyse the financial performance of ICICI Bank pre- and post-merger. The Financial performance has been analysed with the help of ratios, specifically in the areas of Profitability, Liquidity and Leverage. Further, a T-test has been used to determine the significance differences in these financial performance areas. Analyses show that a significant benefit has been achieved by ICICI Bank after the acquisition. Analysis also shows that there is significant improvement in the company's Return on Equity (ROE), interest coverage, Earnings per Share (EPS) and Dividend per Share (DPS) in the post-merger period.

Keywords: Merger & Acquisition, Financial Performance, Profitability, Liquidity, Synergy, ICICI Bank

INTRODUCTION

For any business organization, there are two ways to grow: Organic, which is related to the revenue of the business and Inorganic that is pass over a few steps of the business ladder and adopt corporate restructuring and business combinations. To improve shareholder's wealth, changes in the ownership, business mix, finance mix and asset mix are the various ways of corporate restructuring. Continuous evaluation of the portfolio of business securities, capital mix, ownership and asset management can help to locate the opportunities to increase the shareholder's wealth. Due to rapid changes in technology, market, competitors, product, customers, and even their preferences, it becomes necessary to use inorganic growth strategies like mergers, acquisitions, takeovers, or spinoffs.

Restructuring, as per Oxford Dictionary means to give a new structure to, rebuild or rearrange. The wealth of the shareholder or synergy is not the only benefit of corporate restructuring as it also provides other non-financial benefits like innovation, competition master, cost leader, etc.

MERGER AND ACQUISITION (M&A)

M&A both are the aspects of strategic management and dealing with the buying, selling, dividing, and combining of different companies or similar entities which can help companies to grow rapidly in its sector or location of origin, or a new field or new location.

Merger

Whenever two or more companies combine together it is called a merger. It can be done through either absorption or consolidation.

Acquisition

When two firms combine after one firm acquires another, and the acquired firm ceases to exist, it is termed as an acquisition. It can be said that one company takes over another company and establishes itself as a new company. This takeover can be friendly or hostile.

Forms of M&A

Mergers and Acquisition can be done with different forms as firms can combine with-in or from outside the industry. Let us say two firms, A and B combine together; the various possibilities of a merger are:

$$A + B = A \text{ or } B \quad \text{...(1)}$$

Equation 1 is the example of a merger through absorption where two different entities form an existing one, either A or B.

$$A + B = C \quad \text{...(2)}$$

Equation 2 is the second form of merger where two entities A and B form a new one which is C. This is known as a merger through consolidation and also known as Amalgamation.

$$(A - a) + (B - b) = A + B + C \quad \text{...(3)}$$

Equation 3 indicates another form of merger, that is, Spin-off. A and B both divest a small business a and b respectively and create C with the divested business a and b. Change in the values of A and B will be:

$$A > a, B > b, C = a + b$$

Merger and Acquisition provide benefits in both ways financial or non-financial to the companies involved. The major benefit received by the companies is the benefit of synergy, that is,

$$2 + 2 = 5 \quad \text{...(4)}$$

The value (V) of the combined entity will always (in most cases) be higher than the value of the entity alone. It can be represented as

$$V(A + B) > V(A) + V(B) \quad \text{...(5)}$$

Merger of various companies which happened in the past cannot be identified as distinct entities but there are mergers which were not successful.

In the list of corporate couplings, which worked, the best example is of the Disney and Pixer merger that took place in the year 2006 with the amount of US $7.4 billion in a stock deal with the success of movies like WALL-E, UP, Bolt, etc.

Exxon and Mobil merged in the year 1999 and signed an agreement of US $81 billion to form ExxonMobil and became the leaders in the oil market.

This paper is all about one of those successful mergers between ICICI and Bank of Rajasthan (BoR) in the year 2010. The financial performance has been analysed with various indicators and conclusion has been drawn.

INDIAN BANKING INDUSTRY

In the ancient period accomplishment of needs was done by exchange of goods commonly known as the Barter System. Without using money, 'Barter was the only medium of exchange and livelihood.' With the growth of needs and wants, barter became inconvenient, which necessitated the invention of money. In ancient days, the business of money changing was done by banking. Prof. Marshall wrote about money changers of the temples of Olympia in his book, 'Money, Credit and Commerce'[1] in 1923. In India, *ManuSmriti*[2] has also referred banking as a money lending business.

The word 'Bank' was derived from the Greek word 'banque' or the Italian word 'banco' meaning benches or bench. The Oxford Dictionary defines a Bank as 'an establishment for the custody of money, which pays out on a customer's order.'

The Banking Companies Act 1949 defines banking company in India as,'which transact the business of banking which means the accepting, for the purpose of landing or investment, of deposits of money from the public, repayable on demand or otherwise and withdrawable by cheque, draft, order or otherwise.'

In India, there is a single major source of institutional finance, that is, the Indian joint stock banks, which occupy an essential place in the organized sector of the Indian money market. Indian joint stock banks are commercial banks running in a western style. Modern banking in India was originated by the English agency house of Alexander & Co. Calcutta,with its first bank named the Hindustan Bank, in 1770. The real growth of modern banking began with establishment of the first presidency bank, Bank of Bengal, in Calcutta in the year 1806. The Government of India started a central bank in 1935, named the Reserve Bank of India (RBI), as a private sector bank.

Banks in India can be classified in different ways but the most popular classification is the banks working as Public or Private. State Bank of India (SBI) was the first public sector bank which started operating in 1955. The expansion of public sector banks was done through the nationalization of 14 banks by the Government of India in 1969 with the State Bank of India and its subsidiaries, and added six more banks in 1980. By January 2015, due to the scheme launched by Prime Minister of India, Narendra Modi, Pradhan Mantri Jan Dhan Yojna, 11.5 crore accounts were opened, with

---

1 Marshall, A. (1923). Money Credit and Commerce.

2 Jha, G. (1926). Manusmriti. *University of Calcutta.*

around INR 8698 crore. About 185 commercial banks are currently working in India with more than one lakh branches in India and around 300 branches abroad.

ICICI

In 1955, with the initiative of the World Bank, the Government of India and representatives of the Indian Industry, the Industrial Credit and Investment Cooperation of India (ICICI) was formed, which became the parent company for ICICI Bank formed in 1994, and later merged with the bank. ICICI Bank has been created with the principle objective of development of such a financial institution which fulfils medium and long-term financial requirements of Indian businesses. In 2000, it became the first bank or financial institution, non-Japan Asia based,to be listed on the New York Stock Exchange (NYSE).

The bank has a network of around 4,000 branches all over the world, present in 19 countries. It is operating with more than 11,000 ATMs in India. Along with SBI, Punjab National Bank (PNB) and Bank of Baroda (BOB), ICICI ranks in big four banks of India. Financial services for corporate, as well as retail customers are available with the bank with a wide range of banking products through different delivery channels and specialized subsidies.

In 2002, shareholders of the bank approved the merger with two of its subsidiaries-ICICI Personal Financial Services Ltd. and Capital Services Ltd. The bank has also merged with other different companies like it merged with ITC Classic Finance Ltd in 1998, Bank of Madura Ltd in 2001, Standard Chartered Grindlays Bank in 2002, Sangli Bank Ltd. in 2007, and Bank of Rajasthan in 2010.

Bank of Rajasthan

The Bank of Rajasthan (BoR) was incorporated in 1943 with an initial capital of 10 lakh at Udaipur under the Companies Act 1956. The bank has 463 branches in 24 states in the country with 111 ATMs. It is working with its central office at Jaipur and registered office at Udaipur.

The BoR had total assets worth INR 173 billion according to the balance sheet as on March 2010. Profit and Loss Account of the bank shows that bank was suffering from losses of INR 1.02 billion for the year, which shows the poor financial condition of the bank.

The BoR merged with ICICI Bank in the year 2010 for which ICICI paid INR 30 million. The deal was agreed upon with the conversion of each 118 shares to 25 shares of ICICI Bank.

LITERATURE REVIEW

Sarbapriya Ray (2003) has given an analysis on the performance of Indian banks after mergers with special reference to the merger of Centurion Bank of Punjab to HDFC. Different financial parameters have been taken to analyse the operating performance of the bank for the post-merger period. Analysis shows that the operating performance improved after merger in terms of Liquidity, Leverage, Profitability, and shareholders wealth.

Mehta & Kakani (2006) discussed the various motivations for M&A in the Indian Banking Industry. The paper also discussed about the international M&A scenario and compares it with the Indian market. Authors have explained the role of the central bank with respect to customers' rights and size of international players. The paper concluded by giving the implications for the nation with special emphasis on the Indian Banking Industry.

Goyal and Joshi (2011) have focused on the motives of M&A with reference to the banking industry, with a sample size of 17 mergers. The study was conducted on the basis of number of branches, geographical penetration in the market and benefits from the merger. Aspects of Financial, Human Resource and Organizational Behavior have also been analysed in this paper. Analyses show that small and local banks are unable to bear the global economy impact, which becomes the major reason of merger.

Goyal & Joshi (2012) have studied the growth of ICICI Bank Ltd through merger, acquisition, and amalgamation. The article explained merger as a strategy of three phases- Pre-merger, Acquisition and Post-merger. Authors have analysed the success of ICICI Bank with all its nine mergers with different banks and non-bank institutions. Quantitative analysis has been done which comprises retail network, economies of scale, technology banking, etc. Authors concluded that with the creation of synergy a merger also provides sustainable competitive advantage. But due to a merger severe problems arise for both individual and company.

S. Devarajappa (2012) studied the motives of mergers in the Indian Banking Industry. The author focused on the merger of HDFC and Centurion Bank of Punjab in the year 2008. Comparison of financial performance between pre- and post-merger has been done with the help of parameters such as Gross Profit margin, Net profit margin, Operating profit margin, ROCE, ROE and Debt-Equity Ratio. T-test has been used to analyse the statistical significance. Analyses show that there is a positive impact of a merger on banks.

OBJECTIVES

Literature review showed various studies of M&A in the Indian Banking Industry. But no study has been found which gives a comparison of pre- and post-merger performance of ICICI and BoR. Following are the major objectives for the current study:

1. To examine the post-merger effect on the liquidity position of ICICI Bank.
2. To examine the post-merger effect on the leverage standards of ICICI Bank.
3. To examine the post-merger effect on the profitability standards of ICICI Bank.

RESEARCH HYPOTHESIS

1. H0: There is no significant progress in the liquidity position of ICICI Bank.
2. H0: There is no significant progress in the leverage position of ICICI Bank.
3. H0: There is no significant progress in the profitability position of ICICI Bank.

RESEARCH METHODOLOGY

Following methodology has been used for the present study:

Sampling Technique

Convenience sampling has been used to choose the sample company for the present research paper. Such sampling technique is selected because of the proper data availability and proximity to the researcher.

Sample Selection

In the present research paper, selected merger of two companies is from the Indian Banking Industry. ICICI Bank has been selected for the analysis for pre- and post-merger.

Data Collection

Data has been collected from 2006-10 for pre-merger and from 2010-14 for post-merger of ICICI Bank in the Indian Banking Industry. Data has been compiled from the annual reports of the Bank.

Statistical Tools

To analyse the data financial ratios has been calculated and the mean and standard deviation were used for pre- and post-merger period. Paired sample t-test (2 tailed with 95 per cent significance level) has been used for the testing of the hypotheses. MS-Excel is the only statistical application used for the study.

Data Description

The current study analyses the effect of M&A on pre- and post- financial performance of ICICI Bank for 4 years. Data for the years 2006-07, 2007-08, 2008-09, and 2009-10 have been taken to analyse pre-merger financial performance and the data of 2010-11, 2011-12, 2012-13, and 2013-14 has been taken to analyse post-merger financial performance. For this study relevant ratios have been identified and calculated for the period specified. Table 1 presents the broad categories of ratios which have been classified in to various relevant ratios.

Table 1: Classification of Ratios

Ratios	*Description*	*Standard*
Liquidity Ratios		
Current Ratio	Current Assets/Current Liabilities	High
Liquid Ratio	Liquid Assets/Current Liabilities	High
Leverage Ratios		
Debt-Equity Ratio	Debt/Equity	Low
Interest Coverage Ratio	EBIT/Interest Charges	High
Profitability Ratios		
Net Profit Margin	Net Profit/ Net Sales	High
Return on Capital Employed	EBIT/Capital Employed	High
Return on Assets	NPAT/Total Assets	High
Return on Equity	(NPAT-Preference Dividend)/Equity	High
Dividend Payout Ratio	DPS/EPS	High
Dividend per Share	Dividend Paid/Shares Outstanding	High
Earnings per Share	Earnings for Equity/Shares Outstanding	High

Analysis

To test the hypotheses pre- and post-merger financial ratios have been calculated and compared to see if there are any significant statistical changes in the financial performance by using paired sample t-test at a confidence level 0.05 or 95 per cent (2 tailed). Table 2 provides the details of financial ratios and changes in financial ratios in the form of statistical calculations.

Table 2: Paired Sample t-test for Financial Ratios

Ratios	*Mean*		*Mean Difference*	*Standard Deviation*		*t-value*	*p-value (two-tailed)*
	Pre	*Post*		*Pre*	*Post*		
Liquidity Ratios							
Current Ratio	0.1175	0.315	0.1975	0.0221	0.4438	–0.9	0.0431
Quick Ratio	8.275	11.7675	3.4925	4.2883	2.8423	–1.28	0.0289
Leverage Ratios							
Debt- Equity Ratios	5.775	4.3125	–1.4625	2.5459	0.1873	1.078	0.0359
Interest Coverage Ratio	0.77	0.54	–0.23	0.5552	0.06733	0.779	0.0492
Profitability Ratios							
Net Profit Margin	10.8075	16.6725	5.865	1.0139	1.0886	–10.57	0.0018
ROCE	9.7675	9.185	–0.5825	0.7096	0.5094	1.187	0.32
ROA	398.99	553.6125	154.6225	87.7513	67.3327	-6.977	0.006
ROE	9.37	11.4825	2.1125	2.6029	1.8103	–0.983	0.397
Dividend Payout Ratio	35.23	28.8725	–6.3575	2.0372	1.8957	3.37	0.0433
Dividend per Share	11	18.375	7.375	0.8164	3.9449	–4.611	0.0191
Earnings per Share	35.455	64.4975	29.0425	1.6025	17.6954	–3.272	0.0466

TESTING OF HYPOTHESES

Following are the results based on the Table 2.

Liquidity Ratios

1. There is a positive change in the current ratios as it has been increased by almost 20 per cent in the post-merger period. This is showing the ability of the company to pay off its short-term liabilities in a year.
2. Increment in the Quick ratio shows the improving position of the bank as the mean difference between pre- and post-merger ratio is 3.49. This indicates that the Bank is able to meet its immediate current liabilities.

Based on the results of the t-test (95 per cent significance level), the null hypotheses H0 –'there is no significant progress in the Liquidity position of ICICI Bank' has been rejected. Data reveals that there is a statistically significant difference between pre- and post-values because p value > 0.05 for all the selected liquidity ratios under study.

Leverage Ratios

1. Post-merger Debt-Equity ratio shows a negative 1.46 indicating the higher leveraged policy adopted by the Bank.
2. Interest coverage ratio shows a negative value of 0.23 indicating the inability of the company to pay off its debt.

Based on the results of t-test (95% significance level), the null hypotheses H0-'there is no significant progress in the Leverage Ratios of the Bank', is rejected. Although values the negative trend, but statistically data reveals that p value > 0.05 for all the selected leverage ratios under study so the null hypotheses has been rejected and alternate that there is a significance difference after merger has been accepted.

Profitability Ratios

1. Profitability ratios reflect the good and effective banking services provided by the bank. All the profitability ratios are showing the positive values except two, that is, Return on Capital Employed and Dividend Payout Ratio.
2. Net profit margin has been increased in the post-merger period which indicates the increment in the net profit after the merger.
3. Return on Assets (ROA) and Return on Equity (ROE) ratios are positive which indicates that profits are worth according to assets and equity capital invested.
4. Dividend per Share and Earnings per Share also increased in the post-merger period by generating high profits that the Bank is distributing among shareholders as well.

Based on the results of t-test (95 per cent significance level), the null hypotheses H0 – there is no significant progress in the Profitability Ratios of the bank, is accepted. Data reveals that pre- & post-merger values are p value < 0.05 for ratios such as Net profit margin, ROA, Dividend payout ratios, DPS and EPS as well. The overall p value is less than 0.05 as it is 0.025 for all selected profitability ratios during the time period studied.

SIGNIFICANCE OF THE STUDY

The focus of this research paper is on the merger of ICICI and BoR for which the financial performance has been analysed by the comparison of pre- and post-merger. The study is significant for the purpose of analyzing the financial performance of various other mergers. The methodology can be further used for such similar analysis.

CONCLUSION

Results of the analyses showed that there is a significant improvement in the various ratios of the Bank for the pre- and post-merger period. The null hypothesis of the study have been accepted which stated that there is a significant progress or improvement in the financial position of the Bank in the pre- and post- period. ICICI is proficient to encash the benefits of synergy. It can also be said as that the post-merger impact or synergy benefits have worked for the Bank. The Bank witnessed an increase in its EPS, as for the year 2010 it was only INR 36.1 which increased to INR 84.95 for the year 2014. In the post-merger period the Bank is not only receiving the benefits, but also distributing it with its stakeholders in the form of dividend. The DPS for pre-merger period was INR 12 for the year 2010 which increased to INR 23 for the post-merger period (2014).

REFERENCES

A. Alam, S. Khan and F. Zafar, 'Strategic Management: Managing Mergers & Acquisitions', *International Journal of BRIC Business Research*, vol. 3, no. 1, 2014, pp. 1–10.

B. Banerjee, *Fundamentals of Financial Management*, PHI Learning Pvt Ltd, Delhi, 2008.

D.M. Mithani, *Money, Banking, International Trade and Public Finance*, Himalaya Publishing House, New Delhi, 1985.

ICICI Bank, Annual Reports, 2006-2014. Accessed on 12 September 2014, from www.icicibank.com.

Internet search engines www.google.com, www.wikipedia.com. Accessed for various terminologies.

K.A. Goyal and J. Vijay, 'Merger and Acquisition in Banking Industry: A Case Study of ICICI Bank Ltd', *International Journal of Research in Management*, Issue 2, no. 2, 2012, pp. 30–40.

K.A. Goyal and V. Joshi, 'Mergers in Banking Industry of India: Some Emerging Issues', *Asian Journal of Business and Management Sciences*, vol. 1, no. 2, 2011, pp. 157–165.

K.G. Ray, 'Mergers and Acquisitions: Strategy, Valuation and Integration', PHI Learning Pvt Ltd, Delhi, 2010.

M. Pandey, *Essentials of Financial Management*, Vikas Publishing House Pvt Ltd, Delhi, 2009.

M.R. Baye, and D.W. Jansen, *Money, Banking, and Financial Markets: An Economics Approach*, Boston: Houghton Mifflin, 1995.

Mary DiMaggio, 'The Top 10 Best (and Worst) Corporate Mergers of All Time...Or, the Good, the Bad, and the Ugly', Retrieved on 24 September 2014 from http://www.rasmussen.edu/degrees/business/blog/best-and-worst-corporate-mergers/.

R. Vadapalli, *Mergers, Acquisitions and Business Valuation*, Excel Books India, Bangalore, 2007.

R.K. Kakani, and J. Mehta, 'Motives for Mergers and Acquisitions in the Indian Banking Sector – A Note on Opportunities & Imperatives', SPJCM Singapore Working Paper No. 6–13, 2006.

S. Devarajappa, 'Merger in Indian Bank: A Study on Mergers of HDFC Bank Ltd and Centurion Bank of Punjab Ltd', *International Journal of Marketing, Financial Services & Management Research*, vol. 1, Issue 9, 2012, pp. 33–42.

Sarbapriya Ray, 'Impact of Merger Performance of Indian Banks: A Case Study on Specific Bank Merger in India', *United States of America Research Journal*, vol. 1, no. 3, 2013, pp. 14–31.

Early Indicators of Bank Mergers
An Analysis of Public Sector Banks in India

Poonam Singh
Department of Management, Jamia Hamdard University, New Delhi
e-mail: poonam96@gmail.com

ABSTRACT

It has been witnessed that merger and acquisition in the banking sector in India has been very instrumental in preventing banks' failure. It has become more pertinent in the present context where globalization emerging with fast pace. It has increased the degree of competitiveness and posed many challenges before the banks for sustaining their operations efficiently. Therefore, the process of consolidation of banks assumes more significance to make the banks stronger in terms of increasing business turnover and manage it to improve return of investment (ROI), increase profitability, and serve the customers more effectively at reasonable cost. Considering the advantages of banks' mergers, there is a loud thinking for a large scale consolidation of public sector banks (PSBs) in India. In the present paper an attempt has been made to evaluate the health of PSBs based on certain financial parameters over a certain period of time. For a purposeful assessment and to make the findings more discreet, an approach of discriminate analysis has been used. In order to make the findings more analytical and to achieve accuracy, the concept of 'Altman Z-score model' has also been adopted. Based on these two different approaches, few selected banks have been identified to indicate more possibilities of a merger in near future. This analysis can be more useful in constructing a model to forecast the banks for probable merger in the immediate future. In addition, an attempt has also been made to establish relationship between banks merged in the past to understand the impact of merger on their performance in the post-merger era.

Keywords: Merger and Acquisition, Compete, Altman Z-score, Financial Performance, PSBs

INTRODUCTION

Merger and amalgamation is a concept which has been used in the corporate sector since long across the globe to gain synergic advantages of merger and acquisition in business operations. The process of consolidation, merger and amalgamation has been found much more lucrative in the banking sector to make the banks more strong, and at the same time prevent failure of banks. Failure of a bank has severe consequences, as a bank's survival is dependent on the faith of customers. It can be observed that the Reserve Bank of India (RBI) and the Government have made all efforts to prevent the instances of bank failures. Rather, timely steps were taken to merge weak banks with the stronger one and continue to serve the customers. In addition to this, the increased global competition has posed serious challenges before the competing banks having international presence. The banks in India have to face stiff competition from the large sized banks across the globe. Therefore, the size of banks has received greater attention of policy makers, more particularly in India. Therefore, the issue of merger and acquisition of banks have two-fold considerations—first in terms of survival of weak banks, and second to increase the size of banks to face global competition.

There are many other considerations which are also important and well argued in favor of the merger and amalgamation of banks. Among others, the capital structure of banks in India, which calls for radical changes in view of the implementation of Basel III norms, is a major cause of concern and the process of merger and amalgamation can be very helpful. The increased level of capital and higher provisions for cyclical effects may force many banks to use the process of merger and amalgamation. Another area of concern is the increased level of non-performing assets where merger and amalgamation can be quite advantageous. The efficient mechanism of asset management and increased level of standard assets minimize the capital level and other financial provisions in banks. There are basically two scenarios—one, to find out the weak banks with early warning signals to forecast the early and likely merger of banks and arrest further deterioration in the health of weak banks; and the other scenario is the merger of banks on account of size and making the banking system more strong and competitive as a whole.

In the present paper, an attempt is made to develop a framework for forecasting the banks facing likely mergers in the near future. This will help in two ways—first to initiate adequate timely steps for turn-around strategies, and the other is to merge the banks with stronger counterparts in appropriate time if turnaround is not feasible in order to prevent further deterioration of financial health of the weak bank.

LITERATURE REVIEW

The research study by Pradhan (2011) predicted bankruptcy of selected private sector banks based on the Z-score for private sector banks considering the lending activities of these banks. In this paper a comparison was made among several banks, viz., Axis, HDFC and ICICI to assess internal parameters of banks based on the Z-score approach using the data for 8 years during the period 2001–08. Based on the findings, the study made forecasts for the years 2009 and 2010. Further, as per results of the analysis, the paper had drawn predictions for a period of 5 years, that is, from 2011–15. In the study, it was also found that Z-score value for ICICI was maximum, followed by HDFC and Axis. Similar results were observed in the area of priority sector lending of these banks. In another study, Grant et al. (2012) have also used the Z-score prediction model to assess the collapse of financial research firms. In this study 20 firms engaged in Finance were identified and data over a period of 5 years prior to their collapse was analysed. The study concluded that timely information about a firm can help in making better decisions and avoid further deterioration. The study also observed that the likelihood of the failure of firms can be predicted.

Beaver (1966) used univariate analysis to evaluate the financial ratios which have a fairly strong ability to predict business failure of the firm. The study used many ratios among the six key groups, such as cash flow ratios, net income ratios, debt to total asset ratios, liquid asset to total asset ratios, liquid asset to current debt ratio, and turnover ratios. The paper further analysed one key ratio from each of the ratio groups, such as cash-flow to total-debt ratio. The study concluded that the strongest predictor of financial failure can be determined by the net-income to total-assets ratio.

A research paper by Aneja and Makkar (2013) made a comparative study to assess the internal determinants of insolvency of Indian commercial banks, based on book value, through Z-score model. This study considered 47 Indian commercial banks and analysed the results during the period of 2006–11 to make a comparison between private and public sector banks. The study found that the size of a bank is the major determinant factor impacting the solvency of Indian commercial banks. This was followed by another component of non-performing assets which leads to greater insolvency risk of a bank. The study also concluded that the private sector banks have inadequate risk management systems as compared to public sector banks (PSBs). There is another study conducted with similar approach by Sinha et al. (2010), who analysed the risk and book value insolvency of 15 Indian commercial banks during the period 2006–08 using the Z-score model of predicting probable bankruptcy of firms. In this study, they found that the instances of the probability of book value insolvency have been reduced during the period of study. Further, the study by Charles and Goodluck (2010) assessed healthy and unhealthy banks in the state of Nigeria using the Z-score model and certain financial ratios and found that the health of banks could be predicted.

Going through the research literature it is observed that not many studies were undertaken to measure financial performance using Z-score. Therefore, it is evident that the Z-score model has not been used extensively to measure the efficiency of banks, and predict likely failure of banks and decide about a possible merger. There is a need for undertaking research studies based on the Z-score model to analyse the financial performance of banks in India. This becomes more imperative in the fast changing and competitive environment. The preset study is an attempt in this direction.

RESEARCH METHODOLOGY

The nature of this study is analytical and is based on the secondary data. The data collected for the study is from RBIs publications. A sample of 26 public sector bank has been selected for the study for the period of 2009 to 2013. As per the gap of study, the objectives have been situated. And in a way to achieve potential results, the individual banks financial ratios have been assessed according to altman's Z-score pre-defined cutoff.

Objectives

- To make an assessment of the individual banks based on financial performance needing immediate consolidation in near future.
- To identify and segregate healthy and unhealthy banks based on past performance of individual banks.

Tools and Parameters of Research

In this study, Altman's score model has been used for analysing the performance of PSBs. The Altman's predictive model was developed in 1968 to measure the viability and performance of business firms based on selected financial ratios. Technically, this model is applicable in all kinds of firms for analysing the viability of business at a particular point of time. In this model reasonable weight is assigned to each financial ratio to design predictive model about the future sustainability of business.

Altman (2000) described the multivariate method (Multiple Discriminate Analysis) as a statistical technique to be used to classify an observation into one of the several priori groupings. This depends on the observation of individual characteristics. It makes predictions of problems where the dependent variable is in qualitative form like, healthy or unhealthy, bankrupt or non-bankrupt, etc. The analysis under multivariate method is transformed into the simplest dimension, the discriminating function of the firm. The model is defined as:

$Z = V1X1 + V2X2 + V3X3 + \ldots.VnXn$

This is done through transforming the value of individual variables to a single determinant score or Z value. The value so arrived is then used to classify the objects, where V1, V2....V*n*, are determinant coefficients and X1, X2.....X*n* are independent variables.

1. *Working Capital to Total Asset Ratio:* it measures the net liquid assets (i.e. current assets less current liabilities) to its total capital.
2. *Retained Earnings to Total Assets Ratio:* This ratio measures the cumulative profitability of a firm over certain period of time. If there is no cumulative profit over the particular time period, there will be an adverse RA/TA ratio (Retained earnings/Total assets).
3. *Earnings before Interest and Tax to Total Assets Ratio:* It measures the true productivity of the firm's assets. It is a very significant ratio for undertaking studies concerning business failure.
4. *Market Value of Equity to Total Liabilities Ratio:* This shows the extent of reduction in a firm's equity value before the liabilities exceed the assets, which is a likely sign of insolvency. The value of equity is the combination of market value of preference and common shares.
5. *Gross Earnings to Total Assets Ratio:* This measures the extent of asset utilization of a firm. It also evaluates the management capacity in dealing with competitive conditions.

The Z-score is a linear analysis where five components are given weights objectively. The weights are summed up to arrive at an overall score. This becomes the basis for classification of firms into one of the priori groups (healthy and unhealthy). The variables in the Z-score are X1, X2, X3, X4 and X5 (Altman, 1968). There are three different models, viz.:

1. Altman's Z-Score – Publicly Traded Manufacturing Firms
   $Z = 1.2(X1) + 1.4(X2) + 3.3(X3) + 0.6(X4) + 0.999(X5)$

X1 = Working Capital/Total Assets
X2 = Retained Earnings/Total Assets
X3 = Earnings before Interest and Taxes/Total Assets
X4 = Market Value Equity/Book Value of Total Debt
X5 = Sales/Total Assets
Z = Overall Index

2. Altman's Z-Score – Privately Held Firms
   $Z = 0.717(X1) + 0.847(X2) + 3.107(X3) + 0.420(X4) + 0.998\ (X5)$
3. Altman's Z-Score – Non-Manufacturing Firms
   $Z = 6.65(X1) + 3.26(X2) + 6.72(X3) + 1.05(X4)$
   However, the above models cannot be used to evaluate the banks as the above models have been designed for the industries, whereas, banking is a financial service entity and the modus of banking business operations are quite different. Nevertheless, it is observed that this model has been used by some of the researchers to measure banks' performance (Pradhan, 2011; Aneja and Makkar, 2013).

On the other hand, it can be observed in the equations that the weights assigned are different and they mainly focus on manufacturing and non manufacturing firms and the results obtained are more relevant to these firms. Therefore, the approach of prediction of failure through the Altman model is not very relevant for banking firms. However, the predictive model can be used to judge the viability of banking business and initiate appropriate caution and desired improvements to avoid future deterioration in the health of banks.

Table 1: Altman's Pre-determined Cutoffs[1]

Prediction	*Publicly Traded Manufacturing*	*Privately Held Manufacturing*	*Non-Manufacturing Firm*
Bankrupt	< 1.81	< 1.23	< 1.1
Zone of Ignorance	1.81 to 2.99	1.23 to 2.90	1.1 to 2.6
Non-bankrupt	> 2.99	> 2.90	> 2.6

DATA ANALYSIS

An analysis has been made to measure the banks' performance using the Altman's Z-score model of predicting the probable bankruptcy of firms. A bank is a service provider entity, therefore the pre-defined score of the

[1] R. Rusuf , Financial Ratios: Use, Predictive Power and the Z-Score ,Retrieved from http://www.rufusandrufus.com/financial_ratios.pdf

Z-score model, as applicable to non-manufacturing firms, has been used. The data on relevant parameters has been considered for a period of 5 years (2009–13) for each PSB to evaluate healthy, unhealthy, and banks needing more attention.

Table 2: Public Sector Bank's Categorization as Per Altman Z-Score Pre-defined Standard Model (refer Annexure)

S. No.	*Healthy Banks*	*Progressive Attention*	*Mixed*	*Need for Attention*
1.	Allahabad Bank	IDBI Bank	Bank of India	Bank of Maharashtra
2.	Andhra Bank	Punjab and Sind Bank	Union Bank of India	Central Bank of India
3.	Bank of Baroda	United Bank of India	Vijaya Bank	Dena Bank
4.	Canara Bank	Corporation Bank		Indian Overseas Bank
5.	Indian Bank			Syndicate Bank
6.	Oriental Bank of Commerce			UCO Bank
7.	Punjab National Bank			

The criteria for categorization is as follows: those banks which have performed well under all parameters during the past 5 years have been categorized as healthy banks; the banks which performed lesser in the past 5 years are categorized under progressive attention category; the banks whose performance showed improvements in the later years are kept under mixed category; and lastly the banks needing attention are categorized as unhealthy banks. This has been done on the basis of performance measurements of the Z-score model. The last category of banks needing attention, have been predicted for probable mergers in the very near future. The observations can be referred in Annexure.

The Bank of Maharashtra, Central Bank of India, Dena Bank, Indian Overseas Bank, Syndicate Bank, and UCO Bank are categorized in the category of banks needing attention based on their performance during the period of 2009–13. Therefore, suitable turn-around strategies are recommended in case of these banks to avoid further deterioration. The analysis has been done as per the Z-score model.

The Vijaya Bank, Bank of India, and Union Bank of India showed mixed performance results as their performance is seen to have improved in the later years of the data analysis.

Further, the performance of Punjab and Sind Bank and IDBI Bank has not been very significant during the period 2009–11, but it improved in the later years, that is, in 2012 and 2013. Similar was the situation with Corporation Bank and United Bank of India.

There are few banks whose performance has been quite encouraging during the period 2009–13 on various financial parameters according to the Z-score model. These banks include, Allahabad Bank, Andhra Bank, Indian Bank, Bank of Baroda, and Oriental Bank of Commerce.

FINDINGS AND CONCLUSION

According to the analysis, the study concludes that nearly half of the PSBs need immediate attention for taking required measures for better performance. Based on these findings, possibilities may also be explored for merging these banks under different groups to make them more vibrant, and strengthen the banking system. On the other hand, one fourth of the PSBs have mixed performance. They may adopt suitable strategies depending on their performance from time to time. The remaining one-fourth PSBs are performing significantly well. Thus, it could be concluded that Z-score model has certain relevance and indications in evaluating the performance of PSBs in India and help in predicting the bankruptcy of banks in India.

REFERENCES

E.I. Altman, 'Financial Ratios, Discriminant Analysis and the Prediction of Corporate Bankruptcy', *The Journal of Finance,* vol. 23, no. 4, 1968, pp. 589–609.

E.I. Altman, 'Predicting Financial Distress of Companies: Revisiting the Z-score and ZETA Models', Working Paper, New York University, New York, 2000.

E.I. Altman' 'The Success of Business Failure Prediction Models: An International Survey', *Journal of Banking and Finance,* vol. 8, no. 2, 1984, pp. 171–98.

R. Aneja and A. Makkar, 'A Comparative Study of Book Value Insolvency of Indian Commercial Banks: An Application of Z-Score Model', *The IUP Journal of Financial Risk Managemen'*, vol. X, no. 2, 2013.

R. Pradhan, 'Prediction of Z-Score for Private Sector Banking Firms', *International Referred Research Journal,* July, vol. II, Issue 22, 2011.

S. Grant, L. Mary and A. Tracy, 'The Use of Z-Scores to Predict Finance Company Collapses: A Research Note', *New Zealand Journal of Applied Business Research,* vol. 2, no. 2, 2012.

W.H. Beaver, 'Financial Ratios as Predictors of Failure', *Journal of Accounting Research,* vol 4, no. 3, 1966, pp. 71–111.

O. Charles and A. Goodluck, 'Financial Ratios and the State of Health of Nigerian Banks', an unpublished paper, 2010.

P. Sinha, V.S Taneja, and V. Gothi V, 'Evaluation of Riskiness of Indian Banks and Probability of Book Value Insolvency', *International Research Journal of Finance and Economics*, vol. 38, 2010, pp. 7–12.

Reserve bank of India-Liabilities and Assets (2014, April 26), Data Base on Indian Economy-RBI Data warehouse retrieved from http://dbie.rbi.org.in/DBIE/dbie.rbi?site=publications

ANNEXURE

Altman Z-Score Analysis of Public Sector Banks' Performance

Year	*Bank*	*CA-CL/TA* (6.65)	*Retained Earnings/TA* (3.26)	*EBIT/TA* (6.72)	*Equity/Total Liabilities* (1.05)	*Total*	*Remark*
2013	Allahabad Bank	0.3839	0.0112	0.0925	0.0245	3.2370	Healthy
2012	Allahabad Bank	0.3840	0.0101	0.0920	0.0273	3.2333	Healthy
2011	Allahabad Bank	0.3385	0.0070	0.0819	0.0315	2.8568	Healthy
2010	Allahabad Bank	0.3497	0.0103	0.2094	0.0367	3.8046	Healthy
2009	Allahabad Bank	0.3373	0.0098	0.1947	0.0457	3.6314	Healthy
2013	Andhra Bank	0.3375	0.0067	0.0954	0.0382	2.9474	Healthy
2012	Andhra Bank	0.3558	0.0080	0.0979	0.0449	3.0974	Healthy
2011	Andhra Bank	0.3388	0.0269	0.0844	0.0514	2.9619	Healthy
2010	Andhra Bank	0.2468	0.0222	0.2003	0.0537	3.1163	Healthy
2009	Andhra Bank	0.2214	0.0223	0.1881	0.0708	2.8834	Healthy
2013	Bank of Baroda	0.3621	0.0006	0.0710	0.0077	2.8951	Healthy
2012	Bank of Baroda	0.3333	0.0010	0.0740	0.0092	2.7267	Healthy
2011	Bank of Baroda	0.3531	0.0010	0.0689	0.0110	2.8256	Healthy
2010	Bank of Baroda	0.3045	0.0009	0.1773	0.0131	3.2332	Healthy
2009	Bank of Baroda	0.2643	0.0010	0.1899	0.0161	3.0542	Healthy
2013	Bank of India	0.2239	0.0005	0.0788	0.0132	2.0338	Need for attention
2012	Bank of India	0.1749	0.0006	0.0827	0.0149	1.7362	Need for attention
2011	Bank of India	0.0682	0.0006	0.0695	0.0156	0.9389	Unhealthy

Year	Bank	CA-CL/TA	Retained Earnings/TA	EBIT/TA	Equity/Total Liabilities	Total	Remark
		(6.65)	(3.26)	(6.72)	(1.05)		
2010	Bank of India	0.2206	0.0005	0.1711	0.0191	2.6382	Healthy
2009	Bank of India	0.2337	0.0005	0.2420	0.0233	3.2065	Healthy
2013	Bank of Maharashtra	0.2153	0.0125	0.0900	0.1068	2.1896	Need attention
2012	Bank of Maharashtra	0.1559	0.0489	0.0862	0.1292	1.9107	Need attention
2011	Bank of Maharashtra	0.1243	0.0478	0.0797	0.1399	1.6649	Need attention
2010	Bank of Maharashtra	0.0191	0.0401	0.1146	0.0606	1.0917	Unhealthy
2009	Bank of Maharashtra	0.0449	0.0217	0.1344	0.0729	1.3492	Need attention
2013	Canara Bank	0.2561	0.0006	0.0903	0.0107	2.3228	Healthy
2012	Canara Bank	0.3008	0.0007	0.0903	0.0118	2.6221	Healthy
2011	Canara Bank	0.2890	0.0011	0.0767	0.0132	2.4540	Need for attention
2010	Canara Bank	0.3247	0.0010	0.1912	0.0155	3.4631	Healthy
2009	Canara Bank	0.2376	0.0009	0.1805	0.0187	2.8152	Healthy
2013	Central Bank of India	0.2169	0.0001	0.0877	0.0993	2.1363	Need attention
2012	Central Bank of India	0.1538	0.0001	0.0894	0.1024	1.7313	Need attention
2011	Central Bank of India	0.0300	0.0001	0.0786	0.1929	0.9303	Unhealthy
2010	Central Bank of India	0.0101	0.0001	0.1127	0.0970	0.9263	Unhealthy
2009	Central Bank of India	-0.0303	0.0001	0.0973	0.0895	0.5463	Unhealthy
2013	Corporation Bank	0.2940	0.0006	0.0876	0.0079	2.5541	Need for attention
2012	Corporation Bank	0.2664	0.0007	0.0887	0.0091	2.3796	Need for attention
2011	Corporation Bank	0.3014	0.0008	0.0724	0.0103	2.5040	Need for attention
2010	Corporation Bank	0.2350	0.0008	0.1913	0.0128	2.8650	Healthy

Year	*Bank*	*CA-CL/TA*	*Retained Earnings/TA*	*EBIT/TA*	*Equity/Total Liabilities*	*Total*	*Remark*
		(6.65)	*(3.26)*	*(6.72)*	*(1.05)*		
2009	Corporation Bank	0.2279	0.0009	0.2016	0.0165	2.8899	Healthy
2013	Dena Bank	0.2000	0.0005	0.0842	0.0309	1.9305	Need for attention
2012	Dena Bank	0.2702	0.0008	0.0844	0.0401	2.4084	Need for attention
2011	Dena Bank	0.2574	0.0008	0.0786	0.0471	2.2916	Need for attention
2010	Dena Bank	0.2234	0.0008	0.1460	0.0498	2.5211	Need for attention
2009	Dena Bank	0.1895	0.0007	0.1499	0.0592	2.3317	Need for attention
2013	IDBI Bank Limited	0.3563	0.0280	0.0876	0.0413	3.0927	Healthy
2012	IDBI Bank Limited	0.3760	0.0232	0.0878	0.0440	3.2122	Healthy
2011	IDBI Bank Limited	0.2891	0.0243	0.0816	0.0389	2.5908	Healthy
2010	IDBI Bank Limited	0.1165	0.0201	0.1167	0.0310	1.6577	Need for attention
2009	IDBI Bank Limited	0.1005	0.0041	0.0799	0.0420	1.2631	Need for attention
2013	Indian Bank	0.3830	0.0055	0.0932	0.0510	3.2450	Healthy
2012	Indian Bank	0.4593	0.0063	0.0952	0.0587	3.7762	Healthy
2011	Indian Bank	0.5257	0.0073	0.0866	0.0682	4.1733	Healthy
2010	Indian Bank	0.5336	0.0087	0.2710	0.0818	5.4838	Healthy
2009	Indian Bank	0.4715	0.0102	0.2446	0.0987	4.9160	Healthy
2013	Indian Overseas Bank	0.2388	0.0001	0.0926	0.0378	2.2499	Need for attention
2012	Indian Overseas Bank	0.2205	0.0003	0.0891	0.0363	2.1038	Need for attention
2011	Indian Overseas Bank	0.1680	0.0004	0.0745	0.0346	1.6554	Need for attention
2010	Indian Overseas Bank	0.2218	0.0004	0.1407	0.0416	2.4652	Need for attention
2009	Indian Overseas Bank	0.2561	0.0003	0.2084	0.0450	3.1516	Healthy

Year	Bank	CA-CL/TA	Retained Earnings/TA	EBIT/TA	Equity/Total Liabilities	Total	Remark
		(6.65)	(3.26)	(6.72)	(1.05)		
2013	Oriental Bank of Commerce	0.4075	0.0000	0.0965	0.0145	3.3731	Healthy
2012	Oriental Bank of Commerce	0.4063	0.0000	0.0961	0.0164	3.3651	Healthy
2011	Oriental Bank of Commerce	0.4230	0.0000	0.0809	0.0181	3.3758	Healthy
2010	Oriental Bank of Commerce	0.3406	0.0000	0.1762	0.0182	3.4686	Healthy
2009	Oriental Bank of Commerce	0.3584	0.0001	0.1483	0.0223	3.4040	Healthy
2013	Punjab and Sind Bank	0.2707	0.1917	0.0964	0.0564	3.1323	Healthy
2012	Punjab and Sind Bank	0.2571	0.1951	0.0945	0.0596	3.0438	Healthy
2011	Punjab and Sind Bank	0.2088	0.1711	0.0783	0.0617	2.5374	Need for attention
2010	Punjab and Sind Bank	0.2174	0.1551	0.1549	0.0676	3.0631	Healthy
2009	Punjab and Sind Bank	0.2079	0.1444	0.1745	0.0926	3.1226	Healthy
2013	Punjab National Bank	0.4084	0.0008	0.0963	0.0074	3.3730	Healthy
2012	Punjab National Bank	0.3258	0.0009	0.0888	0.0074	2.7740	Healthy
2011	Punjab National Bank	0.2681	0.0010	0.0809	0.0084	2.3385	Need for attention
2010	Punjab National Bank	0.2997	0.0010	0.2470	0.0106	3.6671	Healthy
2009	Punjab National Bank	0.2931	0.0003	0.2305	0.0128	3.5120	Healthy
2013	Syndicate Bank	0.2426	0.0007	0.0850	0.0280	2.2169	Need for attention
2012	Syndicate Bank	0.2681	0.0006	0.0896	0.0330	2.4216	Need for attention
2011	Syndicate Bank	0.2764	0.0005	0.0790	0.0366	2.4093	Need for attention
2010	Syndicate Bank	0.1961	0.0005	0.1347	0.0375	2.2507	Need for attention
2009	Syndicate Bank	0.0943	0.0003	0.1283	0.0401	1.5326	Need for attention
2013	UCO Bank	0.1965	0.1064	0.0891	0.1297	2.3886	Need for attention

Year	Bank	CA-CL/TA (6.65)	Retained Earnings/TA (3.26)	EBIT/TA (6.72)	Equity/Total Liabilities (1.05)	Total	Remark
2012	UCO Bank	0.1679	0.1170	0.0864	0.1378	2.2231	Need for attention
2011	UCO Bank	0.1836	0.1031	0.0753	0.1500	2.2200	Need for attention
2010	UCO Bank	0.1472	0.0982	0.1242	0.1238	2.2638	Need for attention
2009	UCO Bank	0.1196	0.0721	0.1076	0.1119	1.8706	Need for attention
2013	Union Bank of India	0.3392	0.0000	0.0887	0.0227	2.8760	Healthy
2012	Union Bank of India	0.3182	0.0000	0.0895	0.0252	2.7440	Healthy
2011	Union Bank of India	0.2654	0.0000	0.0784	0.0269	2.3200	Need for attention
2010	Union Bank of India	0.2438	0.0001	0.1875	0.0259	2.9085	Healthy
2009	Union Bank of India	0.2038	0.0001	0.1915	0.0314	2.6751	Need for attention
2013	United Bank of India	0.2294	0.0002	0.0900	0.1025	2.2388	Need for attention
2012	United Bank of India	0.2891	0.0005	0.0852	0.1138	2.6159	Healthy
2011	United Bank of India	0.2299	0.0004	0.0775	0.1271	2.1847	Need for attention
2010	United Bank of India	0.2173	0.0003	0.1137	0.1125	2.3287	Need for attention
2009	United Bank of India	0.1233	0.0003	0.1092	0.2873	1.8563	Need for attention
2013	Vijaya Bank	0.2048	0.0864	0.1108	0.1528	2.5485	Need for attention
2012	Vijaya Bank	0.2546	0.0976	0.0889	0.1771	2.7952	Need for attention
2011	Vijaya Bank	0.2935	0.1112	0.0778	0.2040	3.0510	Healthy
2010	Vijaya Bank	0.2039	0.1216	0.1505	0.1330	2.9036	Healthy
2009	Vijaya Bank	0.2075	0.1203	0.1441	0.1496	2.8978	Healthy

Size Premium or Liquidity in Drag?

Ashok Bhardwaj Abbott
West Virginia University, Morgantown, West Virginia
e-mail: ashok.abbott@mail.wvu.edu; ashok.abbott@gmail.com

ABSTRACT

The goal of this article is to examine the role of firm size and liquidity on expected asset returns in the US stock markets. The impact of company size and level of liquidity on asset returns is examined in the Fama and French cross-sectional framework. We find that the observed level of liquidity is a superior predictor of future performance as compared to the market value of equity. Liquidity impact may be a substantial part of the explanation for size premium. We also introduce a new measure of liquidity, which is independent of the stock price impact.

Keywords: Size Premium, Liquidity Premium, Half-life, Market Returns, Investment Strategy

INTRODUCTION

Size effect, initially reported by Banz (1981) and Reinganum (1981), has been researched extensively. Fama and French (1992, 1993), for example, have proposed a three factor model which incorporates size and value as two value factors augmenting the traditional Capital Asset Pricing Model(CAPM.). However, the original question posed by Banz, 'It is not known whether size *per se* is responsible for the effect or whether size is just a proxy for one or more true unknown factors', is still unanswered. Recent papers suggest that the size effect may have diminished after the early 1980s. In fact, Eleswarapu and Reinganum (1993), (sample period 1980–90), Dichev (1998), (sample period 1980–95), Horowitz et al. (2000a, 2000b) (sample period 1979–95 / 1982–96), and Amihud (2002) (sample period 1980–97) find no size premium over their sample periods and suggest that the size premium may be disappearing after its discovery and exploitation in market participants. The empirical results presented in this paper suggest a strong role for liquidity in explaining higher raw and excess returns realized by investors in smaller, less liquid stocks.

CONCEPTUAL FRAMEWORK

While traditional CAPM-based asset pricing literature has skirted the liquidity issue, a parallel stream of research starting around the same time has examined the role of liquidity in explaining asset returns. Liquidity risk has been recognized as a significant factor in asset pricing. Constantinides (1986) hypothesized that illiquid assets need to offer higher returns than similar risky assets in order to compensate for the higher risks associated with lack of liquidity. Grossman and Miller (1988) followed up with the concept that the residual demand curve facing active traders is not infinitely elastic and price concessions are necessary to accommodate order flows. Earlier studies of liquidity studied the role of transaction costs for stocks traded on the New York Stock Exchange (NYSE). Perhaps the most influential study of liquidity in asset pricing is that of Amihud and Mendelson (1986), exploring the relationship between market micro structure and asset pricing by showing that bid-ask spread and asset returns are positively related. This study spawned a large body of literature dealing with bid-ask spreads in explaining stock returns, as well as on the determinants of bid-ask spread. Amihud (1989), Chalmers and Kadlec (1998), and Jones (2001) found positive relationship between stock returns and bid-ask spreads. Heaton and Lucas (1996), Vayanos (1998), and Lo et al. (2001), among others, explore the relationship between liquidity and asset prices and show that significant price discounts exist for less liquid, but otherwise comparable assets. Brennan et al. (1998) separated the cost of transactions into variable and a fixed cost and found that illiquidity tends to result in higher stock returns. Similar results have been reported by researchers using different proxies for liquidity. For example, while the bid-ask spread measure used in Amihud and Mendelson (1986) relates to the trading cost dimension, Pastor and Stambaugh (2003) construct their measures based on the concept of price impact to capture the price reaction to trading volume. Amihud (2002) used the ratio of absolute stock returns to Dollar volume as a proxy liquidity measure for the price pressure. These studies reported that even after controlling for common risk factors, stocks' liquidity and returns remained negatively related.

At the macro level more recent studies have started addressing the role of market liquidity and the sensitivity of the individual asset to the market level of liquidity as components of the illiquidity risk premium analogous to the equity risk premium. Chordia et al. (2000) show that there is a common component of liquidity that should be considered as a systematic risk factor within a market. Pastor and Stambaugh (2003) and Porter (2008) examine individual stocks' sensitivity to aggregate market liquidity and explore the relationship between stock returns and changes in market wide liquidity. Both studies report that stocks with high sensitivity to aggregate liquidity offered substantially higher returns. Acharya and Pedersen (2005) estimated liquidity risks of individual stocks by studying their sensitivity to market conditions and market liquidity. Predictive accuracy for expected returns has been shown to improve with inclusion of liquidity as an explanatory factor. Jones (2001) finds empirically that the expected annual stock market return increases with the previous year's bid-ask spread and decreases with the previous year's turnover. Amihud (2002) finds that illiquidity predicts excess return, both for the market and for size-based portfolios. These results strongly suggest that liquidity risks provide valuable insight and should be considered in asset pricing. The available evidence indicates that liquidity is an important factor in asset pricing. However, most studies do not explicitly examine whether the size effect can be explained by liquidity factors, and the few studies that do present mixed evidence. This interaction between the size effect and liquidity effect is being examined in the current paper. The results suggest that a substantial part of the observed size premium may simply be a manifestation of the underlying liquidity impact.

A cross-sectional analysis of the relationship between liquidity and returns can be potentially contaminated by the existence of risk factors other than liquidity. Any discussion of a liquidity premium, therefore, would be incomplete without accounting for security risk. Amihud and Mendelson (1986), for example, adjust for risk by analysing asset returns in a CAPM framework. The Fama-French three-factor model (Fama and French, 1993, 1996) adjustment for risk factors is used by Brennan and Subrahmanyam (1996). Both studies find that asset returns include a significant premium for illiquidity, even after accounting for the market risk, and in case of Brennan and Subrahmanyam, adjusting for market risk, size premium, and market value / book value ratio. The incremental impact of liquidity as a pricing factor is assessed inside an Arbitrage Pricing Theory framework for its contribution to the required risk premium for holders of illiquid assets. Using various approaches, these studies come to similar conclusions, essentially confirming that significant price discounts exist for less liquid, but otherwise comparable assets. The recent financial credit crisis, (2007–09) has dramatically illustrated the impact that lack of liquidity can have on entire economies.

This paper presents a simple measure of liquidity, uncorrelated with unit stock price, which can be used to measure the relative role of liquidity and size in explaining asset returns and address this fundamental question. The measure of size is the market value calculated as the product of the closing price for the month, multiplied by the number of shares outstanding at the end of the month. The measure of liquidity is the half-life for each stock based on a constant flow model. The number of shares outstanding and the observed monthly trading volume are used to construct our liquidity measure λ. It is a natural log transformation of the turnover measure.

Given:

The number of shares issued and outstanding at time t is S_t.

Volume for one time period time t is V_t.

The stock remaining in hands of the original holders at time $t+1$ is

$$S_{t+1} = S_t - V_t.$$

Assuming that the rate of deal flow is constant (λ) at time t

$$S_{t+1} = S_t e^{-\lambda}$$

Or $\lambda = \text{Log}_n(S_t) - \text{Log}_n(S_{t+1})$.

The advantage of using the natural log transformation is that half-life, or the time a Dollar invested in the stock/portfolio is held before being reinvested, can be estimated as Log (2)/λ.

Results suggest that between size and liquidity, liquidity may be the dominant factor in asset pricing.

The rest of this paper is organized as follows. Next section describes the analysis performed, detailing the data sources and empirical methodology employed. Third section presents the empirical results, and conclusions and some suggestions for further research.

ANALYSIS, DATA AND METHODOLOGY

The data set consists of 11,89,707 firm-month observations spanning all listed primary securities (Share Code 10 and 11) for the three equity markets (NYSE, AMEX, and NASDAQ) for January 1993 to December 2012. Firms with an Initial Public Offering (IPO) or delisting during the month are excluded from the sample. This results in reassigned monthly portfolios containing 11,77,797 firm-month observations. This time period was selected such that a more precise measure of liquidity can be devised. Trading volume reporting was standardized across the three equity markets only in June 1992. The trading volume reported by NASDAQ before June 1992 was the aggregate of volume reported by all dealers in the security, leading to inflated counts as dealers/market makers reported each buy and sell transaction separately. The analysis period (1993–2012) is appropriate as it covers two cycles of Pre Bubble, Bubble, and Post Bubble data, allowing us to observe significant changes in liquidity and pricing behaviour. Market capitalization, bid, ask, closing price, total returns, shares outstanding, and trading volume for all stocks traded on the three exchanges were obtained from CRSP data base provided by the Center for Research in Security Prices at the University of Chicago.

Securities are reassigned to size and liquidity portfolios at the end of each month. The geometric annual returns for each stock, as well as the market indices were calculated, starting with every month.

High and low stock portfolios based on monthly levels of market value and liquidity are formed at the end of each month. In addition, sub-portfolios are formed using alternate sort orders (size followed by liquidity/liquidity followed by size) for every month, and used to measure the between and within portfolio return differentials. A comparison is made between the observed annual geometric annual returns following the portfolio assignment. Geometric annual returns are used instead of arithmetic returns as averages of arithmetic returns tend to get inflated in the presence of high volatility. Size and liquidity premiums are calculated following the Fama-French procedure as the difference between returns on larger stocks and smaller stocks, and between stocks with higher liquidity and lower liquidity. Further, similar differences are calculated for each of the size and liquidity portfolios further sorted by liquidity and size and averaged to generate size adjusted liquidity premium and liquidity adjusted size premium. The sample consists of 228 monthly portfolios in each series. The first portfolio formation month is January 1993 and the last is December 2011.

FINDINGS AND CONCLUSIONS

Data distribution follows the expected pattern. Mean market value and liquidity differentials are high when compared across size and liquidity sorted portfolios. Larger market value and higher liquidity portfolios exhibit lower returns as compared to portfolios with smaller market value and low liquidity. Small stocks in aggregate are about half as liquid as the larger stocks. Half-life for small stocks is 6.73 months ($\lambda = 0.10296$), while it is 3.27 months ($\lambda = 0.21201$) for the larger stocks. When the sample is segmented by liquidity, the difference in observed half-life is significant. The illiquid stocks exhibit a half-life of 19.41 months ($\lambda = 0.035713$), while it is 2.48 months (λ

= 0.279274) for the liquid stocks. The difference becomes even more striking when illiquid and liquid stocks are further parsed by size. While illiquid small stocks exhibit a half-life of 25.1 months ($\lambda = 0.027646$), it is 15.8 months ($\lambda = 0.043776$) for the illiquid large stocks. However, for the liquid large and small stocks the difference in half- life virtually disappears. Liquid small stocks exhibit a half-life of 2.61 months ($\lambda = 0.265093$), and it is 2.36 months ($\lambda = 0.293401$) for the liquid large stocks.

The observed returns indicate that the difference in annual geometric returns between large and small market cap, as well as the high and low liquidity portfolio returns, are significant. In addition, small stocks exhibit significant returns' differentials for high and low liquidity portfolios. Overall liquidity premium is significant and positive, and the average liquidity premium after adjusting for size is also significant and positive. The overall size premium, particularly the size premium after filtering out the liquidity impact, is relatively small. This suggests that the origins of 'size effect' may lie in the small stock/low liquidity quadrant, and it may simply be a manifestation of the 'liquidity' effect. We find that the relative liquidity and returns differential between large and small stocks is dwarfed by the considerably higher relative liquidity and returns differential between liquid and illiquid stocks. The data appear to indicate that the liquidity impact may be significant in explaining the excess returns generated by the stocks. These results are summarized in Table 1a, b, and c.

The analysis indicates that between size and liquidity, liquidity may be the driving factor explaining the realized returns. In addition to comparing the portfolio returns across the size and liquidity spectrum, the excess returns (Alpha) generated by the size and liquidity sorted portfolios, which appears to rise monotonically with the decline in liquidity, is also presented. Results of regression models with stock excess returns (Annual Geometric return minus the risk free rate) as the dependent variables and the equally weighted market excess returns (Annual Geometric return minus the risk free rate) as the explanatory variable are also given. Tables 2a and b show the impact of illiquidity across the size spectrum. Illiquidity has a strong impact that overrides the size premium impact. Tables 3a and b explore the impact of size across the liquidity spectrum. The cross testing strongly supports the thesis that liquidity impact is strong, persistent, and considerably larger than the size effect. Once again, liquidity alpha is positive and significant across all specifications, indicating that less liquid stocks generate higher returns across all size segments. These regression results indicate that liquidity premium is significant in explaining stock excess returns. The results suggest that the

Table 1(a)

Market Value $'000	*N Obs*	*Variable*	*Mean*	*Std Dev*	*Minimum*	*Maximum*	*Lower 95% CL for Mean*	*Upper 95% CL for Mean*	*t Value*	*Pr > |t|*
Small	588829	Annual Geometric Return	0.1677494	0.728847	-0.99843	5.7118569	0.1658878	0.1696111	176.61	<.0001
		Market Value $'000	74116.95	79745.9	219.875	510244.22	73913.26	74320.64	713.19	<.0001
		Liquidity	0.1029604	0.20838	0	9.5185601	0.1024282	0.1034927	379.15	<.0001
Large	588947	Annual Geometric Return	0.1291173	0.558746	–0.99893	5.6449685	0.1276903	0.1305443	177.34	<.0001
		Market Value $'000	4482973.98	17547746	68681.25	626550334	4438158.1	4527789.9	196.06	<.0001
		Liquidity	0.2120104	0.313433	0	9.0827604	0.2112099	0.2128109	519.1	<.0001

Annual Geometric Returns are higher for smaller firms. Liquidity is higher for larger firms.

Table 1(b)

Liquidity	*N Obs*	*Variable*	*Mean*	*Std Dev*	*Minimum*	*Maximum*	*Lower 95% CL for Mean*	*Upper 95% CL for Mean*	*t Value*	*Pr > |t|*
Illiquid	588840	Annual Geometric Return	0.1592659	0.610524	-0.99843	5.711857	0.157707	0.160825	200.18	<.0001
		Market Value $'000	1816790.7	13452210	309.21	5.81E+08	1782431	1851150	103.64	<.0001
		Liquidity	0.0357125	0.028224	0	0.19302	0.03564	0.035785	970.95	<.0001
Liquid	588956	Annual Geometric Return	0.1376017	0.686409	-0.99893	5.644969	0.135849	0.139355	153.84	<.0001
		Market Value $'000	2740666.64	11674525	219.875	6.27E+08	2710850	2770483	180.16	<.0001
		Liquidity	0.2792738	0.342296	0.036957	9.51856	0.2784	0.280148	626.14	<.0001

Annual Geometric Returns are higher for illiquid firms. Liquidity is higher for larger firms.

Table 1(c)

Liquidity	*Market Value*	*N Obs*	*Variable*	*Mean*	*Std Dev*	*Minimum*	*Maximum*	*Lower 95% CL for Mean*	*Upper 95% CL for Mean*	*t Value*	*Pr > |t|*
Illiquid	Small	294357	AnnualGeometric Return	0.178901	0.698439	–0.99817	5.6653899	0.176378	0.181424	138.97	<.0001
			Market Value $'000	38246.01	31049.17	309.21	188762.16	38133.84	38358.17	668.3	<.0001
			Liquidity	0.027646	0.022632	0	0.1924516	0.027564	0.027728	662.75	<.0001
	Large	294483	AnnualGeometric Return	0.139639	0.506895	–0.99843	5.7118569	0.137808	0.14147	149.49	<.0001
			Market Value $'000	3594574	18855337	47201	581098859	3526473	3662676	103.45	<.0001
			Liquidity	0.043776	0.030836	0	0.1930202	0.043664	0.043887	770.39	<.0001
Liquid	Small	294414	AnnualGeometric Return	0.149322	0.777474	–0.99824	5.6449685	0.146514	0.152131	104.21	<.0001
			Market Value $'000	203532.6	246131.5	219.875	1580832.3	202643.6	204421.7	448.69	<.0001
			Liquidity	0.265093	0.329711	0.036975	9.5185601	0.263902	0.266284	436.26	<.0001
	Large	294522	AnnualGeometric Return	0.12588	0.581054	–0.99893	5.5284518	0.123781	0.127978	117.57	<.0001
			Market Value $'000	5276870	16112478	86232.75	626550334	5218680	5335061	177.73	<.0001
			Liquidity	0.293401	0.353827	0.036957	9.0827604	0.292123	0.294678	450.02	<.0001

Smaller firms exhibit a larger impact of liquidity on returns. Small firm returns differential 3%, larger firms 1%.

origins of the previously observed size premium, neglecting liquidity, may in fact lie in the small illiquid stock quadrant.

Liquidity risk is priced by the markets and has a positive economically significant contribution to expected returns. In periods of crises, as a flight to safety occurs, liquidity premium is expected to rise. Regression

Table 2(a): Illiquidity has a Strong Impact for Large and Small Firms: Sort Order Size followed by Liquidity

Sample	*Large and Liquid*	*Large and Illiquid*	*Small and Liquid*	*Small and Illiquid*
N	294531	294416	294475	294354
Intercept	0.00698	0.03395	0.01305	0.04607
t Value	5.65	38.23	8.55	36.94
Pr > |t|	<.0001	<.0001	<.0001	<.0001
Index Return	0.86995	0.55107	1.16466	0.84287
t Value	176.7	155.59	191.38	169.5
Pr > |t|	<.0001	<.0001	<.0001	<.0001
Dependent Mean	0.09461	0.08949	0.1303	0.13105
Adj R-Sq	0.0958	0.076	0.1106	0.0889

Table 2(b): Impact of Illiquidity Overrides the Size Premium for Large and Illiquid Firms

Sample	*Large and Liquid*	*Large and Illiquid*	*Small and Liquid*	*Small and Illiquid*
N	294531	294416	294475	294354
Intercept	0.00956	0.03244	0.02182	0.04953
t Value	7.74	36.49	14.47	39.75
Pr > |t|	<.0001	<.0001	<.0001	<.0001
Index Return	0.70832	0.64524	0.61563	0.62701
t Value	101.1	127.94	71.94	14.47
Pr > |t|	<.0001	<.0001	<.0001	<.0001
Liquidity Averaged Size Premium	0.43691	–0.25455	1.48417	0.5835
t Value	32.37	–26.2	90.03	42.85
Pr > |t|	<.0001	<.0001	<.0001	<.0001
Dependent Mean	0.09461	0.08949	0.1303	0.13105
Adj R-Sq	0.0991	0.0781	0.1344	0.0946

Table 3(a): Illiquidity has a Strong Impact for Large and Small Firms: Sort Order Liquidity followed by Size

Sample	*Liquid and Large*	*Illiquid and Large*	*Liquid and Small*	*Illiquid and Small*
N	294522	294483	294414	294357
Intercept	0.01552	0.04039	0.00195	0.04213
t Value	13.83	41.14	1.32	31.6
Pr > |t|	<.0001	<.0001	0.188	<.0001
Index Return	0.72732	0.61714	1.09466	0.9896
t Value	162.53	157.59	184.89	186.09
Pr > |t|	<.0001	<.0001	<.0001	<.0001
Dependent Mean	0.08881	0.10257	0.11225	0.14183
Adj R-Sq	0.0823	0.0778	0.104	0.1053

Table 3(b): Size Adjusted Liquidity Premium for Large Firms Overrides the Size Impact for Illiquid and Large Firms: Sort Order Liquidity followed by Size

Sample	*Liquid and Large*	*Illiquid and Large*	*Liquid and Small*	*Illiquid and Small*
N	294522	294483	294414	294357
Intercept	0.03298	0.03271	0.0302	0.04383
t Value	29.01	32.65	20.17	32.15
Pr > |t|	<.0001	<.0001	<.0001	<.0001
Index Return	0.54093	0.6992	0.79305	0.97144
t Value	105.9	155.36	117.89	158.6
Pr > |t|	<.0001	<.0001	<.0001	<.0001
Size Averaged Liquidity Premium	–0.58186	0.2562	–0.94163	–0.05671
t Value	–73.52	36.74	–90.34	–5.98
Pr > |t|	<.0001	<.0001	<.0001	<.0001
Dependent Mean	0.08881	0.10257	0.11225	0.14183
Adj R-Sq	0.0988	0.082	0.1282	0.1054

results presented in Table 4 show that liquidity premium alpha is positive, significant, and relatively similar across the full sample, and small and large stocks. Liquidity premium is negatively related to the level of the prevailing market liquidity, as well as the market returns, as expected. In periods of low liquidity and economic downturns, preference for liquidity creates a larger

Table 4: Regression Results Dependent Variable Liquidity Premium

Variable	*Full Sample*	*Small Stocks*	*Large Stocks*
Intercept	0.05648	0.05655	0.05641
t	306.54	217.03	216.49
Equally Weighted Excess Returns	–0.0861	–0.08656	–0.08564
t	–289.97	–205.82	–204.26
Mean Market Liquidity	–0.33036	–0.33122	–0.32952
t	–180.72	–128.11	–127.46
F Value	55926.3	28116.3	27811.6
Adj. R-Square	0.0759	0.0763	0.0756

discount for illiquid stocks, resulting in subsequent higher returns. This effect is significant across the entire sample, as well as the sub samples partitioned across small and large sizes.

These results suggest that liquidity effect is economically significant in explaining the realized returns. A naïve strategy consisting of investing in long position in illiquid stocks and short position in liquid stocks would generate significant positive economic returns. The role of size effect, neglecting the liquidity component, in generating larger returns is not supported by this analysis. The previously reported size effect, thus, may be a manifestation of the liquidity effect.

The empirical results presented in this paper suggest a strong role for liquidity in explaining higher raw and excess returns realized by investors in less liquid stocks. Size effect has been studied extensively and it has been suggested that it may be a proxy for another unobserved factor. The results of this paper strongly suggest that liquidity may be that unobserved factor. A new measure of liquidity, unaffected by the stock price per share, is introduced here, and it is found that it provides an effective indicator of stock and market liquidity. While market level liquidity and sensitivity of individual stock liquidity has been studied primarily in price impact, there is considerable work that needs to be done in assessing predictability of future returns based on historic liquidity. This paper is a first step in that direction.

REFERENCES

A.W. Lo, H. Mamaysky, and J. Wang, 'Asset Prices and Trading Volume under Fixed Transaction Costs', Working Paper, Cambridge: MIT, 2001.

Dimitri Vayanos, 'Transaction Costs and Asset Prices: A Dynamic Equilibrium Model', *Rev. Financial Studies*, vol. 11, Spring 1998, pp. 1–58.

E.F. Fama and K.R. French, Common Risk Factors in the Returns on Stocks and Bonds', *Journal of Financial Economics*, vol. 33, 1993, pp. 3–56.

Fama, E.F. and French, K.R. (1992), 'The Cross-Section of Expected Stock Returns', *The Journal of Finance*, vol. 47, pp. 427–465.

________, 'Multifactor Explanations of Asset Pricing Anomalies', *Journal of Finance*, 1996, pp. 55–84.

Grossman, S.J. and Miller, M.H., 'Liquidity and Market Structure', *Journal of Finance*, vol. 43, no. 3, pp. 617–633.

G.M. Constantinides, 'Capital Market Equilibrium with Transaction Costs', *Journal of Political Economy*, vol. 94, 1986, pp. 842–62.

I.D. Dichev, 'Is the Risk of Bankruptcy a Systematic Risk?' *Journal of Finance*, vol. 53 1998, no. 3, pp. 1131–47.

J. Heaton and D.J. Lucas, 'Evaluating the Effects of Incomplete Markets on Risk Sharing and Asset Pricing', *Journal of Political Economy*, vol. 104, June 1996, pp. 443–87.

J.M. Chalmers and G.B. Kadlec, 'An Empirical Examination of the Amortized Spread,' *Journal of Financial Economics*, vol.48, 1998, pp. 159–88.

Joel L. Horowitz, Tim Loughran, and N.E. Savin, 'Three Analyses of the Firm Size Premium', *Journal of Empirical Finance*, vol. 7, Issue 2, August 2000, pp. 143–53.

Jones, C. and Lipson, M. (2001), 'Sixteenths: Direct Evidence on Institutional Trading Costs', *J. Finan. Econ.*, vol. 59, pp. 253–278.

L. Pástor and V. Stambaugh, 'Liquidity Risk and Expected Stock Returns', *Journal of Political Economy*, vol. 111, no. 3, June 2003, pp. 642–85.

M.J. Brennan and A. Subrahmanyam, 'Market Microstructure and Asset Pricing: On the Compensation for Illiquidity in Stock Returns', *Journal of Financial Economics*, vol. 41, 1996, 441–64.

M.J. Brennan, T. Chordia and A. Subrahmanyam, 'Alternative Factor Specifications, Security Characteristics, and the Cross-section of Expected Returns', *Journal of Financial Economics*, vol. 49, no. 3, 1998, pp. 345–73.

M.R. Reinganum, 'Abnormal Returns in Small Firm Portfolios', *Financial Analysts Journal*, vol. 37, no. 2, March-April 1981, pp. 52–6.

Porter, R.B., 2008, 'The Multiple Dimensions of Marketwide Liquidity: Implications for Asset Pricing', John Wiley & Sons, Chap. 21, pp. 387–406.

R.W. Banz, 'The Relationship between Returns and Market Value of Common Stocks', *Journal of Financial Economics*, vol. 9, 1981, pp. 3–18.

T. Chordia, R. Roll, and A. Subrahmanyam, 'Commonality in Liquidity', *Journal of Financial Economics*, vol. 56, 2000, pp. 3–28.

V. Acharya and L.H. Pedersen, 'Asset Pricing with Liquidity Risk', *Journal of Financial Economics*, vol.77, 2005, pp. 375–410.

Venkat Eleswarapu and Marc Reinganum, 'The Seasonal Behavior of Liquidity Premium in Asset Pricing', *Journal of Financial Economics*, vol. 34, 1993, pp. 373–86.

Y. Amihud, 'The Effects of Beta, Bid-Ask Spread, Residual Risk, and Size on Stock Returns', *The Journal of Finance*, vol. 44, no. 2, 1989, pp. 479–86.

________, 'Illiquidity and Stock Returns: Cross-Section and Time-Series Effects', *Journal of Financial Markets*, vol. 5, 2002, pp. 31–56.

Yakov Amihud and Haim Mendelson, 'Asset Pricing and the Bid-Ask Spread', *Journal of Financial Economics*, vol. 17, 1986, pp. 223–49.

Authors' Profile

(In alphabetical order)

Ambrish Gupta is a 'Rashtriya Gaurav' awardee. He has been teaching at FORE since 1997. Prior to that, he worked for 14 years in industry, mainly investment banking, as Director and Senior Vice-President: Country head. His teaching and research areas include Investment banking, Project financing, Financial accounting, Financial reporting standards, IFRS convergence and Contemporary corporate reporting practices. He has published 2 Books, namely, *Financial Accounting for Management: An Analytical Perspective* (Pearson) and *Inflation Accounting: The Indian Context*, Edited 1 book, namely, *Gaagar Main Saagar: Self Realization Towards Fulfillment*, 23 papers, 7 working papers, 3 papers in the proceedings of international conferences in Germany, Macau (China) and Thailand and 2 papers in edited books. He has provided research guidance to 1 PhD scholar and 50 major student projects. Prof. Gupta is Co-editor – 'GSTF Business Review', Singapore, Member – Editorial board, 'Public and Municipal Finance', Ukraine and Program Committee of annual Conferences on Accounting and Finance, Singapore. He has attended faculty development programmes in China, Malaysia and Italy. He is a Fellow of the Institute of Chartered Accountants of India (ICAI), Member of Doctoral committee, Department of Management, Jamia Hamdard University, Capital market committee, PHD Chamber of Commerce, CFO Guild of ICAI and Editorial board, Indian Journal of Finance. His Papers have been presented in international conferences in Germany, Macau and Thailand. He has authored reports on restructuring of FORE's PGDM curriculum and salary structure of non-teaching staff at FORE, delivered talks on topics of his interest areas in MDPs and seminars including for IAAS officers and attended numerous seminars. He has been Chairperson (Finance) for 6 years and Programme Director (WMG) for 2 years at FORE.

Anupam Narula has 17 years of rich experience in teaching, research and industry. He is silver Medalist in PGDBM. His other qualifications are PhD,

MA (Eco), PGDBM (Marketing). He was Area Chairman Marketing at FORE from 2012–14 and Professor-in-Charge Alumni Relations at FORE.

He successfully held various administrative & academic responsibilities as Director, Dean, Officiating HOD, Founder and Coordinator for many new Management Education programs. He had undertaken various institutional building activities with premier and upcoming B-Schools in NCR. He has published and presented papers in various reputed national and international forums. He has travelled extensively in Singapore, USA, Italy, China, Malaysia & Uzbekistan as part of his work and also for research. He is on the Editorial review board of two national journals.

His teaching, research and training areas of interest include Consumer Buying Behavior, Service Marketing, Textile Marketing and Educational Marketing. He conducts Management Development and Faculty Development programmes in the area of his expertise.

Ashok Bhardwaj Abbott is tenured Associate Professor of Finance at West Virginia University in Morgantown, West Virginia. He received his MBA and PhD in Finance from Virginia Tech, Blacksburg, VA. Dr. Abbott's areas of research and teaching include Corporate Finance, Mergers and Acquisitions, and Corporate Valuations. He has consulting interests in valuation of closely held businesses. In addition to publishing extensively in scholarly finance research journals, he has presented at national and international finance and valuation conferences and emerged as a thought leader in market pricing anomalies.

Bharti is Assistant Professor at University School of Management Studies, Guru Gobind Singh Indraprastha University, Delhi. She has completed Bachelor of Science from St Stephen's College, University of Delhi and Master of Finance and Control (MFC) from South Campus, University of Delhi. She is UGC NET qualified. She has mentored several projects at graduate and post graduate levels. In addition to the publications in journals of national and international repute, she has participated in various seminars, workshops and national and international conferences. She currently teaches International Banking, Financial Management and Valuations.

Deepak Tandon is Professor in Finance at the International Management Institute (IMI), New Delhi. He is a PhD, MBA–Finance (FMS, Delhi University); LLB (Delhi University); CAIIB (Indian Institute of Banking and Finance, Mumbai). He has 33 Years experience, 103 Research papers, authored

6 books and 4 awards. He has also been a Chairperson/Keynote speaker at various National and International Conferences. He is instrumental in conducting various MDPs and Conferences. He is an Editor-in-Chief in two International Journals and on the Editorial Board for several journals.

Freda Swaminathan comes with 35 years experience in Marketing and Advertising and is a Professor of Marketing at FORE School of Management, New Delhi. Her ad agency experience was extensive, with over 18 years experience in agencies including LINTAS and JW Thompson and with profit-center responsibility, as Vice-President of Advertising & Sales Promotion (ASP – a CK Birla group). She was Head Marketing Communications at Goodyear India Ltd. For 3 years, and was also the Senior General Manager – Marketing at DSS Mobile Communications (a Dalmia Company).

Since the last decade she has been in the academic field as Professor at FORE School of Management in the areas of Marketing, Brand Management and Integrated Marketing Communications. She is on the Governing Board of Jesus and Mary College, New Delhi, and is a founder Board member of Etasha Society. Her areas of interest in research and publication include brand management, advertising and culture. She has also been the Program Director for several seminars in the area of Marketing, Brand Management and Advertising.

Himanshu Joshi is associated with FORE School of Management, New Delhi as Associate Professor in the area of Finance and Accounting. He has more than fourteen years of experience in research and teaching at post graduate levels in Management Education. He holds an MBA (Finance) and PhD Degree. He has published extensively in peer reviewed journals, and presented number of research papers in International and National Conferences. His areas of research interest include Fixed Income Securities, Investment Management, FOREX Risk Management and Corporate Finance. He has successfully developed and delivered various open and in house management development programs like Spreadsheet Modeling for Business Valuation, FX risk management, and Financial Modeling.

Madhu Vij is Professor at Faculty of Management Studies, University of Delhi. Her areas of interest are International Financial Management, Financial Management, Management of Financial Services and Management Accounting. She has written books on Multinational Financial Management and Financial & Management Accounting. She has organised many seminars and case development workshops. There are many research papers and research projects in the areas of Finance to her credit.

MEENA BHATIA has been teaching Accounting and Finance courses to management students at post graduate and undergraduate level since 1997. She has taught at IIFT, IMT, IILM, Bombay Stock Exchange Institute and many other B Schools in NCR region. She has also taught at School of Management, University of Bradford, UK. She also worked as Assistant Manager (Corporate Finance & Investment Banking) with a Merchant Banker.

Her research interest includes financial markets, disclosures and financial reporting. She presented papers at IIM Ahmadabad, IIM Lucknow, IMI, FORE School of Management and Harvard, Boston USA. She has published in journals of repute. She is on the Editorial Board of South Asian Journal of Business and Management Cases (SAJBMC), Sage Publications and also reviewed papers for Journal of Financial Reporting and Accounting, Emerald Publication. She is a PhD guide with Mohanlal Sukhadia University, Udaipur.

She has offered training & development programmes in the area of Costing, Finance, Accounting, Analysis and Investments to executives of NTPC, PowerGrid, and IFFCO, etc. She has provided consultancy to a small and medium scale enterprises.

By way of qualification, she is a PhD, AICWAI, CFA, MBA and B.Com (Hons) from Delhi University. She is a merit holder of ICWAI and scholarship holder of ICFAI.

MEGHA AGGARWAL is pursuing PhD (Thesis submitted) in Management from Banasthali Vidyapith with the topic, 'An Analysis of Indian Union Budget using Crystal Maze: A Holistic Approach', under the supervision of Dr. Siddharth Shastri, Prof. of Economics, Dean, Faculty of Social Sciences, Banasthali Vidyapith, Rajasthan.

MBA (Finance, Marketing) from IILM Academy of Higher Learning, Greater Noida, UP Technical University, Lucknow and Graduate in Commerce from MD University, Rohtak.

Currently working as an Assistant Professor with WISDOM (Faculty of Management), Baansthali Vidypith, Rajasthan from 2010.

Research area: Emerging fields of Finance & Accounts and currently working on multidisciplinary areas related to financial economics.

Mukta Mani is Assistant Professor in Department of Humanities and Social Sciences, Jaypee Institute of Information Technology, Noida. She has done MBA with specialization in Finance and PhD in Management. She has around 14 years experience of teaching to Post graduate classes of Business Management and undergraduate classes of Engineering. She is actively engaged in research on Banking, Financial markets and Entrepreneurship. She has authored many research papers which are published in international and national journals. She has also supervised doctoral research in the area of Banking and Mutual Funds.

Namita Rajput is Associate Professor at Sri Aurobindo College, Department of Commerce, University of Delhi with teaching experience of more than 23 years. She is an expert in research with major focus on Finance, International business, Marketing and other subjects in commerce. Proficient in handling graduate, post graduate students and research scholars by using interactive discussions and 'hands-on' approaches to help them learn and apply concepts in subjects. She has a distinction in planning, executing and monitoring various research projects. She has also been a part of various seminars, paper presentations, business reviews and has authored several books and papers in various national and international journals. She has been vastly successful in continuously acquiring new knowledge and applying innovative pedagogies and has always aimed to be an effective educator with a global outlook which is the need of today.

Neelam Tandon is Associate Professor at Bhartiya Vidya Bhavan's Usha & Lakshmi Mittal Institute of Management (BULMIM) New Delhi in the area of Economics and Finance. She is PhD, M Phil, MBA in Economics and Finance, has over 15 years academic experience and published over 53 research papers, authored 5 books and guide to various Ph.D students. She has been instrumental in conducting National Seminars and International conferences in the areas of Finance, Risk Management, International business at the PHD Chamber of Commerce in New Delhi.

Neha Agarwal is pursuing PhD in Management as a full time scholar from Amity Business School, Amity University, Noida (UP) in the area of behavioural Finance. She completed her MBA Master's Degree in year 2009 from Amity Business School, Amity University, Noida. She completed her Bachelor's Degree BBA from Seth Padam Jain Institute of Commerce,

Business Management and Economics, Agra. Area of expertise is Financial Decision making, Behavioural finance, Investment.

Neha Taneja is MBA Gold Medalist in Family Business and Entrepreneurship from Nirma University, JRF and UGC NET certified in management and has done her Bachelor of Science in statistics. She is having more than 8 years of Industry and Academic experience of teaching variety of subjects ranging from Entrepreneurship, Establishing and Growing your Venture, Business Plan, Research Methodology, Advanced Business Statistics, Business Statistics, Business Mathematics to Fundamentals of Mathematics. She has presented various research papers and cases at national and international conferences. Her major areas of interest are Entrepreneurship Education, Succession Planning and Entrepreneurial Finance. She has also attended programs at University of Cambridge for Entrepreneurship and at China.

Nehal Joshipura is Assistant Professor in Finance at Durdadevi Saraf Institute of Management Studies, Mumbai. She earned MBA in Finance from Bhavnagar University and MCA from Gujarat University. She is currently pursuing PhD on 'Exploring risk anomaly in Indian stock market: The test of market efficiency.' She has nearly a decade long experience in industry and academia. She has published a number of papers in refereed management journals. In addition, she has presented papers at national and international conferences. She was with Alliance University, Bangalore in last assignment. She teaches courses of Portfolio Management and Corporate Finance. Her research interests lie in market efficiency and portfolio theory.

Pawan Kumar Jha is Assistant Professor of Finance at the School of Management, Kathmandu University, Nepal. He has been awarded the PhD degree in Management in 2015 from the Faculty of Management Studies, Banaras Hindu University, Varanasi, India. He completed M Phil. (Management) in 2011 from the Faculty of Management, Tribhuvan University, Nepal. He received his Master in Business Studies (Finance) degree in 2006 from Peoples' Campus (Tribhuvan University), Pakanajol, Kathmandu. He has also completed Post Graduate Diploma in Financial Management (PGDFM) from IGNOU, New Delhi in 2007.

He started his academic career in 2006 and since then he has made decisive contribution to the areas of Financial Management, Corporate Finance, Investment Management, Financial Markets and Institutions, Banking and Insurance, and International Finance by way of teaching and research. He has published and presented eight research papers in the area of finance to national and international conferences. Dr. Jha is a young and dynamic academician, full of potentials and sense of engagement in academic activities. In the past, he has taught in different academic institutions of Kathmandu, Nepal. In a short period of time, he has proven himself as a successful academician and professionalism.

Pervin A. Gandhi is working as a Senior Lecturer (Finance and Accounting), with over 9 years of academic and industry experience, at B.K. Majumdar Institute of Business Administration, Ahmedabad University, Ahmedabad. She is an Associate Chartered Accountant and has done her Masters in Commerce (M Com) in Advanced Accounting from Gujarat University. Her industry experience ranges from various audits of Companies, Trusts, and Firms to statutory Audit of various Banks. Her academic arena includes teaching Finance and Accounting related courses like, Financial Management, Advanced Financial Management, Corporate Finance, Financial Markets, Financial Services, Personal Finance, Financial Statements Analysis, Strategic Financial Management, Financial Accounting, Corporate Accounting, Cost Accounting, and Tax Planning at undergraduate level and at Final Year of Chartered Accountancy. She has researched in the area of Corporate Finance, Financial Markets and Entrepreneurship. She has visited University of Cambridge and National University of Singapore for her research study. She has to her credit various research papers presented at national and international conferences, published cases and reviewed a book on Financial Management. Her areas of interest include Corporate Finance, Financial Markets, Derivatives, Behavioral Finance, and Emerging issues in Accounting.

PK Gupta is a post-graduate from Faculty of Commerce and Business Studies, Delhi School of Economics, University of Delhi and Ph.D. in Finance. He is a fellow member of the Institute of Cost and Works Accountants of India, Fellow member of the Institute of Company Secretaries of India, Chartered member of the Institute of Chartered Financial Analysts of India and fellow of the Insurance Institute of India, Mumbai. He has experience of more than twenty-three years in industry and academics.

He has presented papers in various international conferences and has won outstanding research awards. He has organised various Seminars, Workshops and Management Development Programmes in the area of Finance and Risk Management and has been involved in various consultancy assignments in the area of corporate restructuring. His corporate training endeavours include Risk Management in Banks, Financial Risk Management, Project Risk Management, Cash Flow Analysis, etc. He has also undertaken many UGC sponsored research projects and consultancy assignments in the area of risk management.

He is the author of the six books, which include Insurance and Risk Management (2004 & 2012), Human Resource Information Systems (2004) and Legal Aspect of Insurance (2006). He has won the second prize for case study competition organised by Emerald Worldwide.

He is the founder of Society for Professional Development (Regd.), Delhi and President of Delhi Professionals' Association (Regd.), Delhi. He is also the Co-Regional Director of the Delhi chapter of PRMIA, USA.

He is presently associated as Associate Professor (Finance & Risk Management) with Centre for Management Studies, Jamia Millia Islamia University, New Delhi. He has supervised PhD in various areas of Finance, Risk Management and Knowledge Management. He is also a visiting faculty with various management institutions including IIM Shillong, Faculty of Management Studies, University of Delhi, Delhi School of Management, Delhi Technological University, Delhi, Symbiosis, Bangalore, Lal Bahadur Shastri Institute of Management, New Delhi, School of Management Studies, NIT, Neemrana, I.P. University, etc.

Pooja Misra, Assistant Professor has a work experience of 19 years+ in academics and the Corporate industry. She has spent 12+ years in the Industry with organizations such as American Express, Standard Chartered Bank and Lazard Creditcapital. She shifted to the Academic world in 2008 and has completed her PhD in Management from Gautam Buddha University in the area of: Compensation Components and its effect on Employee engagement and turnover intent.

Her research interests include Macroeconomic dimensions of an economy, Corporate Strategies, Compensation, Employee engagement and Current trends in Business Environment. She has published several research papers and articles in international and national journals and has presented papers in various national and international conferences.

Poonam Singh is pursuing PhD from Jamia Hamdard University; her area of research is Merger and Acquisitions of Indian Banking Industry. She has qualified NET/JRF form University Grant commission (UGC) and at present availing Senior Research Fellowship (SRF) for her PhD. She has written several research papers and also published in International journal of financial management (IJFM), Global business review (GBR) and Journal of research in management (Optimization).

She has presented and attended several conferences and seminars in India. Also wrote few case studies and one of it for (Indian Institute of Management) IIM Raipur. Moreover, her interest area of research is in corporate finance, Mergers and Acquisitions and Commercial banks performance, Banking synergies and Micro-finance.

Pushpendra Singh is Associate Professor (Finance), GL Bajaj Institute of Management and Research, Greater Noida.

He has 14 + years of rich and diverse experience in Teaching, Training, Research, Consultancy and Academic Administration in various Business Schools of repute.

Experience of teaching all kinds of students – Full time fresher, Part time working executives and students in correspondence and distance mode. Have always been rated as an excellent teacher by his students.

Experience of working as Program Director/Coordinator of PGDM program where shouldered the overall responsibility of the program – strategy formulation, admission, review of curriculum, delivery, examination, placement, convocation and overall program administration.

Having adequate industry exposure – first in the role of a Credit Appraisal professional and now on an individual level. Maintain a strong network of top-notch industry practitioners in the area of Finance to keep abreast of the latest developments in the field.

In the current role, the primary emphasis is on teaching and research. However, he is actively involved in institution building activities as well. He is an active member of the Admission Committee, Placement Committee, Library Committee, etc., and help the institution in maintaining a healthy industry-academia interface.

Areas of teaching interest are Corporate Finance, Investment Management, Financial Derivatives, Mergers, Acquisitions and Corporate Restructuring.

Areas of research interest are Dynamics of Capital Markets, Equity Research, Enterprise Valuation and Inclusive Finance.

Rachan Sareen is Associate Professor at the Department of Commerce in Sri Guru Tegh Bahadur Khalsa College, University of Delhi, New Delhi. She has been teaching the Under Graduate classes in Commerce for about 19 years.

Her research areas of interest are corporate governance and credit ratings. She has recently completed her Doctoral thesis on corporate credit ratings at the Faculty of Management Studies, University of Delhi.

Sandeepa Kaur is holding three post-graduations to her credit namely; M Com, MBA and CFA. She is a research scholar pursuing PhD in Finance from Centre for Management Studies, Jamia Millia Islamia. She has done Executive Education Program on Risk Management of Banks & Financial Institutions from Indian Institute of Management (IIM) – Bangalore. She has been working for more than 6 years on the post of Assistant Professor – MBA (Finance) prior to joining PhD.

She holds an industry exposure of working with ICICI Bank - SME Division as Credit Manager handling Loan Appraisals and sanctions thereof. She has presented papers in various international conferences and has won outstanding research awards. She has been an Associate Editor of Institute's National level Refereed Journal. She has organized National events such as Case Folio, Case Writing Workshops, Inter-College Business Quiz competitions, seminars.

Her research interest includes Banking, Risk Management, Corporate Finance, Mergers & Acquisitions, and Project Planning & Analysis.

Shalu Mahajan is Assistant Professor at the Department of Commerce in Acharya Narendra Dev College (University of Delhi), New Delhi. She has been teaching the Under Graduate classes in Commerce for about fifteen years in the University of Delhi. Her research areas of interest are finance, business policy and banking. She has recently submitted her Doctoral thesis on Banking at the Faculty of Management Studies, University of Delhi.

Shelly Oberoi is Assistant professor at Sri Aurobindo College, Department of Commerce, University of Delhi. She is MPhil in Human Resource Management and UGC NET qualified. Been a part of various National and International seminars, paper presentations, and has authored several papers in national and international journals, displayed vast knowledge of subject matter, effective discipline skills, teaching methods and good classroom management skills.

Siddharth Shukla is post graduate in Business Management and Certified Associate of Indian Institute of Banking and finance, Mumbai. He has managerial experience of more than 9 years in banking sector. He is presently working as Manager with IDBI Bank Limited. He has worked with various departments like retail branch operations, collection, clearing, etc., besides managing overall administrative function in branch banking in private as well as public sector bank. He has been awarded for his efforts for fraud prevention measures and considered for faculty position during his banking career.

He is perusing his PhD in field of Banking Regulations from Pandit Deen Dayal Petroleum University Gandhinagar, Gujarat. His areas of interest are banking laws and practices, credit and risk management in banks, security measures for alternate banking channels and internal control for banking operations. Presently he is working on the paper related effect of global banking regulations on Indian banks.

Tanvi Babbar, student of PGDM (2014–16), Birla Institute of Management Technology, is doing her specialization in the area of Finance. She has completed her Engineering in the area of Computer Science.

Taral Pathak has over 12 years of academic and industry experience and is currently engaged as a faculty with the Amrut Mody School of Management, Ahmedabad University, in the area of Accounting and Finance. A qualified ACA with masters in commerce, Mr. Pathak, is pursuing his PhD in Asset Price Bubbles and their Implications on Monetary Policy. He has to his credit selected quality national and international publications; has presented research papers in national and international conferences and has been a part of a 4 week international study program to Cambridge University for 2 consecutive years.

Mr. Pathak's academic and research interest lies in the area of Economics of Finance with a special focus on its impact and resultant policy making in developing and emerging economies.

TV Raman is Doctorate from Mohanlal Sukhadia University, Udaipur (Rajasthan) in the area of Managerial Decision making related to Risk and Return in Portfolio Construction. Presently working as a Associate Professor, Department of Accounting and Finance, Amity Business School, Amity University Uttar Pradesh. He is into academic field since 1995 and Published & Presented more than 20 research papers in national and international journals. Area of expertise is Financial Decision making, corporate Tax Planning, Corporate Restructuring, Cost and Management Accounting, Behavioural aspects in Finance and Management Control System. As a Corporate trainer he has given training in the area of Finance for non-finance executives, Working Capital Management, Direct and Indirect Taxes, Cost Control Techniques, Financial Decision making, Financial Reporting in corporates like, BEL, IFFCO, Delhi Transco Ltd, NTPC, SAIL, JCB Ltd, Department of Science and Technology, etc.

Vandana Mehrotra has a vast corporate and teaching experience in the field of Finance and Accounts which includes work on International Finance, Resource Mobilisation, Securitisation, Asset–Liability Management, Derivatives and Financial Accounting. She has taught Accounting & Finance courses to management students at both post-graduate and under-graduate level. She has conducted many Management Development Programmes for working executives at PHD Chamber of Commerce, Delhi. She has also conducted classes for IBM Daksh executives.

Her research interest includes intellectual capital, corporate disclosures and financial reporting. She has authored research papers for national and international conferences at FORE School of Management, Ansal University and Harvard, Boston USA. She has reviewed papers for Journal of Financial Reporting and Accounting, Emerald Publication.

Her education is from reputed educational institutes like Delhi School of Economics and Shri Ram College of Commerce (SRCC), Delhi University.